Boxing's Mister President

by

Bill Beadle

First published 1997

ISBN 0952 448 94 7

Typeset by:
In-House Typesetting

Printed and bound by:
Redwood Books
Trowbridge
Wiltshire

Published by:
Wat Tyler Book
PO Box 17
Dagenham
Essex

In Memorium

William Henry Walford Beadle

my late Father who believed in this Book and wanted it to suceed, and without whom it could not have been published.

"The wistful savings of a vanished hand"

Acknowledgements and thanks to Stanley Paul and the late Peter Wilson for permission to quote from 'More Ringside Seats', to Thomas Hauser and Robson Books, 'Muhammad Ali: His Life and Times', and Everett M Skehan and Robson Books, 'Rocky Marciano'.

Other sources either could not be contacted or failed to respond. I have however duly acknowledged them in the text.

Introduction: The State of Boxing in the 1990s

This book is about the Heavyweight Championship of the World. But it is impossible to write a serious book about the sport without passing comment on what is happening to it as a whole.

Boxing has always been a money making business, 'show business with blood', to echo an oft quoted remark. But the huge financial rewards that are now on offer within the sport have seen it degenerate into anarchy. It is worth taking a little time to examine the situation. We begin with the way boxing should be organised and the way it is organised.

Ideally boxing should have one World Champion in each weight division, followed by ten leading contenders, an International Champion (a good idea now devalued by anarchy), a second tier of ten contenders and then the rest divided by merit into 'A' group, 'B' group and so on. To progress up the lists boxers would fight men rated either in their own group or the bottom half of the next group up. Champions would defend purely against their No. 1 contenders, and contenders would fight only each other.

But the ideal is a long way from the reality.

In common with other major sports, boxing's paymaster is television. This should enhance boxing as it has with better regulated sports. Instead the windfall profits have led to disarray. There are now no less than nine regulating organisations offering their own 'world champions', contenders and 'championship' bouts. The regulatory bodies are themselves in the grip of powerful promotional interests.

Of the nine, known derisorily as 'the Alphabet Boys', four are accorded widespread recognition, the W.B.C. (World Boxing Council), W.B.A. (World Boxing Association), I.B.F. (International Boxing Federation) and W.B.O. (World Boxing Organisation). Slipstreaming along in their anarchic wake are the lesser known I.B.C. (International Boxing Council), I.B.O. (International Boxing Organisation), W.B.F. (World Boxing Federation), W.B.U. (World Boxing Union), and W.A.A. (World Athletics Association). In the U.S.A. anybody with $300.00 to spare can set up his own sanctioning body and get in on the act.

Criticising the 'Alphabet Boys' is like shooting fish in a barrel. One cynical comment made about W.B.O. titles is that they often seem to have replaced British domestic titles. When W.B.O. World Middleweight Champion Chris Eubank and his No. 1 contender, the ill-fated Michael Watson, decided to move up to super middleweight they were immediately installed as the No. 1 and 2 contenders to fight for the then vacant 'world' title; the existing top contenders simply disappeared from view. Johnny Nelson, a British cruiserweight who had twice failed in dismal fights for versions of the 'world' cruiserweight crown, suddenly became the W.B.F.'s heavyweight claimant after beating an Australian nonentity. W.A.A. director Pat O'Grady installed his prospective son-in-law Monte Masters as the W.A.A.'s 'world' heavyweight champion; when Masters split with O'Grady's daughter, O'Grady stripped him of it! The list of examples could go on and on indefinitely, filling this book and many others, but to continue the aquatic metaphor they are simply water off a duck's back to the Anarchy, sorry Alphabet Boys.

There are now a staggering 154 versions of a 'world' title, as opposed to 8 genuine world crowns forty years ago. Each of the nine bodies offers a world championship in 17 weight divisions and one has created an 18th , a 'super cruiserweight' division. Of the proliferation of weight divisions more later. For the moment we concentrate on the multifarious organisations. They have produced a galloping inflation in 'world' title fights and champions. Britain provides a classic example of this. In the decade of the 1950s Britain produced just two world champions, middleweight Randolph Turpin, who reigned only 64 days, and flyweight Terry Allen who also lost his crown on the first defence. This situation can be explained very simply: the overwhelming majority of British fighters were just not good enough to win genuine world titles.

By the time the Sixties arrived there were two sanctioning bodies (which was one too many), the W.B.C. and W.B.A.*, and 11 weight divisions. The British haul doubled, John Caldwell, Terry Downes, Walter Macgowan and Howard Winstone winning W.B.C. versions of world titles. This situation remained static in the Seventies, five Britons gaining world titles including a rare undisputed title-holder, lightweight Ken Buchanan. But the Eighties saw boxing throw off the last vestiges of sanity. Sanctioning bodies and weight divisions mushroomed. So did British 'world' champions. In the sixteen year period 1980–1995 (inclusive) Britons held versions of world titles at all bar super flyweight. The roll of 'honour' during those years amounts to heavyweight (4), cruiserweight and light-heavyweight (1 each), super-middleweight (2), middle (4), light-middle (2), welterweight, light-welter, lightweight and super-featherweight (1 each), featherweight (5), super-bantamweight and bantamweight (1 each), flyweight (5) and light-fly and strawweight (1 each), a total of 32 world championships held by British boxers. 14 were under the strictly dubious auspices of the W.B.O., an organisation which seems to some to be British boxing's house sanctioning body. Only Alan Minter and Lloyd Honeyghan can claim to have been undisputed champions. At the other end of the scale Paul Weir won the W.B.O. strawweight title in only his sixth paid fight and their

* then under different names

light-flyweight bauble in his eleventh. Weir has yet to fight for a domestic title.

Some have claimed that this has been good for boxing; more title fights have generated more interest and therefore more television money. But the outset of runaway inflation creates a feeling of prosperity with money chasing goods. Then, as its momentum gathers, inflation devalues currency and destroys living standards. That is what is happening in boxing; soaring inflation in both titles and title fights devaluing and destroying their validity, audiences increasingly turning their backs on phoney championships. Nobody knows who the real champions and the genuine contenders are anymore. The party lasts only for the evening; in the morning comes the hangover.

Boxing's weight divisions have multiplied with the growth of the sanctioning bodies. In the '50s there were eight, in the Sixties and Seventies eleven, now there are seventeen. Purists long nostalgically for the good old days of eight, but here the issue is by no means as clear cut. Two hundred years ago there were no weight divisions. The middle of the nineteenth century saw the introduction of first a lightweight and then a middleweight class below heavyweight. This allowed smaller men access to the prize ring. The gradual introduction of the Queensbury rules saw the implementation of the welterweight, featherweight and bantamweight divisions. Doubtless purists then mourned for the good old days of the three classes, just as some bemoaned the passing of the bareknuckle era. But men were getting bigger and stronger; the disparities in physiology more evident.

The light-heavyweight division was created in America at the turn of the century. Ten years later the British approved a flyweight and a paperweight division but the latter was never implemented. In the 1920s the Americans created three 'light' divisions at lightweight, welterweight and middleweight. Light-welter flourished for a while but fell into abeyance during the Thirties. One problem was the lack of a clear identity; the divisions were viewed by both fighters and fans as synthetic junior versions of real weight categories. The light-heavyweight division also struggled in its early years. But the Sixties saw the revival of the three classes. The Eighties saw six more added and although the creation of a 'super cruiserweight' division (by one of the minuscule bodies) is premature, it seems likely to become an eighteenth division one day as heavyweights continue to get bigger. Jack Johnson, Jack Dempsey and Gene Tunney were genuine heavyweights in their era and would probably have grown apace today through improvements in living standards. But looked at purely in 1996 terms they and their contemporaries were actually cruiserweights.

Overall, the seventeen divisions today are seen by purists as part of boxing's negative inflationary spiral, phoney divisions set up to create more titles and secure greater pickings for promoters and sanctioning bodies. They have a point. New weight categories have been added by simply halving existing ones, and without creating any real identities for them (save for cruiserweight and strawweight). Even amongst small men it seems anomalous and unnecessary to have categories ranging over a mere three or four lbs (1.36 and 1.83 kilos), and the name game is even more ridiculous than with the Alphabet boys themselves. For example, is the 154 lbs (70 kilo) class the super-welterweight, light-middleweight or junior-middleweight division? Fans continue to regard them as synthetic.

But there is a need for more than eight weight divisions, just as there was a need for more than three a hundred years ago and for the same reasons. Amateur boxing has twelve and professional boxing would benefit from copying its unpaid counterpart. Without the absurd 'half divisions' each category could have a clear identity and shed its synthetic image. The Heavyweights are boxing's bums on seats, deluxe models, and this reality would be reflected in the top three divisions, namely:

Heavyweight	above 91 kilos (200 lbs)
Middle-Heavyweight	91 kilos (200 lbs)
Light-Heavyweight	81 kilos (178 lbs)
Below them:	
Cruiserweight	75 kilos (165 lbs)
Middleweight	71 kilos (156 lbs)
Welterweight	67 kilos (147 lbs)
Lightweight	63.5 kilos (140 lbs)
Featherweight	60 kilos (132 lbs)
Paperweight	57 kilos (125 lbs)
Bantamweight	53.5 kilos (118 lbs)
Flyweight	51 kilos (112 lbs)
Strawweight	48 kilos (106 lbs)*

Last but not least is the justification for boxing itself. The arguments over whether boxing should continue have been put for and against over and over again. Both sides can pick holes in each other. For example, although it is the official policy of the British Medical Association to ban boxing only 12% of its delegates actually voted in favour of this policy. In the 'Split Screen' television debate about boxing soon afterwards, the B.M.A.'s representative implied that boxing was an immoral sport by citing the fact that the Kray twins had boxed professionally: he forgot to mention that 'Nipper' Reid, the policeman who brought the Krays to justice, was the Deputy Chairman of the British Boxing Board of Control! Doubtless, opponents of boxing could point to similar flaws in the arguments of its defenders. Neither side is ever likely to convince the other.

* All rounded up to the nearest lb.

Basically, there are two real arguments, safety and morality. Viewed purely in terms of safety boxing is on firm ground. Of the major sports it is only the twelfth most dangerous in terms of deaths and serious injuries. Risk cannot be eliminated from life. I write these words three days after a terrorist bomb ripped through East London killing two people and injuring 140 others. Thousands die in road accidents every year and even a pastime as seeming innocuous as gardening claims its death toll. Some psychologists believe that a minimum level of risk is good for our mental health; that there is an acceptable level of danger on which the human psyche thrives. But boxing's opponents often couple the safety arguments with the morality of the sport and here they are on a much surer footing; the purpose of boxing is for men *to inflict physical damage on one another.* In this context, boxing is anomalous to other combat sports. Strict safety procedures prevent fencers from harming each other, and in karate heavy blows are severely penalised. The purpose of both is to score hits without injury. But these sports along with others such as amateur wrestling, judo, taekwondo and kendo have only limited spectator appeal by comparison with boxing and the reason lies in the very nature of mankind: men like to fight and others enjoy watching them do it. Boxing, with its pain and its brutality is a reflection of the innate aggression in us. Robert Louis Stephenson outlined it in his classic novel Dr Jeckyll and Mr Hyde. Boxing is Hyde with a rulebook; the primordial instinct which lurks within us all. For that reason men will always fight.

Bill Beadle
February 1996

Volume One

James Figg to John L. Sullivan

Round One: Beginnings

Boxing is one of the oldest sports of all. Precisely when it began is unclear but it appears to have originated in Greece. The Greeks celebrated the fall of Troy with a festival of sport which included boxing. Later it was included in the ancient Olympics. Today the sport has passed from the country of its origin. No Greek has won a boxing Gold medal in the modern Olympics, and only Light Heavyweight Anton Christoforidis (domiciled in America) has held a professional world championship.

Rome succeeded Greece as the world's great superpower and boxing became an event in the Roman Games. Like the rest of the Games it degenerated into a sickening spectacle. The Greeks had boxed with leather gloves to protect their hands. The Romans had spikes embedded in them. Later they fought with wooden gloves — Caestus boxing as it was termed. Death was common, serious, often crippling injury the norm. Few survived long and the name of only one champion, Entellus, has come down to us. Entellus seems to have won three or four fights after which he was presented with the prize of a steer which he killed with a blow between the eyes. He was then permitted to retire undefeated.

Excess destroys and the orgiastic slaughters of the Games mirrored Rome's decline. With the dismemberment of the Roman Empire, the Games, and with them boxing, went into abeyance. But not the vicious side of man's sporting instinct which resurfaced during medieval times with teams of knights fighting mock battles against each other. Fought with real weapons by men clothed in chain mail and wearing protective helmets, there was nothing very 'mock' about these encounters. They were miniature bloodbaths derived from the war games of the Roman Coliseum and replete with death and serious injury.

As time went on opposition to this sporting carnage grew. The Church, performing the role of a sort of twelfth century B.M.A., attempted to have such combats banned and refused to bury those killed in them in consecrated ground. Few took any notice, but more practical opposition came from kings and nobles who were sacrificing too many of their best men to these contests. In England in 1194 Richard I introduced a licensing system and properly organised tournaments rather in the fashion of the Boxing Board of Control today. During the course of the next century there were improved safety regulations, blunted weapons replacing real ones and specialist armour introduced to avoid the most serious injuries. Once again there is a parallel here with boxing where improved safety measures have been progressively introduced over the last 200 years. Another parallel with boxing: the tournaments provided a route to fame and fortune for men of poor birth. William Marshall (1145–1219) rose from humble origins to become the greatest knight in the kingdom and a member of the

Council of Regents who governed England during the boyhood of Henry III. Five hundred years later prize-fighting would enable John Gulley to rise from a debtors' prison to fame, fortune and the House of Commons.

By the 14th century the tournaments had become more-or-less harmless spectator sports with heavily armoured knights jousting across tilted safety barriers to unseat one another. But the age of the knight was in fact over. The longbow revolutionised warfare and knights on horseback became redundant. Their tournaments did not survive them, possibly because it was a new era, possibly because the sport had become too safe and non-violent. The age of the knight flourished not during its period of chivalry but during its dark earlier days when it epitomised savagery and aggression. Boxing grew out of its violent hydra's limbs.

Interestingly, as side shows to the jousting tournaments bands of strolling players would enact old battles; the tail of the dog, so to speak. By the end of the seventeenth century the position had been reversed: the play was now the dog and the combat the tail. It is here that we find our first references to boxing, prize-fights being staged as violent pot boilers to the plays at the Theatre Royal, London. The interest which these contests generated was noted by a young athlete-cum-entrepreneur named James Figg who in 1719 opened an amphitheatre off Tottenham Court Road in which he featured prize-fighting, fencing with the backsword and cudgelling. In Figg's eyes prize-fighting was the least significant of the three but it would survive and prosper whilst the other two fell by the wayside.

In those days the term 'boxing' was itself unknown. The sport was generally called pugilism reflecting its Greek origins. The contestants used gloves only in sparring. The actual contests were fought with bare-knuckles. Wrestling was included as well as more dubious modes of fighting such as kicking, gouging and hitting below the belt. There were no formal rules; nor were there any weight limits as in modern-day boxing. Naturally this favoured the big, powerful men.

Initially fights were held only on the stage of Figg's amphitheatre but as prize-fighting became gradually more popular so Figg began to tour the fairgrounds where he set up the first boxing booths and challenged all-comers to beat him. Figg was acknowledged as the champion of England and whilst at this time nobody thought in terms of World Championships, the fact that prize-fighting was practised almost exclusively in England meant that the champion of England was, *de facto*, champion of the world.

When Figg retired he was succeeded by James Broughton, one of his pupils. Broughton accession proved to be a stroke of good fortune for prize-fighting. Unlike Figg, who considered cudgelling and fencing as his premier sports, Broughton favoured prize-fighting and concentrated on it to the decline and extinction of the other two. Yet ironically Broughton owed his position to his ability with the sword for as a protégé, of Figg's he trounced the Duke of Cumberland in a fencing contest. After Figg's retirement Cumberland became Broughton's backer.

In 1741 Broughton defeated George Stephenson, a Yorkshireman, in a vicious and sadistic bout for the championship, after which Stephenson died. Two years later Broughton introduced prize-fighting's first set of rules. The major innovations were that it became illegal to hit or seize a man below the waist, and that if a contestant was either felled or thrown he was allowed 30 seconds in which to recover. The latter rule meant that matches were now divided into rounds, but not as we know them today: as the round only ended when one fighter went down it could last any length of time.

Unhappily, Broughton's career ended in disgrace when he was beaten by a mediocre fighter named Jack Slack. Slack was so outclassed during the opening minutes of the fight that the odds in Broughton's favour soared to 10–1. What happened next resulted in boxing's first great controversy.

According to Broughton, Slack caught him with a lucky punch between the eyes which temporarily blinded him. Unable to see, Broughton was hammered to defeat in the third round. Cumberland and his friends, who had wagered heavily on the champion, saw it differently and accused him of throwing the fight.

The exact truth will never be known. Broughton was a great fighter and a man of pride and courage, but that does not mean that he was impervious to making easy money. Whatever the truth of it, both he and prize-fighting had made a dangerous enemy in Cumberland. The third son of King George II, he had defeated the Scots at Culloden four years earlier and had acquired an odious reputation there as 'Butcher' Cumberland. Although he later forgave Broughton (and provided him with a pension), Cumberland turned his back on the sport and was instrumental in having it banned. The message would seem to be that you can get away with upsetting the Church and the medical establishment, but don't antagonise the Royal Family!

Broughton never fought again and boxing went underground. Bans only work when they have the full support of the public; the reaction to this one was ambivalent. In particular a large section of the aristocracy — including the future George IV — were loyal to the sport. Prize-fighting became a fun day out. A fight would be announced for a particular venue. The local magistrates would then ban it. With the proposed contest now public knowledge, it would be switched to a new, secret locale. Instructions were then issued to meet at specified taverns on a certain morning. Once assembled, the patrons and contestants travelled to the destination where the fight was now being held, a ring was pitched in a field and the fighters went to work. Generally the magistrates got wind of it too late and the contest was over by the time they arrived. The fans savoured not only the fighting but outwitting the authorities as well, all accompanied of course by vast consumption of liquid refreshment!

However, all was not well with the sport. Indeed, had the authorities left it alone and not cloaked it in clandestine glamour then it is very possible that boxing would have destroyed itself. The forty years following Broughton's defeat saw a procession of poor champions and fixed fights. Slack reigned in corrupt mediocrity for ten years. In 1760 he was bested by Bill Stevens who promptly 'threw' his first defence to George Meggs, who in turn was beaten by Tom Milsom. One, Tom Jachau, succeeded Milsom and was swiftly conquered by Bill Darts. Darts was champion for five years. In 1769 he lost his crown to Tom Lyons but reclaimed it when Lyons quit the ring. Two years later Darts dismal career cam to an end when he was swiftly beaten by Peter Corcoran, a fight which was certainly fixed. And on and on the carnival of corruption went, Corcoran arranging to 'lose' the title to Harry Sellers in 1778.

Boxing's reputation was now at a very low ebb. Sellers four year tenure did not enhance it and in 1782 he was trounced by Jack Fearns in a fight which although very short may at least have been honest. So too, seemingly, was Fearns loss on his first defence to Tom Johnson. Although not particularly skilled, Johnson possessed enormous power and defended the championship in a series of bruising encounters until he lost to Ben Brain in 1791. The fight was a most violent one and ruined both men. Neither fought again and Brain died three years later, Johnson's blows apparently a contributory factor.

In need of a charismatic champion, pugilism now at last found one in the shape of Daniel Mendoza, a Jew from the East End of London. Mendoza was short but very skilful and a hard hitter. He is sometimes said to be the first scientific fighter (Broughton's admirers would certainly have disagreed), deploying fast footwork, tight defence and adroit ringcraft in a manner not seen before. He wore his hair gypsy style in dashing ringlets and was easily recognisable as a personality. His accession to the title was bitterly disputed by another first rate young fighter, Richard Humphries, and as often happens in boxing their three fight rivalry created immense interest. Mendoza gained the ascendancy and went on to claim the title. This was rather ludicrously disputed by Bill Warr, a West Countryman who had previously quit cold in the first round of a title fight with Tom Johnson. However, when Mendoza and Warr met on November 12th 1794, the fight seems to have generally been recognised as a decider for the vacant championship. Mendoza won in 23 rounds.

Astonishingly he reigned for only five months losing at Hornchurch, Essex, to 'Gentleman' John Jackson, so called because he seems to have had some claim to noble birth. But there was nothing gentlemanly about the way Jackson relieved Mendoza of the title. Seizing hold of Mendoza's mop of curly hair he battered him into unconsciousness in nine minutes. Jackson retired without making a defence and boxing now had its first disputed title situation with both Mendoza and Jem Belcher, a teenager from Bristol, laying claim to the championship. They were not destined to meet and in 1800 Belcher was afforded recognition.

Jem Belcher was prize-fighting's greatest 'might have been'. The grandson of Jack Slack, he is said to have been a brilliant scientific fighter with tremendous speed of hand and foot. Whether this was true, or are the misted reflections of wistful old men recalling a tragic figure, we do not know, but in 1803 Belcher lost an eye during a game of racquets and at the age of only 22 his days as a top notch fighter were over. He was succeeded by his friend and fellow Bristolian, Henry 'Hen' Pearce, a colourful character who was known as 'the game chicken'. Unwisely, Belcher — who had hit the bottle — came out of retirement to face Pearce and was thrashed back into it.

Pearce is best remembered for a tremendous championship battle with John Gulley whom he had once sparred with when the latter was imprisoned for debt. It is said that Pearce encouraged the young man to take up fighting. They met in 1805 and Pearce won with a terrible blow to the throat. Sadly, Pearce also died young (of tuberculosis) and Gulley was 'awarded' the championship. He declined it and went on to a successful career as a businessman and Member of Parliament.

The period Mendoza to Gulley had seen the arrival of an age of greatness and integrity (although boxing was still outlawed). The next champion put the seal on it: Tom Cribb.

Round Two: Transatlantic Rumblings

Tom Cribb is considered by some historians to have been the greatest of all the bareknuckle fighters, a teak tough colossus with a devastating punch. That at any rate was the image and it was a good one for boxing which flourished during his era. But perhaps the image was greater than the substance.

Cribb mounted the pugilistic throne astride the body of poor Jem Belcher who was twice again lured out of retirement. On the first occasion Cribb defeated him in 41 rounds but the half-blind Bristolian had much the better of the fight until he broke his right hand in the 18th. Their second encounter came two years later in 1809 and was for the vacant championship. Belcher was by now a drink sodden wreck and Cribb won as he pleased in forty minutes (31 rounds). Belcher died in 1811 at the age of 30.

Cribb's lustre actually emanates from his two fights with the black American Tom Molyneux*. Boxing was originally one of Britain's least successful exports to America: there is some evidence of prize-fighting in the 18th century but very little.

Molyneux arrived in England in 1810. According to the pre-fight hype of his first tilt with Cribb, he was a former slave who had won his freedom by defeating other black slaves in the plantation fields of the South, but there is no evidence of this whatsoever. Circa 1809 he apparently resided in New York where he worked for a restless, fitful period as a porter before taking a ship to England. We have no evidence that he had ever taken part in a prize-fight, but in England he came under the wing of another black American, Bill Richmond. Domiciled in England, Richmond had fought in the ring with some success. Molyneux was big, powerful, and possessed a natural aptitude with his fists, and Richmond was certainly not disposed to let a good meal ticket go begging. Under his tutelage Molyneux defeated two average English fighters and was then ballyhooed into a fight with Cribb.

Cribb and his backers were certainly on the look out for easy pickings and one-eyed, one-armed alcoholics were in short supply. Molyneux seemed the ideal choice, a virtual novice in terms of technique and experience, but a fighter who could be 'sold' to the public. And sold he was. It has been cynically observed that nobody ever got rich by over-estimating the public's intelligence. Cribb-Molyneux provides a classic example, the latter being fraudulently built up as Champion of America and credited with a string of bogus victories in the cotton

* Spellings of the name vary.

fields. It was white versus black and Britain versus America (with the clouds of a real war looming), in a contest for the 'world' championship and the public bought it hook, line and sinker.

The fights itself gives some idea of Cribb's real abilities. During the first twenty-eight rounds Molyneux exposed his lack of genuine class at championship level, first matching him punch for punch then, growing in confidence, beginning to outclass him. By round 26 Molyneux was completely on top and in the next two he handed out fearful punishment. Cribb's backers watched their expectations falling apart with mounting horror. When time was called for round 29 Cribb remained in his corner, beaten into a stupor. His chief second saved the day with a piece of quick witted chicanery, darting across to Molyneux's corner and accusing Richmond of putting bullets in his fists. During the ensuing row Cribb recovered and now his greatest strength, his endurance, came into play. Molyneux, by contrast, was exhausted and psychologically beaten. He took a sustained hammering during the 29th and 30th, falling without a blow to end the latter. Faced with disqualification, he retired instead. Afterwards his seconds claimed that he had succumbed to the cold (it was a December day), but New York winters are harsher than England's. In reality he had been beaten by his lack of ring experience. Plus of course some sharp practice by Cribb's handlers.

The Molyneux fight seriously suggests that Cribb was overrated. However his popularity was undiminished and the public wanted more of Molyneux and he. They met again at the rather prosaically named Thrislteton Gap, Rutland, on September 28th, 1811. On the evidence of their first fight Molyneux should have won. Interim, he had fought again and won impressively. But he had also been wined and dined and was not in tip top condition. This time Cribb had the easy victory which he had expected in the first fight, Molyneux retiring with a broken jaw at the end of round 11.

Tom Molyneux's road from Thristleton Gap was a downhill one. The rest of his ring career was undistinguished and 'this tremendous man of colour', as the English press dubbed him, died of drink in Dublin at the age of 38. With more experience and seasoning he would undoubtedly have become 'world' champion and a fistic legend. The raw natural talent was there. Unfortunately it remained raw; he was pushed in at the top too soon.

Cribb more-or-less retired after Thristleton Gap but remained champion in name until 1823 when he 'bestowed' the title on his foster son Tom Spring. Cribb was a lucky champion, always in the right place at the right time. He just missed the Mendoza–Jackson–Humphries era, Belcher had the cruel luck to lose his eye and turned to the bottle where his luck got even crueller in his jousts with Cribb; Pearce died young and Gulley did not want the title. Cribb was fortunate that Molyneux was almost a novice in their first fight, luckier still he was tripping down the primrose path by the time of the second. But it has to be said that Cribb's good fortune spilled over onto boxing. His fights, and the image which they created of him as a British Bulldog figure, captivated the public and cloaked the fight game in a rosy glow. It *seemed* then, and has done ever since, a golden era.

The next ten years were not. Spring suffered by comparison with his mentor and fought again only once before retiring. In his wake trailed the likes of Tom Cannon, Jem Ward, Peter Crawley and Ward again who retired in 1832. The man who took his place was excellent but fated with tragedy. However, because of it, James 'Deaf' Burke became the first champion to take his talents to America. It is to what was then a fledgling country in fistic terms that we now turn.

Mighty oaks grow from small acorns. One would have thought that Molyneux's battles with Cribb would be that acorn but not so. Their fights generated very little interest in the U.S.A. Some journals reprinted the reports of the bouts from their English counterparts, but they were greeted with an apathy bordering on disdain.

The first bout sometimes regarded as being for the American championship took place in 1816 between Jacob Hyer and Tom Beasley. But Hyer and Beasley would have been amazed at their humble scrap being elevated to such heights: it was actually a personal quarrel settled between them under Broughton's rules which ended when friends intervened and agreed on a draw. There was nothing more to it than that, but as Hyer's son later became champion the legend has persisted.

Eight years passed. During this time ring battles took place but the participants were generally not thought worthy of name. However, in 1824 George Kensett, an Englishman from Liverpool, and Ned Hammond, a Dubliner, took to the ring in New York. Their first fight was broken up at bayonet point; the second ended in Hammond being disqualified after having the better of the exchanges. Bad feelings fermented for two years before the two men fought again. The rematch was a duplicate of the first except that on this occasion Kensett was superior but was disqualified. The unsatisfactory outcomes notwithstanding, prize-fighting began to gather momentum as a sport, the press reporting the outcome of fights while maintaining a lofty, and hypocritical, contempt for them.

James Burke arrived in America in 1836 as champion of England. Three years earlier he had defended against Simon Byrne of Ireland. The fight was the longest then on record, lasting three hours and sixteen minutes. Byrne was carried from the ring and died shortly afterwards. Burke and his seconds (among them Tom Spring and Jem Ward) were indicted for manslaughter. They were acquitted at the judge's direction, Byrne's death being deemed an occupational hazard. Which is what happens when the law is used to stifle libertarianism and promote the cause of 'nanny state'. Burke and Byrne had engaged in the bout for reward and of their own free will; each was aware of the risks and accepted them. But because boxing was banned Burke and his handlers were charged with manslaughter. The law was a contradiction; such laws always are.

But what can be aptly described as a contradiction of morality now took over. Burke was ostracised from the ring; even sidestakes as low as 100 found no takes. It was not that he was feared, but that convention demanded a penalty for breaking a law which few respected. Outcast by hypocrisy, Burke went to America to ply his trade.

While he was there Broughton's rules were radically revised. Just as George Stephenson's death led to the first set of rules so Simon Byrne's accomplished the second. Whether they would have prevented either death is highly doubtful. But that is not the point: boxing needed to advance into the nineteenth century; more than that it had to soothe the guilt complexes of those who thrilled to this violent sport but were disturbed by their own feelings.

The new regulations — called The London Prize Ring rules — numbered 23 in all*. Many of them concerned codes of etiquette and defined the duties of trainers and officials. These need not concern us. The most important new rules set the size of the ring at 24 square feet and outlawed butting, gouging, kicking and hitting a man whilst he was down. It was around this time that weight classes also came into being, Lightweight (10 stone – 63.6 kilos) and Middleweight (11 stone – 70 kilos).

Burke meanwhile was earning his bread on the other side of the Atlantic. Initially he engaged in sparring exhibitions, touring with a young Irish immigrant named Sam O'Rourke. However, on May 9th, 1837 Burke and O'Rourke attempted to stage a proper contest in New Orleans. The result was a fiasco. A large Irish contingent turned out looking for blood — Burke's. His reputation as the man who had killed their fellow countryman, Simon Byrne, had preceded him. In the third round Burke struck O'Rourke's chief second and the crowd invaded the ring. Burke succeeded in making his escape during the confusion but a full-scale riot now ensued, spilling over into the streets of New Orleans and only ending when the mayor called out the militia. Subsequently Burke engaged in a second contest in New York with a man named O'Connell whom he defeated in 10 rounds. This passed off without incident.

It is tempting to think of Burke–O'Rourke as the first transatlantic contest on the American side of the pond. Burke was the English champion and a visitor; whereas although O'Rourke was Irish born and bred he had emigrated to the States. But whether it was or not, the bout augured badly for the future of the

* These were refined and added to in 1853.

American fight game. Crowd trouble was not entirely unknown in England — there had been ugly scenes during one of Tom Spring's fights — but the New Orleans riot spread alarm throughout the country. New Jersey had already formally banned prize-fighting two years earlier. Massachusetts would follow suit in 1849, followed by New York ten years later, and then many other states. Even when not banned state-wide the sport was subject to local ordinances and the laws governing riotous assembly, and newspapers were in full cry after prize-fighting, hypocritically reporting contests on one hand and condemning them as immoral and degrading on the other.

Despite this boxing continued to stealthily advance, rather as a suitor's looks grow on a young lady. A sports-hungry public was there to be seduced and from the 1840s through to the end of the Civil War prize-fighting would become America's premier spectator sport. In 1849 the American championship was finally pulled from the rock where it had lain like some loathsome excalibur. The contestants were Tom Hyer, son of Jacob, and James Ambrose a.k.a 'Yankee' Sullivan. Sullivan was an Irish immigrant with a chequered past*. During his early life he was no stranger to the British courts and had originally been transported to Botany Bay. On completion of his sentence he emigrated to America and successfully took up prize-fighting, winning nine ring battles in America and Britain. Tom Hyer also had a bruising reputation, but had only won one previous prize-fight.

They met at Still Pond Heights, Maryland on February 7th. Not without difficulty. Local magistrates had secured writs banning the fight but ended up arresting the wrong men! Snow lay lightly on the ground as the two contestants got down to business. It was a hard, dour fight which lasted just over seventeen minutes before Hyer, who had considerable advantages in height and weight, won.

It was not really an auspicious beginning for the championship, but a beginning it was.

Meanwhile the prize ring in Britain had fallen into decay. Burke's leading challenger was William Thompson, alias Bendigo, from Nottingham. Bendigo was really only a big middleweight weighing 12 stone (76.4 kilos) and standing 5ft 9". Burke should have whipped him but fell foul of the new rules and was disqualified for butting. Not long afterwards Bendigo broke his knee and announced his retirement from the ring. The title picture was now thrown into confusion. Burke re-claimed it, Jem Ward's younger brother Nick advanced his claims and so did Ben Caunt who had earlier won and lost to Bendigo on fouls. The procession of fouls continued with Caunt being disqualified against Ward

* And a sad future. He was lynched by vigilantes in 1876.

when they were matched for the vacant title. A re-match however ended in Caunt's favour. The big loser would seem to have been the unpopular Burke who had effectively been given the elbow by the 'fancy', as boxing's cognoscenti termed themselves.

Caunt followed in Burke's footsteps by undertaking a tour of America. He returned with a 250 lbs (114 kilos), 6′ 10″ behemoth from Michigan named Charles Freeman. Matched with Caunt's leading contender, Bill Perry, 'The Tipton Slasher', Freeman won convincingly and should have gone on to fight Caunt for the 'world' crown. But Caunt instead chose to defend his laurels against Bendigo who had emerged from retirement. It was in the usual nature of things with Bendigo that he won on a foul. To say that he was lucky is an extreme understatement. Having gone down time and again to avoid punishment, which should have led to his disqualification, Bendigo saw his opponent thrown out instead when Caunt sat down after mistakenly believing the round had ended. Bendigo was even luckier that his next proposed fight, with Charles Freeman, did not materialise; the huge American contracted tuberculosis and died. It seems certain that had he lived America would have had a 'world' champion long before Paddy Ryan.

Bendigo has received a surprisingly good press from history*, 'colourful' being the adjective commonly applied. In fact he was a highly unsatisfactory performer constantly dropping to the turf with a huge grin on his face whenever an opponent closed with him. The 'fancy' considered such tactics at best unmanly, and Bendigo both embarrassed the sport and tarnished its image with his antics outside the ring. Forever being hauled before the magistrates for drunkenness or assault, he was imprisoned no less than 28 times. Crowd trouble was often in evidence at his fights. Contemporary opinions of him were hardly flattering: 'A clown' wrote one reporter; another, more trenchantly, 'dirty and treacherous'. Perhaps his only real distinction was that he was boxing's first southpaw champion, but this served only to heighten his unpopularity with the majority of fans. When he retired again in 1846 boxing was in another trough.

The next champion, Tom paddock, was a fighter of limited ability and distinction. In 1850 Bendigo was taunted out of retirement (by his mother so he claimed) to face him. And yes, you've guessed the outcome, Bendigo won on a foul, giving him the dubious distinction of being the only fighter in the game's history to have won a final 'eliminator' and three championship challenges all via the disqualification route. It was a typical Bendigo performance. He ran like a thief, dropped down all over the place, and gained the 'victory' when the frustrated Paddock finally hit him while he was on his knees. Bendigo now

* Bendigo in Australia is actually named after him.

retired again, this time for good, but refused to give up the championship belt. Later he reformed and turned to religion, becoming a lay preacher.

Tom Paddock and Bill Perry were now matched for the vacant title. It took them three fights to sort it out. The first two were declared draws; the third, a dreadful offering, ended all too predictably on a foul, Paddock being banished for illegal hitting.

The awful merry-go-round of fouls continued with Perry being disqualified for hitting Harry Broome when he was down, a verdict which resulted in a near riot. Broome in turn was beaten by Harry Orme, for once a fight ending without a disqualification. But the rot now set in a different way. Orme retired; Broome was awarded the title; he retired. And the new champion was — Bill Perry!

It was a foretaste of the coming extinction of the prize-rings, down and almost out. Shades of Bendigo, Perry's next opponent would be the middleweight champion.

But this time what a middleweight.

Round Three: In Desperate Battle

Boxing has always found a saviour at its darkest moment. This time it was an illiterate thirty-one year old who stood 5′ 8″ tall and weighed eleven stone (70 kilos): Tom Sayers.

Sayers was born in Brighton in 1826 but grew to manhood in London. He had his first actual prize-fight at the age of sixteen, the contest terminating in a draw. Several impromptu fights of a personal nature are recorded over the next few years, but he was 22 before he next duelled for money, winning handily. Two years later he again entered the prize-ring — a draw — and at the rather late age of 24 decided on a career in the ring. Three victories later he fought Nat Langham for the middleweight championship and suffered his only career loss. Langham however retired after the fight and nominated Sayers as his successor.

Pickings in the middleweight division were not rich and Sayers defended that title only once before he began to take on heavyweights, beating Harry Paulson and drawing and winning against Aaron Jones. It is perhaps symptomatic of the state boxing was in that these contests paved the way for a challenge to Perry. They fought on the Isle of Grain, Kent on June 16th, 1857 and Sayers won in an hour and forty-two minutes. Although Sayers had been confident, most had expected Perry to be too big for him. The new champion was to be England's last great bareknuckle fighter.

Sayers cleaned up the heavyweight division, defending the crown four times over the next two years. Amongst his victims was Tom Paddock making his penultimate challenge. Had Sayers retired at this point — he was 33 — then he would be well remembered, but not a legend. Instead he stayed on to participate in the most famous match in bareknuckle history. Eyes turned once more across the water.

Tom Hyer never defended the American championship. His inactivity caused Sullivan to lay claim to it but as Hyer had not formally retired his claims were not taken seriously.

In 1853 Hyer was challenged by an Irish-born New Yorker named John Morrisey. Up to this point Morrisey had engaged (victoriously) in only one formal prize-fight but he had a formidable reputation as a bar-room brawler. In fact he was just about the most odious thug in New York. The leader of a gang of bully boys, Morrisey fleeced immigrants and enforced the control of corrupt politicians. In one bar-room fight (over a woman) his opponent held him down over hot coals until his flesh began to burn. From this he gained the nickname 'Old Smoke'.

Hyer agreed to meet Morrisey but demanded more stake money than Morrisey could raise. Instead 'Old Smoke' turned his attentions to Yankee Sullivan. In October 1853 they clashed at Boston Corners on the Massachusetts-Connecticut-New York borders. Sullivan looked — and quite literally was — old enough to be Morrisey's father, but for 37 rounds he dealt the younger man a wicked beating, mashing his face into pulp. With their man on the verge of defeat, Morrisey's handlers attacked Sullivan's corner. When time was called for the 38th Sullivan was brawling with Morrisey's chief second. Morrisey claimed the fight on the grounds that Sullivan had not come to scratch. Clearly anxious to be somewhere else, the referee agreed. Morrisey turned a deaf ear to Sullivan's demands for a re-match. Although the fight had not technically been for the championship, it was plain that Hyer had no further interest in it and Morrisey was now afforded general recognition*.

His reign was degenerate. On one occasion he pulled a pistol in a New York bar and opened fire at the waiters; on another he and Hyer agreed to have a gunfight (they were dissuaded by friends). The most infamous incident occurred in 1855. Morrisey was beaten bloody by a rival gang leader named Bill Poole who announced that that made him the champion. Two days later Poole was shot to death by five of Morrisey's henchmen. Morrisey escaped indictment for this one, but in 1857 he was arrested on three occasions for assault with intent to kill. Political influence got him off each time.

In 1858 Morrisey was challenged to defend his title by a young Californian**, John Camel Heenan, nicknamed the 'Benecia Boy'. Morrisey accepted the challenge and the two men faced each other on October 19th. To avoid brushes with the law the ring was pitched just across the Canadian border at Long Point. The fight generated intense interest as a struggle between good and evil, age and cunning against youth, and beauty versus the beast.

Only the last has any degree of accuracy. Heenan was a handsome young man and the possessor of what is termed 'star quality'. The rest was simply hype. Heenan was in actuality a thuggish gang leader himself who performed the same sort of political boot boy errands on the West Coast as Morrisey did on the East. The 'Benecia Boy' was certainly young, 23, but at 27 'Old Smoke' was hardly Methuselah. And incredibly, given the upsurge of activity in prize-fighting, a two fight 'veteran' would be defending against a man who had never participated in an organised contest before.

Heenan had been in bed ill for several days prior to the fight and was feeling weak. He therefore pinned his chances on an early knockout. Some believe he

* Except in Pennsylvania where one Dominick Bradley was feted as champion. Bradley however slipped into obscurity.

** Though originally from Troy, N.Y. where Morrisey also grew up.

might have gotten it too but for bruising his knuckles against a ring post. But Morrisey's strength was his strength. He survived a whirlwind opening from Heenan, and the next few rounds in which the Californian retained the upper hand, and then came back to wreak havoc as the effects of Heenan's illness overtook him. Heenan could not continue in the 11th and the fight was Morrisey's. But the lustre was with the 'Beneria Boy'. This boxing fight, plus his charisma, made him a hero and set the stage for an epic battle with Sayers.

Overtures for a Sayers-Heenan contest began early in 1859 with a formal challenge and a 200 sidestake from Heenan. Sayers was interested but had already accepted a sidestake from his old foe Aaron Jones for a title match. Negotiations rambled on throughout the summer and then in October a letter arrived from Heenan's principal backer to say that Jones had agreed to waive his right to fight Sayers first. Whether Jones accepted what we today call 'step aside money' is unclear, but he had become friendly with Heenan during a visit to the States and had trained him for the Morrisey fight. Very possibly, Heenan guaranteed Jones a fight should he win. At any event Sayers and Heenan agreed to meet the following year for a sidestake of 500 in a contest billed as being for the 'first international championship'. The fact that Cribb and Molyneux had already fought two such bouts, and to a lesser extent Burke as well, was conveniently shunted aside.

John C. Heenan's ship sailed from New York on December 31st. No bands played salute nor crowds cheered. In fact he was smuggled out, the legacy of having beaten up two of Morrisey's gang who had then issued a summons against him. Nor did crowds or bands greet him in England; the police had orders to arrest him on sight to prevent the contest taking place. Throughout the build-up to the fight he was to be consistently harassed by the authorities, on one occasion being arrested in his underwear. But no deportation followed: just a small fine and release. No such travails seemed to plague Sayers, and Heenan suspected — possibly with justification — that he was being deliberately harried to disrupt his training.

The fight created a dilemma for the authorities. With the exception of a minority of anti-boxing busy-bodies, everyone was looking forward to it, including Queen Victoria who had asked to be informed of the result immediately. Possibly no other contest in history has ever captivated the British public's imagination quite like Sayers–Heenan. Sayers himself had long been a hero, a 'Jack the Giant Killer' in the eyes of the public. He enshrined the way in which Britons liked to see themselves, a small nation defeating giants. Heenan was the handsome young Adonis from America who had carried all before him. The fact that at 185 lbs (84 kilos) and 6′ 1″ he was hardly bigger than most of the heavyweights Sayers had bested, and had fought just one losing ring contest, was entirely ignored. So too was the fact that he was not actually the American champion. Although Morrisey (who was in Britain to support Sayers) was declaring that he would not fight again he was equally adamant that Heenan had no right to his title. This initially posed something of a problem but in their time honoured way the British wheedled their way out of it: Morrisey was not actually an American because he had been born in Ireland which made Heenan America's legitimate representative! This of course was nonsense, particularly when joined together with the fact that Heenan had never actually won a prize-fight, but nonsense suffices when people want it to.

The day of the fight was Tuesday, April 17th, 1860. The Home Secretary had ordered the police out in force to stop the contest. One spectator who hoped that they wouldn't was Lord Palmerston, the Prime Minister! With Palmerston was a sizeable proportion of the British aristocracy, including several Dukes.

Secrecy over the venue was strictly maintained: rail tickets were sold leaving the destination blank. It turned out to be Farnborough.

To further bamboozle the authorities it was decided to travel overnight with the contest taking place on the morning of the 17th. By 3 a.m. an estimated 6,000 people were milling around in the darkness. Prodigious sums had been wagered, on today's values seven million pounds. If one makes the somewhat complex equation between the population of Britain in 1860, the much lower living standards, and the amount of money actually then in circulation, then in relative terms it was probably the equivalent of what would today be spent on betting on the Grand National. Dawn brought the contestants; just after seven the fight got underway.

It lived up to expectations. Those who were at Farnborough that day saw a spectacle thrilling in its sheer brutality. On neither side of the ropes was that Farnborough field a place for the faint hearted.

Heenan had much the better of the early stages, but it seems that Sayers was shrewdly pacing himself and looking to take advantage of the American's inexperience. But if that was Sayers' game plan then it came to naught in the 7th because a savage punch from Heenan ruptured a tendon in his right arm. It was Sayers' right hand punch — a devilish weapon — which primarily enabled him to fight on equal terms with men so much bigger than he was. Now the arm was useless.

But he still had his speed, which Heenan had no hope of matching, and raw courage still stemmed from his heart so he concentrated on closing the American's eyes with his left. And as round succeeded round so those eyes gradually disappeared under mounds of swollen, discoloured flesh. By the 18th Heenan's right eye was closed; by the 30th the left was just a slit. In addition the American's right cheek was gashed to the bone and his hands were hideously swollen making his punches less and less potent. At this point Sayers appeared marginally to be on top, despite having been knocked down or thrown to end most of the rounds.

The proceedings became desperate after that. Both men were on their last vestiges of strength. In the 37th Heenan, almost blind now, made a last desperate effort. Closing with Sayers, he seized him around the neck and pushing him across the top rope used all his strength to keep him there, strangling him as he did so. There was a serious possibility that Sayers would be choked to death.

At this point a body of police, who had been fighting their way through the crowd for some time, reached the ringside and somebody cut the ropes. Both men tumbled over, thankfully causing Heenan to release Sayers. But it had been a close run thing. Precisely who cut the ropes was never established. It could have been spectators*, Sayers' handlers or the police who now proceeded to dismantle the ring and tell everybody to go home. But it takes a long time to disperse such a large crowd and whilst the police were at it Sayers and Heenan incredibly kept on fighting. For five more rounds they mauled at each other until finally they had the sense to see that it was futile. The official result was a draw.

Arguments still rage between historians over who was the better man. Heenan was on top at the outset but lacked the experience and ring know-how to finish off a one-armed man. Sayers came back in the fight despite effectively losing the use of his right arm and used his knowledge, experience and speed to great effect. Although it was he who ended up on the turf in 25 of the 37 'official' rounds, he seems to have had slightly the better of the contest as it wore on, and appears also to have been marginally the stronger man at the finish. After a few hours sleep he was able to drink tea with his friends that evening, whereas Heenan is recorded as being in a deplorable state. It is reasonably certain that had Tom been able to use his prodigious right hand punch then he would have won convincingly. But it also has to be said that Heenan had given clear evidence that he had the potential to become a great fighter.

That potential was not to be realised. Three years later Heenan returned to Britain to fight the new champion, Tom King. In that time the picture had altered radically. Sayers retired after the great battle at Farnborough. the champion elect was Sam Hurst, 'the Staleybridge Infant' who turned back Tom Paddock in his final tilt but then succumbed to another fine middleweight, Jem Mace. Mace was in turn beaten by King. When King and Heenan met at Wadhurst, Kent, on December 8th, 1863 the Briton was this time the bigger man and made it tell, besting Heenan in just 35 minutes. But the American had certainly gone back since his fight with Sayers. He retired from the ring with a record of fought three, lost two and drew one. The bleak statistics mask the real story which is that Heenan had tremendous natural aptitude but really was bent on using the ring only as a brief stepping stone in his life. Certainly, his three contests brought

* Some actually suggested Morrisey!

him fame and the love of one of the most beautiful women of his day, the controversial actress Adah Mencken, bewitcher of Dickens, Dumas and Swinburne. Sadly, neither lived a long life. Mencken died in Paris in 1868 and Heenan, of lung disease, in Wyoming on October 25th, 1873.

Tom Sayers also succumbed to an illness of the lungs on November 8th, 1865. He was six months short of his 40th birthday. As both he and Heenan died young from lung complaints, it has to be asked whether this was due to the tremendous punishment they had inflicted on each other. But on the other hand early death from lung problems was common in the 19th century. Sayers' condition was not helped by the fact that he deteriorated into alcoholism after retiring from the ring.

He was a fighter of exquisite ability, Britain's greatest middleweight and probably, after Jimmy Wilde, our best ever pound for pound fighter. He would probably have vanquished most British heavyweights of the 20th century, although the better ones would possibly have been just a bit too big for him. Sayers' secret lay in the fact that he had the punch of a heavyweight. His right hand hitting power was stupendous. Against both Paulson and Jones he weathered crises and came back to win on the power of his punch. To this must be added courage, durability and the speed of a welterweight. Jem Mace also recalled that Sayers had very sharp knuckles which in bareknuckle fighting enabled him to cut his opponents easily. Some will argue that fighters of olden times cannot be compared to those of subsequent eras because of the improvements in technique, but this is wrong: natural talent will always adapt to technical developments.

Tom King retired after defeating Heenan and Jem Mace resumed as champion by defeating Joe Goss who was also a middleweight. The reality was that there were now very few big men of any consequence. Mace stood 5′ 9″ and weighed 150 lbs (68 kilos) and he was a popular fighter but the days of the bareknuckle warriors were over. Their death knell was sounded in 1867.

John Chambers was an all-round sportsman and a fan of boxing. In the early 1860s he drew up a radical new blueprint for the sport. The motivation was the fight game's survival. As a spectator orientated combat sport boxing had a big following; it also had vociferous opponents who succeeded in keeping it banned. The middle ground was held by the majority of the population who thrilled to the excitement of the prize ring, while affecting to dislike the sport's brutality, and its images of sleaze and vice. Commenting on their American counterparts, the *New York Times* tried to come to terms with this apparent contradiction:

> *'With all the benefits of a different education; with a press strong in upholding the moral amenities of life, with a clergy devout, sincere and energetic in the discharge of their duties, and a public sentiment opposed to animal brutality in any shape;... it is inexplicable, deplorable, humiliating, that... Morrisey and Sullivan could have occurred.'*

The leader-writer forgot that it was the very iniquities he was condemning which sell newspapers! It is the immoral things in life which fascinate us, the kept-under-wraps aggression in us which finds outlets in sports like boxing. People like the image of respectability but not its tenets. Chambers perceived this. He set out to build a bridge between contradictions by toning down the sport's violence and improving its image. Thus from the chrysalis of prize-fighting emerged the much more acceptable sport of Boxing.

Chambers proposed that fighters wear gloves to alleviate the worst injuries and that rounds be of three minutes duration with a minute's rest in between. Wrestling was outlawed, and when knocked down a contestant would have ten seconds to regain his feet or be considered knocked out. Fights would no longer be to the finish but over an agreed number of rounds, at the end of which the referee would decide on a points winner. The referee would be able to stop a contest at any time if he considered a man was outclassed, taking too much punishment, or was too badly injured to continue. The maximum size of the ring would be twenty square feet. These rules, Chambers hoped, would replace the existing ones — considered by him to be barbarous — and make fighting respectable.

The game itself proved resistant to change. Fighters sneered at Chambers' proposals as weak-kneed and unmanly. The fact that for the most part boxing was going nowhere fast eluded them. Chambers decided to try a different tack by finding a wealthy patron to represent his ideas. The man he lit on was John Sholto Douglas, the eighth Marquis of Queensberry.

Today, Queensberry is best remembered as the father of Lord Alfred Douglas, the homosexual lover of Oscar Wilde. On the face of it Queensberry was an unlikely candidate to represent anyone's plans successfully. A strong strain of insanity ran throughout the Douglas family (some believed the eighth Marquis to be a sandwich short of a picnic), and they were known in society as the 'mad, bad line'. They certainly were not very popular (Queen Victoria later blamed them for the death of her beloved Gillie, John Brown). But Queensberry was at the end of the day a Peer, and if he had one redeeming quality it was his passionate devotion to the fight game. The Marquis persevered and Chambers' new rules — known as the Queensberry rules — gradually replaced the London Prize Ring rules. Under them boxing eventually became a legal sport.

Hand in glove with the Queensberry rules went the gradual introduction of three new weight classes, welterweight 145 lbs (66 kilos), featherweight 115 lbs (52.5 kilos) and bantamweight 108 lbs (49 kilos), with lightweight being reduced to 133 lbs (60 kilos)*. Light-heavyweight (175 lbs 79.5 kilos) and

* The weights were later refined to welterweight 147 lbs (67 kilos), middleweight 160 lbs (72.5 kilos), lightweight 135 lbs (61 kilos), featherweight 126 lbs (57 kilos) and bantam weight 118 lbs (53.5 kilos)

flyweight (112 lbs 51 kilos) were to follow early in the next century.

It was the end of one era — bareknuckle — and the beginning of another, boxing. It was also the end of British dominance.

Round Four: This Man of Dynamite

John Morrisey kept his promise not to fight again and became a political figure of some dimensions. He was twice a State Senator for New York, and twice won a seat in the U.S. House of Representatives. In 1878 he won a bitterly fought campaign for the U.S. Senate. He was only 47 at the time which means that he might well have become one of Americas most influential politicians. The country was spared this dubious prospect. Worn out by the campaign, Morrisey died before he could take his seat.*

After Morrisey's retirement from boxing, Heenan was considered champion. May 5th, 1863 one, Joe Coburn, and another, Mike McCoole, faced each other in a fight grandly billed as being for the vacant title. This is best described as an act of sheer effrontery. Heenan, who could certainly have thrashed either of them, was still active and was actually in England preparing to face Tom King. Neither Coburn of McCoole was exactly a distinguished pugilist. Coburn had fought only once in the ring before (a draw) and that had been nearly a decade earlier. The Ring Record Book credits McCoole with two previous victories, and his own hype awarded him many conquests in rough and tumble encounters, but the latter were probably as fictitious as the long lists of 'victories' attributed to certain wild west gunfighters. However the newspapers went along for the ride and wrote the affair up as a 'Championship' contest. Coburn won in 67 undistinguished rounds. As Heenan retired after losing to King, Cheesecake Joe was afforded recognition.

American pugilism, which had prospered during the decade of the Fifties, was now in a parlous state. It was widely banned and in this underworld atmosphere vice and corruption flourished. Proposed 'fights' never came off — they were simply betting swindles — those that did were often fixed, and crowd riots were commonplace. One Mississippi contest ended in a pitched gunbattle leaving several dead and wounded.

Coburn's main ambition was to get an international contest with Jem Mace. A proposed bout in Ireland fell through after which Coburn retired.

The title was now not so much vacant as in a vacuum. Into it stepped two worthies named Dunn and Davis. What followed can perhaps be summed up by quoting Winston Churchill's remark about Clement Atlee; 'Mr Atlee's taxi drew up and nobody got out.' Dunn won and nobody was champion. He retired and Davis claimed it. McCoole stepped back into the fray and defeated Davis. His

* New York States political establishment were amongst 50,000 mourners at his funeral.

only defences were against English émigrés, Aaron Jones and Tom Allen. Allen was apparently winning easily until he was jobbed out if it on an alleged 'foul'. McCoole seems to have retired (temporarily) after this leaving Allen to claim the title. Ring-a-ring-a-roses, we all fall down.

Tom Allen was a relatively experienced ring practitioner in both Britain and America, but experience by itself does not make a good fighter and when Jem Mace visited America in 1870 he easily trounced the 26 year old in a so-called world championship contest, breaking both his jaw and collarbone into the bargain. Mace at the time was 39 and nearing retirement.

According to Mace, he was then amazed to receive a challenge from his earlier erstwhile foe, good old Joe Coburn, 'old' being the operative word because Coburn was nearly as ancient as Mace. They met in Canada in 1871 and shared a ring for almost two hours. However the fight itself was as abortive as the earlier Irish non-event, the entire unfunny farce consisting of feints, footwork and dirty looks with never a punch landed. For once nobody was displeased when the police put an end to the miserable affair. (Mace conveniently downgrades it to an exhibition in his memoirs.) The little circus now moved south to Mississippi and this time the elderly couple managed a 'draw'. According to Mace, the referee was intimidated into giving the verdict when it became clear that he, Mace, was on top. Others saw it differently, maintaining that Coburn was the better man before the contest deteriorated into the same irksome frolics as their first fight. Ho hum.

Mace went back to England and retired. His British title was claimed by Joe Goss. Nobody cared; the bareknuckle era had joined the Dodo in England.

Goss moved to America in 1876 and was challenged by Tom Allen, who had scored a revenge win over McCoole in 1873. Goss won a mediocre encounter on a foul. It was four years before he fought officially again and at long last America had a victory, Goss being defeated in 87 rounds by Irish-born Paddy Ryan.* It was only Ryan's second fight and enabled him to claim both the World and American baubles. At this point American boxing was, at least at the top, in a near terminal condition. But already punching furiously in the wings was a young man who was to change that forever: John Laurence Sullivan.

Two things brought American boxing out of the doldrums; the Queensberry rules and John L. Sullivan.

Sullivan was born on October 15th, 1858 in the Boston suburb of Roxbury. His parents were Irish immigrants, Mike from Tralee, County Kerry and Catherine nee Kelly, a somewhat Amazonian lady from Roscommon. Later at the height of John L.'s fame, Mike Sullivan would often put a stop to his son's

* It was Gosss last proper contest.

notorious bragging by telling him that there were at least 15 Sullivans in Tralee who could whip him!

The Sullivans were not 'lace curtain' Irish, but they were not impoverished either. Mike Sullivan worked steadily as a labourer and always provided for his family. His first born son grew into a husky if rather poorly educated young man standing 5′ 10½″ tall and weighing 190 lbs (86.4 kilos). John L. always believed that he got his powerful physique from his father; others believe he favoured his mother.

After leaving school John L. was apprenticed to a plumber. It was not what he wanted; neither was tinsmithing, or the building trade in which he spent a couple of years. There was a restlessness about him which often marks the teenage years of an achiever. He respected and loved his parents but eschewed their ordinariness. Today we recognise this as the bench mark of a 'high dominance' individual.

Sullivan's first love was baseball, a sport at which he demonstrated some talent and played semi-professionally. But his natural aggressiveness and individualism, coupled with the fact that there was more money to be made, led him to the fight game.

Prizefighting had been outlawed in Massachusetts for almost thirty years, but the law permitted 'exhibitions' under Queensberry rules to take place. In reality, these were generally full blooded hitting sessions. Beginning in 1878 Sullivan engaged in a succession of such contests and built up a strong local reputation as an aggressive fighter with a powerful punch. Amongst his fellow Irishmen he became known as the 'Boston strong boy', a ring-de-guerre which was to stay with him all his life.

Two of his early exhibitions were with Joe Goss for whom Sullivan developed a lifelong affection and friendship. That did not stop him cutting loose and flooring Goss in their first match. The Englishman afterwards commented ruefully that Sullivan's right hand punch was like the kick of a mule.

Sullivan's first 'proper' contest was against 'Professor' John Donaldson in Cincinnati, Ohio, Christmas eve 1880. It was a rather odd bout fought with gloves but held under London Prize ring rules. Nobody could find an actual ring so the spectators formed a human one.

It was not much of a scrap. Donaldson, who claimed victory in five previous contests, back-pedalled furiously and dropped at the merest hint of a punch. Sullivan finally caught up with him in the 10th and a full blooded right swing dissuaded Donaldson from taking any further interest in the proceedings.

Next day the police spoilt the fighters' Yuletide festivities by arresting them. The case did not get very far. Questioned as to whether he had watched a prize-fight one spectator replied; 'no; a foot race!' The charges were dropped.

Sullivan had now emerged as a force to be reckoned with. It did not make him humble. The less attractive side of his personality began to take centre stage, boasts, taunts and overwhelming self-confidence. The dominance had emerged without the intellectual development to temper it. This was fine with Sullivan's Boston cronies — especially as he was paying for the drinks! In March of 1881 Sullivan, in a nineteenth Century forerunner of Muhamed Ali's 'name the round' game, issued a declaration that nobody could last four rounds with him under Queensberry Rules. His opponent on this occasion, an ex-coroner known variously as Steve Taylor or John Mahon, certainly couldn't and quit halfway through.

John Flood proved to be of only marginally sterner stuff in Sullivan's second 'official' contest. Flood really had no right being in the same ring with Sullivan; he was simply a bar-room brawler. But he had a big following in his native New York and the fight was easy money for Sullivan. They fought with gloves but under London prize ring rules on a barge moored on the Hudson, off Yonkers, New York. Flood was completely outclassed and comprehensively beaten in eight minutes.

Much the same fate befell Paddy Ryan eight months later when he defended the championship against Sullivan. Ryan was little better than a nonentity. Born in Ireland in 1853, he had grown up in Troy, New York like Morrisey and Heenan before him. His victory over Goss in 1880 was to be the only one of his career. Goss himself was a much abler fighter than history has given him credit for; aside from Ryan, only Jem Mace ever defeated him in an official contest. But by the time he fought Ryan he was nearing 42 and was really only a middleweight conceding around three stone (19 kilos) to the American. Even so, it took Ryan 87 rounds to beat him.

The historical significance of the Sullivan–Ryan fight is that it was the first time that two Americans did battle for the world title*. Curiously, Sullivan himself did not consider it a world title fight — only American — but there can be no doubt that Ryan did have the right to claim the world crown. Goss was the best English fighter around after Mace's retirement and his 1876 fight with Tom Allen was considered to be for the world title. Outside of Britain and America, only Australia had any real boxing pedigree and in 1882 its two greatest heavyweights, Peter Jackson and Frank Slavin, had yet to commence their careers.

Of the actual Sullivan–Ryan contest itself there is not a lot to be said. Sullivan trained hard for it and entered the ring in peak condition. Ryan was in nowhere near as good shape. A photograph of him around this time suggests the beginning of a paunch despite the fact that he was only 28 (Sullivan was 23).

* Allen and McCoole billed their 1873 contest as being for the world title but nobody took them seriously.

The fight was held under London prize ring rules in a ring pitched outside a hotel in Mississippi City, Mississippi. It lasted only eleven minutes, Sullivan winning with almost contemptuous ease and taking only one good punch, a right to the neck. It was the last time that the heavyweight title changed hands under London prize ring rules, and the first time that an action photograph was taken of a heavyweight title fight. And the ring now had a charismatic new champion.

But in fistic terms the Ryan fight was actually the zenith of John L.'s career. Although his popularity was to grow to unprecedented heights, the champion spent more time in bars than rings. His appetite for liquor was prodigious. The stories of Sullivan's drinking saloons dry whilst boasting that he 'could whip any man in the house' are only too well known. They did nothing to dent his popularity, but then the majority of his fans were never on the receiving end of his boorish behaviour. Much less public was his womanising, but in 1883 he and his manager Billy Madden parted company after Sullivan apparently bedded Maddens girlfriend.

A great deal of Sullivan's popularity can be attributed to the fact that he was the first champion to show himself off to a sports happy public. This was done by a series of barnstorming tours of the U.S. in which Sullivan offered $1,000 to any fighter who could last the four rounds with him. Until July of 1882 none could, but then the quality of the opposition was such that they were guaranteed not to anyway. Jimmy Elliot is a prime example. He had fought only once in 15 years, most of which had been spent in prison. Aged 45, Elliot also had poor eyesight. The only surprise was that he lasted into the third.

Two weeks later another ageing pug, an Englishman named Tug Wilson, did succeed in staying the distance. His tactics, repeatedly clinching and dropping to the canvas to avoid punishment, angered Sullivan and the crowd, but the bare facts are that Wilson was an overweight and under-trained middleweight (a double chin emphasised the point). Sullivan's lifestyle was beginning to catch up with him.

On May 14th, 1883, Sullivan defended the world title for the first time, against Charlie Mitchell of England. Some would argue that this was not an authentic title fight; it was billed only as a standard four round 'exhibition' and Sullivan himself did not consider that it was for the championship. However, Mitchell was the best Britain now had to offer and the reason that the fight was billed only as an exhibition was to get round New Yorks anti-boxing laws. The build up to the fight and the fans' anticipation of it was as a genuine contest and there can be no doubt that Mitchell would have claimed the world crown had he won.

Not that there was much possibility of that. Mitchell was in reality yet another beefed up British middleweight. He had a reasonable record of five wins and two draws under London prize ring rules, and had won middle and heavyweight competitions in England under the Queensberry rules. He was also two years younger than Sullivan. But Mitchell was nowhere near the champion in strength and power. His only real chance lay in the fact that John L. had been having problems outside the ring. One was his marriage to a girl named Annie Bailey who was pregnant by him*. It was an unhappy union which ended the following year. The other was that Sullivan had been bed-ridden for much of the early part of the year following a near fatal haemorrhaging of the lungs. Heavy drinking was blamed.

Sullivan appeared to have recovered by the evening of May 14th. He opened like a bull and quickly floored Mitchell twice. But the Briton replied by getting in under John L.'s swings and peppering him with fast lefts. Then came sensation. Mitchell planted a left on Sullivans forehead and down he went for the first time in his career. In the second round an enraged Sullivan tore in again only to meet more of Mitchell's clever boxing. But at this stage the Englishman fell out of the ring and hurt his back. In the third he was down several times and taking a hiding on the ropes when the police decided it was not an 'exhibition' after all and put a stop to it. They undoubtedly saved Mitchell from being knocked out and so Sullivan justly claimed a victory. But he had not been impressive and seems to have done much of his training in the bars. Asked about the knockdown, he claimed that he had had his legs crossed at the time. This may be true as his feelings seem to have been the main thing hurt.

If we accept Sullivan–Mitchell as a genuine world title clash then it was the first at heavyweight under Queensberry rules. A second followed in August although its credentials are very much more dubious. Once again the contest was arranged as a four round 'exhibition' at Madison Square Garden, New York, and once again the opposition was foreign. But Herbert Slade of New Zealand, protégé of Jem Mace, hardly had any business fighting John L. Sullivan for anything. A lumbering, good natured 27 year old who was billed as 'the Maori' (which he wasnt), Slade weighed around the same as Sullivan and was 3 inches taller, but bore only the outward similarity to a fighting man. It is not clear whether he had actually engaged in any serious contests before (Mace makes no mention of any), but he had certainly received a shellacking in an unofficial contest with a novice middleweight named Bob Fitzsimmons two years previously (Mace makes no reference to this either).

Sullivan–Slade was guaranteed to keep the anti-boxing lobby happy. The hopelessly outclassed Kiwi was knocked clean out of the ring in the first round. In the second he quite literally turned and ran; Sullivan caught him and sent him sprawling through the ropes again. He was again on the floor when the police, fearful of a possible fatality, halted the carnage in the third. Sullivan made money

* The child, a boy, died in infancy.

out of it; as for Mace, he ditched his hapless protégé and wandered south in search of fresh pickings.

John L. made no serious defence of the title again until November, 1886, if indeed his rematch with Paddy Ryan can be classified as a serious fight. Predictably, he knocked Ryan out in three rounds. Taking it as a title fight, it was the first at heavyweight between two Americans under Queensberry rules. The rest of the time was spent in whistle stop tours of the country — or rather its bars and saloons. Sullivan appears during these years as a man who was being paid a lot to become an alcoholic. His once magnificent torso became a bloated caricature of its former self: training disappeared from his roster. There were fights of the 'I can beat anyone in four rounds' variety but they cannot be taken seriously — certainly not as championship contests. There were also fights outside the ring. As Sullivan's drinking increased and his fitness decreased, so he became morose and vindictive. On one occasion he butted a young man in a bar and then slugged an onlooker who remonstrated with him. When he left America in October, 1887 for a British tour there was a feeling in America that his time in the sun was over.

In Britain he was feted as Royalty. Huge crowds turned out to see him, he breakfasted with the Scots Guards and sparred with the Prince of Wales. Waiting in the shadows was his old foe Charlie Mitchell.

Mitchell had been needling Sullivan ever since their first fight. A clever, egotistical boxer who analysed and then played upon his opponents' psychological weaknesses, the Englishman had been concentrated on 'getting' Sullivan's goat to lure him back into the ring. A return bout had almost come off two years previously; now the champion's tour of Britain seemed to provide the opportunity for Mitchell to get a world title shot in his own country.

In fact it didn't. Although they agreed to meet under London prize ring rules for a purse of $2,500, the contest did not take place in Britain. Ostensibly the reason was the country's anti-boxing laws. When the fight was announced Sullivan was hauled before the magistrates and bound over to keep the peace. But this was no worse than Heenan had endured. In reality there was very little demand for the match. The face of boxing had changed irrevocably in Britain. There had not been a big man of genuine quality for a long time. (Next to Mitchell was Jem Smith, another middleweight.) Opinion had also shifted decisively in favour of the safer and less brutal Queensberry rules. To top it all, Mitchell himself was hardly a Sayers or a Cribb in the eyes of the public. In the three years following his first bout with Sullivan he had campaigned exclusively in America, touring the country in pseudo exhibition bouts like his conqueror. Back in Britain, his main fistic activity was as a debt collector for racecourse bookmakers. Even in this sleazy profession Mitchell was less than trustworthy. One story told of him was that he had been hired to collect a debt of £200 for a fee of half of it. On inquiring with Mitchell about his money, the unfortunate creditor was allegedly told: 'I've got my half; don't know about yours.' All in all the public no longer wanted bareknuckle brawling, they didn't like Charlie Mitchell and they didn't think he had a ghost of a chance of beating Sullivan anyway. No sale.

Eventually, Sullivan and Mitchell were forced to take their diluted extravaganza across the Channel to France. John L. seems to have had a penchant for 'firsts' — this was the first time that a world title had been contested in that country. Contested but not decided. On March 10th, 1888 the two gladiators plodded their way through 39 wearisome rounds encompassing much clearing of air from Sullivan and a great deal of running and dropping by Mitchell. A good fight it was not. After 3 hours and 11 minutes everybody had had enough and Tweedledum and Tweedledee agreed to halve their battle. The post fight recriminations were more entertaining than the fight. Sullivan derided Mitchell for his hit and run tactics; Mitchell responded that they were designed to wear John L. out and were succeeding admirably (but why then had he accepted a draw?). Although the bout was on private property — Baron Rothschild's estates in Chantilly — the Gendarmerie turned up and arrested everybody in sight*. It was a fitting climax.

Back again in America, Sullivan was challenged by Jake Kilrain, an artless slugger from Long Island who had campaigned mainly along the Eastern seaboard (including Boston). Like Sullivan, his career had consisted principally of pseudo 'exhibition' bouts. Kilrain had never been defeated, but his most notable battle had been a 106 round draw with England's Jem Smith in France, his only outing to date under London prize ring rules**. There was nothing very distinguished about Kilrain either as a fighter or a man. He was surly and introverted and became a virtual hermit in later life. (He once threw boxing historian Nat Fleischer off his property when Fleischer tried to interview him.) However, by 1888 he was the main American challenger and on December 7th Sullivan and he signed to fight each other under London prize ring rules, $5,000 being posted as a sidestake. The fight took place the following July and the champion needed those eight months.

Early in the new year he commenced serious training for the first time in years. His handlers were shocked. Sullivan was obese, slow, a mere shell of the blazing young hitter who had barnstormed his way through all opposition a decade earlier. What was more Sullivan made it quite clear that he had no intention of packing in his drinking whilst he was in training. His handlers knew that Kilrain was fit and determined. In this condition Sullivan stood no chance of victory. There was one hope and they seized it. They called in William

* They were all released without charge.

** Strangely, it was billed as being for the championship of England.

Muldoon, the world wrestling champion and Sullivan's friend, reputed to be the one man whom John L. actually feared.

Muldoon took complete charge of the situation. He forbade Sullivan to drink and concentrated on an intensive training programme. He bullied, threatened and cajoled Sullivan into some semblance of physical fitness. It was enough for one last hurrah.

On July 8th Sullivan and Kilrain stepped into the ring at Richburg, Mississippi.

The battle proved to be a marathon one. Sullivan needed every iota of the conditioning that Muldoon had ground into him. For 2hrs and 16mins under a blazing sun the two men battled it out. Sullivan was the better man but at times it seemed that Kilrain might outlast him. In the 44th round Sullivan was sick and Kilrain asked him if he wanted to quit. Sullivan replied with a crushing right that sent Kilrain sprawling on his back. As the fight wore on Ringsiders reflected humorously that Sullivan was sweating champagne. But finally it was Kilrain who cracked. At the end of the 75th his corner threw in the sponge.

It was the last heavyweight title fight under London prize ring rules. It was also Sullivan's last sojourn with fitness. The contest over, he was soon back to his old ways. By September he was apparently suffering from a form of D.T.s which one might term as 'P.T.s', or 'political tremors' because he rather grandiosly announced that he was available for a draft to the U.S. House of Representatives. Nobody else saw a politician in him, merely a pink elephant coming out of the wall. Massachusetts political bosses made their excuses and left, so to speak.

But humour aside, the endurance test with Kilrain had rekindled John L.'s waning popularity and he was on much safer ground with his next venture, a play entitled 'Honest Hands and Willing Hearts'. The play itself was a good old fashioned piece of American schmaltz — honest woodcutter gets the girl and so on, and Sullivan's presence guaranteed success at the box office. He toured with it from August 1890 to June 1892 and earned a lot of money which he just as quickly spent.

Meanwhile his challengers were queuing up. And there was a good crop of them in every sense of the word. Three from the emergent Australian boxing scene, Joe Goddard, Frank Slavin and Peter Jackson, the last a gifted black fighter. England's Charlie Mitchell continued to ask for more in far less humble tones than Oliver Twist, and there were three good Americans, two white, James J. Corbett and Joe Choynski, and one black, George Godfrey. The Sullivan era had glamorised boxing and reaped a distinguished crop of heavyweights.

Sullivan responded to the various challenges in March 1892:

'I give precedence to Frank Slavin of Australia, he and his backers having done the greatest amount of bluffing. My second preference is the bombastic sprinter Charlie Mitchell whom I would sooner whip than any man in the world.

My third preference is James Corbett of California who has achieved his share of bombast. But... I will not fight a Negro. I never have and never will.'

In fact, Sullivan really didn't want to fight anybody as he made clear when outlining his terms for the fight. The $25,000 purse (around $1.5 million on today's values) was not a drastic stumbling block, but a $10,000 sidestake was. It seemed unlikely that any of the specified challengers would be able to raise it. Slavin and Mitchell quickly fell by the wayside.

There was no possibility either that Peter Jackson or George Godfrey could secure such backing, but just to make sure Sullivan had drawn the colour line against them. However, in saying that he would never fight a black man John L. was being economical with the truth. He had in the past expressed willingness to meet Godfrey if the latter could raise a suitable sidestake. In reality the champion was using race to mask a very real fear of losing to Peter Jackson. He knew that Jackson was a formidable fighting machine.

Which left Corbett. In all probability Sullivan regarded him as the least of the challengers. They had agreed to spar together in an exhibition the previous year but John L. had reduced it to a farce by insisting that they both appear in full evening dress (including the tuxedo!). The result was a shambles, lustily booed by the audience. But as Corbett left the ring he told his manager, William Brady: 'I can beat this fellow; hes a sucker for a feint.' Another of Sullivan's stipulations played right into Corbett's hands: the champion was insisting on Queensberry rules which particularly suited Corbett. The Californian was determined to raise the sidestake. He and Brady scraped up a tenth between them, then begged and borrowed the rest from high rollers. And they had a fight. Sullivan–Corbett was on for September 7th, 1892 at the Olympic Club, New Orleans.

Sullivan vowed that win or lose this would be his last contest. He was being realistic. Since the Kilrain fight his weight had ballooned to an abysmal 264 lbs (120 kilos). His best fighting trim was between 190 and 200, but at almost 34 and with a decade of sustained dissipation behind him there was never a chance of his getting down to it. In the event he came in at 212 lbs (96.3 kilos). Under the ring lights he looked like a fat old whale glistening in a polar sunlight.

Corbett was in his prime, trained to the minute. The contest was scheduled for 45 rounds and was the *pièce de resistance* of a unique triple header. On September 5th, at the same venue, Jack McAuliffe retained the world lightweight title against Billy Myer, the next evening George Dixon annihilated Jack Skelly (it was Skelly's first professional fight) in defence of his featherweight crown and on the 7th Sullivan retained the heavyweight laurel by beating Corbett. Well, that was the way his script read. Unfortunately, Corbett had been handed a different one.

The fight turned out to be totally one-sided. The champion did not win a single round. A wildly pro-Sullivan crowd roared him into the ring. But as round succeeded round they sat stunned and silent as John L. was revealed as a burnt out shell of the once great 'Boston strong boy'.

From the opening bell Sullivan lurched forward sluggishly, trying to connect with his devastating right swing and missing by yards. Corbett revealed a brand of fighting that was almost totally new at the time. Not for him wild swings and ponderous lunges. He moved lightly on his toes, never remaining in one place for more than a fraction of a second, and tied Sullivan up in knots with clever feints and fancy footwork. He rammed the left over time and again, a fast jab to keep Sullivan off balance, a ramrod straight punch from the shoulder to jolt his head back, and a swift hook whenever Sullivan did get to close quarters.

For round after round Corbett boxed Sullivan's ears off. As the fight wore on, and the champion was reduced to a battered, bleeding, exhausted hulk, it became obvious that there was no way he could last 45 rounds. From the 15th onwards Corbett began to follow through with straight rights. In round 20 Sullivan was hurt and befuddled and the end was in sight.

It came in the next round. A volley of lefts and rights drove Sullivan to the ropes and a right hand smash left him face downwards on the canvas. They don't get up usually from that position, but then they're not all John L. Sullivans. Somehow he did. Corbett jabbed him around the ring and then unleashed another torrent of punches. Sullivan fell — once for the death of the bareknuckle days — rose splay-legged and fell again, this time for his own straddling era, rose and again fell, whilst Corbett looked on silently. The last fall was for himself and it was over. Sullivan was still conscious; there was just no strength left.

After the formalities were over he came out to the centre of the ring and told the crowd: 'I'm glad I was licked by a fellow American.' But he spared no glance in Corbett's direction, nor did he congratulate him — instead he hated him always.

The defeat of a great champion always stuns a nation and none more so than this one. It is recorded that men wept who had never cried before. They too would always hate Corbett.

John L. did not entirely keep his promise to retire in 1896 and he boxed a three round exhibition with 'Sailor' Tom Sharkey, a leading contender. Later, though it is not well recorded, an exhibition with James J. Jeffries who in 1899 would assume the mantle of champion. And in 1905, at the age of 46, he fought an actual contest with a young hopeful named Jack McCormick, knocking him out in two rounds. But his main enemy in the long years of retirement was alcoholism. He married again in 1910 and found a measure of happiness; alas brief, his wife died only six years later. In the main the quarter of a century after New Orleans was bitter, people, well meaning but unintentionally cruel, patronised him, the worst fate of all for a dominant personality. On February 2nd, 1918 he died from heart failure. His funeral was of the variety normally afforded to

Presidents and indeed amongst the mourners was a future Chief Executive, Calvin Coolidge. It was a bitterly cold day and in order to consign John L. to the ground they had to dynamite it, a fitting tribute to this man of dynamite.

And thus passed into legend John Laurence Sullivan. According to the hype he was a Hector, a Lysander, a Hercules. But was he?

I will not attempt to fit Sullivan into his times. That has already been done admirably by his most recent biographer, Michael Isenberg[1]. As a man John L. was a contradiction. On one hand a drunken, loutish bore; on the other, a generous man who reflected the warmth of his family upbringing. He made, and kept, close friendships. Billy Madden forgave him and returned to the fold and virtually every one of Sullivan's opponents became his friend, even Charlie Mitchell. But sadly the one man who probably would have prized the old Lion's friendship more than anyone was always excluded. We either hate or love those who destroy us; Sullivan could never forgive James J. Corbett for dethroning him.

As a fighter it is difficult to assess Sullivan. Even analysing his record is a nightmare because most of his bouts were either real fights posing as exhibitions or exhibitions posing as real fights. The Ring Record Book awards him 75 contests of varying descriptions; Sullivan himself claimed 48 whilst Michael Isenberg shaves off the Sharkey exhibition and comes up with 47. The historian has to make decisions and I have described what I consider to be John L.'s major contests (he himself lists Donaldson as his first). Some will disagree and argue that the list should include Dominick McCaffrey (won on points over six rounds); also possibly Patsy Cardiff and England's Alf Greenfield. It is a matter of individual judgement.

When we analyse the quality of John L.'s opposition he appears to be the luckiest fighter in history. His opponents are best summed up by repeating Oliver Cromwell's description of the first Parliamentary Army: 'Old decaying men and tapsters.' But that hides the fact that they were the best around at the time. Not until Sullivan had passed his peak did fighters of genuine merit come along to challenge him. The nobodies and never wassers of his salad days he boxed with ridiculous ease. One might be tempted to argue that John L. lost to his first quality opponent, but Corbett himself, never a man to underrate his own abilities, always refused to speculate on how he would have fared against Sullivan in his prime.

Technically Sullivan appears just a crude slugger. He used his left simply to beat down his opponents' guard and pave the way for his right. It might be argued that any good boxer could have run him out of town. Dominick McCaffrey, who had fought both he and Corbett, was emphatic before the Sullivan–Corbett contest that Corbett would be too good for John L. But once again this

1 'John L. Sullivan and his Times'

masks the truth. Sullivan never learnt the rudiments of his trade because he didn't need to. The opposition was poor and his slugging style was the style of the day. Seventy years later a similarly crude Massachusetts fighter, Rocky Marciano, got to good boxers and destroyed them. If we look closely at John L. then we can see that he had one of the most powerful right hand punches in history. We have already heard what Joe Goss had to say about it; Paddy Ryan likened it to being hit by a telegraph pole. Jake Kilrain attempted to outlast Sullivan but was under no illusions about their respective fistic merits: 'My God, I am licked. He is too strong, too powerful, and can hit too hard.'[1] But hard punching is not purely about power. Timing, accuracy and execution are essentials. At his peak Sullivan's timing was excellent and he shrewdly placed his blows just under the ear. His bodily strength and stamina — especially for a man who trained on booze — were also phenomenal. All in all he was a tremendous fighting machine.

But perhaps the greatest part of his legend is just that, the legend and the stature which he gave to boxing. Sullivan straddled the era between bareknuckle fighting and glove fighting. He had star quality. Abraham Lincoln once described military glory as an attractive rainbow which came up under showers of blood and one Civil War general was heard to comment that if war was made a spectator sport the public would never tire of it (the Jury is still out on that one). Sullivan's glory lay in putting this forbidden fruit in front of the public in the guise of individual combat. And winning. He made boxing what it is today. His legend is not untainted, but it is not destroyed either.

1 Sullivan — 'I can lick any son-of-a-bitch in the house' p.160

Volume Two

James J. Corbett to Tommy Burns

Round Five: 'Gentleman Jim'

James J. Corbett is often credited with being the first scientific boxer. In fact Broughton, Mendoza, Belcher and Jem Mace were also considered to be 'scientific' in their eras. Corbett was the logical progression of their improvements of technique. His brand of left-handed boxing was thought of as revolutionary at the time. For the heavyweight division it was, but there had already been similarly skilful champions in other weight classes, 'Nonpareil' Jack Dempsey at middle and Tommy Ryan, the welterweight kingpin. Moreover, Corbett's style was very limited by today's standards. He had a highly educated left hand and had developed the technique of hooking with it, but his right was not especially good, he was not a particularly hard hitter, and he did not put his punches together in combinations. This has led many modern boxing writers to suggest that Corbett was overrated. Certainly, he cannot be considered as one of the great heavyweight champions, but it needs to be emphasised that technique is a constantly developing feature.

All of the champions of Corbett's era until well into the 20th Century seem very limited when seen on film today. They punch singly, possess only a small repertoire of punches and appear static in terms of footwork and upper body movement. But that does not mean that the outstanding fighters of yesteryear would not reach the top today. Technique has also developed in other sports, golf being a good example. A century ago tournaments like the British Open were being won with scores of around the 300 mark. This was partly due to poorly set up courses and inferior equipment, but also the fact that the modern golf swing had yet to evolve. (Bobby Jones is often considered its pioneer.) However the great champions of that era, the Morrises, Braid, Taylor, Willie Anderson and Harry Vardon would without doubt have still won majors today. The same can be said for boxing; great fighters like Jack Johnson, Stanley Ketchel and Joe Gans would have mastered modern techniques and been exceptional in any era.

James John Corbett was born on September 1st, 1866 in San Francisco. In his prime he stood 6′ 1″ and weighed an approximate 180 lbs (82 kilos). He was the first heavyweight champion to fight all his bouts under Queensberry rules.

The movie of Corbett's life, 'Gentleman Jim' is a highly entertaining Errol Flynn vehicle. It portrays Corbett as the devil may care sibling of a poor but happy Irish family renowned for brawling with each other and everyone else in sight. Corbett's parents were certainly Irish, father Patrick from County Mayo and mother Catherine from Dublin. And they were certainly poor; ten children on a shoestring budget was not calculated to breed financial stability. The eventual outcome was horrendous. Patrick Corbett sunk into chronic depression.

On August 15th, 1898 he shot Catherine to death as she lay sleeping and then turned the gun on himself.

The Ring Record Book's photograph of James Corbett seems to reflect this family tragedy. There is a careworn look around the eyes and an expression of angst on the features. It is not the face of a happy man.

Catherine had ambitions of the Priesthood for her son, but James' young life was dominated by sports. He was a fine all round athlete who excelled at running and baseball. His education was only basic but his appearance was good and helped secure him a job in the Nevada bank. He began to box at about the age of seventeen under the auspices of the Olympic Sporting Club, San Francisco. At this stage he had not settled on a career in the ring; a social climber, Corbett was seeking a status above his working class origins. The Bank originally appeared to hold the right route.

Up to 1889 Corbett boxed sporadically, mainly at the Olympic Club but also as far afield as Salt Lake City. Officially these contests were amateur, although exactly how 'amateur' is open to speculation. One early fight was with 'Professor' John Donaldson of Sullivan 'footrace' fame; Donaldson had been fighting for money for quite some time. Corbett's record up to 1889 lists 13 bouts with only one loss, a points defeat by Billy Welch which was swiftly avenged with a first round knockout.

According to Corbett in his autobiography, the decision to fight professionally came about when the Bank, noting a black eye, gave him the option: quit boxing or quit them. He resigned. Whether this was the exact truth or was part of the image of austere pride which he liked to cultivate, is open to question. Although he had been promoted from messenger to assistant teller a poorly educated shamrock boy from the wrong side of the tracks really did not figure to rise all that much higher. If he was going to make anything of himself then the choice now lay between boxing and baseball. Like Sullivan, Corbett chose boxing.

Being in the right place at the right time is an important ingredient of success in life. In 1889 the coming boxer in San Francisco was Joe Choynski (pronounced Ko-in-ski). Two years younger than Corbett, Choynski had won the amateur championship of the Pacific Coast before turning professional with three straight victories. He was not especially big, 5′ 10½″ and 170 lbs (77 kilos), but was renowned for his punching power. Choynski and Corbett came from the same neighbourhood. According to Corbett, there was no personal enmity between them but their respective friends created some and natural Irish-Jewish rivalry did the rest. A match was swiftly arranged. The two men later became firm friends and in all probability the so-called rivalry was mainly hype for a contest which both men saw to their financial advantage.

The fight was originally venued for a barn near Fairfax, May 30th, 1889. They had boxed only four rounds before the police stopped it. Corbett had damaged his right hand but when Choynski's side suggested that they try again six days later he made no objection. The new venue was of all places Benecia, famed for John C. Heenan, and the contest would take place on a barge moored on the Benecia river. The contest was under Queensberry rules but to a finish and became a legend in ring history.

Before the bout, Choynski's manager contrived to lose his gloves and then proposed that they should fight with bare knuckles. This posed an agonising dilemma for Corbett. The spectators had already assembled and he could hardly refuse to go on with it. Yet Corbett's right hand was already damaged and fighting without the protection of a glove would quickly worsen the injury. Before Corbett could make up his mind, a well meaning spectator offered Choynski his gloves. Choynski had to accept, but for Corbett this only proved to be a case of from the frying pan into the fire for the gloves were braided with rawhide and they lacerated his face dreadfully.

Corbett's right hand was virtually useless. Throughout the fight he used it sparingly, each punch searing his brain with a spasm of agony. The rawhide gloves tore his face to pieces. Jim's mouth was so badly damaged that at one point his seconds had to cut away shreds of bloody flesh hanging from it with scissors. It was like fighting a man with razor blades imbedded in his gloves!

Despite such appalling disadvantages Corbett made the early running, boxing superbly with his left hand and bemusing Choynski with his adroit footwork. But from the 15th Choynski began to come on, surging forward and pounding away with both hands. At the end of 26 rounds the two men were level. Yet Corbett was now desperate. It was the hottest time of the day during the hottest time of the year, and the sun was beating down on them, a fiery furnace taking a savage toll of both, particularly Corbett whose exertions had been greater than Choynski's. Corbett knew that Choynski must outlast him.

He had to gamble; and he did so brilliantly.

At the outset of the 27th Corbett threw a series of haymakers with his right, all carefully calculated to miss although Choynski did not realise it. Smiling, Choynski kept moving away to his right to avoid the swinging punches. He saw Corbett winding himself up for yet another big one and grinned as he stepped gingerly to his right to evade it. A minute later Choynski was being brought round in his corner by smelling salts. He had ducked straight into a savage left hook that carried every ounce of Corbett's fading strength behind it. Corbett's right swings had moved Choynski inch by inch into the path of the left. It was the hardest single punch that Jim ever threw.

Thirty years earlier Benecia's name had helped make John Heenan a celebrity. Now, the Battle of Benecia brought James J. Corbett public attention in his first professional fight. He acquired a manager, William Brady. Brady was shrewd and had a flair for publicity. He would go on to manage a second heavyweight champion, and later become a movie mogul. In some respects

Corbett was a publicist's dream. A tall, slim man, crowned with a pompadour hairstyle, he looked more at home in a tuxedo than boxing trunks. Thus was born the image of 'Gentleman Jim', the myth and the nickname which Corbett would always carry.

Another gimmick, possibly suggested by Brady, was a variation on Sullivan's 'I'll knock anybody out in four rounds' routine, in this case offering a draw to anyone lasting the distance. It was tried out with one, Dave Campbell in July, 1889 and swiftly abandoned; Campbell got his draw. But the following February Corbett made his next big career move, a six round contest in New Orleans with Jake Kilrain whose marathon with Sullivan was still fresh in the public's mind. Kilrain was expected to crush the Californian mannequin but instead had his ears boxed off with ridiculous ease. Poor Jake spent the eighteen minutes cutting huge swathes in the air with his haymakers, while Corbett's left seemed attracted to his face by a magnet. After four professional fights the Brady boy was now a serious contender.

On May 21st, 1891, Corbett stepped into the ring for his sternest test. he fought Australia's Peter Jackson in a fight to the finish at the San Francisco Athletic Club. It was to be another epic and one of the longest clashes ever under Queensberry rules*.

Peter Jackson is regarded in some quarters as the greatest heavyweight never to win the title. Possibly; there are other contenders for this unlucky sobriquet. What does seem certain is that at this stage of their careers he would have beaten Sullivan had John L. not drawn the colour line against him.

West Indian in origin and Australian by naturalisation, Jackson had become a professional fighter in 1883. His first joust for the Australian heavyweight crown betrayed his greatest weakness; he was vulnerable to body punching. After outboxing champion Bill Farnan for two rounds, Jackson was kayoed by a right to the midriff in the third.

Jackson arrived in America in 1888. There were not too many black fighters around at the time although one, George Dixon, was signalling their development and would soon win the world's bantam and featherweight titles. The best black American heavyweight was George Godfrey, 'Old Chocolate' (Dixon was 'Little Chocolate'), who years later when he was dying insisted that his friends lift him onto his feet so that he could die standing up. After 10 rounds with Jackson he looked as though he had fallen down a manhole. Next came Joe McAuliffe, a white heavyweight whom most avoided like the plague. Jackson

* The longest recorded fight was under London prize ring rules, a 110 round draw between Andy Bowen and Jack Burke in 1893 which lasted 7 hours and 19 minutes. The shortest under London prize ring rules was 7 seconds, and the shortest under Queensberry rules was timed at 10.5 seconds including the count!

knocked him out in 24 rounds.

A barnstorming tour of Britain followed, amongst his victims hardy perennial Jem Smith and Ireland's Peter Maker who was later to feature in the title picture. But back in Australia in October 1890 Jackson was held to a draw by Joe Goddard — 'the Barrier Champion' — who set up a non stop body attack. Peter was coming off this result when the fight with Corbett was arranged. But he was still favourite to beat the American. Corbett had nowhere near his experience or power and most believed that he would not be able to cope with Jackson's famed 'one-two', a right to the body followed by a left uppercut to the jaw. They were wrong.

For the description of the fight — and its controversial outcome — we have to rely on Corbett's memoirs and naturally they are slanted towards himself. They do however convey the flavour of one of the ring's greatest classics.

For over three hours the fans witnessed an epic of scientific boxing. Initially Corbett fought defensively, moving at great speed and feinting and weaving to avoid Jackson's blows. The Californian used every inch of the ring, jetting forth a constant stream of lefts whilst Jackson attacked with both hands, seeking to land his dreaded 'one-two'. In the 17th he landed a right hook on Corbett's side which badly hurt him and as Corbett returned to his corner he instinctively clutched his side. Manager Brady angrily pulled his hand away but too late for he had already betrayed how hurt he was to Jackson's watching seconds.

Encouraged, Jackson redoubled his efforts but Corbett met him with superior tactical thinking. Every time the Australian got set to throw the right, Corbett stepped quickly inside with his own sharp left hook to the body. After ten rounds of this a much discouraged Jackson virtually abandoned his attempts to land rights to the body and from this point on Corbett effectively had the fight won, for Jackson was now unable to complete the 'one-two'.

The 27th, 28th, and 29th rounds were the best of the fight. Jackson launched an almost despairing two-handed assault in the 27th, driving Corbett into the ropes, but the Californian then took him completely by surprise by opening up himself and punching the Australian back across the ring. In the 28th they brought the crowd to its feet as they stood toe-to-toe, trading punches for the full three minutes. At the beginning of the 29th Corbett pounded Jackson around the ring on the end of a fusillade of punches but in doing so he left himself open for the Negro to launch a stunning counter-attack with a battery of right hooks to the ribs. Corbett was sent hurtling into sharp retreat.

From the 1st through the 29th the fight had been fought at a searing pace and now the two men were beginning to tire. From round 30 onwards the action slowly de-escalated, and by round 50 — they had now fought for 2½ hours — they were punching only spasmodically. Between the 50th and 60th rounds hardly a punch was thrown, but in the 51st Corbett surprised Jackson with a good right and saw his eyes roll. Corbett knew now that Jackson was virtually out on his feet. At the end of the round Corbett and Brady huddled together in conference in Jim's corner: Corbett felt that he had one good rally left in him, after that he wouldn't be much good. It was now three minutes past one o'clock in the morning and whilst they were engrossed in their tactical discussion they failed to notice referee Hiram Cook leave the ring and confer with the Club's directors. Several directors had bet heavily on Jackson. Cook's actions were not only unusual — they were in fact improper.

When he returned to the ring Cook suddenly announced that he was terminating the contest — the result was a draw — all bets were null and void.

Corbett was furious. He was ahead on points and felt that he had enough left to knock the exhausted Jackson out. His assessment of Jackson's condition was correct. As Jim left the ring he heard a thud behind him: Jackson had collapsed! His handlers carried him to his dressing room. Afterwards Corbett met him in a Turkish bath and found him holding his stomach and groaning. (It does need to be said however that Jackson's training had been interrupted by injury.)

Corbett never forgave the club for their behaviour and never set foot inside it again.

The drawn verdict also meant that neither man got paid for the purse money was on a winner takes all basis. Many club members, feeling that Corbett had been badly treated, raised a subscription for him. Jackson received nothing.

'Gentleman Jim' had risen like a meteor. A shrewd meteor. He and Brady had picked Corbett's fights carefully, Choynski at the outset of his career, Kilrain just after his sun drenched hiding from Sullivan and Jackson who may possibly have been just about to slide. Significantly though, after winning the title Corbett showed no inclination to fight any of them again. There was talk of a rematch with Jackson in 1893 but it fell through. In all probability Corbett had little to fear from the Australian by this time;— or his fellow Antipodean Frank Slavin. Even before Corbett fought Sullivan, Jackson and Slavin had effectively ruined each other in a savage encounter in London.

James J. Corbett was not a popular champion. He had made the mistake of dethroning a legend. But he did not help his own cause either. A month after beating Sullivan he opened in a play, 'Gentleman Jack' (it was his second having earlier debuted in 'Sports Macallister'). Acting and not fighting was to be his main occupation for the next five years.

During that time he defended the championship just once. Now whom would you least want to see getting another title shot, least deserved it and was the least likely to succeed? Yes, Charlie Mitchell!

Nearly six years had elapsed since the Sullivan fight when Mitchell stepped into the ring at Jacksonville, Florida to fight Corbett. During that time he had done nothing except outpoint a nobody and share a ring with Jem Mace! Although officially an exhibition, it was billed as being for the British title, and for a purse of 1,000. At 28, Mitchell was exactly thirty years younger than Mace. How does it feel to hit somebody old enough to be your grandad!

Preparing for Corbett, Mitchell tried his usual pre-fight antics, taunts and insults, designed to make Jim mad. They did. Over 70 years later Jacksonville was to be a happy hunting ground for another British sportsman, golfer Tony Jacklin. For Mitchell it was the burial ground of his career. Corbett, enraged, punched him around the ring for two rounds and then despatched him in the third with a blistering right. But although nobody could then know it, this was to be Jim's last unimpeached victory.

Aside from exhibitions, Corbett did not fight again for three years. One of these, six two minute rounds against Peter Courtney, is worthy of note because it was the first 'fight' ever to be filmed. In the main, Corbett concentrated on acting, opening in a third play 'The Naval Cadet' in 1895. That year he also announced his retirement; and tried to inaugurate his successor!

The new champion, so Corbett and crafty Bill Brady hoped, would be his sparring partner, Steve O'Donnell, an Australian of Irish descent who was also managed by Brady. Corbett announced that he would 'recognise' as champion the winner of a bout between O'Donnell and yet another Irishman (get the picture?), Peter Maher, formerly of Galway.

Whatever Steve O'Donnell's pedigree was has been lost in the mists of antiquity*. Maher had a reasonable record on paper as long as nobody looked at it in detail. Then the cracks started to appear — alarmingly. His only victory of note had been over a faded George Godfrey in Godfrey's penultimate fight. Against this Peter Jackson had knocked him out, ditto Joe Goddard. Also, Bob Fitzsimmons whom we first met pounding lumps out of Herbert Slade and who was now world middleweight champion and contracted to fight Corbett before his retirement. Fitzsimmons was being lost in a fast shuffle. As Maher clearly did not catch as well as he pitched against Antipodeans, then the favoured O'Donnell appeared to be in with a chance. Alas not. Maher destroyed him in 63 seconds and went on to make something of a career out of using O'Donnell as a punchbag**.

Nobody recognised Maher as champion. There was much public support for Fitzsimmons; hecklers made Corbett's life something of a misery during performances of 'The Naval Cadet'. Corbett had agreed to fight him over a year earlier but the authorities had run them out of town in Dallas and had them arrested in Little Rock. Most reluctantly, Corbett agreed to recognise the winner of a Maher-Fitzsimmons bout as champion.

The surroundings of the fight were more colourful than the contest. It was

* Although Nat Fleischer describes him as an 'exceptionally clever boxer.'
** Two more 1st's and a 2nd round kayo.

scheduled for Langtry, Texas (named after the actress-cum-prostitute Lily Langtry), on February 21st, 1896. Langtry was the personal fiefdom of famed wild west character Judge Roy Bean. However, on the day of the fight the Texas Rangers turned up to stop it. Everybody (Rangers included) was happy when the fight moved just across the border into Mexico. Everybody bar Maher that is. He lasted an approximate 90 seconds before one of Fitzsimmons rights sent him into dreamland.

Corbett on the other hand came out of dreamland. Piqued by the destruction of his (and Brady's) plans, he announced that he was returning to the ring. But even now he contracted to defend against a fellow Irishman, 'Sailor' Tom Sharkey, originally from Dundalk. However, public opinion demanded Corbett settle matters with Fitzsimmons and the champion ultimately agreed to defend against first Sharkey, and then Fitzsimmons within 60 days, or March 1st, 1897 if the Sharkey fight had not taken place by the end of 1896. It was a tight contract as far as Fitzsimmons was concerned; not so Sharkey who was quietly ditched. Corbett-Fitzsimmons was eventually arranged for March 17th, 1897 in Carson City, Nevada, for a purse of $15,000 and a sidestake of $10,000.

Corbett and Fitzsimmons actively disliked one another and this time there was no hype involved. Corbett was of Irish extraction, Fitzsimmons English. Irish boxers seemed prone to fatalities around Fitzsimmons. 'Nonpareil' Jack Dempsey had died of tuberculosis four years after losing the middleweight title to Bob; some said his body punches had hastened the end. Con Riordan, one of Fitzsimmons' sparring partners, had been fatally injured in an exhibition bout with him. Physically, the two men were poles apart, Corbett handsome and fastidious, Fitzsimmons freckle faced and balding and with pipe-stem legs which made some refer to him as a freak. Corbett's dislike of his challenger had previously boiled over in a hotel lobby when he had tweaked Fitz's nose and insulted him. Insults flew again when they met whilst doing roadwork; the pair of them had to be pulled apart.

Although Corbett was the aggressor in these affairs, they seem to have played on his mind more than Fitzsimmons. During training he was moody and surly. This is a good sign during the final stages of training but not throughout. Jim does not appear to have been in the right frame of mind for the contest. He was, however, a firm favourite in the betting.

Corbett–Fitzsimmons was the first world title fight to be filmed (the contestants were both on a third of the proceeds and at least one print still exists today). There was also a curious forerunner of the closed circuit, satellite transmission that has become fashionable in recent years with telegraph links being set up between Carson City and various other cities to carry blow by blow accounts of the fight. The telegraph was linked to giant electric boards on which two figures, one representing Corbett, the other Fitzsimmons, electronically re-enacted the fight blow-by-blow as it came over the telegraph wire. Large excited crowds stood watching as the two figures performed the movements.

Throughout the first six rounds the only movements to see came from Corbett. Never had the champion boxed more brilliantly. His left dominated Fitzsimmons. In the sixth Corbett put everything into a vicious right uppercut to the jaw. Fitzsimmons was floored for a count of '9'. He appeared groggy and on the verge of defeat. At this point the odds on Corbett looked to be a 1,000 to 1. When Fitzsimmons returned to his corner — having barely lasted out the round — his face was a bloody mask.

But amazingly Fitzsimmons seemed to be getting stronger in round 7. He landed enough punches to even this stanza and went on to just shade the 8th. No matter how hard or how often Corbett hit Fitzsimmons, the challenger only seemed to get more powerful. By the end of the 8th Corbett was wondering just what sort of man he was fighting. But he gritted his teeth and spurted through the next three rounds, his left hand seemingly attached to Fitzsimmons' face. The challenger was being outclassed at this point but he kept cool and refused to be disheartened. As he went back to his corner at the end of the 11th Fitzsimmons' wife Rose, sitting at the ringside, began to call out a steady stream of encouragement.

In the 12th Corbett took a breather after his exertions of the last three rounds, and Fitzsimmons stole the round. But in the 13th Corbett launched a sustained drive for victory and he punched Fitzsimmons from one side of the ring to the other. At the end of the round however Fitzsimmons was still strong; Rose began to anticipate victory. She kept up her encouragement: 'Hit him in the slats*, Bob.' Fitzsimmons looked at her and nodded.

In the 14th they were boxing on even terms when Fitzsimmons slung over a heavy right to Corbett's neck. Corbett reeled into the ropes. Following up, Fitzsimmons did a brief shuffle of his legs to set himself up for a left hook and then drove it into Corbett's body. Corbett dropped on all fours, his head clear but his body temporarily paralysed. The spasm passed as the referee counted '10', but Corbett was no longer the world heavyweight champion. He charged wildly across the ring at Fitzsimmons but the new champion held him off until Jim's cornermen broke it up.

Before they left the ring Corbett asked Fitzsimmons for a return: Bob refused. Corbett angrily threatened to attack him on the street whenever he saw him: Fitzsimmons coldly replied that if Corbett ever attacked him then he would shoot him!

Corbett left the ring unmarked: Fitzsimmons' face was a relief map of cuts and bruises. No matter: he was the champion.

* Stomach — although some might put a different interpretation on it!

Round Six: 'Ruby Bob'

Robert Fitzsimmons (he had no middle name) was born at Helston, Cornwall on May 26th, 1863. He was the twelfth and final child of James, the village policeman, and Jane, nee Strongman. James was from Ireland (which gives that tiny country an ancestral claim on all first three modern champions) and Jane was a Cornish girl.

Bob Fitzsimmons has often been claimed as a British world heavyweight champion. That however is blinkered patriotism. When Bob was nine he emigrated with his parents to New Zealand where he grew up. He visited Britain only once as an adult, never boxed here and took out American citizenship in 1893. Afterwards he always lived in America. The Duke of Wellington once remarked that because a man is born in a stable it does not make him a horse and that sums the situation up most succinctly.

The Fitzsimmons settled in Timaru where Bob's elder brother Jarrett opened a blacksmith's shop. When he grew older Bob worked in the forge, an occupation which is normally credited for providing him with his phenomenal punching power. He developed a tremendous upper torso with huge shoulders and a powerful chest. By sharp contrast his legs were mere spindles. He had the upper body of a heavyweight and the lower of a lightweight with his actual weight (generally an approximate 165 lbs — 75 kilos) coming to rest at middle. On reaching manhood he stood 5′ 11¾″.

In 1880 Jem Mace visited New Zealand on the look out for talent to develop (or more likely to exploit). He organised an amateur lightweight competition in Timaru. Fitzsimmons, who at that time weighed around 140 lbs (63.5 kilos), entered and won it defeating four opponents. The following year Mace returned, this time with Herbert Slade in tow, and held a middleweight competition. Fitzsimmons also returned and won that too, scoring five victories. After the final he engaged in the aforementioned contest with Slade which Mace was forced to halt because his protegé was getting a hiding (the termination almost caused a fight between Fitzsimmons and Mace).

The next nine years of Bob's life are very sketchy. Possibly deliberately so on Fitzsimmons' part. He claimed to have been victorious in a number of bare knuckle fights around Timaru and names sometimes appear on his record to support this. But whether they were made up is another question; nobody has ever actually located details of these fights. What is known is that in 1883 he departed New Zealand for good accompanied by his first wife, Alice.

They did not travel far, just to Sydney, Australia where Bob found work as a blacksmith. he also boxed in a desultory fashion; around two dozen professional contests (Queensberry rules) are recorded, but over the space of seven years. Not all actually took place. One, billed as for the 'Championship' of New Zealand, was cancelled, but Fitz still included it as a 'victory' on his record. In fights which did come off he had no end of trouble with a Mick Dooley who beat him three out of four. Dooley proved easy meat for the young Frank Slavin* who twice flattened him, and at this point nobody marked Fitzsimmons down as a coming man in the ring.

Life however often hinges on events which ostensibly have nothing to do with us. In 1890 Jim Hall, the Australian middleweight champion, was offered a possible title shot against world champion 'Nonpareil' Jack Dempsey in America. But he needed a good victory to enhance his reputation. Fitzsimmons came to mind; reasonable record but not too ambitious and always on the lookout to make a shilling. Would Fitz like to go through the motions of a title shot and take a dive for a share of the purse? Bob was not averse. They first staged a mock fight to practise the ending of the 'real' one. Fitzsimmons later had the cheek to claim this as a first round knock-out 'victory' on his record! Two days later he and Hall engaged in their so-called 'genuine' match, Fitz doing his high diving act in the 4th. Hall was later to deny this was a fix — historians do not believe him, and at least one newspaper report of the contest strongly implies that it was faked.

Hall booked his passage but was stabbed in a brawl. Instead the chance of fighting Dempsey was offered to Fitzsimmons. Nearly 27, going nowhere in Australia, and with a wife and baby son to support, Fitz seized the opportunity.

He turned up in San Francisco in May, 1890 with a letter of introduction to the California Athletics Club who were sponsoring the challenger for the Dempsey match. It may initially have been a put up job to provide the champion with an easy defence, but later the Club's directors bet heavily on Fitzsimmons to win. At first though they were not even sure the odd looking New Zealander was a fighter, and insisted on him working out with a local middleweight named Frank Allen. Fitz promptly floored Allen who in falling broke his wrist. Suitably impressed, the Club matched him in two contests, one with Dempsey's last challenger. Bob won both and the Dempsey contest was arranged for January 14th, 1891 in New Orleans.

The Irish born American had been a great champion but eighteen months earlier was knocked out by George Lablanche with a back fisted blow which left him unconscious for some time. The 'pivot' punch was promptly outlawed. Some believe Dempsey never fully got over it; he was anyway in the early stages of tuberculosis when he fought Fitzsimmons.

The fight was horribly one sided. With the torso of a heavyweight and the

* Then a middleweight.

punch to match, Fitzsimmons was simply too powerful. Dempsey was bounced up and down off the canvas like a yo-yo. He had nothing left in his knapsack save pride and courage. Even Fitzsimmons begged him to quit. By the 12th, when Dempsey went down four times, it had become something which only a psychopath could enjoy watching. Two knockdowns into the 13th it was finally over, much to Bob's relief. A year earlier he had been an unknown blacksmith, grubbing along with the odd fight to help pay the bills. Now he was the middleweight champion of the world.

What had wrought the transformation? On the evidence of the Mace competitions Fitz had always possessed a degree of natural talent, but it is accurate to say that he was not a particularly skilful fighter. His strengths were punching power, unorthodoxy and durability. He was a good body puncher and developed what became known as the 'solar plexus' punch, in reality a good old fashioned wallop to the stomach for which he made good use of his legs to bring him square onto the target. When he arrived in America he was determined to make the most of his opportunity, trained hard and concentrated purely on fighting. He had not given evidence of great hitting power in Australia — only seven stoppages — but in the much more professional Gyms of America he learnt how to harness his raw strength to timing and accuracy.

However, there is also an explanation of a much darker hue for this sudden conversion to demon puncher — he loaded his gloves.

It is a fact that when Fitz fought Jim Jeffries for the second time he sprinkled cement powder on his bandages to make his fists rock hard*. This accounted for the facial injuries which Jeffries suffered. it was also responsible for the damage to Fitz's own hands. Many of Fitzsimmons' opponents sustained bad facial injuries and his hands have been described by one biographer as 'a mess of broken bones and mangled ligaments'. The effect of his famed 'solar plexus' punch was to leave opponents on all fours gasping for breath as though they had been hit by somebody with a brick in his fist. As the solar plexus is the most fleshy part of the body, it also minimises damage to the hands. This punch seems to have been developed by Bob in America; like his overall knock-out power, there is no evidence of it in Australian days. When we add all this up it tends to suggest that Fitzsimmons acquired status as a kayo artist may not have been entirely due to improvements in technique and training.

His next fight of substance took him back to New Orleans to meet Peter Maher for the first time. The Irishman took a sustained hammering and quit at the end of the 12th, a bloodstained wreck. However, both men took a count in a wild first round, and Fitz was possibly saved from being knocked out by Joe

* The cement turned hard due to the hands sweating and soaking the bandages.

Choynski* who kicked the time-keeper's gong to end the round early**.

Domestic travails occupied the next portion of Fitzsimmons' life. As part of his newly found fame he toured with a vaudeville company. There he met the Julian trio, two acrobatic sisters and their brother, Martin, who handled the trio's affairs. Bob was attracted to one of the sisters, Rose, a shortish but very good looking young woman. Martin Julian in turn fell for Alice Fitzsimmons. The upshot was that Bob and Alice divorced, Bob married Rose and Alice married Martin who became Fitz's manager. Rose was to provide Bob with three more children before she died in 1903. All in all he married four times. No photograph apparently exists of Alice but Fitzsimmons other wives were all highly attractive women. Fitzsimmons himself could not be described as handsome; in addition to his disproportionate frame, he was covered in freckles and his red hair — which gave rise to his nickname 'Ruby Bob' — receded while he was still young. But he seems to have had an engaging personality which people found attractive.

Back in the ring, Bob's challengers for the middleweight crown came from Australia. First was Jim Hall, spitting fury over Fitz's usurpation of his position as challenger to Dempsey. He went back to Australia sadder, wiser and knocked out in four rounds. After that Fitzsimmons hung a two round kayo on the chin of Dan Creedon in a second and final defence, although he kept the crown until he won the heavyweight title***.

It was towards getting Corbett into the ring that Bob mainly directed his energies. He threw out his first challenge immediately after Corbett's victory over Sullivan. A five round pummelling of Joe Choynski in 1894 did his cause no harm. Although technically a draw because the police stopped it, Fitzsimmons blasted Choynski to the canvas several times whilst it lasted.

Not long afterwards came the first of two ring tragedies. Fitzsimmons agreed to box an exhibition match with one of his sparring partners, Con Riordan. Riordan was a washed up Irish-Australian heavyweight who had been drinking heavily for some time. He was drunk when he got into the ring that night, and probably attempted to turn it into a real fight. Riordan was knocked out and died shortly afterwards. The Inquest verdict was that he had lost his life from exhaustion following heavy drinking. However, a contributory factor to the exhaustion may well have been Fitzsimmons' solar plexus special, with which he finished the match. Tragedy would strike again nine years later when an ex pro footballer named Con Coughlin died after an exhibition bout with Fitzsimmons. Though both deaths upset him, he carried on with his career.

The circumstances leading up to the Corbett fight have been described in

* Choynski was working in Fitz's corner.

** In another version it was a spectator who had bet heavily on Fitzsimmons.

*** Ex-welterweight champion Tommy Ryan won the vacant title in 1898.

the last chapter, save one; Fitzsimmons' first contest with Tom Sharkey, in San Francisco on December 2nd, 1896. This was one of the more mysterious bouts in boxing history. Sharkey was supposed to get a title shot before Fitz but Corbett had shelved him. Instead Tom, a squat, brutish ex-sailor unbeaten in 24 fights with 22 knock-outs, signed to meet Fitzsimmons who was secure in the knowledge that win or lose he was going to get a championship fight. The referee for the contest was Wyatt Earp who turned up wearing his gun until the police ordered him to remove it. Before the fight started Earp told the spectators: 'no matter what happens I'll be accused of dirty work.' They call that covering your back.

Fitz, a 3–1 favourite in the betting, gave Sharkey a systematic beating flooring him in the 1st and then again in the 8th, this time for the count. The final punch was a left hook to the jaw but after the count was completed Earp announced that he was disqualifying Bob for a low blow delivered immediately beforehand. He then strapped his gun back on and asked whether anybody had a problem with it!

The result, and its aftermath, threw an ugly stain on boxing. Martin Julian took legal action claiming that Earp had bet the purse money of $10,000 on Sharkey and then divided the winnings between himself, Sharkey's manager and the two joint promoters. Julian's star witness was one Billy Smith, Sharkey's sparring partner. The accused countered that Smith was a blackmailer. The Judge threw it out on the grounds that prize-fighting was illegal in California anyway!

Later Earp's friend and fellow wild west character, Bat Masterson, spread a story that Earp had indeed bet the purse on Sharkey, but had actually divvied up the winnings between himself (Earp), and Fitzsimmons! The whole thing leaves a nasty taste in the mouth. One thing can definitely be relied upon; there was a betting coupe and Earp was a party to it. Far from being the heroic figure of legend he was provably a gambler, pimp and con-man (and that was his good side!). Exactly who his co-beneficiaries were is a matter of conjecture: Masterson was a bullshit artist on a par with Earp himself and hardly reliable. But it is conceivable that the entire contest may have been arranged both to compensate Sharkey for not insisting on his right to first crack at Corbett (he received the purse money — whether he also bet on himself is unknown), and to provide a gigantic betting swindle for *all* the other parties involved, after which they fell out. Whatever the truth of it, Fitzsimmons went blithely on with his preparations for Corbett, and boxing received a black eye. Fortunately, Earp and Co did not think as big as Arnold Rothstein who fixed the World Baseball series in 1919.

Equally fortunately, no stigma attached itself to Fitz's victory over Corbett in his next contest. That came afterwards and for a different reason — like his predecessor 'Ruby Bob' showed absolutely no inclination to be a fighting champion. Instead he copied 'Gentleman Jim' and took to the stage with an opus entitled 'The Honest Blacksmith'. Well, the 'Blacksmith' might have been accurate, but the 'honest' is disputable.

By 1899 Fitzsimmons had more or less retired. But he was still susceptible to a spot of easy money; 6′ 2½″ and 220 lbs* of it to be exact. James J. Jeffries was, according to the East Coast sporting press, a monolithic, muscle bound ape who needed a straw foot to tell right from left. Fitz picked up on the vibes, particularly when lumbering Jim laboured to a points victory over his, (Fitzsimmons') ex-sparring partner Bob Armstrong. The fact that Jeffries was managed by Mr Smooth himself, William Brady who had taken Corbett to the title, cut no ice with Bob. It should have done.

Brady was delighted when Fitzsimmons agreed to defend the championship against Jeffries at Coney Island on June 9th, 1899. He had every reason to be. Jeffries was a gorilla. He had prodigious strength, could punch and moved as lightly on his feet as an Olympic runner. Joe Choynski had driven his teeth up into the roof of his mouth; he had survived for a draw. The only thing which worried Brady was Fitz's famed body punch — he had seen what it did to Corbett. So into camp was summoned Bob's middleweight successor, crafty Tommy Ryan, and from Ryan's tutelage was born the Jeffries crouch. In reality it was a forerunner of Floyd Patterson's 'peek-a-boo' defence, head buried behind the gloves with the forearms protecting the body. Ready for you, Bob.

Brady also had a psychological trick up his sleeve. After the fighters were installed in their dressing rooms, he contrived to start a row about how they would break from a clinch. The debate ended up in Fitzsimmons' dressing room. Whilst Brady was arguing with Julian, Jeffries strolled in (by prearrangement) and demanded to know what the row was about. When told he sniffed disdainfully, caught hold of Fitzsimmons and said, 'This is how we'll break' — and with that he lifted Fitz off his feet and hurled him hard against the wall. Jeffries strolled out leaving Fitzsimmons badly shaken.

When the fight commenced, Jeffries promptly took refuge in the crouch Ryan had devised. Neither Fitzsimmons or the audience knew what to make of it. The latter didn't have to solve it; Fitz did — and couldn't. The only target he had to aim at was the top of Jeffries' head and that was like punching a slab of concrete. Fraught with danger too. When Bob tried to attack in the second, the siege gates flew open, out boomed a left hook and the champion found himself on the seat of his pants!

Round succeeded round tediously. Whenever Fitzsimmons attempted anything Jeffries either lashed him to head and body or gripped him in a bear hug designed to wear the older, lighter man down. Not until the fifth did Fitz have a success, finally getting through with a left which split Jeffries' left eye

* 100 kilos.

open. But the challenger remained calm.

The beginning of the end came in the 10th. Fitzsimmons looked old and frail and Jeffries finally came out of his shell and launched a sustained attack, flooring the champion twice. The 11th saw the finish. Big Jim whaled away savagely to the body until Fitz was ready for the cleaners. Then he ended it with a mighty left hook to the jaw. There was never a chance of Bob beating the count.

For Jeffries it was the beginning of an auspicious reign. But as we shall see, Fitzsimmons still had a few shots left in his locker.

Round Seven: The Boilermaker

It was in the nature of James Jackson Jeffries that not a lot is really known about him. Essentially, he was a private man who, in the vernacular of the trade, let his fists do the talking.

His dour personality can probably be attributed to his ancestry; his father was Scottish and his mother Dutch. His education — in Burbank, California, where the family had moved to from his birthplace of Carroll, Ohio — was equally unsuccessful in developing his communication skills; Jeffries was expelled from school at the age of 14 for beating up a teacher!

His nickname 'The Boilermaker' stemmed not from any colourful image associated with him, but from the fact that he was apprenticed to that trade during his teens. It was a hard, demanding occupation which helped to develop Jeffries' tremendous physique and powerful muscles.

Jeffries began to box, for money, in 1896 on the Pacific coast and won his first five fights inside the distance. But it was as a sparring partner to James J. Corbett that he first made an impression. Jeffries was hired to help the then champion prepare for his title defence against Fitzsimmons. Withdrawn and snappish during training, Corbett seems to have allowed his ego to get the better of him where Jeffriēs was concerned. The new sparring partner was taller and more powerfully built than he was, and at that stage of his career Jeffries had the finely chiselled features of an Ancient Greek Olympian. He also matched Corbett for running; during roadwork the champion could never shake him off. Jeffries was extremely fast for a man of his build. It has been suggested that he could run 100 metres in 11 seconds. This is certainly a gross exaggeration; the world record was then 10.8 and the first modern Olympics in 1896 was won in a time of 12 seconds. But the young Californian may well have been a sprinter of near international standard.

None of this made Corbett very fond of him. Later, Bill Brady was to plant a story in the press that bad blood erupted between Corbett and Jeffries during sparring and that the two men went off alone to a barn to settle things. This famous non-fight has been slavishly repeated by historians down through the years and is almost certainly non-sense. Corbett would hardly have taken such a risk, and his handlers would certainly not have allowed him to. The story surfaced later during Jeffries' title build up, and it suited Corbett to go along with it. In other words it was hype, pure and simple. The most important thing which happened to Jeffries in Corbett's training camp was that he attracted the attention of Brady, who became his manager.

Exactly four months after Corbett was beaten by Fitzsimmons, Jeffries nearly lost his own unbeaten record. He fought Gus Ruhlin, a gangling, flame haired giant from Canton, Ohio, and was held to a draw. His next contest also went the same way. Joe Choynski was still a very good fighter although destined never to win the ones which mattered. On November 30th, 1897 he and Jeffries battled to a twenty round draw in San Francisco. Battled is the operative word. At the mid-way stage one of Joe's pet left hooks badly damaged Jeffries' mouth and he fought the second half of the contest in a haze of blood and pain. Brady decided that there was an easier route to the top for his young hopeful.

Joe Goddard was still a name although now his talent was more a memory. Jeffries chopped him down in four rounds the following February. A month later he was back in the ring to meet another Australian — Peter Jackson.

Jackson was now a sepia shadow of his once great self. Just over a year after the titanic struggle with Corbett, he had fought his great Australian rival Frank Slavin for the British Empire* title in London. It turned out to be a vicious, hate filled battle which Jackson won on a tenth round knock-out after taking a brutal beating around the body. The aftermath was tuberculosis.

When he fought Jeffries, Jackson had been out of the ring for nearly six years; he was thirty-six and dying. Even so, he gave evidence of what might have happened had he met the crude young slugger at his peak. In the first round Jackson handed the Californian a boxing lesson, three times stepping inside Jeffries' guard with his famed right hook to the heart. Jeffries winced but the punches lacked the wicked venom which Jackson brought to bear at his peak and it was Jeffries who ended the round the better with a right swing that sent Jackson reeling into the ropes, an ominous portent of things to come.

Early in the 2nd Jackson tried to score a knockout with a double right hook to Jeffries' heart and head. The younger man was hurt but shook it off and stormed back firing punches with both hands. They met in a wild *mêlée* in the centre of the ring and Jackson called on all his old skill to slip and ride Jim's punches whilst he fought back with a barrage of short arm rights to the ribs which forced Jeffries to back off. But the respite was only momentary; Jeffries switched his own attack to the body and the effect was instantaneous — Jackson's consumption ridden frame was unable to withstand the shock and he doubled up in agony. Then Jeffries unleashed a left hook to the head and Jackson fell to his knees. He arose shakily and walked straight into another one which put him down again. Only the bell saved him from being counted out.

Effectively the fight was over. At the beginning of the third Jeffries pounded home a thunderous volley of punches to the head and then draped Jackson across the ropes with a right swing. Humanely, the referee walked in between them and led Peter to his corner.

* Now termed the Commonwealth Title.

Peter Jackson died three years later of the dread disease which had fastened onto him.

One of the sadder truths about boxing is that it is sometimes victories of no consequence which make a fighter's reputation. Jeffries had beaten not Jackson but his shell. However, that win brought him nation-wide attention. He capitalised on it six weeks later when he took on Tom Sharkey in San Francisco. Sharkey was also a 'name', but had done little to enhance it since the so-called 'victory' over Fitzsimmons. True, he had scored five knock-outs but one was over Goddard, and the other four were nonentities. Another nobody had held him to draw, so too had Choynski, and he had failed to match Fitzsimmons' feat of kayoing Peter Maher, the police halting the contest when both men ignored the bell to end the seventh. At this point the ex-sailor seemed to be heading nowhere in particular and, with a disadvantage in weight of almost three stone and height six inches, he appeared ideal for Jeffries. In the event, the Boilermaker got his victory but had to fight very hard for it. The points verdict over 20 rounds was a narrow one in a venomous, ill-tempered slugfest.

But it was a victory and Brady now decided to unfurl his prospect on the East Coast. Amidst a blaze of publicity, Jeffries was scheduled to fight two men on the same night in Madison Square Garden ten rounders. Selected as the sacrificial goats were Fitzsimmons ex-sparring mate, Bob Armstrong, and Corbett's former crown (or clown) prince, Steve O'Donnell.

Things might have worked out better had Jeffries tackled the glass chinned O'Donnell first, but for once one of Brady's gimmicks went awry. Armstrong, an average but experienced black fighter, spent the ten rounds retreating and covering up and Jeffries — minus the technique to corner or open him up — damaged his hands on Armstrong's ebony skull and was unable to go through with the O'Donnell fight. Next day the press was uniformly hostile and the big fellow got panned. But the Armstrong fight had positive spin-offs. First, it tempted Fitzsimmons into what he thought would be an easy pay-day. Secondly, Armstrong's defensive style may have provided the germ of the idea for the crouch which Jeffries used against Fitzsimmons.

James J. Jeffries became world champion in his thirteenth fight, lucky for some at least. Unlike his predecessors he was a fighting champion. He needed to be. He had no flair for acting and a play featuring him was not a success. (One is irresistibly reminded of Sylvester Stallone's advert scene in 'Rocky 2'.) Therefore fighting was his main form of income whether he liked it or not. Technically, he was a very limited fighter. He had strength and hitting power but little else. The things which most distinguished him from other sluggers were his sheer size (he was a Goliath by nineteenth century standards) and his speed of foot. He is best remembered for his crouch but on the available evidence he only used it to any pronounced degree in his first fight with Fitzsimmons. Afterwards he adopted a semi-crouch. Old times also credited him with his own particular brand of left hook, a sort of half-hook, half uppercut, but here again the evidence suggests that this was a one-off against Corbett. A gifted fighter the big man was not.

His first defence took him back to Coney Island on November 3rd, 1899. In the other corner was Tom Sharkey, the close decision in their earlier fight and subsequent Sharkey victories over Corbett (a foul), Gus Ruhlin (one round) and Kid McCoy, securing him his one and only title shot. The nineteenth century had just eight weeks left to run and in the drumbeat of the 25 rounds which Jeffries and Sharkey fought at Coney, we can almost hear the thunder of the new century. The fight was total war, juggernaut against juggernaut with civilisation cast aside.

The two men began as they meant to continue — toe to toe, punch for punch, no quarter given, no prisoners taken, for there was more than money or a title involved — there was pride and bitter personal enmity. In the 2nd round Jeffries almost tore Sharkey's head off with a right uppercut that lifted him clean off his feet! But Sharkey was up at '2' and attacking with a berserk fury. For the next 23 rounds the two men stood centre ring giving and taking frightful punishment. It was a ferocious spectacle which kept a packed house on its feet.

So murderous were the exchanges that Jeffries feared one of them might be killed! — Ringsiders thought that both might die!

In the 18th round Sharkey fired in a right hook to the head, the hardest punch that Jeffries ever took. As the champion reeled, Sharkey screamed at him:

'Fall, damn you — fall.'

But Jeffries did not fall. By a superhuman effort he kept his feet and recovered sufficiently to get through the round. And in the next he almost knocked Sharkey out. One right hook broke three of the challenger's ribs — then a right uppercut almost ripped his left ear off, the bloodstained lobe hanging on by a mere strip of flesh!

By the 23rd both men were a grim sight.

There now occurred a bizarre incident which brought back memories of bareknuckle days. Jeffries' left glove came off as they broke from a clinch and he had to use his bare fist to ward Sharkey off before it was replaced. The last two rounds swung the fight in Jeffries' favour, including a knock down which decked Sharkey for '3'. It was the champion's fight, but only just.

The bout was fought under ring lights so powerful that spectators even several rows back fainted. The effect on Jeffries and Sharkey was to burn their hair right through to the roots. Both men went at least partially bald. Sharkey collapsed afterwards and was seriously ill in hospital for several days. He recovered sufficiently to carry on fighting (it is doubtful whether it would be permitted today), but was never the same force afterwards. However, a lasting friendship developed between Jeffries and he out of those burning 75 minutes at Coney Island.

James J. Corbett repeatedly challenged Bob Fitzsimmons during the latter's tenure as champion. His demands were ignored. It was no more than Corbett deserved, having himself kept the title in mothballs for most of his reign. Nor did he enhance his claims by being any more active as an ex champion. Nineteen months elapsed before he got into the ring again, with Sharkey in New York. The fight was a controversial one. Corbett administered a boxing lesson for eight rounds but was ruled out for a low blow in the 9th. Corbett's supporters claimed that Jim lost his temper after being repeatedly fouled himself. Possibly: Sharkey was a 'to hell with the rules' fighter. But others thought more cynically that it was a put up job with Corbett deliberately throwing the fight. Two years later he was to be embroiled in an even greater controversy.

Sharkey, as we have seen, got the opening crack at Jeffries, whilst Corbett lapsed back into inactivity. But when the new century opened it was 'Gentleman Jim' who received the call to make up its first heavyweight title pairing. It seemed a typically shrewd Brady move. Corbett was 33, and had engaged in only four serious contests in eight years. In his three championship fights he had beaten a washed up alcoholic, and knocked out one ageing middleweight and then lost to another. But record books do not tell the whole story. No modern champion was to actually regain the title until Floyd Patterson in 1960, but at Coney Island on May 11th, 1900 Corbett had the greatest victory of his career.

Right from the opening bell he gave a superlative display of boxing which had the champion floundering like a raw novice. From the 1st through the 22nd, Jeffries landed only two effective punches. In round two he smashed home a left hook to Corbett's body. Corbett was hurt but retaliated superbly, stringing together a succession of left jabs. In the fourth Jeffries again got through with his left hook to the body but Corbett put on a display of feinting which totally bemused Jeffries and prevented him from following up. From the 5th through to the 20th Corbett moved farther and farther ahead on points until his lead was unassailable, taking every round with his dazzling left jabbing and jolting hooks, and making use of every inch of the ring to dance away from Jeffries' bull-like rushes. The champion tried everything he knew — but nothing prevailed — he was being outclassed!

From the 16th onwards Corbett began to regard Jeffries with an arrogance bordering on contempt, producing little pieces of trickery that a champion normally reserves for an exhibition. He was unashamedly playing to the gallery and making a fool of Jeffries. But in the 21st and 22nd he stopped fooling and stood his ground, actually outpunching Jeffries in several fierce exchanges and topping it off with a scorching right to the head which almost floored the champion. The blow shook Jeffries from head to foot.

There were now three rounds left and Jeffries title appeared to have slipped from his grasp. The Matador had annihilated the Bull.

Down at the ringside the pre-fight betting odds, favouring Jeffries, had swung so dramatically that odds were not being given against him lasting the distance. That however was not in Corbett's mind; he had decided against trying to knock Jeffries out. Instead his thoughts were on tomorrow's headlines — 'Corbett regains title' — 'Gentleman Jim is champ again'. When the bell sounded for round 23 Jim was already toying with the idea of a vaudeville show built around his comeback.

Then James J. Corbett stepped out into the centre of the ring — and into history.

Jeffries propelled himself forward again, lunging desperately with his left. Corbett smiled and moved away, easily avoiding the wild blow. The next thing he remembered was being brought round in his corner.

For once Corbett had misjudged his distance from the ropes and found himself rebounding off them. Straight into Jeffries' path. Jeffries originally intended a left hook to the body but changed his mind and went for the head. What emerged was a sort of hook-cum-uppercut which crashed against Corbett's jaw. Down he went and out. The fairy story had been written without the ending.

The rest of Corbett's career was bitter anti-climax. In August he took the ring in New York against Kid McCoy. Real name Norman Selby, McCoy was a charismatic fighter who had achieved near legendary status. He is credited with being the inspiration for the saying 'the real McCoy'. McCoy had won the welterweight title but outgrown it, and by 1900 was boxing at around 170 lbs (77 kilos). His victims read like a 'who's who' of boxing in the 1890s, Tommy Ryan, George Lablanche, Dan Creedon, Gus Ruhlin, Joe Goddard, Joe Choynski (twice), Steve O'Donnell and Peter Maker. When he fought Corbett he was 26 and in his prime. Even so, the betting favoured Corbett, but as the day of the fight approached rumours of a fix spread. The contest itself was one sided, Corbett flattening McCoy in the fifth. Afterwards the shit hit the fan. Corbett's wife announced that it was a fake and the newspapers fell over themselves jumping on the bandwagon. A film of the fight appeared to confirm it as a fix.

In fact, Mrs Corbett was piqued over an affair Jim was having with an actress, and the so-called 'film' turned out to be a fake itself, actors playing the parts of Corbett and McCoy. Sensation sells newspapers, and nobody wants to be left out in the cold as the mug who couldn't see through something crooked. In reality, there was no hard evidence of a fix and the earlier rumours were confounded by Corbett's victory. In all probability the fight was on the level. But the damage both to Corbett's reputation and boxing had been done. The sport had been legalised in New York State by the Horton Law of 1895. This was repealed to take effect from August 31st, 1900 because of the number of crooked fights. Corbett–McCoy, staged the previous evening, appeared only to emphasise that the authorities were right to ban boxing again.

Corbett did not fight again for three years. He was less than three weeks away from his thirty-seventh birthday when he climbed through the ropes to tackle Jeffries again on August 14th, 1903 in the city of his birth. San Francisco was where it started and where it ended. As a fighter Jim Corbett had come home to die.

Yet for six rounds he gave a peerless exhibition, once again, the master outfencing the pupil. Then the weight of the years descended, and from the seventh round on he could no longer dance away from the powerful left hooks with which Jeffries savaged his body. The champion rapidly reduced Corbett to a ghost boxing on memory. At the beginning of the 10th a left hook to the body dropped Corbett for '9'. Now it was the end. Corbett arose to take the final two punches he would ever have to take in the ring, another left hook to the body swiftly followed by a right hook to the jaw. He fell, yet rose again at '7'. Then the towel came fluttering in. His seconds could see that it was hopeless. James J. Corbett had passed beyond the twilight of the Gods!

In retirement Corbett opened a restaurant and later took up journalism as a boxing reporter. He became famous for tipping losers. On February 18th, 1933 while reporting at ringside in Long Island he collapsed and died of a heart attack.

☛☛☛☛☛

Bob Fitzsimmons was also destined for a second helping of the Jeffries' lumps round. The old warrior (he was thirty-six when he lost the title) retired after their first fight, calling Jeffries a 'crackerjack' fighter who was too big and strong for him. But rest heals the body and time the memory and the following year 'Ruby Bob' was back again, seemingly better than ever. Ed Dunkhorst was known as the 'human freight car'. He was 6′ 3″ and weighed anything between 230 and 300 lbs*. Unhappily for Ed he was a dumkopf in fistic terms and Bob derailed him in two rounds. Afterwards came Gus Ruhlin, now the leading contender by virtue of a revenge decision over Sharkey. He no longer had no. 1 status after Fitzsimmons was through with him. Fitz beat his face to pulp, dropped him several times and finished it in the 6th.

Fitzsimmons was back in the ring only two weeks later to try conclusions with Tom Sharkey again. The ex-sailor had a ship tattooed on his chest which Bob promised to sink. 'You ain't got guns enough' snarled Sharkey. But he hadn't got Wyatt Earp this time out. It was a wild slug feast while it lasted, with Fitzsimmons down at the end of the 1st and needing to produce one of his heart stopping body punches in the 2nd. For Sharkey this was too much after 40 punishing rounds with Jeffries and Ruhlin. Fitz floored him twice, the second time for the count.

Barring exhibitions, Fitzsimmons was inactive throughout 1901 and the

* 104 and 136 kilos.

next title shot went to Ruhlin, in San Francisco on November 15th, 1901. It was predictably one sided. The 'Akron Giant', as Ruhlin was known, had not the skill to perplex Jeffries, or the power to outpunch him. The champion simply slogged him to defeat. At the end of the 4th Ruhlin's handlers threw the sponge into the ring. The referee either didn't see it or ignored it, and counted Ruhlin out as he sat on his stool*, the only time this has happened in heavyweight title history.

Just as he had done with Corbett, the 'Ruby One' relied on public opinion to get him a return with Jeffries. The champion spent part of 1901 touring in vaudeville, and at each stop on the circuit was met by newspapers asking when he was going to fight Fitzsimmons again. Fitz kept up the pressure with a series of well publicised exhibitions against hopeful, — or rather hopeless — young giants (the largest stood 6′ 7½″ and weighed 240 lbs) whom he swiftly despatched into slumber. He shrewdly avoided any real fighting — at 39 there were only a limited number of top level performances left in his antiquated limbs.

The best of them was to be against Jeffries. Probably the greatest tribute which can be paid to the 'Boilermaker' is that three of his championship contenders, Sharkey, Corbett and Fitzsimmons, fought their greatest fights against him. He and Fitz met at San Francisco on July 25th, 1902. It was to be a night of blood and pain.

From the first bell Fitzsimmons took command, unleashing savage volleys of punches to Jeffries head and then skipping away before the champion could retaliate. As round succeeded round so Jeffries' face was pounded into raw meat. But despite the punishment he stuck to his guns and from the 6th began to reach Fitzsimmons with piledriving smashes to the body. In the 8th a tremendous left to the ribs almost cut Fitzsimmons in half. Ringsiders saw him say something to Jeffries and then the champion thumped home two mighty lefts, one to the body, the other to the head and Fitzsimmons collapsed to the canvas and was counted out. He had fought a superb fight, clearly the better all round fighter, but in the end Jeffries' size and strength had told.

It is a pity that such a contest had to be marred, but it was next day. The *San Francisco Examiner* started the ball rolling declaring the match a 'fake'. According to its Editor, he had received a letter before the fight stating that the contest had been arranged for Jeffries to win in the 8th. The *Examiner's* ringside reporter attested that he had heard Fitzsimmons say 'hit me' to Jeffries immediately before the knock-out. Other journalists enlarged on this claiming that they had heard the words: 'hit me and get it over'. It was of course quite impossible for anybody to have heard anything in that din; it was simply

* It went into the record books as a 5th round kayo.

journalistic invention to help fuel the Canard, Pardon, story. Fitzsimmons himself stated that he had told Jeffries to 'keep away' because he was badly hurt. Accusations that the fight was rigged have persisted to this day: the evidence makes nonsense of them. Fitzsimmons tried everything he knew to win; he even sprinkled cement on his bandages. Because of it he chopped Jeffries' face to ruins: 'as if I had been run over by a mowing machine' the champion commented ruefully, and mashed and broke his own knuckles. No spectator thought he had seen anything other than a strictly honest fight until the newspapers came out. It was gutter journalism at its worst.

San Francisco should, by any logical standards, have been the end of Bob Fitzsimmons' career. Bob did not function on logic. Sixteen months to the day later, he was back in San Francisco challenging George Gardner for the world Light-heavyweight title. Gardner, a native of County Clare, was fourteen years Fitz's junior and had been beaten only four times in 47 contests. But he should have remembered that Fitzsimmons was the nemesis of Irish world champions.

It has been observed that experience and guile will always triumph over youth. Not necessarily, but it did on the evening of November 25th, 1903. Fitzsimmons used every iota of the ringcraft he had acquired in almost a quarter of a century of fighting to confound, frustrate and out manoeuvre the champion. For fifteen rounds he held the upper hand, flooring Gardner five times, one a spectacular flip-flop, and then holding on down the straight to win a twenty round points decision. At the age of 40 he became the first man to officially win titles at three different weights (although 'Nonpareil' Dempsey also has a claim*).

He held the 175 lbs laurel for over a year before losing it on his first defence to 'Philadelphia' Jack O'Brien, for once an Irish boxer overcoming the jinx. O'Brien, whom we shall meet again, was not a powerful puncher (only 36 kayos in over 180 bouts), but he had a left hand like a rapier and on the night of December 20th, 1905 he used it to cut the old man to pieces. By the 13th Fitz was wallowing in his own blood which ran down his legs and formed puddles on the canvas. He surrendered at the end of the round and needed a transfusion to make up four pints of lost blood.

Still he was drawn to the ring. In 1907 he boxed the leading heavyweight contender Jack Johnson and was knocked out in two rounds. Afterwards Johnson told reporters that he could feel Fitz's punches whistling past his ears like bullets. In 1909, age 46, Fitzsimmons boxed Bill Lang for the heavyweight championship of Australia and was kayoed in 12 rounds. In 1914 he boxed two 'no

* Dempsey held the welterweight title before the middle, and also claimed the lightweight crown.

decision' bouts and then had his licence withdrawn by the New York Commission. Other bodies followed suit despite Bob's protests that he was fitter than men half his age. The sad truth was that he needed the money. He was broke. Later he was converted to evangelism by his fourth wife. On October 22nd, 1917 he died of pneumonia in Chicago.

Bob Fitzsimmons was not one of the great heavyweight champions, but he was one of the great *figures* of boxing. He won three world titles and his ring career spanned an astonishing thirty-four years. As a character he was irresistibly colourful and if at times he was a rogue then he was always a loveable rogue. Bar Corbett, everybody seems to have liked him. He was a child of many nations but perhaps only America can really claim him. America and the ring. He deserves his place of honour in the history of boxing.

Round Eight: Hiatus

James J. Jeffries made his sixth and final defence of the world heavyweight title on August 26th, 1904. Sharing the ring with him was a Canadian ex-miner named Jack Munroe. For Jeffries, the fight was a matter of personal pique more than anything else. Following their San Francisco bout he and Fitzsimmons had embarked on an exhibition tour. In Butte, Montana, Jeffries boxed a four rounder with Munroe. In the 2nd Munroe clipped him on the chin as he slipped and Jeffries found himself on the canvas for the first time. It was not a real knock-down and would have been quickly forgotten but for Munroe's boasts that he had 'floored' the champion. Seeking revenge, Jeffries gave Munroe a title shot in San Francisco.

Jeffries–Munroe is deservedly one of the least remembered world heavyweight title fights. Munroe would later be decorated for bravery during the first world war, but personal combat against a human grizzly with a score to settle is something quite different. Jeffries spent most of the first round catching up with Munroe, floored him at the end of it and then decked him three more times in quick succession at the start of the second, whereupon the referee stopped it. Having thus disposed of Jack Munroe, Jeffries hung up his gloves.

He was 30 and had saved his ring earnings. The fights with Sharkey, Corbett and Fitzsimmons had been punishing ones. Moreover he was toying with the idea of another venture into the theatre, this time playing Davy Crockett (and before John Wayne was even born!). But the reason which big Jeff gave for his retirement was that he had run out of opposition. Not true. The white contenders were a very sickly and undistinguished lot, but there were a number of first class black heavyweights, most notably Jack Johnson. Johnson had been throwing out challenges to Jeffries for some time and held a bauble called 'the Negro heavyweight championship of the world'. It is said that on one occasion Johnson bearded Jeffries in a San Francisco restaurant and was offered a fight in the cellar. The champion was not disposed to meet him in the ring. Jeffries refused point blank to defend against any black fighter. At least that is what he said. In reality, he had very real fears about Johnson who was a master boxer. Jeffries knew only too well his own limitations in this department.

The formal announcement of his retirement was made on May 2nd, 1905. Following Corbett's abortive precedent, he nominated Marvin Hart and Jack Root to fight for the vacant title. In retrospect it is clear that the timing of this announcement was dictated by the fact that Hart had been awarded a verdict over Johnson five weeks earlier. The decision, which Johnson termed as 'robbery', had been given by referee Alex Greggains who also promoted the bout. Greggains was one of the co-promoters of Jeffries' defence against Fitzsimmons.

There is no actual evidence of collusion, but Jeffries was determined that Johnson should not occupy one of the corners in the upcoming title bout.

The paucity of white talent is amply demonstrated by Jeffries' choice of Jack Root to contest the title with Hart. Root's claim to fame (apart from being the only Austrian born fighter to win a world title) is that he had outpointed a fading Kid McCoy to win the inaugural bout for the light heavyweight title. His reign of 73 days is one of the shortest for any world champion. Gardner removed his crown via a 12th round stoppage. That should have put the Irishman in the other corner, but Gardner was in turn outpointed first by Fitzsimmons and then Root. Any last hopes Gardner may have entertained vanished when Mike Schreck knocked him out. So it was Root who got the call. The Austrian had a good left hook but precious little else.

Hart–Root went on at Reno, Nevada on July 3rd. To emphasise his approval of the bout, Jeffries refereed. As a fight it lived down to expectations. Nothing much happened between the two men of limited ability. Hart seems to have been something of a protégé of Jeffries and was managed by his old crouch-master, Tommy Ryan. He was bigger all round than Root and Jeffries no doubt expected an emphatic victory from him. Shocks were in store. The early rounds were even-steven, Root flurrying with both hands, Hart stealing rights to the body. But from the 6th Root began to forge ahead, and towards the end of the 7th he laid Hart flat on his back with a right to the temple. Only the bell saved Hart from being counted out.

Root kept the upper hand going into the 12th. Hart needed something spectacular. He got it. Midway through the round Root left himself open to a pulverising right uppercut to the heart and went down and out. Jeffries breathed a sigh of relief, raised Hart's hand and wondered who the hell had written that script!

So began the reign of boxing's forgotten champion. As successor to Jeffries, Hart was really a joke. Big Jeff could have whipped him with one hand. But that of course was not Hart's fault. He had, in effect, been over promoted. Born in Jefferson County, Kentucky on September 16th, 1876, Hart weighed around 190 lbs (86 kilos) and stood 5′ 11¾″. His face betrayed a profession he was not auspiciously good at, battered features, mashed lips and a flattened nose. Unbeknown, he fought throughout his career with only one eye.

Hart became a professional boxer in 1899 and won 14 in a row (13 by knockout) before walking into a right hand from an average middleweight named Billy Hanrahan. Thereafter his record was patchy. Boxing at light-heavy and heavy he beat the not-so-goods but lost to Root and Gardner. As he got higher up the scale so the knock-outs were harder to come by. Washed up Gus Ruhlin held him to a draw, but he outpointed Sandy Ferguson, a white heavyweight who was no mug. And on March 28th, 1905 Hart had his career best victory over Jack Johnson. Johnson himself describes the fight as: 'not an auspicious event for me'[1] and claims that Greggains pointed to Hart by mistake. But Johnson gave different excuses to different people, and is also alleged to have said: 'One white man did beat me and beat me good — Marvin Hart.' Actual reports of the fight suggest that Johnson boxed very lackadaisically; Greggains himself said that he gave it to Hart because he was the aggressor. The truth probably is that Johnson, a moody, complex man, had one of those nights when he simply couldn't be bothered. Hart most decidedly would not have been able to repeat the victory.

His reign lasted just 235 days, the shortest undisputed tenure in heavyweight history. On February 23rd, 1906 he defended against Canada's Tommy Burns. Burns must have appeared an easy mark; on his last outing he had been beaten by middleweight contender Jack 'Turn' Sullivan. But, as we shall see, Burns was nothing if not crafty, and may not have tried too hard against Sullivan in order to set up the Hart match.

Hart–Burns venued in Los Angeles. Exciting it was not, although purists of the type who enjoy defensive strokes in cricket might perhaps have fawned over Burns' defensive capabilities.

He lured Hart into all kinds of errors with clever feints, tied him up at close quarters, and kept the champion off balance with a fast left jab which also rattled up the points. There were two highlights — round 14 in which Burns cut loose with a two-handed attack that caught Hart unawares, and round 15 when the challenger scored with a succession of crisp rights to Hart's head. Well ahead, and completely in command, Burns consolidated his position down the final straight by left hooking Hart to the body at close quarters. At the final bell Burns had a huge points lead and the world a new heavyweight champion.

The rest of Marvin Hart's career was a downhill run. Mike Schreck wrote finis to him as a contender by knocking him out twice. His last fight was in 1910 when he was kayoed in three rounds by Carl Morris, more of whom later. Hart died in Kentucky in 1931, the day after his fifty-fifth birthday.

It is fashionable today to deride Tommy Burns as an insignificant champion. In fact no champion is ever insignificant except by comparison. Burns suffers from the fact that he was freakish in build. At 5′ 7″ he is by far the shortest of all the heavyweight titleholders. He never weighed more than 175 lbs (79.5 kilos), the light heavyweight limit. But he had a heavyweight's reach at 74½″ and a barrel chest which gave him a heavyweight torso.

Because of his physical stature, Burns had been underrated as a fighter. He was not one of the greats; he had few attacking moves. But he was an excellent defensive boxer, full of cunning feints and clever counters. He made maximum use of his long left and adopted a crouching, tightly knit defence. And Burns

1 Jack Johnson — In the Ring and Out (F/B) p.50

could punch. His right hand was a heavyweight weapon.

He was born Noah Brusso on June 17th, 1881 in Hanover, Ontario. Burns is usually described as French Canadian and on reaching manhood bore an uncanny resemblance to Napoleon Bonaparte. However, only his father was French; his mother was German.

We have few details of his early years, but we do know that he had a passion for sport. He played Lacrosse to distraction and excelled at a variety of other sports including soccer, swimming and baseball.

Burns drifted into boxing when he was nineteen. The story is that he volunteered to take part in a show in Detroit one night when a fighter did not show up. He certainly began his career in Detroit, and was based there at least until 1904.

He began as a middleweight notching up eleven straight winds (nine kayos) before handy Mike Schreck outscored him late in 1902. He then went unbeaten again for almost two years before losing to Philadelphia Jack O'Brien. By this time Burns was flirting with the light heavies while maintaining a position as a solid contender in the middleweight division. In 1905 he drew and lost with Jack 'Twin' Sullivan, and shared braces with two other 160 lb contenders, Hugo Kelly (two draws), and Dave Barry (both wins).

The middleweight ranks were then awash with talent. Tommy Ryan was still champion, and jockeying for position with Burns, Sullivan and Kelly were the likes of Joe Thomas and Johnny Thompson. Coming through the pack in spectacular fashion was a dynamic young slugger from Michigan; Stanley Ketchel. The scene was a mite crowded and Burns had no qualms about being selected as Marvin Hart's first sacrificial goat.

Burns was a fighting champion. The only trouble is that he did not fight the right people. Like Jeffries he was deaf to any ears coloured black. In particular he avoided Johnson like the black death. Johnson threw out a constant stream of challenges. Burns did not actually ignore them; instead he engaged Johnson in a war of words. The Negro was 'yellow', and, in best 'Dad's Army' tradition, 'didn't like it up him', i.e. body punches. Johnson was to make him pay bitterly for those taunts. It is doubtful that Burns was actually a committed racist; he had grown up in Canada amongst Red Indian children, and as a member of that country's French community knew only too well what it was like to be part of a minority. But he played the race card very shrewdly, pandering to racist views and fears. It really masked the fact that he didn't think he could beat Jack Johnson.

He picked his first defence very shrewdly as well, 'Fireman' Jim Flynn. Flynn was an Italian masquerading as an Irishman, and a light heavyweight pretending to be a heavy. He had a good record against the likes of 'Dummy' Rowan, but had lost to Root and been held to a draw by Gardner and Jack 'Twin' Sullivan.

Flynn's greatest victory was eleven years in the future when he pasted a young fighter named Jack Dempsey. Against Burns at Los Angeles on October 2nd, 1906 he promised little and achieved same. Burns took it easy during the opening rounds, picked up the pace in the middle and then finished it in round 15, dropping Flynn three times with stunning rights to the head.

Meanwhile, Philadelphia Jack O'Brien was going around grumbling that he had whipped both Burns and Hart* and wasn't it time he had a go? Burns obliged him eight weeks later on November 28th at Los Angeles. The fans who witnessed this 20 rounder left wishing they hadn't. The fight consisted of cunning feints, artful footwork, and carefully planted left jabs. The general opinion — amongst the few who cared enough to have one after the waltz was over — was that O'Brien had done enough to win. The referee was James J. Jeffries, come to see how two light heavyweights were getting on with his crown, and he called it a draw, the first under Queensberry rules. The following day Jim explained that he thought Burns had a slight edge, but that both fighters had asked him to give a draw in preference to a hairline decision. This admission gave rise to suspicions that there was something not quite right about the fight; that the two men merely went through the motions for not one pay-day, but two.

The return took place at the same venue the following May. It showed Tommy at his most devious. Before the fight he offered O'Brien money to 'lay down'. O'Brien refused. Burns tried another tack; how much would Jack pay *him* to take a dive? O'Brien thought it over and offered $3,500. Burns accepted and O'Brien, unaware that Tommy was planning a double cross, did not train as hard as he should have done. The charade continued until they were actually in the ring. Then Burns announced to the spectators: 'All bets are off; I agreed to lose to O'Brien but I am here to win.' He emphasised the point with his first punch of the fight, a swinging right which gunned the Philadelphian into the ropes. Half trained and taken unawares by the champion's perfidy, O'Brien took a lacing for much of the twenty rounder. Had he a punch then he might have pulled it round, but in trade parlance Philadelphia Jack, 'couldn't break an egg with a hand grenade'. Burns won the fight by a clear margin and without anybody noticing had also taken O'Brien's light-heavyweight title as both were under the 175 lbs limit**.

Burns mean mood lasted until July 4th when he defended against the Australian heavyweight champion, Bill Squires at Colma, California. (Los Angeles had seen enough of him.) For trivia fans, this was the first heavyweight title fight under Queensberry rules between two non-Americans, and the first contested by two men from the British Empire who were not British. As for the

* In fact his two fights with Hart were officially 'No Decision' bouts.

** He never defended it and O'Brien later reclaimed it.

fight itself, Burns got into the spirit of independence day by liberating Squires from his senses in two minutes and four seconds*.

England now beckoned, or, to be more exact, Johnson was pressing too hard and he needed to get away. There was a lot of money to be made from the heavyweight championship, but only if you had it in the first place, and the British wanted him to fight their champion Gunner Moir.

Boxing in Britain had been legalised under the Queensberry rules. Bare knuckle fighting had finally been flushed down the toilet along with cudgelling and dog fighting. Before the British Boxing Board of Control was established in 1914 the (unofficial) ruling body of the sport was the National Sporting Club. (Only British title fights held at the N.S.C. were recognised as such.) The N.S.C. wielded power in similar fashion to the F.A. in soccer and M.C.C. in cricket. Like these august bodies the N.S.C. was autocratic and imperious, its committee culled from the ranks of the privileged. As the aristocracy were no longer running the important things such as Politics and Commerce they were given sport to play with.

Their first meeting with Burns can accurately be described as a shock to the system — in more ways than one. Committee members were used to dictating to dog-faced little managers in bowlers and loud suits, with cigars hanging from their mouths, whilst the boxers hung around outside tugging their forelocks. Burns was his own manager and certainly not disposed to doff his cap to a gaggle of aristocrats. He trusted nobody and had very much a sense of his own worth. Psychologically, he was not a little man and would not be treated like one. On meeting the N.S.C. Committee he at once took charge and outlined his own terms, take them or leave them. In particular, he wanted the money in his hand before entering the ring. It is recorded that Committee members stared at him with stupefaction!

The fight with Moir took place at the N.S.C. on December 2nd. A Christmas present for the British it wasn't. Britain had recently produced a whole host of world-beating little men, but the heavyweight division remained in the dumps. 'Peggy' Bettinson, the N.S.C.'s promoter described Moir as a 'big muscular man', and that was it. For two rounds he roused a few expectations but ringsiders could see that Burns was merely biding his time. From the 3rd Tommy uncoiled his long left, and in the 10th he unwrapped the right and left the Gunner well and truly spiked.

Pickings in London being easy, Burns stayed around to give Moir's main challenger, Jack Palmer, a go. The contest was arranged for February 10th at the

* Squires was managed by John Wren, a corrupt business magnate who was the subject of the 1976 television series 'Power without Glory'.

'Wonderland' arena in East London. On the day of the fight Tommy breezed into Wonderland, changed all the locks, locked all the doors save the box office, and then sat down and counted the takings as the spectators filed in. Once his purse money was in the till he pocketed it and went off to get changed. Oh yes, the fight. Well it didn't last long, and Jack Palmer was not in Wonderland when the referee rescued him in the fourth.

Next Burns skipped across the sea to Dublin to face the Irish champion Jem Roche on St. Patrick's Day. Roche was the first and to date only Irish national to contest the heavyweight title and not for very long. Eighty-six seconds to be precise, a right uppercut doing the trick. It is reported that one quick witted fan dashed outside and told would-be spectators: 'I can't watch it; Roche is after murdering him. Who'll buy my ticket for £2?'

Paris was next on the itinerary. In April Burns defended against another leading (I use the word loosely), British heavyweight, Jewey Smith. In the 5th the fight was going along very pleasantly, nobody getting hurt, when someone shouted that the building was on fire. Burns promptly knocked Smith cold, grabbed his winnings and fled without waiting for the count! Nobody could say that things weren't interesting when Tommy was around.

Burns stayed in Paris long enough to give Bill Squires a second helping — eight rounds of it. Then he was off to Australia to see what the pickings were like in the Antipodes. The persistent Squires arrived before him and demanded a third meeting. 15,000 people filled the stadium at Rushcutters Bay, Sydney, on August 24th. An estimated 25,000 milled around outside. Burns boxed with a heavy dose of flu and after 12 rounds Squires was ahead. Didn't matter much though because Tommy knocked him out in the 13th. He had now won Bill Squires outright.

Nine days later Burns was in Melbourne to face Australia's No. 2 heavyweight Bill Lang. The paying audience was even bigger, 19,000, but the result was the same. Lang went in six. (Presumably Burns' virus had cleared up.)

Whilst Burns had been charging across the globe knocking over Joe Palookas, Jack Johnson had not been idle. He had kayoed Fitzsimmons, Kid Cutler — a John L. Sullivan protegé, and 'Fireman' Flynn. Early in 1908 his manager, Sam Fitzpatrick, borrowed $5,000 and they followed Burns to England. The champion was then still in the country. Fitzpatrick and Burns sought the good offices of the N.S.C.; would they be interested in promoting a fight between Burns and Johnson? Yes, but only for a purse of £1,000 and each man to bear his own expenses. The offer was derisory. Johnson turned it down out of hand. Burns had already announced his terms: he told Bettinson: 'I shall want £6,000 ($30,000) win, lose or draw — I don't think I can beat him.' Then he lit out for Dublin and Paris.

Johnson stayed on to fight Ben Taylor, the 'Woolwich infant'. If Moir the British champion had muscles and nothing else then one dreads to think how bad Taylor must have been. Allegedly he was a man of considerable durability*, and the arrangement was that he would receive the decision — and the purse — if he lasted the distance. Johnson entered the ring red eyed from a three day drunk. He shuffled his way through the first seven rounds. In the 8th he knocked Taylor out.

The purse money bought the tickets for Australia. At times this long chase resembles a Fifties' western with the gunfighter, Johnson, doggedly pursuing his quarry until they finally meet on a dusty street at high noon. Unfortunately, heroic images like that have very little to do with boxing. It is a business and a hard and bloody one at that. Burns did not think he could beat Johnson, but he was not physically scared of him. He was frightened of losing his meal ticket. If it had to go then it would be at his price, an unprecedented $30,000. Who in Australia would pay such a sum? One man would.

Hugh D. ('Huge Deal') McIntosh was an Australian rags to riches success story who seemed to have stepped straight out of the pages of *Boy's Own*. McIntosh had been a miner, labourer, racing cyclist, member of Parliament and boxer, but it was as a pie salesman that he slugged his way to fame and fortune. He was an entrepreneur par excellence having once bought up every piece of bunting in Australia prior to a visit by the U.S. Navy and then selling it to the Government at a massive profit. Lately, he had turned his attention back to boxing, promoting Burns' two title defences and building the Rushcutters Bay Stadium for his bout with Squires. Hugh D. McIntosh was willing to meet Burns' price.

Burns and Johnson signed to meet at Rushcutters Bay on December 26th, 1908. By comparison with Burns, Johnson would receive only $5,000. The fight needed no selling. Few sporting events have attracted such world-wide attention. But there was a sombreness in the air that has been commented on by all historians. This was not the anticipation of a great occasion that had marked Sayers–Heenan; it was more the atmosphere surrounding the last days of a King, a boxing match played to the death march from Saul. Nobody wanted Johnson to win; everybody feared he would.

In training Burns appeared confident. What private doubts assailed him when his bedroom door closed at night can only be guesses at. It is enough that we know he had them. Johnson appeared to be going through the motions, but that was the impression he liked to give. In reality he trained hard. McIntosh would referee, the only party both camps could agree on. Privately though he disliked Johnson. Stories of McIntosh threatening him with a gun are probably untrue, but it is known that he kept a lead cosh rolled up in newspaper in case Johnson attacked him.

* Although another top black American, Sam McVey, had stopped him twice.

And so to Rushcutters Bay, Boxing Day (appropriate), 1908. The stadium was packed to capacity; the eyes of the world were on Sydney.

At 1.30 p.m. Johnson made his way to the ring. By custom the challenger always enters first, but with Johnson it was a superstition. First into the ring was always written into his contracts.

Burns arrived in an old blue suit and stripped off in the ring. There was a contretemps about some tape on his elbows. Finally he removed it. Then they were on their way, as Shakespeare put it: 'If not to glory then hand in hand to hell.'

The film of the fight is old and quirky and never seen in its entirety. Missing from the first round is the knockdown, yet we know that Johnson floored Burns with his pet punch, a right uppercut. The knockdown in round 14 is also missing, the explanation being that the police stopped the fight at this point. But the police did not stop it until *after* the knockdown. In the footage Burns appears unmarked, but all newspaper reports of the fight say that he suffered extensive facial damage and bled profusely. In other words what we are watching is not a chronological account of the fight but edited vignettes taken from a couple of the early rounds. This editing is not of recent origin — there would be no reason — it was clearly done at the time and done so that white audiences would be spared the sight of Burns being floored and marked.

The film does show that Burns fought the wrong fight for him. His tactics were to attack Johnson to the body where he was supposedly weak. This was a racial fallacy, but is only half the story anyway. Burns had no option but to attack. Johnson was almost six inches taller, and although their reaches were almost identical* Jack was a much faster puncher who would have chopped Tommy to pieces at long range, particularly as Burns' punches to the head had, diagonally, a longer distance to travel. Burns' strategy, categorised by boxing historian Jim Jacobs as: 'impaling the face on the other man's glove', was in effect dictated to him. He could not box defensively and win.

Johnson looks, and was, far superior. He bosses the clinches, pushes Burns on to his backfoot, and lashes him with whiplash punches. In close he rakes Tommy with uppercuts. It is doubtful whether the Canadian won a round (some reporters gave him the fifth). Johnson himself described it as: 'One of the easiest of the more important fights of my career.'[1] According to one source Jack was so much in command by the 12th that he concentrated not on Burns but the antics of an Aborigine boy, perched on a wall, who was imitating his moves. When Johnson ducked a Burns' haymaker so did the boy — and fell off the wall! It is

1 'Jack Johnson in the Ring and Out' (P/B) p.58

* Burns 74½ — Johnson 74

a good story; its authenticity may be doubted.

As the fight progressed so Johnson is alleged to have taunted Burns with remarks like: 'Come on, Tommy, you can hit harder than that' and 'poor little Tommy, who told you you were a fighter'. The actual words are almost certainly journalistic licence, but the film does show Johnson talking to Burns and nobody has ever suggested that he was saying anything pleasant!

Time was finally called by the police in round 14 when Burns was decked for the second time, by a right cross. The fighters had agreed that if the police halted it then the verdict would be given to whoever was ahead at the time. McIntosh had no hesitation in pointing to Johnson.

After years of trying to land a title shot, Jack Johnson was finally the heavyweight champion of the world.

Some people do not like to face facts.

In the aftermath of Rushcutters Bay it was claimed that the police were too hasty in stopping the fight. Well alright, Tommy was a bit behind on points; okay, yes, he had taken some stick, but that was to be expected because he had to take the fight to Johnson, and he was beginning to come on strongly. And, so the legend ran, Johnson spent the next day in hospital whilst Tommy, being a good sport, went to the races and gambled his purse money away.

Yes, and there are fairies at the bottom of my garden. The police stopped the fight because Burns was being brutally beaten. There is no evidence that Johnson went to hospital afterwards. As for blowing a sum adjacent today to $1.5 million on a day's racing, that really is preposterous. Nor does it sound like Tommy Burns whose grasp of financial affairs was never anything less than shrewd.

Burns showed no inclination for a return. In fact, at the age of 27, he was more-or-less finished with the ring. Sixteen months later he boxed Bill Lang and won on points. Three years later he boxed a 'no decision' bout with rising heavyweight Arthur Pelkey, and in 1920 came out of retirement to promote a fight between himself and British champion Joe Beckett at London's Royal Albert Hall for the Empire title. Now 39, Tommy showed glimpses of his old skill for three rounds, but then age and Beckett's left hooks to the body caught up with him and he was stopped in the 7th. But the outing netted him a handsome profit of £4,000 (circa £200,000 today).

Later in life Tommy became a Presbyterian minister. Speaking of his boxing career he described himself as 'vicious and full of hate'. He died of heart failure on May 10th, 1955 in Vancouver.

Jack Johnson's victory at Rushcutters Bay was the end of an hiatus in the world heavyweight championship. Although Burns was a better fighter than he is sometimes given credit for, he and Hart were really only interim champions. The man who succeeded them may well have been the greatest heavyweight in history. He was certainly the most controversial. His was to be a troubled reign.

Volume Three

Jack Johnson to Jack Dempsey

Round Nine: American Othello

Legend has it that Shakespeare's 'Othello' was the outcome of a boozy evening spent with the actor Richard Burbage. Burbage bragged that he could interpret any role ever written; Shakespeare promised to come up with a character whom no actor would ever completely master. The result was 'Othello, the Moor of Venice'.

Jack Johnson was the living embodiment of Othello. There have been some fine biographies setting him into his times, but as a character nobody has ever mastered this infinitely complex man who was a mass of inherent contradictions. On the surface as transparent as glass, beneath the surface as deep as the ocean. Whenever you think you have solved the puzzle you find a bit which doesn't fit. He was a man who acted out his whole life.

That life began on March 31st, 1878 in Galveston, Texas. John Arthur Johnson was the third of six children who survived infancy. His father, Henry, was an ex-slave. His mother was known as 'Tiny' — nobody ever called her anything else.

The fashionable image of Johnson is of an uneducated boy born into deep poverty. It isn't accurate. Although partially crippled, Henry Johnson had a secure job as a school janitor and all the children were educated. In manhood John Arthur was a great reader of Dumas, Hugo, Shakespeare, Milton and Bunyon, and learnt to speak — and read — Spanish and French.

Johnson's early years are vague. According to his own colourful reminiscences he ran away from home at the age of 12 and for five years lived a hobo existence, learning to box as a sparring partner for Joe Walcott, an outstanding turn of the century welterweight who gave his name to a future heavyweight champion and once stopped Joe Choynski in a catchweight bout*.

None of this can be factually established. records indicate that Johnson was living in Galveston up to 1901. He did become friendly with Joe Walcott later and the two often trained and travelled together. But the fight he claims to have originally helped Walcott prepare for — against 'Scaldy' Bill Quinn — took place in 1896 when Johnson was 18 and a year after he said he returned to Galveston.

What motivated Johnson to become a fighter we do not know. The simple answer of course would be money. He appears to have started out in 'battle royals', a form of combat in which eight or more black youths were put into the

* Although Choynski had a broken rib at the time.

ring and fought each other until only one was left standing; for the amusement of white audiences. Single combat variations on this included contestants fighting in the nude. The sort of mentality that this, and battle royals, appealed to is best described as degenerate.

The earliest records which we have of Johnson in proper contests emanate from 1897. He had a number of fights, four in all, with one Jim McCormick, whom he first drew with and then otherwise defeated. All in all, up to May, 1899 he had seven bouts, winning five and drawing two. He then made his first trip to Chicago where he was stopped in five by a black heavyweight calling himself 'Klondike' Haynes. These days of course promising young fighters are feather-bedded with easy opposition early in their careers. In Johnson's day you learnt your trade the hard way.

The 'Klondike' reverse seems to have disheartened Johnson for a time. Over the next twenty months he fought only twice — a draw and a win — before taking on the veteran Joe Choynski in Galveston on February 25th, 1901. The fight was preceded by the ultimate in degradation, two one-legged black youths pitted against each other. Anybody who could find this entertaining had to be sick. The main event ended with Choynski kayoing Johnson with a left hook to the temple in the 3rd round after which the Texas Rangers arrested them. The two fighters spent the next 25 days in gaol but for Johnson it was a blessing in disguise. Had he simply lost to Choynski, who was then at the tail-end of his career, Jack might have gone home and called it a day. Instead the two men sparred daily in the prison yard and Jack learnt much that he had not gleaned from his earlier fights. He was not to be beaten again for four years and 36 contests.

Galveston saw the last of him in late 19012. He had beaten everybody of note locally, although 'Klondike' made the trip south and held him to a draw (Jack finally kayoed him the following year). It was time to expand his horizons.

On the West Coast his career really began in earnest. He stopped Jack Jeffries, younger and less able brother of Jim, a victory which did nothing to endear him to the champion, acquired a gun-toting manager named Frank Carrillo, and began to move up in class, besting good black fighters like Frank Childs and Sam McVey, although he could never quite get the hang of Hank Griffin, a fine defensive boxer who held him to a draw three times. Possibly their styles cancelled each other out; equally possibly, neither saw any reason to damage the other's earning potential. There was a largely unspoken agreement between black fighters of that era. They very rarely went all out against each other. When Johnson defeated 'Denver' Ed Martin for the 'negro heavyweight title' early in 1903 he floored him five times in the 11th but then eased up and allowed Martin back into the fight in the later rounds. Blacks saw no reason to ruin one another for the gratification of white audiences who jeered them and threw lighted cigarettes at their backs while they fought. But just to show the mean side of his nature, Johnson later annihilated Martin in two, and terminated a tame 20 rounder with McVey by suddenly knocking him out with 20 seconds to go.

White fighters posed a different problem. It was unwise to flatten them in front of white spectators, particularly when liquored up, as many generally were. Black fighters therefore often boxed under wraps, doing just enough to win but not trying for a knockout. George Gardner and Sandy Ferguson (three times*) lasted the distance with Johnson in this manner.

By the beginning of 1905, when he dropped the decision to Hart, Johnson had become an outstanding fighting machine. His defence was well nigh impregnable. Harry Wills once recalled surprising him with a good right while they were sparring. Later he repeated the punch and Johnson blocked it. Nothing significant about that except that Johnson had turned away to speak to his wife at the time! Old timers are prone to exaggeration, but according to them Johnson could feint a man into knots with his eyes alone. They also credited him with extraordinary reflexes and anticipation, blocking punches and riposting with the same hand in one fluid movement, and anticipating a blow just as it started so that his opponent's glove was driven back into his face with double the force. Jack was also said to deliberately target his opponent's biceps so that as the fight wore on they became too swollen and sore for his adversary to raise his arms properly. Perhaps, but nobody seems to list fights in which this ploy was used to effect.

Even from the jerky motions of old films, Johnson comes over as a consummate master boxer. He had a superb left, executed every punch well and was particularly admired for his uppercutting skills, eulogised by some as the best in boxing history. He could deliver the blow without moving his feet, sometimes even leaning into an opponent. Some say that he had a short variation of it, delivered with a turning motion of the wrist. If so, then it was the bolo punch years before its time and before anybody had a name for it. His upper body movement was also ahead of its time, enabling him to turn punches aimed full tilt for his body into just glancing blows.

Jack is not normally credited with being an offensive fighter. He liked to do his work out of defence. But when required he possessed the necessary attacking skills. 'Denver' Ed Martin was simply overwhelmed in their second fight, and after seeing him cut loose on Ben Taylor the British press unanimously picked him to beat Burns.

Equally, 44 kayos in 113 does not sound like a puncher's record. It is 39% as against Jeffries 70%, Burns 59%, Dempsey 60%, Louis 76% and Marciano 88%. But unlike them Johnson, sometimes by choice — sometimes not — often kept his heavy guns locked away. When he wanted to he could hit devastatingly, the essences being, as with Fitzsimmons, perfect timing and accuracy. Accord-

* Ferguson lost a fourth fight on a foul.

ing to one journalist, Sam McVey, 'Could stand up for 20 rounds lashed to a post and let the other man take an axe'. Johnson knocked him spark out with a lightning combination to the head which McVey knew nothing about. When he came round he asked: 'Was it a draw?' One white boxer whom Jack did unload upon was Kid Cutler. Goaded by Cutler's mentor, John L. Sullivan, Johnson walked out of his corner, waved his left in leisurely fashion and Cutler was suddenly staring up at the ringlights. Turning to a now speechless Sullivan Jack asked: 'How did you like that one Cap'n John?'

After the Hart fight Johnson lost again only once in ten years and that was on a foul. His conqueror was Joe Jeannette, a superb black fighter whom Johnson boxed nine times, winning two, drawing two, losing one, with four 'no decision' bouts. Jack also outpointed the man who was to become his No. 1 contender, Sam Langford. In all, between Hart and Burns he went to the post 30 times. During this time he shelled managers like peas. Carrillo went; Morris Hart, Johnny Connors and Alec McLean came and went. Sam Fitzpatrick came; two months after winning the title Johnson split up with him as well.

Alas, as champion, Johnson was a grave disappointment. The search had begun for a white fighter to beat him. The morning after his defeat of Burns the writer Jack London, a man as complex and contradictory as Johnson himself, wrote:

> *'One thing remain. Jim Jeffries must now emerge from his alfalfa farm and remove that golden smile from Jack Johnson's face. It's up to you. The white man must be rescued.'*

But Jim Jeffries didn't want to emerge from his alfalfa farm, where he had quite happily ballooned up to 300 lbs. And there was really no-one else. Hart had gone back too far, Burns was defeated, ditto Sandy Ferguson. A lanky ex-sailor named 'Gunboat' Ed Smith was beginning to make an impression but had far to travel yet. The best white 'heavy' around was 'Fireman' Jim Flyn, in actuality a pudgy light heavyweight.

It is fair to say that in 1909 all the real contenders were black. Sam Langford, Joe Jeannette, Sam McVey, Jim Barry and 'Black Bill', probably in that order. About to come on stage were Harry Wills and Jeff Clarke. But Jack Johnson now drew his own version of the colour line against Langford and co. Two blacks fighting for the title wouldn't draw a crowd; besides he'd beaten them all already. True, he had. But equally true he knew just how good Langford, Jeannette and McVey were, and that he would need to be in tip top condition to beat them again. And that sort of conditioning was becoming increasingly hard for Jack Johnson.

He had been living a life of drink and debauchery for some time. It was part of a multi-faceted character within whom the elements were often at war. Jack Johnson was no ordinary bruiser attracted to drink, gambling and women because that was his simplistic way of life. He was a highly intelligent, dominant individual. But like many other such men he was attracted to the dark, squalid side of life. He drank heavily and sought the company of prostitutes. It meant that Johnson was often facing in three directions simultaneously: the well read, educated man seeking the respect of his peers, the aspirant to success in the boxing ring and the dissipated low life. The last two, at least, were directly contradictory.

Johnson's first 'wife' was Mary Austin, a light-skinned negress. Although Johnson often referred to her as his spouse, there is no evidence they ever married, and he seems to have left her in Galveston in 1901. The following year he began to live with Clara Kerr, another 'wife', but in reality a black prostitute. Whether Jack sometimes lived off her earnings is unknown; she later said he did, but there is no evidence of him doing this with other prostitutes. After Kerr, he began to frequent white prostitutes, often travelling with two or three of them at a time. These peccadilloes were not well known until he won the championship. Then everything changed.

There is an enormous difference between being the champion and the No. 1 contender. The contender has his nose pressed against the shop window — the champion is in it. Johnson was now effectively living in a goldfish bowl. He was already hated by whites because he was the heavyweight champion; and feared by them as the symbol of an emergent people. They felt even more threatened when they discovered his predilection for white women.

After returning from Australia Johnson settled in Chicago and opened a restaurant, the Café de Champion. It was in Chicago that he met and started living with a white prostitute named Belle Shrieber.

To look at the photographs of Shrieber and the three women whom Johnson subsequently married, Etta Duryea, Lucille Cameron and Irene Pineau, is to look at the photographs of four women who might be sisters, oval faced, pale skinned and dark haired. They form a 'type' which was obviously Johnson's.

Lucille Cameron was a prostitute when she met Johnson; Etta Duryea almost one. This too was Jack's type. Whether this was bound up with his sexuality — the composer Tchaikovsky trawled the midnight streets seeking young male prostitutes — or whether it was because he was afraid of giving and receiving love, we do not know. Irene Pineau contradicts both schools of thought. Nor do we know whether, like Tchaikovsky, Johnson loathed himself for his behaviour: he was always close to his mother, a deeply religious woman. What we do know is that when no white boxer could be found to beat him, his lifestyle was used against him instead.

The champion spent most of 1909 fighting exhibition bouts, although on his record they are listed as 'no decisions' which means that the title could have changed hands if any of his opponents had stopped him. There was never any possibility of that. Victor McLaglen — later an Oscar winning actor — and Tony Ross were preliminary fighters, Philadelphia Jack O'Brien couldn't have knocked over his granny, and Al Kaufman was Jack's sparring partner. Johnson's first recognised defence of the title took place on October 16th and it speaks volumes for the lack of white heavyweight talent that it was against the middleweight champion, Stanley Ketchel.

According to one scribe Ketchel was: 'a God who came down from Mount Olympus to dwell briefly amongst mortals.' Other less admiring writers have branded him a psychopath. At 5′ 9″ and 154 lbs (70 kilos) he was much smaller than the 6′ 0″, 190–200 lbs heavyweight champion. At the contract signing Ketchel appeared in platform shoes and a padded jacket to make himself appear bigger. By fight time Ketchel's weight was 170 lbs but the added poundage did not increase his strength; it was merely flab. The fighters had anyway reached a secret agreement that Johnson would carry Ketchel for the stipulated 20 rounds in order to help the revenue from the fight film which they were getting a cut of. Jack was not normally trusting; this time he was and almost paid the price.

For 11 rounds at Colma, California, it was a poor fight. Ketchell shuffled forward, Johnson fended him off and the paying customers were not amused. In the 12th Stanley sprang his double-cross.

The middleweight champion was one of the most fearsome punchers in the division's history. Now he put everything into a ferocious right to the head. Jack hit the canvas. He rolled over and at '2' was squatting on his haunches eyeing Ketchel with a look of murderous hatred. He rose at '8' and met Ketchel's rush with a perfect right uppercut which left him inert on the canvas, his whole body quivering with shock. The force of the punch tore out several of Stanley's teeth. Two of them were embedded in Johnson's glove. The fight film shows Jack brushing them off while the count is completed.

On the corner of Reno's 4th and Toano streets stands a junkyard. It is all that is left of the huge wooden stadium built for boxing's first 'fight of the century'. Today, a plaque on the wall commemorates it. Most people pass by without a glance.

Nobody seriously believed that Ketchel, outstanding middleweight though he was, could win the heavyweight title back for the white race. Throughout 1909 pressure built up inexorably on Jim Jeffries to come out of retirement. Even the most senseless arguments were used. Jeffries was still champion even though he had retired — by which token there would have been no new champion until 1953; Johnson was actually only the No. 1 contender. Why, we're helping him get s title shot! Logic stood on its head and kicked in the testicles. These however are the arguments we can smile over. The rest we can't; they were bound up with racism at its most naked.

James J. Jeffries did not want to fight again. He was happy with his wife, his farm and the expanding waistline which said that after years of abstinence he was now enjoying life. He was a taciturn inarticulate man who only relaxed in the company of family and close friends. Imagine then the effect of newspaper advertisements featuring a little girl asking: 'Please, Mr Jeffries, are you going to fight Mr Johnson?' Children used to promote an unworthy cause. But of course that was not the way it appeared to Jeffries. White supremacy was never questioned in the first decade of the 20th century, and Jeffries was being hailed as its ultimate repository. Whipping Jack Johnson, the arrogant, uppity nigger who perverted white women, was, they told him, his duty. Slowly, reluctantly, the ex-champion began to succumb to the pressure. Early in 1910 he travelled to Baden-Baden in Germany to take the spa waters. Even here he could not escape Johnson's long black shadow. Britain's King Edward VII — who would not live to see the fight — shook his hand and told him to do his duty for the white race. In fact Jeffries had already made up his mind — hence the health trip — but a touch of royal racism, albeit from a libertine of the same stamp as Johnson, made it all seem so respectable. But poor Jim was mining fool's gold.

Arguably no sporting contest in history has ever created so much interest. That is because it was not a sporting contest. On one side it was a haunt of fears which found expression in a neo-fascist hoe-down. On the other, laudable aspirations intermingled with blind revenge. There was no part of it which was wholesome or inspiring. One anecdote sums Johnson-Jeffries up perfectly. Several months after the contest a whaling ship in the northern seas espied a rowing boat approaching. The rowers were eskimos; in the bow sat a grizzle-haired old white man. When they got within hailing distance the old man shouted, 'the fight; who won the fight?' When told Johnson, the whalers could hear him cursing as the boat rowed away.

The Ring Record Book lists 35 different promoters and syndicates from as far afield as London and Dublin who originally bid for the contest. Purse offers began at $50,000 and went up to $150,000. On today's values this does not seem excessive at around $7.5 million. But in 1910 it was the subject of much inflammatory comment by the press. They would not of course have questioned their own right to make such profits, but 'ordinary' people were not then supposed to earn that sort of money.

The winning bid, $120,000 in gold, came from a man few had heard of: Tex Rickard. Out of this sum, Rickard guaranteed $10,000 each to both contestants purely on signing — he put the money down on the table in front of them — plus two-thirds of the film rights.

This was not Rickard's own money but that of his backer, a millionaire mine owner named Thomas Cole*. But it was Rickard who was in the limelight. He was a natural showman, an ex-frontier lawman, gambler, saloon owner and

* They made a profit of $120,000, about $6,000,000 today.

gold miner who a few years earlier had promoted the epic Joe Gans–Battling Nelson lightweight bout at Goldfield, Nevada.

Rickard wanted to stage the fight in San Francisco. Moralising reactionaries objected. Initially they cut no ice with California's Governor John Gillett. But when a cable arrived from the Federal Government threatening to withdraw the Panama–Pacific Expo from California, Gillett suddenly discovered that he found Johnson–Jeffries 'demoralising', 'offensive' and 'a public nuisance'. Apparently he took a more lenient attitude towards coercion. But the pressure throws an interesting sidelight on thinking in Washington. Ostensibly the Government was worried about race riots, but it is a pretty safe bet that there would have been no objections had they thought Jeffries was likely to win. The undiscerning might have swallowed the legend of the invincible Boilermaker; but where hard heads ruled the real truth was known.

Rickard took the disappointment in his stride and moved the fight to Reno where he was assured of no interference. In 1910 Nevada was no more than a few sparse communities and the revenue from Johnson–Jeffries would be a boon to its economy.

The open air stadium which Rickard built sat 16,500*. By later standards this was hardly a significant live gate, but the astronomical ticket prices were for the moneyed class. Joe Public could queue up later at his local movie theatre to see the fight. Boxing has always been an exploitative business.

Jeffries was the pre-fight betting favourite, but behind the scenes all was not well. In the first place he was upset about the fight being drummed out of California. In the second, training was a nightmare. Rickard had originally wanted Jeffries to have a warm-up bout. One look at him disposed of that notion. James J. Corbett was brought in to supervise his training. Corbett sweated 70 lbs off his corpulent frame but the effort left Jeffries a shell. John L. Sullivan turned up to see how things were going and Corbett curtly told him to get lost. Only with great difficulty was Rickard able to persuade the three ex-champs to pose together for the cameras. Necessity forced the Jeffries camp to exclude reporters from the training sessions, forcing them to rely on invention and imagination.

By comparison the Johnson camp seemed an oasis of tranquillity. Johnson appeared to be doing nothing special but in fact was working hard. His inestimable advantage was that he had not been out of the ring for almost six years. However, at 32 he was only three years younger than Jeffries and needed to condition himself well. Sadly, this was to be the last time for five years that he would be in anything like good shape.

* Another 1,500 gate-crashed.

The day of the fight, symbolically July 4th, brought the high and the low, the respectable and the riffraff, to Reno. They sang the popular song of that independence day, 'All Coons look alike to me'. That too was symbolic: racism had desecrated liberty.

It was a boiling hot day, yet the fight was scheduled for 45 rounds, the triumph of illusion over reality. Jeffries' handlers were relying on his much vaunted strength over the long haul. But like a punctured air-bag, not much of it remained in the trappings of a once great physique. As in the Burns fight, the promoter, Rickard, would referee. Uniquely, there were no preliminary bouts.

It was never a contest. Jeffries was in the ring, Corbett in his corner and Sullivan, Fitzsimmons and Burns were at ringside. It was as though Johnson was imposing mastery on all of them. At no point did Jeffries win a round or share one. The limit of his success was in re-opening a cut lip which Jack had sustained in training. Johnson on the other hand tore Jeffries' face to shred, turning him into a walking blood saturnalia.

There were no highlights. Clump-clip, rip-rap went Johnson's fists as they thudded into the ex-champion. He could have finished it at any time but an early knock-out would have damaged the film revenues and boxing is a business. As facile round succeeded facile round so Jack could be seen talking to his old arch enemy. As usual reporters made up their own dialogue, 'C'mon Jeff — this is for the title', 'C'mon Jeff — where's the punch that caved in all Sharkey's ribs' and so on. What could however be clearly heard above the hub-bub, at ringside and in the ring itself, was the steady stream of insults which Corbett shouted at Johnson. 'Gentleman' Jim had a racial theory of his own: that if you insulted a black he would lose his temper. But Johnson's grin just got wider and wider and Corbett himself just got angrier and angrier until by the 12th he was hopping up and down red faced with rage. One cannot help but be reminded of the 'Kemptown Races' scene from 'Blazing Saddles'.

And so to the 15th. 'Nuff. The proles in the downtown cinemas had their money's worth and it was time to get out of this blazing sun. The end was simply a little poignant rather than dramatic. A right uppercut followed by a trio of left hooks left Jeffries sitting in a huddle against the ropes. He arose. Another left hook put him through them. Eager hands helped him back in to the ring, but other spectators called out to Rickard: 'Don't let him be knocked out.' In vain. Jack drove him across to the far side of the ring with another volley of left hooks, Jeffries collapsed against the ropes again and this time he did not beat the count.

It is said that boxers always reveal their true feelings immediately after a fight. On reaching the sanctuary of his dressing room Jeffries said:

'I could never have beaten Jack Johnson; not even at my best'

He retired again into such obscurity that when he visited troops during the Second World War they had to be told who he was. Jeffries' recreation in later life was fishing on his farm with Tom Sharkey. They died within six weeks of each other, Jeffries on March 3rd, 1953 and Sharkey on April 17th.

Reno, July 4th, 1910 was Jack Johnson's finest hour. It is said that when Roman Emperors returned in triumph slaves stood beside them whispering: 'All glory is fleeting.' One of the first people Jack called after the fight was Belle Schrieber.

Round Ten: The Magic Black Circle

Imagine the works of Shakespeare being turned down by the whole of the publishing world; envisage every art gallery rejecting the Mona Lisa. Impossible? Ridiculous? Well, equally impossible and ridiculous was the fact that Sam Langford could wander through a 22 year career without even fighting for a world title, let alone winning one.

Langford was a black Canadian from Nova Scotia. He began boxing professionally in 1902 when he was either nineteen or twenty-two, depending on which source you accept. Known as the 'Boston Tar Baby', Langford fought in the country of his birth only once. The bulk of his fighting was done in the U.S.A. with excursions to London, Paris, Australia and Mexico. He claimed a staggering 640 contests. This is certainly an exaggeration but the Ring Record Book, which credits him with 252 admits that the record is incomplete. Remarkably, Langford boxed most of his career with only limited vision in his left eye (the result of an accident), and finished up more-or-less blind in both eyes.

Sam Langford is a serious contender for the title of greatest pound for pound fighter of all time. On pure skill Sugar Ray Robinson probably shades them all but no fighter in history ever tackled and beat the quality of opposition that Langford did.

After less than two years as a professional Sam fought Joe Gans, the world lightweight champion, and outpointed him. Old timers saw Gans as the greatest 135 pounder ever. It was an over the weight bout, (Langford was 142 lbs (64.5 kilos), which meant that he could not claim the world title. Nine months later he met the great Joe Walcott. Walcott had flattened middleweights like Dan Creedon and Billy Hanrahan (Hart's conqueror), outpointed George Gardner and drawn with Philadelphia Jack O'Brien, and despite standing a mere 5′ 1½″, kayoed Choynski and held Sandy Ferguson even. But he got no better than a draw with Langford and some said he did not deserve that. Shortly afterwards Walcott reclaimed the welterweight title; Sam Langford did not feature in his plans.

Nor in those of other world champions. Jack Johnson knocked him down and outpointed him in 1906. The fight was sparsely reported and Langford's manager, Joe Woodman, later claimed that it was a close decision, with Jack taking a count as well. Johnson angrily refuted both claims, and it does seem that Woodman was being elastic with the truth. But Johnson showed no inclination to defend against Langford after winning the championship.

Stanley Ketchell might conceivably have put the 160 lbs crown on the line against Langford. Unfortunately, six months after they boxed a tame six rounder (apparently they agreed to take it easy) a farm-hand named Walter Dipley sent Stan back to Mount Olympus at the end of a shotgun.

It is possible that Langford could have claimed the light-heavyweight title, but the reasoning is somewhat tortuous. As Burns never bothered with it, Philadelphia Jack O'Brien was generally recognised as champion again. O'Brien was eventually knocked out by Ketchel, but Stanley never claimed the title and was killed a year later. With no other bidders — the 175 lbs division was then about as popular as typhus — O'Brien was still considered title-holder when Langford stopped him in 1911. It seems certain that both men were within the weight limit, but Langford made no claim and did not dispute Jack Dillons when O'Brien retired in 1912.

The heavyweight championship was a different matter. Although he stood only 5′ 7½″ and never weighed more than 180 lbs (82 kilos), Sam was indisputably the No. 1 contender from 1909 to 1918. His record was astonishing. He fought Joe Jeannette 14 times, winning 4, losing 3 and drawing 2 with 5 no decision bouts. He also had six no decision bouts with Jim Barry but bested him on six other occasions, five inside the distance. He also twice knocked out Sam McVey, and without needing an axe! All in all they fought 15 times, Langford winning four to McVey's two with four draws and five no decisions. Later, when Jeff Clarke and Harry Wills came on the scene, Sam showed them who was boss too. He knocked Clarke out three times and outpointed him against a solitary loss, and stopped Wills twice before blindness started to overtake him.

Few white fighters, if they had any pretensions to glory, could be persuaded to share a ring with this mini-titan. Certainly none of the infamous white hope brigade*. Fireman Jim Flynn did and was knocked out three times. Another Flynn, 'Porky', who got to be a fair to middling performer, was kayoed twice. 'Gunboat' Smith did actually 'beat' Sam but the fight appears to have been fixed, and when they met again Langford batted him out in three. Fred Fulton holds the only inside the distance win over Langford up to 1918, but it was a freak circumstance. Fulton caught him with a punch to the Adam's apple and Sam quit, unable to breathe.

The genesis of Sam's extraordinary ability lay in what most men would consider defects. He seemed to be made up from a collection of ill-assorted spare parts. He had a barrel chest, shoulders described by British boxing writer Jimmy Butler as the widest he had ever seen, and little lightweight legs. Like Fitzsimmons and Sayers before him, this ungainly combination gave Sam both speed and power. His reach was incredible. Butler records that, 'the tips of his fingers

* See next Chapter.

drooped below his knees.'[1] The British once built a warship along these lines, the battlecruiser, which had the speed of a cruiser and the power and range of a battleship. Unfortunately they could not provide it with an adequate defence. But Langford, a human battlecruiser, had a superb defence, on a par with Johnson's. His long, raking lefts cut opponents to pieces and his right hook carried within it a glimpse of Hades. Above all Langford was a superb body puncher, considered by some its greatest exponent and credited with inventing the maxim: 'kill the body and the head dies too.' Sam might have been constructed from bits and pieces but they were amongst the best parts of Sayers, Fitzsimmons, Burns and Johnson.

As Langford never officially fought for a championship there are no great title dramas to unfold. But he left behind a fund of humorous stories which seem to convey the essence of him, both as a man and a boxer. Langford inspired a certain dread in other fighters. Even as late as 1916 when Sam was either 33 or 36, the young Jack Dempsey wanted absolutely no part of him whatsoever. One opponent, whom Sam agreed to take it easy with, refused to go anywhere near him in the 1st round. At the start of the 2nd Langford reached out and touched his gloves. 'Why Sam, this isn't the last round?' 'It is for you,' replied Sam grimly and over flashed the right hook. John Lester Johnson, who a few years later was to smash Dempsey's ribcage in, fled from the opening bell in such a state of terror that he did not notice that Langford was not even chasing him. Instead Sam lolled on the ropes until Johnson scurried past and then flattened him with a right to the spine! But then the 'Tar baby' had seen it all before. Two years earlier Jim Smith had turned and ran. Not until the 5th could Langford catch up with him. Then he left Smith flat on his face with a right to the buttocks!

In 1917 Langford discovered that the optic nerve of his left eye was burnt out and he could no longer see with it. Then a cataract grew over the right. A maturing Harry Wills started to beat him regularly. Even now he won more than he lost, but was drifting down the leagues. In 1922 somebody called 'Tut' Jackson halted him in five. He had his final fight in May, 1924 when by any yardstick he was in his 40s. He won by a third round knockout. It is said that he boxed completely blind, located his opponent by feel, and caught him flush with that famous right hook of his. The story may be apocryphal, but it provides a fittingly brave finale for a hero.

Many years later a sports journalist, Al Laney, decided to track down the old 'Tar Baby'. He found him alone and blind in a slum apartment in Harlem. The article which Laney wrote helped start a small trust fund which enabled Sam to eke out his remaining days in decent surroundings. It also brought back a measure of respect; Langford became a regular visitor to Joe Louis' training

1 'The Fight Game' p84

camp. His words of thanks to those who cared about him were poignant: 'If I had my eyes, I'd cry.'

Today Sam Langford, history's greatest contender, is forgotten. He should not be. Of the 58 men who since 1892 have held either the undisputed world title, or a version of it, Langford in my view would have beaten all but ten of them. His challenges to Jack Johnson went unanswered. Had they met for the title at their peaks then it would have been the greatest series in boxing history, although not necessarily the most exciting because both were primarily defensive fighters. Johnson realised this; two black chess masters added up to zero at the box office. But that was not the whole of it. The financial return was matched at the other extreme by the physical outlay involved. Jack could earn more by training in bedrooms and bars to beat white dummies. Fully fit he would have one a series with Langford because he was just that bit better. But it wasn't worth his while.

Langford's two greatest rivals in the magic black circle were Joe Jeannette and Sam McVey. Jeannette was also a master of defence, a fine boxer with a good punch. McVey was a sawn-off human tree-trunk. He had the image of a thuggish street fighter, according to one reporter, ugly enough to 'frighten the rising moon'. In fact McVey also had a tight defence and could hit very hard indeed.

Jeannette and McVey fought Langford so often that they could have joined the golf tour. Each other not so often. In all they met five times and ended up with one win each, two draws and a no decision. But their third fight was worth not only their entire series but those of all the other contenders put together. They had been doomed to wander in the twilight world of the perpetual contender, odyssey without end until age frayed their limbs and the fists of younger men wrote 'might have been' across their brows. The frustration of it exploded one night in a contest which echoes down the years as perhaps the greatest of all time.

The year was 1909. They met in Paris in a tepid 20 rounder. McVey won and the crowd booed them both. Eight weeks later they agreed to fight again in the same city, this time to a finish. Literally.

On the day of the fight the fans blew it a gigantic raspberry. When they climbed into the ring Jeannette and McVey could probably have counted the spectators. By the time it was ended, three and a quarter hours later, the hall would be packed to the rafters as the news spread to every bar, bistro and theatre in Paris that two of the greatest fighters of the day were locked in a fight to the death.

The opening bell. McVey hurtles across the ring and pistols a screaming right to Jeannette's head: Jeannette reels into the ropes. McVey follows through with a ramrod left and now Jeannette hits the floor. He only just makes it at '9' and needs all his craft and skill to survive to the bell.

For the next four rounds McVey drives Jeannette before him like chaff in a gale. Time and again Jeannette is ground to the canvas but he survives each searing barrage and turns his head into the very teeth of the maelstrom, bravely ripping both hands to McVey's body. And gradually — almost imperceptibly — Jeannette comes more and more into the fight. McVey continues to batter him to the floor but now Jeannette's fists are pounding out a drumbeat on McVey's ribcage. In the 16th a right hook almost tears Jeannette's head off but somehow he survives — how only he will ever know — and comes up for the 17th. In this round he will catch a glimpse of hell through McVey's hammering fists and at the end of it the police want it stopped.

'No' — scream the crowd, who have not sat down since the first bell, and faced with the French Revolution breaking out again the gendarmes wisely relent.

Jeannette needs oxygen in his corner, but he comes out for the 18th and incredibly, unbelievably, he carries the fight to McVey, welting his body; hurting him.

By the end of the 19th Jeannette has gone down 21 times, McVey not once. But now the tide has turned. Jeannette attacks, McVey retreats. As he goes back he scythes murderous rights at Jeannette and between the 19th and the 31st Joe hits the floor another six times. But each time he gets up and marches forward relentlessly, eyes blazing with a burning will to fell the oak tree of a man before him.

After the 31st the woodcutter begins to slowly but surely cut the tree down.

McVey is floored for the first time in the 39th when an eviscerating left hook to the jaw axes him down. Up he comes and the two men stand in the centre of the ring volleying bone crushing wallops into each other, no quarter given, none asked, and none intended, two human battering rams trying to kill each other in a 20 foot abattoir.

But it is McVey's last fling. Over the next ten rounds, exhausted by punches that have shattered, bruised and shocked his body beyond endurance, he will be knocked down another ten times. His nose will be broken in two places, both his eyes will be shut tight and his mouth will be torn to ribbons. By the end of the 48th he is vomiting blood.

Jeannette is sick also, but he is the one with just the faint reserve of strength left. In the 49th he uses McVey as a target zone. When the bell sounds for round 50 McVey remains slumped in his corner, beaten into a stupor. It is the end.

Back in the U.S.A. Langford will grin as he reflects on the validity of his dictum — kill the body and the head dies too.

Joe Jeannette had now beaten Johnson, Langford and McVey, but the manner of the last named victory was such that Johnson was never going to take the ring against him again, at least not until they were fat old men sparring in front of the cameras for a World War II services benefit. Middleweights and hollow goliaths were far easier.

After Jeffries, Jack did not defend the title for exactly two years, July 4th, 1912, at Las Vegas, New Mexico. He didn't have to train too hard — not for 'Fireman' Flynn. That year Jeannette was unbeaten in 21 fights winning 15 by knockout, while Langford whipped McVey three out of four, twice by kayo, and iced Jim Barry and the other Flynn, 'Porky'. The 'Fireman' went to Canada and stopped Al Williams. Exactly the right credentials for a title shot.

There is not much to say about Johnson-Flynn II — or worth saying. It went nine awful rounds and then the police stopped it, apparently a two-fold act of philanthropy to save Flynn getting hurt and the spectators from terminal boredom. The main, in fact the only, talking point, was whether Flynn should have been disqualified. Like a rotund jack-in-the-box, he consistently jumped up and down butting Johnson in the face. Johnson seemed no more concerned about it than a father with slightly unruly child.

He would have been more perturbed had he known it was his last title bout in the U.S.A.

Round Eleven: Obscenity–
The White Hope Campaign

Racism begins with the theory that one race is superior to another. It ends with the allegedly inferior race being put into gas chambers.

In the immediate aftermath of Johnson's victory over Jeffries, at least ten blacks were murdered as race riots swept America. Scores more were injured. Although whites were also fatally injured, the overwhelming majority of the atrocities were committed by whites against blacks.

Fear of further outbreaks caused many States to prohibit showing of the fight film.

The day after the contest, a 6′ 4″ railway worker jumped down from his locomotive at Sa Pulpa, Oklahoma, and announced his intention of regaining the title for the white race. Ironically, the speaker, Carl Morris, was half Cherokee Indian.

The Ring Record Book lists Morris as the original white hope. This is fair because although other white heavyweights such as 'Gunboat' Smith became caught up in the ebbs and tides of the white hope campaign, they were more swept along by it than through any conscious racialism.

Wrote boxing historian John Lardner: 'Well muscled white boys more than 6′ 2″ were not safe out of their mother's sight.' The search was on for a white boxer to dethrone Johnson. It was a squalid campaign, conceived in prejudice and conducted in bigotry. It also masked a much more perfidious campaign being waged against Johnson by the authorities.

The best of the numerous hopefuls were Morris, Luther McCarty, Frank Moran, Al Palzer and Jess Willard. There was also a British white hope, 'Bombardier' Billy Wells, and a Canadian, Arthur Pelkey. Most came from poor rural backgrounds in the South and Mid West, and were from the social underclass sneeringly referred to as 'poor white trash'. The fact that they actually had more in common with the majority of blacks than large sections of the white community eluded them. Fourteen years earlier banks had threatened to foreclose on farm mortgages if the Democrat nominee William Jennings Bryan was elected President. In Henry Ford's car firm at Deerborn, Michigan, men were sacked if they spoke to each other during lunchbreaks. Racism however divides and rules and keeps those ruled in ignorance. If white hopefuls thought that the campaign offered them a way out of economic servitude then they were very sadly mistaken. The takings went to carpetbagger managers and promoters who scoured hicksville looking to exploit giant palookas.

Meanwhile the effect of all this passion and hatred was stoking up its flames. Shortly after the Ketchel fight Johnson met Etta Duryea. Etta was not a prostitute in the sense that she worked in a brothel or touted for business on street corners, but her favours were readily available to those with large enough wallets to show her a good time. Around the end of 1909 she began to live with Jack as his common-law wife, although it would be more correct to describe her as leader of the pack. Belle Shreiber and other prostitutes were still in the entourage. Belle and Co. continued to ply their trade while they were travelling with him. Whether Jack gained a sexual stimulus from this we do not know. What historians are generally agreed on is that he was not receiving any of the money they made from other clients. Whatever else Jack may have been, he was not a pimp. What he was doing however was building his own funeral pyre. Deep down he may have been aware of this because at the beginning of 1911 he married Etta and parted company with Belle.

May found him in Britain to do battle with 'Bombardier' Billy Wells. Wells may accurately be described as the 'Eddie the Eagle'* of the white hope campaign. The closest he came to Johnson is that like Belle Shrieber he found himself looking up at a lot of ceilings! In 1911 he had had just nine fights (Johnson over eighty) which included being knocked out by Gunner Moir. A photograph of the fight shows an obese Moir (who appears to be wearing swimming trunks) taking a straight left while Wells right seems to be directing traffic. This may explain why the 'Bombardier' became a human punch bag for even mediocre American heavyweights.

Any fight with Johnson was plainly a horrid mismatch, a view endorsed behind the scenes by Lord Lonsdale, Chairman of the National Sporting Club. Home Secretary Winston Churchill quite properly banned it, but unfortunately had to indulge in unsatisfactory reasons for doing so, which allowed various paranoid racists and reactionaries to have their little says. It did however demonstrate the need for British boxing to have a proper controlling body and the nucleus of the Boxing Board of Control was established three years later**.

Losing an easy pay-day was something which Johnson could shrug off. Like his predecessors he found plenty of work touring in vaudeville. His next fight, with Flynn in 1912, was hardly any different from the burlesque routines he performed. He lost little, if any, sleep over the antics of the white hopes. Carl Morris's pugilistic locomotive was hardly gathering steam. He had shunted Marvin Hart into retirement but in May, 1912 was himself detrained in six by fellow white hope Luther McCarty. Frank Moran had gone to the post 25 times

* An unsuccessful British ski-jumper who became a celebrity during the 1988 Winter Olympics.

** Disgracefully though, one of its first acts was to prohibit blacks from fighting for British titles, a ban which lasted until after World War II.

but beaten no-one of note. Al Palzer, unbeaten in nine, seemed lethargic by comparison but Johnson had watched him win something called a white hope tourney. Canada's Pelkey was wandering around the fringes without making an impact. All of them of course had business elsewhere when Langford, Jeannette or McVey were in town. The white hope campaign was however out in the open where it could be seen; the insidious forces which were about to destroy boxing's first black heavyweight champion were not.

Around the time of the Flynn fight, Johnson began to employ an eighteen year old white secretary named Lucille Cameron. Despite her tender age, Lucille was in fact an experienced prostitute. Her duties certainly involved more than typing; equally certain, Etta was aware of it. On the night of September 11th, 1912 Jack arrived home to find Etta in bed with a gun, and half her head missing.

The tragedy at first created a measure of sympathy for Johnson. Claims that Etta was shunned by fellow whites and also disliked by Jack's black friends were not without foundation. But any good will swiftly evaporated when, with Etta still warm in her grave, Lucille openly moved into her bed. Lucille's mother turned up and swore out a charge against Johnson for abducting her daughter. In fact the only abduction was by Federal authorities who held Lucille against her will for six weeks until they were forced to drop the charges against Jack. Just to make sure, he married Lucille on December 4th. But the sluice gates were open. Searching around for witnesses against the champion, the authorities came up with Belle Shrieber.

It is often said that the Mann Act of 1910 was framed (the operative word) with the specific intention of being used against Jack Johnson. That isn't true. Nor was he its worst victim. Twenty years late nine young blacks were to have their lives ruined after being falsely accused of rape by two white prostitutes seeking to evade charges under the Mann law*. The act, which made it illegal to transport a woman across state lines for immoral purposes, was aimed specifically at pimps. Unfortunately, like all legislation which seeks to regulate behaviour it was ill-defined and open to abuse.

Jack Johnson had certainly travelled across state lines with prostitutes, but at worst as a paying customer and, as with Belle Shrieber and Clara Kerr before her, mainly a boyfriend. Like Lucille, Belle was held in close confinement by Federal agents. They had no right to do so, but fed her with lurid and wholly untrue stories that Johnson would have her murdered if she was free. Meanwhile she provided them with reams of testimony about her sex life with the champion. In fact, as far as the Mann Act was concerned, only her dealings with him from

* The infamous Scottsboro Case which fully exposed prejudice in America's Deep South.

July 1st, 1910, when the act became law, and the end of January, 1911, when they parted for good, were relevant. During that time Belle had not crossed any state lines with Johnson. The prosecution — or rather persecution — should have ended here. In no other case would it even have begun; although not against the strict letter of the law it was entirely alien to its concept. But white expectations of a conviction had been raised to fever pitch and the U.S. Government was at one with them. They found a straw. In October, 1910 Johnson had wired Belle $75 to come from Pittsburgh to Chicago to see him. It was a pure technicality and could only succeed anyway if a jury were persuaded that Johnson's perfectly reasonable explanation of a gift was untrue. They were. Which, given that the jurors were a body of white, republican, church-going middle-aged men who disliked both sport and blacks, is hardly very surprising*. On June 4th, 1913, Johnson was sentenced to a year and a day in a federal penitentiary. Shortly afterwards he jumped bail and fled with Lucille to Paris.

The champion was gone. The fly in the buttermilk had been removed. racism had won.

Johnson did not thrive in Europe. He found the same prejudices as in the U.S.A., particularly towards his inter-racial marriage. By November he was chronically short of money. He knocked out a Russian named Andre Spool in a boxer-wrestler contest and then on December 13th made his fourth title defence.

Historically, the Jack Johnson-Jim Johnson bout is of importance because it was the first heavyweight title bout between two black fighters, something which was not to happen again for over a quarter of a century. And that really is it. 'Battling' Jim Johnson was not one of the gifted black fighters of the day. No great scalps hung from his wampun belt. His ambition was limited to lasting the distance which he did by fighting out of an exaggerated crouch. Jeannette had four times failed to knock him out: Langford once. In a career best, 'Battling' Jim had held McVey to a draw, but was stopped in a return. That year the circle was still performing its magic. Langford and McVey had boxed a draw, and a week after the birds had flown, Jeannette outfoxed Langford in Paris.

The battle of the Johnsons ended all square, the last time this has happened in an undisputed title clash. At least that is what the record book says. Those still awake after ten poor rounds thought that Jim had done enough to get it — which wasn't much. Jack, overweight and out of condition, did next to nothing. Afterwards he claimed to have broken a bone in his arm.

* Even so, four voted for acquittal on the first two ballots.

He was in no better shape when he defended against white hope Frank Moran in Paris the following June.

According to his publicity folder, Moran was an ex-dentist. In fact he had dropped out of dental school after a few weeks. He claimed to possess a knockout right swing which he called his 'Mary Ann'. Not that it had connected that often, only 14 times in 36 fights. Cumbersome is probably a flattering description of Moran; he didn't telegraph punches, he sent them by second class post! In addition to Tony Ross and 'Gunboat' Smith, he had lost to such worthies as Frank Appell, Jim Savage, and Jack gayer. Never heard of them? Nope, and you won't again in this book. In his last fight he had stopped Palzer, but the latter was then sliding down the pole.

Perhaps the most interesting thing about the contest was the referee. Georges Carpentier was the European heavyweight champion, and three weeks later would lay claim to the 'white heavyweight championship of the world'. The irony of that was probably lost on Frank Moran.

Johnson–Moran was strictly a non event. War clouds were gathering over Paris; they did not settle on the velodrome d'hiver. For 20 very tedious rounds Moran plodded after the champion who grinned a lot and jabbed occasionally. In the 14th Moran actually connected with a swing. Jack is alleged to have clapped his gloves together and called out, 'My sincere congratulations Frank.' Jack received the decision but was apparently never paid. Well, you get nothing for nothing.

A month after the Paris waltz Al Palzer was shot to death by his father in a family dispute. It was the second tragedy to hit the white hope campaign. Seventeen months earlier Palzer had surrendered his bauble of 'white heavyweight champion' to Luther McCarty, a young cowboy from Driftwood Creek, Nebraska. Photographs of McCarty show a resemblance to the legendary James Dean. There was to be more than a similarity in their brief but meteoric careers.

Of Scotch–Irish ancestry, McCarty was eighteen when he had his first fight. That was in 1911. In his second he stopped Joe Grim. Grim is largely forgotten today; indeed most boxing historians prefer to forget him. Born Saveris Giannone in Italy, Grim became a legend as the iron man of the ring. He is believed to have had over 300 contests, winning no more than about a dozen. But he was only ever knocked out three times and made his name by standing up to terrible punishment. He lasted six round distances with both Fitzsimmons and Johnson despite being floored in the region of forty times during the two 'contests'. McCarty kayoed him in four; nine months earlier it had taken Sam McVey twelve.

That December, McCarty boxed a no decision bout with Jeff Clarke, the 'Joplin Ghost'. Clarke would go on to beat Langford and McVey, and if not quite overall magic circle standard was only a rung beneath it. Of the senior white hopes, only McCarty was prepared to get in the ring with him.

The following year the young Nebraskan fought another leading black fighter, Jim Barry, again a no decision contest. Also 'no decision' was Jess Willard, but McCarty knocked out Morris and 'Fireman' Flynn to set up the meeting with Palzer whom he pummelled to defeat in eighteen rounds.

By May 24th, 1913 when he stepped into a makeshift ring at Calgary, Canada to defend the white hope 'championship' against Arthur Pelkey, McCarty had established himself not only as the top white fighter but as a genuine title contender. Pelkey did not figure to be stiff opposition. Real name Peletier, he was French–Canadian like Burns, who managed him, and seven weeks previously had actually boxed the old champion in a no decision bout. Shortly after the opening bell McCarty and Pelkey went into a clinch. Pelkey appeared to land a light left. McCarty collapsed face down on the ground. The audience screamed 'fake'. But Luther McCarty never rose again in this world.

The post mortem established that death was due to a blow to the head some weeks earlier. McCarty had in effect been walking around with a time bomb ticking away inside him. What put it there has never been satisfactorily established. One account says that a horse threw McCarty heavily against the side of a barn. Another is that he dived into a river and hit his head on some submerged rocks. However, it should be noted that less than a month earlier he had boxed Frank Moran in a no decision contest. Was he injured by some of Moran's crude swipes? We will never know.

We shall also never know just how good McCarty actually was. At 6′ 4″ and 205 lbs (93 kilos), he looked the part. His record was first class. Up to the Pelkey bout he boxed 24 times in just over two years winning sixteen inside the distance and engaging in eight no decision contests. The latter rather irritatingly prevents us from gaining a clear picture. 'No decision' bouts were a halfway house to legality. Many states which had previously banned boxing relaxed their laws to permit contests as long as decisions were not rendered if they went the distance. This was as a sop to moralists who opposed boxing because of its links to gambling and corruption. The gambling fraternity circumvented the rule very easily by agreeing to be bound by whoever the press made the winner. Corruptible journalists could of course make some very easy money. Of Luther McCarty's no decision bouts only the most important, with Jess Willard, has been delved into by historians. Press reports indicate that McCarty was the better man and out-boxed Willard. On the available evidence, McCarty was a fighter of merit who could box and punch, and at only just turned 21 was probably still three years away from his peak. Indisputably, he was the best of the white hopes.

The McCarty tragedy ruined Arthur Pelkey. He carried on for seven more years and 16 contests but never won another fight and was stopped twelve times. He took wicked beatings at the hands of 'Gunboat' Smith, Sam McVey, Bill Lang, Carl Morris, Fred Fulton and Jack Dempsey. He died at the age of only 36. Pelkey may have taken his hidings as a penance for McCarty. If so then it was tragically unnecessary because he was not responsible for his death.

'Gunboat' Smith took the white 'championship' from Pelkey on New Year's Day 1914. It should have led eventually to a real title shot, particularly as, after Luther McCarty, 'Gunboat' was the best white heavyweight around. He was born Edward Eckbladt but as 'Smith' rolled more easily off the tongue adopted that name for his boxing career. 'Gunboat' derived from service in the U.S. Navy. Tall and gangling, Smith possessed a good left hand and a powerful right. Shortly before stopping Pelkey, 'Gunboat' was awarded a 12 round decision over Sam Langford. Sam appears to have merely gone through the motions, possibly to try and lure Johnson into the ring. But the outcome was that by the summer of 1914 'Gunboat' Smith was on top of the heap.

The it all went wrong.

On July 16th Smith defended his cardboard crown against Georges Carpentier in London. The Frenchman, who was then hardly more than a middleweight, spent most of the contest looking up at 'Gunboat's' loose limbed frame from the canvas (Carpentier's own account of the fight is about as valid as the Hitler diaries), and he was down there in the 6th when Smith was adjudged to have hit him and was disqualified. Three months later 'Gunboat' gave Langford a return and was knocked out. The remainder of his career was spent in 'could-have-been' land.

Which left Jess Willard. But for the white hope campaign Willard would have spent his life in peaceful obscurity amongst the rolling prairies of Kansas. He was 29 when he took up boxing, having been born of English parents in Pottawatomie County, Kansas on December 29th, 1881.

The only impressive thing about Willard was his size. He stood 6′ 6″* and weighed 250 lbs (114 kilos). He was discovered by a typical palooka-spotting manager, Tom Jones, late in 1910, while working as a cowhand. It is said that Jones took Willard to breakfast and wondered whether they could make enough to cover the food bill when Jess gulped down 28 eggs! It is also alleged that on his first morning in the gym, Willard walked out after being hit in the stomach by a welterweight!

Despite these tribulations, Willard had his first contest on February 15th, 1911, and became the only world heavyweight champion to lose his professional debut, being disqualified against Louis Fink (no I haven't made it up). In October of that year he quit against Joe Cox, claiming that Cox's friends had threatened him with guns. Two months later Luther McCarty endured no such travails when knocking Cox out at the same venue.

The Big Jessie plodded on. There was an undistinguished no decision

* Although some recent historians have disputed this.

contest with Pelkey, McCarty had the better of him in another, and then 'Gunboat' Smith outboxed him in San Francisco. By the summer of 1913 it looked like a one way ticket back to Palookaville. It was not that Jess was altogether a bad fighter. He had a fair left hand and a good right uppercut when he wanted to use it. He was easy to hit, but so big that punches just seemed to bounce off him. His greatest problem was his attitude. He was lazy and didn't like fighting.

Jones told him to do something and he did; with fatal results. On August 22nd, at Vernon, California, Jess really tore into 'Bull' Young, pounding him over and over again with the uppercut until Young was counted out in the 11th round. Young collapsed after the fight and died several days later without regaining consciousness.

Young's death certainly upset Willard and played a big part in his next contest, a ten rounder against George 'Boer' Rodel, a South African who was trying to cash in on the white hope campaign. Or rather his manager was. Rodel was handled by Jimmy 'the boy bandit' Johnson, a crafty English scavenger. The 'Boer' was hardly a fighter of merit. Even punchbags hit him back and his record contained the sad notation 'Bombardier Billy Wells k.o. by 2'. Johnson used his managerial 'skills'. Poor old George had a dodgy ticker, if Jess cut loose then who knew what might happen, and so on. With the Young tragedy fresh in his mind Willard agreed to take it easy.

He must have been somewhat surprised at the vigour of the 'Boer's' attacks for a man with a weak heart, but whenever he was tempted to hit back there was Johnson at ringside meaning fully tapping his heart. At the end of 10 'no decision' rounds Rodel got the newspaper verdict and Jess had been thoroughly conned. He demanded a rematch and this time gave Rodel a hiding, dropping him for the count in the 9th.

The beginning of 1915 found Jack Johnson in London, broke and fed up. Across the Channel the war of movement between the Allies and Germany had come to an end, and the next four years were to see millions perish in headlong assaults against static positions. Beside such monumental loss of life, boxing and the heavyweight title were of no consequence. Johnson was therefore not in a position to turn away work, and when his friend, boxing promoter Jack Curley, turned up with a proposed contest in Mexico he was all ears. The problem was, who should be in the other corner?

Not Langford, Jeannette or McVey. Between them the three musketeers had gone to bat 27 times in 1914 and only Langford had struck out, dropping a points decision to Jeff Clarke, which also eliminated Clarke. 'Gunboat' was still the best of the whites but his high profile defeats by Carpentier and Langford meant that Jack could shuffle him out of the pack. Arguably he had never even heard of Willard. But Curley had. 30 fights with 21 wins (18 kayos) against 4 losses. It was a good enough record to be sold to the public, while at the same time a points defeat to little known Tom MacMahon in March, 1914 indicated that Willard was hardly top of the form (MacMahon had subsequently been knocked out by Langford). Not uncommonly in boxing, Jess got the call for what he hadn't done rather than what he had.

Mexico proved untenable. Officially, the Johnson-Willard was called off there because of the antics of guerrilla leader Pancho Villa; in reality the Mexican authorities intended deporting Johnson to the U.S. as soon as he set foot in the country. The Cuban Government was altogether more sanguine and the contest was arranged for the Havana race track on April 5th. It was the oldest coupling ever in a heavyweight title bout — Johnson was 37, Willard 33.

How hard Jack trained for it is a matter of dispute, which we will come to shortly. Willard on the other hand prepared as never before and went into the ring in the best shape of his life. With a scheduled distance of 45 rounds he needed to be in condition.

April 5th was a scorchingly hot day. The boxers entered the ring at around noon. 20,000 people paid to see the contest and 15,000 more saw it for free seated on the hills overlooking the race track.

Until the night before the fight Willard did not think he had a chance of beating Johnson. But that evening Jess went for a walk along the beach. Looking up he spotted a black seagull trying to battle its way into land against a strong headwind. The bird finally succeeded after several rebuffs but the strain was too much for it and it dropped dead at Jess's feet. To the uneducated Willard this represented an omen as to how his fight would go. The black champion would fade and die from his own exertions just when victory seemed close at hand.

In fact it could equally have been interpreted that Johnson would win the fight and then collapse. But Jess saw it the way he wanted to.

Possibly it was this psychological momentum which carried Jess through the first 20 rounds of the fight. Jack opened by feinting his defence into ruins and then rocking him with a blistering right cross. From here on he blocked or evaded Willard's long leads, speared the white man with punishing lefts, and pounded his body with hooks and uppercuts. In the 7th Jack opened up a big attack and drove Willard around the ring. Jess barely survived the round.

Johnson continued to pound Willard thoughout the next five rounds and in the 13th he set up another big assault. Again, Jess barely survived the barrage of leather. But at the bell he still stood. Jack continued to have the upper hand thoughout the next seven rounds, but after the 13th the fight was slipping away from him. Age, the blazing heat, and the years of dissipation, were now catching him up. By the 20th Willard looked a mess: his face minced to bloody shreds, body badly bruised, but he was in fact the stronger and could sense that Johnson was weakening. Just like the seagull.

From the 21st onwards Willard marched forward pounding home ramrod lefts to Jack's head and punishing rights to his body. Johnson could see the punches coming but now could not react fast enough to block or avoid them. In the 25th he took a fearful hammering to the body and when he slumped wearily back in his corner he knew that it was all over. He now ordered Lucille to leave the stadium. At the time the action appeared quite innocuous. Later, it would become the centrepiece of a great controversy.

The minute's rest before the 26th was to be Jack's last as champion. When the bell went he walked from fact into legend! He had enough for one last attack but there was no steam in his punches anymore. Willard pushed him away, measured the distance and then unleashed a superb right to the side of the jaw. Jack crashed to the canvas and rolled over onto his back. He made no attempt to beat the count.

Afterwards in his dressing room Johnson told reporters: 'I have no excuses; a better and younger man won the title.'

And there the matter stood for the next twelve months. Until Johnson contacted boxing writer Nat Fleischer* with a story that he had thrown the fight in return for an extra $50,000, and the waiving of his prison sentence in the U.S. He had received the money, but the authorities had double-crossed him. By way of evidence Jack pointed to a photograph of him taking the count, with his right arm across his eyes to shield them from the sun, proof, he said, that he was fully conscious at the time. Fleischer's story sowed the seeds of one of the greatest controversies in boxing history. It still echoes today.

There *was* talk of a fix even before the fight took place. But such rumours attended virtually every championship contest of that era.

Promoter Jack Curley vehemently denied the story. Johnson, said Curley, had received his purse and nothing else. He knew of no arrangements with the U.S. Government. The authorities themselves dismissed the allegations. One would of course have expected both denials, but it has to be said that Curley was a friend of Johnson's and had handled the funeral arrangements for Etta.

Willard also dismissed the ex-champ's story. Again, one would expect him to, but here too there is a caveat. Although they were never friends, Jess was a great admirer of Jack Johnson. He was under no illusions as to what the outcome would have been had they met at Jack's peak, and later declared that Johnson could have whipped both Joe Louis and Billy Conn in the same ring at the same time (not quite, but we get the picture Jess).

It also needs to be said that Fleischer never believed Jack, and this is

* Later editor and publisher of 'The Ring' magazine.

important. He too was a great admirer of Johnson and believed that he was the greatest fighter in history. Like Curley, he also was a personal friend. And, great boxing historian though he was, Fleischer was not wholly objective when it came to men he liked and admired. His 1972 biography of Jack Dempsey is very largely hero worship. Sordid details of Dempsey's private life are glossed over, the allegation that Dempsey loaded his gloves against Willard is omitted, and other major controversies are seen purely from Dempsey's point of view. Given Fleischer's known feelings about Jack Johnson we can be certain that he would have taken Jack's side had there been any truth in the allegations.

Which leaves us with the evidence of the photograph. At the time Johnson made his accusations the fight film was banned in the U.S.A. (it was not shown until the 1920s). When it became available all manner of ring historians rushed into print to say that far from shielding his eyes throughout the count, Johnson's arm fell to his side after a couple of seconds*.

I am afraid this is not correct. Not only Johnson's right arm, but his left glove too are raised above his eyes throughout the entirety of the count!

But that does not mean that Johnson was telling the truth. We need to look at the evidence of the fight as a whole.

First, Jess Willard hardly seems to have been selected with defeat in mind. Quite the opposite. Of the leading white fighters he had the least impressive credentials. 'Gunboat' was the best around, Carl Morris had a superior overall record to Willard's with only three defeats in thirty-five fights (22 kayos).

Secondly, although it was said that Johnson entered the ring in poor condition, the fight film does not sustain this. Jack looked his age — which is only to be expected — but he does not appear to be flabby or overweight.

Third, on the evidence of the fight, Johnson seems to have tried very hard to win. At times only Willard's enormous strength kept him on his feet.

Strength is probably the key word here. After the 20th, Johnson's was clearly running out. At the end of the 25th Lucille left the stadium. Jack claimed that this was a signal to him that she had received the final instalment of the money. But it is more likely that he sent her away to avoid her seeing him knocked out. The fight had already gone 25 rounds under a blazing sun. When it ended it would be the longest heavyweight title bout in history. Yet Johnson still mounted one last despairing attack in the 26th and the punch which sent him to the canvas was a very powerful one, delivered against the jaw of a 37 year old after over an hour and a quarter of gruelling combat in dehydrating conditions. Jack was not actually rendered unconscious — neither was Jeffries at Reno — hence he shielded his eyes against the sun. But, like Jeffries, he did

* Some prints may have been edited to give this impression.

not have the strength to get up.

And that seems to me the most logical explanation. There was no great fluctuation in the betting before the fight — Johnson was the favourite — and on the available evidence he was beaten fairly and squarely. Nobody at the time had any doubts about it.

Fundamentally, Jack Johnson was not a dishonest man, but he was a manipulator who sought to turn any situation to his advantage, particularly where boxing was concerned. During his trial he described boxing as: 'all crooked'. He therefore had no qualms about exploiting it. He was the first black heavyweight champion and believed — entirely with justification — that he had been hounded.

In the years after Johnson lost the title it became fashionable to say that if he had been a different sort of man then he would have been more acceptable as champion. This is racist poppycock. Sullivan behaved in similar fashion and was venerated for it. Johnson was hated not because of his weaknesses, but his strengths. He was no 'Uncle Tom' figure, but a man of pride and intellect. He saw himself not as a representative of his race, but as an individual seeking respect for his accomplishments. He was hated because he was feared. Whites saw in him a man who challenged the belief that a pale skin automatically made them superior. Ironically, in view of the way his philosophy was later distorted by the Nazis, Nietzsche would have recognised in Johnson his concept of the dominant man, beyond race and religion, good and evil. Jack Johnson was not a man for average men to understand, because he was not a man to be understood by them.

After Havana he returned to Europe. He had a few fights and tried his hand at bullfighting. In 1920 he surrendered to Federal authorities and served his 366 days in the penitentiary at Leavenworth. Two years on from this Jack attempted a comeback. His ring career finally ended in 1928 when at the age of 50 he was stopped by a Phil Hartwell in Kansas City. He toured in bit parts in the theatre and for a time ran a flea circus. In 1945 Joe Jeannette finally got Johnson in the ring again; the two elderly warriors sparred for the cameras in aid of service charities.

Jack Johnson died as he lived, in the fast lane. On June 10th, 1946, outside Raleigh, North Carolina, Jack's long and winding road finally ran out and he was killed when his car hit a tree.

The victory over Jack Johnson was Jess Willard's one golden moment in an insipid career. The 'Tall Pine from Pottawatomie', as he was called, cashed in on the title by touring as a circus strong man.

On March 25th, 1916 he defended against Frank Moran. Moran had put together four kayos since losing to Johnson but the quality of the opposition was hardly inspiring, two wins over Jim Coffey, the 'Roscommon Giant' (for 'Roscommon' read 'Palookaville'), and a come from behind victory over 'Bombardier' Wells. Langford, Jeannette and McVey did not of course exist despite their 27 combat missions in 1915. Nor did Harry Wills, a fast rising young black who had outpointed McVey and 'Battling' Jim Johnson in 1915 and kicked off his 1916 season with a verdict over Langford.

Willard–Moran was predictably awful. For trivia collectors it was the only 'no decision' title bout in heavyweight history. For ten rounds at Madison Square Garden Willard prodded Moran with his left and the following morning was awarded the newspaper decision.

Afterwards Willard went into semi-retirement. America joined the First World War in 1917. Willard evinced no interest in the proceedings, refusing even to box exhibitions to raise funds for the war effort. The hero of 1915 who had given white Americans 'renewed confidence in their eight inch biceps, and their twenty-eight inch chests' was replaced by the 'great, hulking, money grabbing slacker', fit only, according to one service newspaper, to be tarred and feathered (and, one supposes, run out of town on a rail if a rail could be found strong enough).

By 1918 a new white contender was exciting the public's imagination, Fred Fulton, a 6′ 5½″ giant, also from Kansas, with a record of 34 wins (30 kayos) and only four defeats — three on fouls. Only Al Palzer had really dented him and that was early on in his career. His wins included 'Gunboat' Smith, Carl Morris, 'Fireman' Flynn, 'Porky' Flynn, Arthur Pelkey and — one definitely for the scrapbook — Sam Langford, although it was something of a fluke*.

Tex Rickard, promoter of Johnson–Jeffries, saw very clearly the money-spinning potential of putting the two Kansas behemoths against each other. Willard too. Unfortunately, Fulton went and ruined the script. On July 27th, 1918 he entered the ring at Harrison, New Jersey, against a hard young slugger from Colorado, Jack Dempsey. Dempsey rushed him to the ropes, doubled him up with a left hook to the body and then crossed a right to the jaw. Time, including the count, 18 seconds!

Rickard did not want Dempsey as a replacement. At 6′ 1″ he was not a giant. Well, what about Carl Morris instead? He was 6′ 4″, had never had a title bout, lost only three of his last 31, two on fouls, the other an insignificant four rounder, and had beaten Fulton.** Fine, but Morris would have to get past Dempsey first. He did better than Fulton; six seconds better! A left hook to the stomach left him face down on the canvas twitching his way through the count.

'Whenever I see you, you seem to get smaller,' Rickard grumbled at

* See page 90.
** On a foul.

Dempsey. But his claims to a title fight could not be ignored. The promoter began to bang the drum for the giant against 'the giant killer', while fervently hoping not only that the public would buy it, but that Dempsey would not get hurt!

Willard–Dempsey was arranged for Toledo, Ohio, over 12 rounds, on July 4th, 1919. The distance was a strange one for its time, and seems to have been the only twelve rounder scheduled in a heavyweight title fight up to the 1980s when it became the regular championship distance.

Willard was an overwhelming favourite to win. Even Dempsey's father picked him! The reasoning was that he was simply too big for a man of Dempsey's size. He had a 5¼" advantage in height, 6½" in reach and 54 lbs (24 kilos) in weight. The champion was overconfident and took his training lightly. Dempsey on the other hand tuned up for it with five consecutive first round kayos. Admittedly, the opposition was not stiff, but it emphasised a frightening statistic: Dempsey had now won 17 of his last 26 fights inside the first round! On the day of the fight his manager Jack 'Doc' Kearns bet $10,000, over a third of Dempsey's purse, on his man to score his sixth consecutive one round knockout.

Rickard had rather ambitiously constructed a 97,000 capacity seater stadium for the contest. Had it been full then he would have had boxing's first million dollar gate and possibly a net profit approaching half a million dollars. In fact, less than 20,000 paid their way through the turnstiles. Even so, an $86,000 profit, around three million on today's values, was hardly peanuts.

The noon-day heat in the open air arena was blistering when referee Ollie Pecord called the two gladiators together to receive their instructions. Willard, perfectly composed, looked calmly at Dempsey. Dempsey, as jumpy as a cat on hot bricks, glowered at the floor. The crowd wondered whether it would not be long before Jack made an even closer acquaintance with it!

What they did not, could not, know was that they were about to witness the most terrifying three minutes in ring history: Dempsey was about to give them a frightening display of grand guignol in boxing gloves.

Pecord finished his lecture and sent them back to their corners to await the bell of destiny. There was just time for Jones to warn Willard for the umpteenth time about the fearsome Dempsey rushes that had destroyed Fulton and Morris in a few brief seconds.

But when the bell rings there is no demonic rush from Dempsey. Instead he comes out cautiously, bobbing and weaving, hands held high. Willard studies him: he flicks out a long left jab which lands high on Jack's forehead. There is no retaliation. Jess flicks out another jab. Still no move from Dempsey. Willard begins to uncoil his left hand again. Afterwards some unkind people will joke that he was ahead on points for 30 seconds.

Dempsey is under it, and a hammer of a left hook is streaking for the champion's ribs. Willard's whole body shudders under the impact, and Dempsey is on him like a tiger. He rips a right cross to Willard's jaw and the Kansan hits the canvas for the first time ever. The crowd leap to their feet: they will not sit down again.

Willard is up at '6' and Dempsey attacks like a demon. Left and right to the body and Jess is almost cut in half. Left and right to the head and the huge frame goes shuddering to the canvas again. Once again Willard takes '6'. Once again Dempsey tears into him, coldly ferocious as he smashes home a volley of punches to the head, literally battering Jess back down again. The champion struggles up, eyes glassy, a ruined fighter. But there is no move to halt the massacre. Dempsey is a berserk tiger, a pitilessly cruel machine of destruction, and Willard is being surgically dissected now as Jack scythes murderous rights into his body and then left hooks once, twice, three times to the head. Down again. Yet Willard is incredibly brave. He has rarely shown a champion's ability, but now, when he needs it, he shows a champion's courage. Alas, it is all merely futile heroism. More ferocious punches send Jess crashing for the fifth time. Around the ring a torrent of noise washes up from the bowels of the stadium like a tidal wave, seeking to batter its way inside the skull, but Dempsey and Willard are oblivious to the commotion. Willard has been battered beyond comprehension — beyond any possible redemption. Dempsey can only hear the thud of his punches as they land. So intense is his concentration that he could be fighting in a tomb. Willard is fighting in a tomb! Dempsey has ridden the rails as a hobo, fought for his meals in mining towns that even their inhabitants want to forget, and gritted his teeth through pain and despair to arrive at this moment. Now he hovers over the stricken champion.

Slowly, Willard climbs to his feet. This time his knees have barely left the canvas and he is still doubled up when Dempsey, snarling, smashes left and right to the rear of his head, and down Willard goes again. The count reaches '9' before he regains his feet for the sixth time.

He reels to the ropes and stands there, swaying and lurching, his left grasping the top strand to keep him upright. Now Dempsey stands off, measuring him for the kill. Jack moves in. A right hook hurled like a tomahawk sends Jess reeling backwards, a second clubbing right smashes against his jaw and now he disintegrates, toppling slowly to the floor. A third right hook thuds into him whilst he is on his way down. He ends up sitting on his behind, propped up against one of the ring posts, completely out, obliterated, and Pecord tolls off the full count as Jess stares pathetically up at him, a bloody, battered hulk with staring eyes, beaten more completely than any other champion in history.

'Ten' — and Dempsey leaps into the air with joy whilst Kearns dances in the corner. Now at last, Jack becomes aware of the tumult. The din hits him with numbing force and all he can think of is to get out of it, to get back to the sanctuary of his dressing room. He is out of the ring and fighting his way through an endless mass of cheering, back-slapping fans, when suddenly the mood changes and he becomes aware that they are chanting for him to come back. He turns. Kearns and Pecord are beckoning frantically from the ring.

Amidst the noise nobody, save Kearns, heard timekeeper Warren Barbour's official count. The bell actually rang at '9'. Hoping to present everybody with a *fait accomplis*, Kearns hustled Dempsey out of the ring. Almost Doc, but no cigar. After Barbour explained the situation to Pecord, Dempsey was forced to return to the ring. The fight continued.

Today, the bell can only save a beaten fighter after the last round. That rule did not exist in 1919. But the rules of humanity did and Pecord should have stopped it anyway. Willard had suffered terrible injuries. Jones should also have prevented his fighter from coming out again. He did not. That Willard was not fatally injured owes nothing to either of these men. The sun blazed down piteously and many ringsiders believed that had it lasted five or six more rounds then one or both fighters might have died from heat exhaustion.

After his manic exertions in the first round Dempsey took it easy in the second. At the beginning of the third Willard scored with a right uppercut according to some writers. The fight film does not evidence it. Dempsey stayed in close working to the body. At the round's end Jones finally decided that Jess had suffered enough and pulled him out. Jack Dempsey, 73″ and 191 lbs of lithe tiger, was the heavyweight champion.

The white hope campaign was finally laid to rest here in Toledo. But not, sadly, the ugliness behind it.

Round Twelve: Tarnished Hero

When William Harrison Dempsey died he was probably the second most popular ex-champion in the history of all sports. It was a remarkable turnaround for a man once criticised as a draft dodger, and who as champion was disliked by the fans because he was too brutal inside the ropes..

He lived a long time, from June 24th, 1895 to May 31st, 1983, and saw changes undreamed of at the time of his birth. The first fight film had been shot less than ten months earlier; in 1971 Dempsey was at ringside for a fight which was beamed by satellite into homes and cinemas all round the world. When he was born men walked in front of the infant motor car carrying red flags. When he died multi-laned freeways were packed with cars travelling in excess of 100 miles per hour. In 1897 Corbett and Fitzsimmons fought for a purse of $15,000; in 1974 Ali and Foreman split $10,000,000 between them.

Dempsey was the fifth son of Hyrum and Celia Dempsey. According to the registrar of births in Manassa, Colorado — from which Dempsey derived his ring-de-guerre 'the Manassa Mauler' — he was 'native American', meaning not red indian but a native of America. However, there was Indian ancestry — Choctaw — in his family, as well as a strong strain of Irish blood.

It was a family tinged with sadness. Hyrum, a former school teacher, never prospered and later he and Celia divorced. One brother, and a sister, died in infancy, another brother committed suicide after shooting his wife, a third was murdered and the eldest, Bernie, died of silicosis. Chronic ill health seemed to plague most of the Dempseys. They were not a very lucky brood. The exception was William Harrison: he was the one who flew over the cuckoo's nest.

Dempsey later told a Congressional Committee that he began to box at the age of ten. This was probably an exaggeration, but he left home at sixteen and became a hobo, drifting around the mining towns of the Mid-West. It was a hard existence and it hardened Dempsey. He rode the rails between towns, lived in hobo jingles and fought with his fists in saloons for eating money. Exactly when he first started to fight in properly organised bouts is unclear, but he used the name 'Kid Blackie'. 'Kid Blackie's' early record was not compiled; Dempsey remembered only the nickels and dimes put into his hand, not the men he knocked out to win them.

The first actual name on his record was Andy Malloy in 1914 when he was moving up slightly in class. Malloy outpointed him. A further 27 contests are listed over the next twenty-two months, most of them wins, mainly inside the distance. But at this stage Dempsey was just a palookaville fighter, boxing for ham and eggs in Nevada and Utah, particularly Salt Lake City.

Today we remember the blazing young hitter who took the world by storm in 1918. But in fact Jack Dempsey had two ring careers which were as alike as chalk and cheese. The first was as a wild young swinger who stopped punches with his jaw, a kill or be killed fighter who seemed destined for nothing more than the scrapheap of the punch drunk. His 1915 fight with Johnny Sudenberg — one of a series — is a vivid illustration of this phase of Dempsey's life. In the first round Jack floored Sudenberg six times but was himself hanging on hurt at the bell. In the 2nd he hacked Sudenberg down another five times but couldn't keep him there. For the next four rounds Sudenberg boxed on the retreat ramming Jack's head back with lefts. In the 7th he stopped back-pedalling and put Dempsey down twice. Jack went down three more times in the 8th, but recovered to outfight Sudenberg over the last two rounds and earn a draw. This fight recalls the comment made by a French General about the Charge of the Light Brigade: it was magnificent but not boxing. It also pointed to a flaw which Dempsey never overcame: he would always have difficulty with fast stepping boxers.

His fight with George Copelin, at altitude, the same year highlighted other flaws. Copelin was down several times in the early rounds but by the 6th appeared likely to outlast Dempsey. Jack managed one last flurry in the 7th and forced the referee to stop it. But he had failed to pace himself properly, and lacked the control and precision in his own boxing to finish Copelin early in the fight when he should have done. Raw power is useless without the technique to apply it properly.

That point was noted by a shrewd, sharp-eyed little man who was working the corner opposite Dempsey in April, 1916. Jack 'Doc' Kearns had boxed unsuccessfully as a welterweight. Now he was doing the Palookaville circuit as a manager hoping to find a heavyweight worth a little pot of gold. 'Australian' Joe Bond wasn't the answer, but managing him beat working for a living. In Ely, Nevada, he watched Dempsey grind out a decision over Bond and saw specks of gold amongst the quartz. Dempsey could hit and be hit, and possessed natural aggression. Kearns liked that.

Kearns would also have noted what Dempsey did six weeks later. Historians have attached no particular significance to the entry on Dempsey's record which reads 'George Christian w. ko1'. In fact Christian, a black fighter, had lasted into the eighth round against Jeannette, and blasted out Arthur Pelkey inside a round, the Canadian's only defeat the right side of the McCarty tragedy. Christian's scalp was a good one and helped persuade Dempsey and his then manager, Jack Price, to leave the sticks and seek fame and fortune in New York.

I was once told a marvellous story about a man who had lived his entire life in a small village. On his 65th birthday the villagers clubbed together to send him to London for the day. He was back by 5.30 in the evening complaining that he didn't think much of London. It transpired that he had simply walked around the shops in the main-line station!

The same feeling hit Dempsey and Price as they first surveyed Times Square. Well, not much to New York. Just a gaudy version of Salt Lake City. They very quickly learnt differently. The Big Apple was as unwelcoming to a two bit fighter and his manager as it was vast. 'Kid who?' They hit on a change of name. 'Nonpareil' Jack Dempsey and William Harrison shared the same surname. Why not take the christian name as well? It did not move any mountains. Promoters sighed. Well, there was a young Fitzsimmons, 'Young Corbett', a 'Young Peter Jackson' and even a 'Young Jack Johnson'. Names didn't butter any parsnips. 'Who'd you beat; Sudenberg, Copelin, Bond who are those guys?' Come back later.

Eventually, the new Jack Dempsey landed a fight with Andre Anderson, a mediocre trial horse who had been belted out by Fred Fulton and light-heavy-weight champ Jack Dillon. The best thing to be said about it is that it was a good fight. Dempsey picked himself up off the canvas three times in the 2nd and came back to outslug Anderson in the later rounds. It led to a bout with 'Wild' Bert Kenny two weeks later. Wild it was too. Kenny was down in the 2nd, Dempsey twice in the fifth and then the see-saw tipped Jack's way again, Kenny being floored three times in the 10th and apparently saved by an early bell. Officially, both fights were 'no decisions', but Jack got the newspaper verdicts.

Jack Price now departed back to Utah, ostensibly because his mother was dying. However there may have been some sharp practice here because Jack's contract was acquired by John 'The Barber' Riesler, a New York manager with a reputation for chicanery. Riesler, who was later to bombard Jack with law suits after he became champion, attempted to match Dempsey with Sam Langford. Not being a complete idiot, Jack declined. Well, what about 'Gunboat' Smith; 'er... no, not really.' Frank Moran: 'I don't think so.' Finally Riesler trotted out John Lester Johnson, last seen in these pages fleeing in terror from Langford. That was more like it.

In fact, on the credit side of the balance sheet Johnson had gone the distance with Jeannette (twice) and Harry Wills in no decision bouts and was a fighter of reasonable ability. In the 2nd Johnson broke two of Dempsey's ribs, but Jack came back hard in the second half of the fight, all guts and determination personified. There was no decision but the press voted it a draw.

Dempsey got his ribs taped up and 20% of his purse. Riesler took the rest. Jack returned to the Mid-West a sadder, wiser man. The next few months were the worst of his life. He signed on as a sparring partner for Carl Morris and came to detest the original 'white hope' for his meanness. He married a prostitute named Maxine Cates who was sixteen years older than himself. The Dempsey legend normally glosses over this, mainly because, one suspects, they lived off each other's earnings during hard times. Later Jack ditched her; a broken down whore had served her purpose when Tinseltown's much more glamorous bed-hoppers were available.

The nadir came early in the new year. 'Fireman' Jim Flynn was 37 years old and since Jack Johnson it had all been steps going down. Given that the 'Fireman's' fistic ceiling was never very high, he did not have far to fall anyway. Kayos by Luther McCarty and 'Gunboat' Smith, and a drubbing by Carl Morris, finished him as a contender.

In February, 1917, Flynn was coming off back to back knockouts by Fulton and Jack Dillon. It must have appeared easy to Dempsey. Instead, he walked on to a right swing and four knockdowns later his corner threw in the towel. After two minutes the fight, and apparently Jack Dempsey's career, were over. That night he walked through the streets of Murray, Utah, with his brother Bernie. Despair was in his eyes and on his lips. But the darkest hour is the hour before the dawn.

We can only really go by the Dempsey legend as to what happened next, but there is no real reason to dispute it. 'Doc' Kearns made contact. He could get Dempsey a series of four round bouts on the Pacific Coast. Jack wired acceptance. The beginnings of the partnership were hardly auspicious. Dempsey lost and drew twice against Willie Meehan, a fat ex-sailor with a reputation as a clown. Al Norton, not exactly top of the heap, also held him twice. But in fact this was the transformation period.

Historians have dismissed Kearns' well publicised claims to have taught Dempsey to fight as newspaper hype. But somewhere during those early months in California Jack added technique to his natural abilities. He acquired a crouching. cross-armed defence. Georges Carpentier later wrote that many young fighters in Europe were trying to copy Dempsey and getting their brains knocked out because they didn't realise how adept Jack was at blocking punches.

Nor did they perfect Jack's upper body movement, his method of constantly bobbing and weaving from the waist up which made him very difficult to tag properly, and enabled him to slip jabs and move inside the other man's punches.

This was a defensive strategy for an attacking fighter. One also dictated by his size. Paradoxically, Dempsey was the natural height and weight for a heavyweight of his day, but the white hope campaign had led to a crop of heavyweights who were abnormally large. Today, Mike Tyson, who is under-size for a heavyweight, fights men who are more naturally bigger and his strategy is modelled on Dempsey's Like Dempsey, Tyson boxes exclusively off his front foot and moves inside with hooks, crosses and uppercuts. This is what Dempsey learnt during those early months of 1917: controlled aggression and precise, well-timed hitting. The swings were replaced by precision hooks, crosses and uppercuts. The raw power was married to technique. Before him Corbett had broken new ground in left-handed boxing, and Johnson had become the master at fighting out of a tightly knit defence. Both had helped take the sport forward technically. Dempsey, under Kearns tutelage, was the great innovator of controlled, attacking boxing. Nat Fleischer rated Corbett the best and fastest boxer, Johnson the best defensive and all round heavyweight and Dempsey the best in-fighter and two handed hitter. Corbett really does not stand any comparison with Johnson, Tunney or Ali, but Nat's other verdicts, on Johnson and Dempsey, are intelligent and authoritative*, although it is fair to say that he never saw Tyson fight.

But did Dempsey also help his punching power by loading his gloves? That allegation was made by Jess Willard after he lost the title to Jack. Jess claimed that Dempsey sprinkled plaster-of-paris on his bandages. There is evidence to support the accusation. Willard's injuries were horrific. His jaw was broken in four places, most of his teeth were torn out at the gums, his nose was broken, right cheekbone splintered, both eyes closed and both ears damaged, one permanently. Jess's body was one great bruise and three of his ribs were shattered. No other fighter has ever sustained such injuries. They were far worse than Jeffries' (which were bad enough) when we know that Fitzsimmons did load his gloves. Jack's far more subdued performance in the 2nd and 3rd rounds is always put down to the heat but equally may have been due to damaged knuckles. His primary assault then was to the body, more fleshy than the head. Outside of the Willard fight there is no evidence whatsoever that Dempsey put plaster on his bandages. His opponents do not seem to have suffered excessive facial and bodily damage, and Jack was not plagued by hand injuries. But it is difficult to avoid the conclusion that he *did* artificially harden his fists against Willard**: not only was the heavyweight title involved but there was also the little matter of the $10,000 which Kearns had bet on a first round knockout.

By the summer of 1917 Dempsey was a wholly unrecognisable fighter from the dub whom 'Fireman' Flynn had annihilated. The results began to flow: Al Norton and Charlie Miller kayo one, Bob McAllister whipped over four. Nothing sensational in these; they were just 'opponents'. But it was the *way* Dempsey handled them. Now it was time for the deep end: 'Gunboat' Smith.

Initially Jack was reluctant; Christ, the 'Gunboat' even had a decision over Langford on paper. But Kearns talked him round. On October 2nd, Dempsey and Smith went on at San Francisco over four rounds.

Jack did well in the 1st, moving inside Smith's long punches and raking him with good short blows. In the 2nd 'Gunboat' lowered the boom on him with one hell of a right hand. Dempsey awoke in his corner. Well, that was it, finis — the end. But nobody was shedding tears. Kearns explained what had happened. After the right, Jack had stayed in close to Smith denying him punching room. In the 3rd he had held him even and in the 4th slugged him all round the ring. Dempsey had fought on sheer instinct since the 2nd: he had not even been

* He also rated Johnson as best feinter and uppercutter, and Dempsey best heart puncher and roughest fighter.

** 'Doc' Kearns later confirmed that he did, but by then they had split acrimoniously.

aware of the referee giving him the verdict!

The following month it was Carl Morris with the new Dempsey technique very much in evidence. He fought on the inside jolting Carl with precise punches and after four rounds had won a clear decision. The missile was now out of its silo and standing on the launching pad.

In 1918 Jack Dempsey decimated the heavyweight division with the explosive power of an atom bomb. Sometimes in the history of sport a competitor has a year in which he or she is transcendent. In 1945 golfer Byron Nelson won an astonishing nineteen tournaments, eleven in a row. He set records for stroke averages and sub-par rounds which no other golfer has ever equalled. In 1992 Britain's Nigel Mansell had a similar year in motor racing. He won the first five Grand Prix in succession and went on to nine overall. These exploits, and his points tally of 108, were unprecedented. At the halfway stage of the season an American T.V. station pulled its coverage of the world Formula One championship on he grounds that nobody was interested in a one horse race!

What Dempsey did in 1918 has to be seen in the same context. He fought 21 times and scored 17 knockouts, 12 in the first round. A year and a day after his one round loss to 'Fireman' Flynn he returned the compliment. Others who didn't make it to the end of the 1st were 'Porky' Flynn, Pelkey, Fulton and Morris; the latter only avoided being knocked out in an earlier contest by deliberately losing on a foul. 'Gunboat' Smith exited as a contender. His handlers scraped him off the canvas after the fifth knockdown of the second round, with blood billowing out of a broken nose. Jack took on world light-heavyweight champion 'Battling' Levinsky. Levinsky was king of the 'no decision' — his career record lists an astonishing 174 — and, reminiscent of D'Artagnan's introduction to Aramis, Athos and Porthos, had once fought heavyweights Bartley Madden and 'Soldier' Kearns in the morning and afternoon and then 'Gunboat' in the evening — all on the same day!* But against this transformed Dempsey, Levinsky's morning, noon and night were encapsulated into three rounds. It was the first time in 209 contests that he had ever been stopped. One historian has written that the Dempsey of this period seemed to burn with a white hot aggression from the opening bell.

Oddly, there was a defeat, Fatso Meehan 'L pts 4'. But it was a joke fight, really an exhibition for the was effort which neither man took seriously. There were also two 'no decisions' against one of Levinsky's leading contenders, Billy Miske. Miske was a toughie; a German-American who had lost only once in 57 fights and that to Kid Norfolk, a light-heavyweight so dangerous that he was on the moon as far as Levinsky was concerned. But the Miske fights are a puzzle. Jack outweighed him by at least a stone and Billy was not really a puncher, only

* January 1st, 1915.

14 stoppages at the time. Possibly Dempsey was either jaded or their styles cancelled each other out; both fights are recalled as repetitive and boring.

Aside from Fulton and Morris, Dempsey's most prestigious win in 1918 is generally recognised as Bill Brennan. In fact Brennan was a cotton-wool fighter who was being cunningly steered towards a title shot by a crafty little manager named Leo Flynn who would one day become Dempsey's manager. Brennan had been carefully kept away from the likes of Smith, Fulton, Morris, Moran and Jim Flynn — even average triers like Charlie Weinert did not make little Leo's blueprint. Brennan had been permitted to box the 'Roscomon Giant' Jim Coffey, but the only enormous thing about Coffey was his inability to spot the telegraph boy delivering Frank Moran's punches. In his next contest after a no decision with Brennan, Coffey failed to last the distance with the very average Bartley Madden.

Light-heavies were more in tune with Flynn's thinking; or rather, one of them. 'Battling' Levinsky, as we have noted, was as tough as old boots and a good shifty boxer, but he had rather luckily won the 175 lbs crown from Jack Dillon and thereafter went deaf at the sound of his name. Levinsky was also one of the lightest punching world champions in history*: he made 'Philadelphia' Jack O'Brien look like a blaster. In consequence, Brennan and Levinsky went to the post four times between October, 1917 and January 1918. The results were not exactly inspiring for a man with pretensions to the heavyweight crown: a win apiece on points and two draws.

Leo Flynn's paper tiger needed a patsy to kickstart his career again. Apparently, man with message in boot of heel had not reached some parts of the East Coast by February, 1918 because Dempsey was chosen as the sacrificial goat. Some goat. In Milwaukee, February 23rd, Dempsey showed Brennan that it takes more than an astute manager to make a fighter. He knocked Bill down in the 1st, and then four times in the 2nd, after which Leo Flynn is alleged to have shouted: 'stay away from his right — and his left too.' In the 6th Jack knocked Brennan out. As he hit the canvas Brennan broke an ankle; a very profitable old ankle that proved to be.

Byron Nelson retired not long after his historic year in 1945. Nigel Mansell left the Formula One circuit for Indy-Car racing. Had Dempsey quit after winning the title from Willard — his golden year crowned by the icing on the cake — then he would probably not be the legendary figure he became. But paradoxically he would have been a better champion. His reign as titleholder was one of the worst frauds ever perpetrated on the sporting public.

* 25 kayos in 272 contests.

Jack Dempsey successfully defended the title five times: a South American who couldn't fight, a mediocrity, and three light-heavyweights.

In Dempsey's defence it is fair to say that until 1925 there was not a lot of white opposition around. He had slaughtered Willard, Fulton, Morris and Smith. Moran was still winning, but had failed miserably in two previous title bids. The best white contender was in fact the ex-light-heavyweight kingpin, Jack Dillon, who had fashioned his career on knocking great lumps out of the likes of Smith and Moran. Unhappily his nickname 'Jack the Giant Killer', said it all. Dillon rarely weighed much above the middleweight limit and stood only 5′ 7½″. As Dempsey himself had to be built up as a giant killer, a title fight with a man almost half a foot smaller and two stone lighter was not going to make the turnstiles go clickety-click.

Image-wise, Billy Miske was more saleable. He was the same height as Dempsey and had twice given him trouble. Critics would later say that Jack made his first defence against a dying man, but this is not entirely fair. Midway through 1919 Miske was diagnosed as suffering from Bright's Disease, a progressive illness of the kidneys. He retired from boxing but came back in 1920 due to financial troubles. Ill he was, but after fighting Dempsey he went undefeated for the rest of his career, 24 bouts in which he knocked out Meehan, Fulton and Brennan. The real problem is that when he stepped into the ring with Dempsey at Benton Harbour, Michigan, on September 6th, 1920, he was just a light-heavyweight weighing only half a pound above the title limit.

In contrast to their earlier fights, Dempsey savaged Miske. Body punches dropped him in the 1st, and in the 3rd he was knocked out by a right to the jaw. Although Miske was sick, this was Jack's best display as champion; in fact it was to be the last impressive performance of his career.

Dempsey–Miske could be classified as unfinished business, but not Jack's second defence. The man who should have been in the other corner was Harry Wills. Wills was head and shoulders above any other contender. The problem was that he was black.

By late 1920 the magic black circle was gone. Johnson was forty-two, fat and in gaol. Jeannette had retired the previous year*. McVey was finished and would die in 1921. Langford was almost blind, and fistically decrepit. Although, astonishingly, he still won more than he lost, the latter now included nonentities like Lee Anderson.

But Harry Wills was still out there and at 31 was in his prime. He was 6′ 4″ and weighed a splendidly proportioned 220 lbs (100 kilos). Like Johnson, Langford and co., Wills was primarily a defensive boxer, an excellent ring

* He opened a car rental business.

technician. He had gone to school on Langford whom he fought 23 times, beating him five times after 1917 when Sam began to fade. Wills also twice knocked out McVey and beat Clarke six times (four kayos). All in all, by December 1920 Harry had had 72 fights and only Langford had legitimately beaten him*. That summer Wills knocked out Fulton in three rounds.

But when it came to a title shot he was given the same run-around as Johnson 15 years earlier. Dempsey himself stated his unwillingness to defend against black boxers. He had of course fought blacks when it suited him — and avoided them when it didn't.

History has been very kind to Dempsey over his refusal to face Wills. Nat Fleischer always detested racism in sport. During the early Twenties he campaigned ardently for Wills to get a title fight. But Fleischer was also a friend and admirer of Dempsey. When he published his second book on Dempsey, in 1972, he absolved him from blame. According to Fleischer, the New York Boxing Commission was the villain of the piece, on one hand insisting that Dempsey fight Wills — even to the point of temporarily taking away his licence — but on the other refusing to let it go on in New York.

Nobody would dispute that this was absurd. But it is not the whole of the story. The New York Boxing Commissioner was William Muldoon, the old wrestling champion and Sullivan's friend and trainer. Boxing was only fully legalised again in New York State in 1920, and the Walker Law had plenty of opposition. Muldoon was seen as a man of impeccable integrity but he was not perhaps the brightest man in the world. Behind the scenes Tex Rickard skilfully manipulated him playing on his fears that a Dempsey-Wills contest could lead to boxing being banned once more in the Empire State**.

Rickard himself had declared after Johnson–Jeffries that he would never again promote an inter-racial clash for the heavyweight title. The reality of course is that money is colour blind. Dempsey was an exciting fighter; Wills an uninteresting master of defence. Dempsey was where the money lay. Business is business and Wills wasn't wanted as champ.

As for Dempsey himself, there were 47 other States in the Union, and Rickard was not the only promoter around. Once again the real-politic was that Wills was simply too big and too good. Later, it became fashionable to use Jack Johnson as a scapegoat. Because of his behaviour blacks were unacceptable as challengers for the heavyweight title. According to Fleischer, Harry Wills was a morally upright, clean living man. Ironically, it was Dempsey who had followed in Johnson's footsteps and married a prostitute. By the end of Dempsey's reign blacks had won the championship of every established division bar

* Wills retired in a contest against 'Battling' Jim Johnson with a broken arm.

** A number of politicians were opposed to the fight.

flyweight*. Yet many whites still felt too threatened to accept them as champions in boxing's premier division. Dempsey and Tex Rickard used this prejudice as a mask to hide the fact that they didn't want Wills at any price.

So the call for Madison Square Garden on December 14th, went out to Bill Brennan! The apologists for this one argue that Brennan was the best of a poor crop of white heavyweights. Poor they must have been and with a capital 'P'. Brennan's only contests of note since being kayoed by Dempsey had been against Billy Miske, a no decision and a loss on points!

But there was always the Bill Brennan ankle. If he hadn't broken it when getting knocked down then he would have whipped Jack's arse off. That was an acceptable argument only to those who left their brain outside in the car park.

It was not a good fight for Dempsey. He seemed to have regressed to the Sudenberg days, as though the clock had struck 'twelve' and Cinderella's ball gown had changed back to rags.

Brennan was down in the 1st and 2nd. Then he hit Dempsey with a right uppercut which left him fighting on instinct. The champion had gotten over-confident.

For the next three rounds Brennan boxed well on the retreat. The Manassan mauled him in the 6th but couldn't finish it and back came Brennan again. In the 10th he produced a right hook which almost tore Jack's left ear off.

Round 12. Dempsey was behind on points. But the challenger was simply not good enough to turn his advantage into victory. Dempsey put together the combination which had wrecked Fulton: left hook to the body, which cut Brennan in half, right cross to the jaw. As Brennan slumped towards the canvas Dempsey crouched low and exploded another right against his chin. Brennan just failed to beat the count.

The following morning the critics were not impressed. It is a pity that they then suspended their critical faculties throughout Dempsey's next three offerings.

By the end of 1920 Dempsey's popularity had waned. He was dogged by persistent allegations of being a draft dodger. Title defences against sick light-heavyweight and men of straw were not calculated to improve this image.

Dempsey had escaped military service in the First World War by claiming to be the sole support of his wife and family. Whether this is true, or was a ruse, is outside the scope of this book. Societies who entrusted their youth to fossilised cretins who estimated that if they sacrificed 3 men for every 2 on the other side they would end up with 10,000 and the enemy none, were hardly fit to make

* No black fighter has ever won the undisputed 8 stone crown.

moral judgements anyway.

But that was not the way it was seen at the time. Rheumy old men and saloon bar patriots grumbled that Dempsey was a 'slacker' who 'hadn't done his bit'. The prevailing attitude was best summed up by the *New York Times*:

> *'Dempsey did not go to the war, while weak armed, strong-hearted clerks reeled under pack and rifle; while middle aged men with families volunteered... There rests the chorus for the Dempsey dispraise.'*[1]

'Business', as Lyndon Johnson once observed, 'makes the mare go', and you can always make a profit, even out of unpopularity. In fact, as Messrs Rickard, Kearns and Dempsey were about to prove, you can make a lot of profit out of it.

In December, 1919, Georges Carpentier of France defended his European heavyweight title by knocking out British champion Joe Beckett in 73 seconds. It was exactly the result which Rickard and co. had hoped for. Rickard had had his eye on the Frenchman for some time.

'Gorgeous Georges', as the press dubbed him, was a national idol in France. A war hero, he had served in the French Flying Corps, been wounded twice, and decorated twice with France's highest awards for gallantry. He was the nemesis of British fighters knocking out 'Bombardier' Wells in four rounds to win the European title and then repeating the dose in 18 seconds. He would later kayo Beckett again — 15 seconds — and Ted 'Kid' Lewis. After the latter fight a dispirited British press corps would claim that Lewis would have won if he had not been knocked out in the 1st round! If that sounds ridiculous it is because *it is* ridiculous. But it perhaps conveys the effect which Carpentier had on the British.

The secret of Carpentier's success was that he possessed one of the fastest and most perfectly timed rights in boxing history. It was not however anywhere near as effective against rugged Americans. 'Gunboat' Smith had bounced him all over the canvas before being freakishly disqualified; Joe Jeannette outpointed him, and middleweight champs Billy Papke* and Frank Klaus savaged his body until his lungs haemorrhaged and the blood cascaded down his chin. Therein lay the dilemma: Georges could fight but was neither big nor strong. He could bat out Brits from the slums of Palookaville**, but his right was a pop gun against men mean and hard.

This however was not a consideration which money men like Rickard and

* Uniquely Papke once defended the middleweight title at the London Palladium!

** That description does not include 'Kid' Lewis who had been an outstanding world welterweight champion.

1 January 28th, 1920.

Kearns allowed to stand in their way. Dempsey–Carpentier was a dream contest: America v Europe, the handsome, debonair Frenchman against the roughneck American; above all, the war hero against the draft dodger. The contest was built up around the latter angle.

Early in January, 1920, the *San Francisco Chronicle* published a letter from Maxine, now Dempsey's ex-wife, charging that Jack's reasons for avoiding the draft were lies. In reality Maxine did not write the letter; she simply put her name to it. Afterwards she went to ground. Who actually inspired it, penned it, and then paid for her to lie low remains a mystery.

Part of Maxine's letter refuted that Dempsey had worked in a shipyard during the war. He hadn't, but he had posed for a photograph wearing overalls. That it was an obvious publicity still was known to the press at the time, but it did not stop them now reproducing the photo as 'proof' that Jack was a draft dodger.

Maxine resurfaced late in February, full of contrition and more-or-less withdrawing what she had said in the letter. The whole thing sounds very suspiciously like a put-up job to help sell the mooted Dempsey–Carpentier fight.

The government now took over and charged Dempsey and Kearns with conspiracy to evade the draft. Given the intense coverage in the press they probably had little choice. In June the two Jacks were tried and acquitted. It is unlikely that things were meant to go this far, but the publicity was still wonderful. The *Atlanta Constitution* could only pray that Georges Carpentier:

> *'Idol of the French nation, fighter in the ring and battlefield, will snatch the world championship.'* [1]

It summed up the general mood of the press.

The stage was now set for the idol of France to make his (carefully timed) entry. In late summer Carpentier arrived in Atlantic City to do battle for the world light-heavyweight title. Up against a man his own height and weight the disparity between Carpentier and a genuine heavyweight was not so evident.

On October 12th Carpentier won the 175 lbs crown by knocking out 'Battling' Levinsky in four very one-sided rounds. Afterwards some doubted that the fight was on the level. It is easy to see why. Levinsky had fought 230 contests, many against rough, tough heavyweights, and only the peak Dempsey of 1918 had ever stopped him. After Carpentier, he had over 40 more fights and never failed to go the distance. Yet he surrendered to the Frenchman without a struggle and in almost the same number of rounds that Dempsey had taken.

Draw your own conclusions, but when Dempsey and Carpentier climbed into the ring on July 2nd, 1921, 80,183 spectators paid $1,789,238 — boxing's first million dollar gate — to see them. Dempsey was on a guaranteed $300,000, Carpentier $200,000. Federal taxes were 25%. Other costs are not known, but

1 June 16th, 1920

it is unlikely that Rickard netted less than $500,000 in profit. Afterwards, Dempsey and Kearns complained bitterly about Rickard putting them on guarantees rather than percentages.

'The Battle of the Century' (it was around the fourth to receive the accolade) was in fact a hoax for which Rickard, Kearns and Dempsey should have been sent up the river to Sing-Sing. During training the Frenchman's scrawny physique was so apparent that Rickard banned reporters from his camp claiming that Carpentier was perfecting a 'secret punch'. Not until the two men got into the ring in a specially constructed wooden stadium at Boyle's Thirty Acres, New Jersey, was it obvious that everybody had been had.

The fight itself hardly merits description. In the 1st Jack clawed away at Carpentier's body. In the 2nd Carpentier had his one tiny moment of hope, a right to the head which staggered the champion. The follow-up was ineffective and Georges later claimed that he had dislocated his right thumb in landing the big punch. Possibly, but his best hadn't put Dempsey down. Jack was too big; too strong. In the 3rd Dempsey set up a ferocious body attack. Whatever strength the Frenchman had drained out of him. Early in the 4th, a left-right to the head dropped Carpentier on his face for '9'. When he arose Dempsey finished it: left uppercut to the jaw, right to the heart, another right to the head.

Dempsey was booed into the ring and out of it. The match was the first coast to coast radio hook-up* and millions heard how unpopular the alleged draft dodger was. Later, when the accusation faded and people realised that Carpentier was only an over-publicised light-heavy, the criticism changed to Jack being a bully boy.

Perhaps the most interested spectator at the fight was another light-heavyweight who fought and won the main supporting bout. Gene Tunney, an ex-marine who had previously held the American Expeditionary Force 175 lbs title, had gotten his billing due to his war service (Rickard was not missing any tricks). But watching Dempsey, he saw a man who could be beaten by a smart boxer.

Gene Tunney went home and began to dream.

After Boyles Thirty Acres, Dempsey did not fight again for two years. In fairness, excluding the ever present Wills, not a lot was really happening in the heavyweight picture. There was 'Fighting' Bob Martin, the former A.E.F. heavyweight champion, whose 32 kayos in 42 fights up to the end of 1922 looked

* Fleischer commentating.

impressive on paper and included the now dilapidated 'Gunboat' Smith and Frank Moran who Martin finished as a top liner. On the debit side, Bob had been outpointed by middleweight contender Fay Keiser, whom he outweighed by around four stone (25 kilos), Bill Brennan and Bob Roper, and stopped by another mediocre heavy named Floyd Johnson. In the cynical world of boxing these statistics made him an ideal contender (bums on seats followed by Bob's bum on its seat), but he went and ruined whatever scenario they were writing for him by being seriously injured in a car crash, after which he wasn't much good.

So for defence number four it was back to the light-heavies again. It was another take the money and run job but at least this time there was a bit of humour about it. Unless you happened to be a citizen of Shelby, Montana that is.

In 1923 Shelby had a population of less than 1,000 but a lot of big ideas. Oil had been found there and the citizens wanted to attract people and investment. What better way of publicising Shelby than promoting a heavyweight championship bout? They were about to find out.

The beginning of the year found Dempsey and Kearns needing to cash in on the title. But the East had temporarily gone dead. Tex Rickard was laying low after a scandal involving under age girls, and Commissioner Muldoon had announced that New York would not allow any heavyweight title bouts at present (although he wanted Dempsey to fight Wills elsewhere).

At this point the civic leaders of Shelby made contact with Kearns about their dream fight. The suggested opponent was a 32 year old light-heavyweight named Tommy Gibbons. Although 3 inches shorter than Dempsey and a stone lighter, he was, overall, slightly better built than the champion and had only been beaten twice in 90 fights, a disqualification against Miske and a points loss to soon-to-be middleweight champion Harry Greb, a snarling, fouling fighter who had once roughed up Dempsey in a sparring session and allegedly spat in his eye. Gibbons was not regarded as a big hitter but had in fact stopped 27 of his last 33 opponents. All round, he was probably the best Dempsey successfully faced as champion. Had Tommy been a genuine heavyweight then the town of Shelby might have been well and truly put on the map.

'Doc' Kearns paid a visit to Chicago to meet an attorney representing Shelby. It probably is an exaggeration to say that when 'Doc' went swimming in the sea the sharks got out, but you get the meaning. He demanded, and got, a guaranteed $300,000, plus $10,000 training expenses, to be paid in three instalments, one-third on signature, one-third on June 15th and the last on July 2nd, two days before the fight. Not as astute as Kearns, Gibbons' manager negotiated 50% of the gate receipts between $3-600,000, and 25% thereafter. They came out with nothing.

There now followed the great Shelby bank raid. The first $100,000 was met; the second had to be scraped together by a consortium of banks after Kearns refused 50,000 sheep in lieu (he was negotiating with some of them anyway!). The third instalment was impossible, so 'Doc' agreed to take it out of the gate receipts, his one and only miscalculation because only 7,000 paying customers turned up.

They did not see a very good fight. Gibbons boxed smartly at long range, but Dempsey smothered him inside where he made his extra poundage tell. After 10 of the scheduled 15 rounds it was about even, but Jack finished the stronger to earn the decision. There were no highlights.

Afterwards Kearns got out of town fast with some $50,000 stuffed inside two hold-alls, appropriate because Shelby had been well and truly carpet-bagged. He and Dempsey made about a quarter of a million dollars, nobody else got a red cent and the four banks involved folded. They should have taken notice of the sharks!

Gibbons could at least fight; Dempsey's next opponent was simply a con trick.

Luis Angel Firpo was a 26 year old from Buenos Aires who stood 6′ 3″and weighed 216 lbs (98.5 kilos). By September 14th, 1923 when he took the ring against Dempsey in the Polo Grounds, New York, Firpo was undefeated in 26 fights with 21 kayos. His early campaigning was done in South America where his record shows two wins over 'Gunboat' Smith. This may possibly have attracted attention to him in the first place. If so then it is symptomatic of the entire Firpo farce because the 'Gunboat' on big Luis's listing was actually a black fighter going by the same name.

Tex Rickard had watched Firpo's career as it unfolded and seen him fight in Argentina. What impressed Rickard was not the Argentinian's ability, but his personal magnetism. Firpo had star quality. After only a handful of fights he was a hero in South America with a variety of products being marketed in his name. Firpo was obsessed by money; Rickard was a kindred spirit. Visions of another million dollar gate began to float before Tex's eyes. He took Firpo to the States and hired Jimmy Deforest, one of the best cornermen in the business, to train him.

Unfortunately Firpo didn't like training. He couldn't fight either. He had no defence, no attacking skills, no recognisable punches, no nothing apart from a powerful right which he never learnt to throw properly. Aside from this he was just brave and durable. But he did sell tickets; the American public was just as captivated by him as the folks down south.

Firpo was unveiled against 'Sailor' Maxted in Newark, N.J., March 1922. He kayoed Maxted, whom nobody ever accused of being a good fighter, in seven. The Rickard PR machine claimed that the final punch literally stood the 'sailor' on his head. No, I don't believe it either.

Three more nobodies followed, and then the final build up to a title fight began. Bill Brennan was knocked out in 12. Several months afterwards Billy

Miske took only a third of that time and then died seven weeks later*. On July 12th 1923, Firpo was matched with Jess Willard!

The 'Tall Pine' was 41 when Rickard lured him out of retirement. Willard lumbered to an undistinguished stoppage of trial horse Floyd Johnson, then faced Firpo at Boyles Thirty Acres. The public reaction to the fight was astonishing. 100,000** people turned up to see it; the interest nation-wide was intense. For seven rounds Willard, who even in his prime had never exactly been a master boxer, gave Firpo a lesson painting his latin features with left after left. In the 8th however youth prevailed and Firpo knocked Jess out with his right. Willard went back to his farm quite a lot richer. He remained on it until his death in 1968.

There were mixed feelings at ringside. Rickard knew that he had another million dollar gate in the offing. He also knew that it needed to be soon; the first decent fighter in his prime who got into the ring with Firpo would take him apart. 'Doc' Kearns, happily surveying the mega crowd, shared both sentiments. Jimmy Deforest, sacked by Firpo because he cost too much, put a voice to them. If Firpo went into the ring with Dempsey now the Argentinian would be 'entering a slaughterhouse'. It was a view endorsed by the press. But not by the public: they couldn't wait to get their money down. And we wonder why people are so susceptible to salesmanship!

Firpo's idea of preparation was a short tour of Palookaville. One opponent, just six weeks before he got into the ring with Dempsey, gives some idea of how good Firpo really was. Five years earlier Homer Smith had been one of Dempsey's first round victims; fourteen months before Firpo, Smith had failed to reach the first bell against Billy Miske. On August 3rd Smith lasted ten awful rounds with Firpo to a 'no decision'.

Didn't deter the punters though. 88,000 of them turned up at the Polo grounds paying $1,188,603. This time Dempsey and Kearns had insisted on a percentage of the gate, 37½, which brought them in $509,000.*** Firpo received 12½%. Rickard's profit is unknown, but it wasn't peanuts.

There was almost no contest. Nat Fleischer later revealed that on the day of the fight Firpo was found to have dislocated his left arm. Commissioner Muldoon, who only six months earlier had put a bar on heavyweight title fights in New York, snapped the bone back into place. The arm was still sore however when Firpo got into the ring.

Probably, more has been written about Dempsey–Firpo than any other bout in history, not because it was a great fight — it was so one-sided that it was

* Brennan did not survive him by long. In 1924 he was shot to death in a New York speakeasy.

** The largest crowd ever to watch a fight live up to that time.

*** $446,000 plus a share of the movie rights.

hardly a fight at all — but because it was a great drama. That it was owed itself to three moments of sheer carelessness by Dempsey. At the opening bell he catapulted across the ring and ran into a right, more a reflex action than anything else, which caused his left knee to momentarily touch the canvas. When he got up Dempsey proceeded to work on Firpo as though he was the heavy bag in his training camp. The Argentinian went down three times, Dempsey hovering over him as the referee counted. It was so easy that Jack became reckless and at the midway point in the round lunged into a right swing which dropped him on both knees this time. But again he was up immediately and resumed his work-out.

Hopelessly outclassed, Firpo went down four more times. On the final occasion Dempsey was sure that he would not get up and relaxed. It was his final error and this time almost cost him dear. Firpo, 'The Wild Bull of the Pampas', took him by surprise and drove him to the ropes with a series of clubbing right hands, followed by a swing to the chest which knocked Jack out of the ring and into the lap of one of the judges. Willing hands pushed Dempsey back — technically illegal — at the count of '9', trampling over a reporter's typewriter in the process. There is no doubt that this time Jack was dazed, but he had little to worry about; Firpo's follow-up attack was utterly inept.

The 2nd round was almost too one-sided for words. Dempsey was punching the bag again, this time without mistakes. Firpo collapsed twice under the onslaught, the second time for the count.

Dempsey–Firpo has been called the most sensational fight in history*. In the sense that it had 12 knockdowns or semi-knockdowns in under four minutes, it certainly was not boring. And it provided two major talking points which have lasted to this day. Could Dempsey have gotten back into the ring in time under his own steam, and should he have been disqualified because he was helped?

On the first point, a boxer is at an obvious disadvantage under the 'ten' count if he goes through the ropes. In the third Patterson–Johanneson fight in 1961 the boxers insisted on a '20' count should it happen. This has been repeated in other world title fights since. Had Dempsey been counted out then it would have been grossly unfair. Firpo's blow was as much a push as punch, and there can be no doubt that had Jack not gone through the ropes then he would certainly have beaten the count. The question therefore is really academic.

Technically, he could have been disqualified. Deforest, sitting at ringside, said he would have insisted on it had he been in Firpo's corner. Kearns later said the same thing. By a strict interpretation of the rules they were right, but it would hardly have been a satisfactory ending. Moreover, it was not uncommon for fighters to be helped back into the ring; Jeffries had been after Johnson had

* One spectator died from a heart attack.

knocked him through the ropes.

But these controversies have been allowed to obscure the real truth about the fight which is that it was a dreadful mismatch interposed with moments of sloppiness by Dempsey. Deforest was right: Firpo was a kicking mule in a slaughterhouse.

After Firpo, Dempsey put the title into his bottom drawer and forgot about it.

Hollywood beckoned. Jack had already made one film, 'Daredevil Jack' in 1920*. Now he embarked on such screen classics as 'The Health Farm Wallop', 'The Winning Way', and 'Manhattan Madness'. Dempsey himself was under no illusion about his acting talents: 'When I started I was really bad and I never got any better.' But he liked the money.

The ladies too. There were plenty of available starlets who, like the champion, enjoyed the bright lights. One, who was rather more than a starlet, was Estelle Taylor who Jack married in 1925. Basically, Estelle was an actress whose name generally appeared in the 'also starring' credits. She had been around the block a few times and it would be naive to imagine that she resisted the casting couch.

Estelle and Jack had little in common. She did not like boxing or boxing people. In particular, she loathed Kearns (the feeling was mutual). But it is unfair to place too much blame on Estelle for the break up of one of the great partnerships in boxing history. Dempsey did not like their agreement, 50–50 (he wanted 67–33) and Kearns owed him money. The split was more-or-less inevitable from 1923 when Dempsey insisted that Rickard pay the purse for the Firpo fight direct to him.

Meanwhile, as Jack performed on celluloid and tried to keep Estelle happy, challengers were beginning to emerge. There was a brace of Bostonians, Jack Sharkey and Jim Maloney; Johnny Risko, the 'Cleveland Rubber Man'; and Gene Tunney who was slowly but surely nurturing his dream to fruition. Harry Wills was still on the scene although disappointment and age were beginning to erode his skills. He continued to be frozen out. Pressed by the New York Commission, Rickard signed Dempsey and he to a contract but without specifying any purse, date or venue in it. Later, Rickard even had tickets printed for November 8th, 1924, at Boyle's Thirty Acres. Nobody, least of all Wills, thought they were anything more than camouflage.

The real fight which finally emerged was against Tunney. New York

* Jess Willard was actually the first reigning heavyweight champ to make a movie, 'A Fighting Chance'. It opened at Toledo on July 4th, 1919, and closed the same day!

refused to sanction it because of the still simmering Wills controversy (although they also continued to ban Dempsey–Wills in New York). Rickard moved the Tunney bout to the Sesqui Centennial Stadium (don't ask me what it means — I'm only a humble boxing fan), Philadelphia for September 23rd, 1926. Dempsey had been out of the ring three years (bar exhibitions), the longest any heavyweight champion has gone without defending his title under peacetime conditions.

This fatal lay-off showed in his preparations. Future light-heavyweight champion Tommy Loughran whipped him bloody in sparring. Dempsey later blamed Kearns for his lay-off. That would only be believable had 'Doc' changed sex and his name to Estelle. However, Kearns was harrying his now ex-fighter in other ways, filing law suits for percentages of phantom fights. Approaching the contest, Dempsey suffered from a bad stomach, in all probability nerves due to his problems outside the ring.

However, for once he was the popular favourite with the fans. Tunney was not liked. An unexciting fighter, he was also snobbish and had a tendency to talk down to people. Few could imagine him beating the invincible Dempsey; they had thought the same about Sullivan and Jeffries. One who didn't go along with the general view was Harry Greb who had fought Gene five times. Greb bet his life savings on Tunney. Some thought the challenger a blown up light-heavy. In fact, he had matured into a genuine heavyweight and was as big all round as Dempsey.

On the evening of September 23rd over 120,000 people filed in to Sesqui Centennial providing gate receipts of $1,895,733, the third million-dollar gate, the largest ever *paying* live audience*, and the most revenue ever generated up to that time. Dempsey eventually garnered $717,000 (Tunney $200,000), somewhere in the region of twenty million today. It was a long way from the embryonic knuckle-ups of a century before.

The match had been made over 10 rounds. Anything more was beyond Dempsey's rustbucket legs.

Tunney was a strategist and psychology was part of his strategy. On the day of the fight he flew into Philadelphia with stunt pilot Casey Jones, a genuine daredevil as opposed to the celluloid one he was about to meet. Six months later Jones would crash to his death.

In the ring before the fight Gene strolled around beaming and shaking hands as though he was at an Ivy League reunion. By stark contrast, Dempsey looked as if he were attending his best friend's funeral.

* 135,000 attended the Tony Zale-Billy Pryor middleweight bout in 1941, but admission was free.

When the fight started Tunney took command. A mistake which Gibbons had made was that although at times he had clearly outboxed the champion he had always been on the defensive. Tunney was different. He moved forward confidently behind his jab, not tip-tap punches but steel whipcords which forced Dempsey onto his back foot and denied him leverage. Gene was getting his punches off; Jack couldn't get his started. Midway through the 1st, Tunney pounded home a series of rights. Dempsey looked shaken and discomforted.

Thus was established the pattern of the fight. It went on round after round, an unceasing torment. Dempsey's right eye was cut, his left closed. His mouth was ripped open, his face puffed up. When he did succeed in attacking he found Tunney's defence well nigh impenetrable. There were a few good individual punches, two rights to the temple in the 4th, and another to the throat in the 6th which afterwards caused Gene to cough blood, but each time Tunney came straight back and regained the ascendancy. Some ringsiders did not give Dempsey a round, others awarded him the 2nd but that was the limit of his achievement.

The stadium was open air and it had started to rain at the first bell. When the last sounded the rain ceased; so did Dempsey's reign. The referee and two judges unanimously awarded the title to Gene by big margins. It was only the second time it had changed hands on points.

As he left the ring a great roaring chant of 'Dempsey – Dempsey' went up, rolling around the stadium like thunder and drowning out any cheers for the new champion. Jack Dempsey had found popularity in defeat. It was also an unhappy augury for Gene Tunney.

Volume Four

Gene Tunney to Joe Louis

Round Thirteen: The Master Marine

Charles Dickens asked in *David Copperfield*: 'Whether I shall turn out to be the hero of my own life, or whether that station will be held by anybody else.'

The sad fact is that Gene Tunney was not the hero of his own life, at least not his fistic life. His career was irrevocably bound up with that of Dempsey who overshadowed him. Tunney fought Jack twice and beat him twice, yet it is Dempsey who is remembered from those contests.

Yet Tunney was one of the greatest heavyweights in history. Nat Fleischer rated him the smartest and best conditioned boxer and the best left jabber of all the heavyweight champions he saw. Tunney was a ring technician par excellence. A childhood disease of the right elbow slightly impaired the use of his right arm and he suffered from brittle hands, but his technique was, by the standards of his era, next to flawless. Tunney had a superb defence and was a boxing master. He had every punch in the book and executed them with speed and precision. Above all he fought with his brain, capitalising on his opponents' weaknesses. He analysed Dempsey as a professor studies a mathematical problem, and when he got into the ring with Jack in Philadelphia knew him inside out.

If Tunney had a weakness it was that he was not a chilling puncher. This has been put down to his suspect hands, but I believe that he lacked natural power. Although Gene grew into a well muscled heavyweight, that by itself does not make a kayo puncher. Jimmy Wilde, a tiny, skinny man and a natural straweight, was one of history's great punchers and knocked out bantamweights and even featherweights. Wilde possessed perfect timing, but within his emaciated frame there was also a natural element of power. Tunney had the timing, the accuracy, the execution and the muscular development, but raw power had been eliminated from his starting line up.

James Joseph Tunney hailed from Greenwich Village, New York. There was certainly Irish ancestry in his family, but Gene never made a point of it. By 1926 the Irish affinity with boxing was beginning to fade. Of the six champions in the other divisions*, none were now of Irish descent. Tunney himself did not originally intend that boxing should be anymore than a minor passing phase in his life. Born on May 25th, 1898 (he may share his birthday with 'Jack-the-Ripper'!), Gene was from what we would classify as 'lower middle class' origins. On leaving school he went to work in a shipping office. At night, he studied law.

* The flyweight title was vacant.

He also began to box for the odd few dollars to supplement his wages. From 1915 to 1918 he was undefeated in twelve contests.

The war decided Tunney on a career in boxing. On May 2nd, 1918 he enlisted in the Marine Corps. His unit was shipped to France but by the time it arrived the war was nearly over and Tunney never saw action. In fact, after the Armistice, Tunney had three contests in France.

According to his memoirs, Gene committed himself to boxing after a conversation with a sports journalist who told him that Dempsey could be beaten by a smart boxer. That may not be the whole truth. Although he later posed as an intellectual, educated people sometimes found Tunney unconvincing. It is plausible that he found his law studies hard going, or thought that establishing himself later might prove either beyond him or too long a haul. Boxing, on the other hand, he proved to himself that he was good at by winning the American Expeditionary Force light-heavyweight title, and then outpointing A.E.F. heavyweight champ Bob Martin in a special bout.

After de-mob in the Autumn of 1919, Tunney's career really got under way. There was a single-mindedness about Gene Tunney which he brought to his ring career. Within him there was a need to be good at something which would put him above the herd. In addition to a desire for wealth, there was a highly developed, self absorbed, ego. Dempsey might burn with aggression from the opening bell; Tunney burnt with ambition. It left him with very few close intimates. He disliked boxing people; considered himself above them. Yet, contradictorily, he became very close to Harry Greb, the great middleweight champion, despite the fact that they were poles apart temperamentally. Greb reflected the baser instincts in boxing but was irresistibly colourful. Tunney also struck up a friendship with Dempsey. Opposites attract, and Tunney certainly respected both men as fighters. But maybe there was something else too, a need to be above yet part of the adulation which the crowd gave to these men. Tunney couldn't join them, but he could beat them and win their friendship. This was egotistical; effectively a gesture of contempt at the masses and the way they conferred their favours. But perhaps it also said that there dwelt a lonely man at the heart of Gene Tunney's concentric circle of ambition and ego, a man who secretly longed to be loved by the crowd himself.

Twenty-two unbeaten fights between November, 1919 and January, 1922 carried Tunney to a fight with 'Battling' Levinsky for the vacant American light heavyweight title. The fight gave Tunney a valuable insight into human nature. He was winning handily when Levinsky whispered 'Let me stay Gene'. Tunney, who by his own admission, disliked the brutal side of boxing, eased up and Levinsky attempted to knock him out. Gene worked him over for the rest of the fight, and was never taken in by anyone again.

Tunney was now a definite contender for Carpentier's crown. As well as beating Levinsky, he had twice had the better of another contender, Leo Houck, in no decision bouts and, five weeks later, leading middleweight Fay Keiser. He was not, however, interested in 175 lbs laurels. The obsession with beating Dempsey was already aglow within him, and he had embarked on an intensive programme of callisthenics to build himself into a legitimate heavyweight. When Tunney won the title he stood 6′ 0½″ and weighed 190 lbs, exactly the same as Johnson in his prime.

But there now followed a setback. In May, 1922, Tunney defended his American title against Greb, one hundred and sixty pounds of foul ridden viciousness. Greb gave Tunney a bad 15 round beating. Nose broken, Tunney only just made it to the final bell. Afterwards he fainted from loss of blood.

If anything, defeat made Tunney even more determined. Six weeks afterwards he was back decisioning Keiser. Tommy Loughran was outboxed in a no decision contest and minor heavyweights such as Charlie Weinert and Chuck Wiggins trounced. Wiggins was more important than the record indicates. A bosom buddy of Greb's, he and Harry engaged in some of the dirtiest fights in boxing history. It was a measure of both Gene's courage and determination that he was willing to twice get in the ring with Wiggins and learn how to cope with the low blows, gouges and flying elbows which Wiggins regularly traded with Greb.

The return with Greb came on February 23rd, 1923. This time it was different; Tunney knew what he was dealing with. The fight was ultra close, but Gene won a split decision. It was again close when they collided for the third time in December, but the verdict for Tunney was this time unanimous. They were to clash twice more, officially no decision bouts but Greb taking a hiding on both occasions. Harry only just made it through the last one, and then told reporters that he wanted no more of Tunney: the son-of-a-bitch was now too big and too strong. Dempsey? Gene would lick him. He put his money where his mouth was and cleaned up.

The onward climb continued. Carpentier, now an ex-champion, was outboxed and outfought for 14 rounds. In the 15th Gene dug a left hook into his body and Georges didn't beat the count. Then Tommy Gibbons. Tunney, swift and sure, boxed him to a standstill with sharp, accurate punches and in the 12th the referee armisticed Tommy.

Onto Cleveland and let's win there. Johnny Risko, the 'India rubber man' who fought like a human pogo stick and was renowned for getting the close ones in his home town. Tunney made sure it wasn't close. Boxing beautifully, he proceeded to take the blades out of this human windmill one by one.

Risko was the third ranked heavyweight contender behind Wills and Boston's Jack Sharkey. Victory over him led Gene to the title fight with Dempsey. The rest, as they say, is history.

On September 24th, 1926, Gene Tunney awoke as the heavyweight champion of the world. But not in the hearts of the public. Their affection was now all with Dempsey.

Dempsey handled the press conference masterfully.

'I don't want any sympathy. I don't need any. The better man won. I have no alibis to offer.'

'Nothing bothered me except what Tunney was doing to me.'

'I lost fairly. Let's not cook up phoney excuses.'

Later, to Estelle: 'Honey, I guess I just forgot to duck.' Those words were to become part of the Dempsey legend. With defeat only a few hours old he was already towering over Tunney.

Tunney himself went down like a lead balloon with the average fight fan. He was a boxer:— 'Oh yeah, a fancy dan.' Loved literature:— 'Lit..., say ain't that something to do with the law?' George Bernard Shaw was a favourite*:— 'Jeez, — who?' And Shakespeare:— 'What weight does he box at?' Above all, Tunney had dethroned the mighty Dempsey: 'Me? Naah, I never went along with all that draft dodger stuff. Still the champ in my book.'

Initially Jack seemed to take himself out of the picture as far as a rematch went. But, as the months went on, so his mood changed.

In every defeated boxing champion there is the feeling that it was an off-night, that he had over or under trained, he was caught cold, it was a lucky punch, had under-estimated the opposition, was robbed of a close decision, and so on. Great boxing champions possess great self-confidence. They do not think that they can be beaten. Self belief is a pre-requisite for success. Nor do boxer's accept easily that they are over the hill. This realisation only comes later amidst the tears and bitterness of further defeat.

By the new year Dempsey had convinced himself that he was capable of regaining the title. Rickard was delighted, but cagey. There was far more money to be made here than just from a straightforward Tunney–Dempsey rematch.

Three weeks after Tunney won the title, Bostonian Jack Sharkey finally removed a long black cloud from all their lives by thrashing Harry Wills to defeat. Officially, the result went into the record books as a disqualification loss in 13 rounds, but Sharkey, on probably the best night of his career, gave the now fading Wills a sustained hammering. It was not merely that Wills could be discarded, but Rickard now had three big names to play with; Tunney, Dempsey and Sharkey.

The money spinning potential went beyond that. There was also Sharkey's great rival from Boston, Jim Maloney, and a trio of foreign heavyweights who

* Shaw, himself a fight fan, became friendly with Tunney and is said to have modelled his play 'Cashel Byron's Profession' on Gene.

were on the up, Spain's Paulino Uzcudun, Denmark's Knute Hansen and from New Zealand, Tom Heeney.

Rickard, who effectively controlled the heavyweight division (he even produced his own rankings), came up with the idea of an elimination series. Uzcudun v Hansen and Sharkey against Maloney, the winners to box each other for the right to meet Dempsey in a final eliminator.

Sharkey had already beaten Maloney two out of three, and stretched the percentage to 75 by stopping him in five. Uzcudun hauled Hansen over the coals, and for good measure whipped Tom Heeney shortly afterwards. That was one victory too many. In boxing you can look too good for your own good. Tex shelved the Spaniard in favour of a straight Dempsey–Sharkey clash*. If Dempsey won then he would re-establish himself; if Sharkey won then he would have beaten Wills, Maloney and Dempsey (plus Risko earlier) in a row. Either way, it added up to another box office bonanza.

In the event Richard got two. 75,000 people turned up at New York's Yankee Stadium on July 21st, 1927 to see Dempsey and Sharkey. With receipts of $1,083,530 it was the fourth million dollar gate, the first for a non-title fight. Dempsey's share was 27.5%.

The ex-champion was favoured to win, but some good judges were not so sure. Sharkey stood an even 6′ and weighed 196 lbs (89 kilos). At 24, he was eight years younger than Dempsey. On the debit side, his rather patchy record (five defeats in thirty-three fights), did not suggest much of a puncher, only ten stoppages. Sharkey was also a man of suspect temperament, given to claiming fouls. This time it was to cost him dear.

The bout was scheduled for 10 rounds and at the halfway stage Sharkey was well ahead. Many ringsiders scored all the first five rounds to him. Sharkey boxed well behind his jab and took the fight to Dempsey, punishing him with hooks to the head and welting him around the body. What really surprised an increasingly hushed crowd was that it was Sharkey who seemed the heavier puncher. He hurt Dempsey on numerous occasions (Dempsey later admitted that he feared he might be knocked out), whereas Dempsey's own punches failed to shake Sharkey. A boxer never loses his power; basically, Dempsey's timing had gone.

At the end of the 5th, Dempsey's new manager, Leo Flynn, told him to go all out for the body. It was a far cry from the days when Jack simply barnstormed the opposition.

Dempsey mauled Sharkey's body throughout the 6th. He never decisively penetrated Sharkey's defence, but probably shaded the round on sheer aggression.

* Another school of thought is that the elimination tournament never really existed; Rickard announced it merely to promote interest in Uzcudun–Hansen and Sharkey–Maloney.

The assault continued in the 7th. Some of Dempsey's punches strayed low and he was warned by referee Jack O'Sullivan.

What happened next has become part of boxing folklore. It runs as follows. Dempsey landed some shots around the borderline. Sharkey dropped his arms and turned to the referee to appeal for a foul. Dempsey stepped in with a left hook to the jaw and knocked Sharkey out.

In fact, it is rather more complex than that.

Dempsey certainly landed two punches in the area of the borderline. Ringside opinion was equally divided on whether they were low or not.

The fight film shows Dempsey landing low punches at an earlier stage of the contest. When he does so, they cause Sharkey's trunks to ride up. They do not on this occasion. Ironically, Sharkey himself is low with a right just beforehand.

When Dempsey's punches land, referee O'Sullivan begins to move towards them with his arms outstretched. Sharkey doesn't actually turn towards O'Sullivan but seeing him, drops his hands to his groin. Dempsey hits Sharkey with the left hook and down he goes. Sharkey is not unconscious, but writhes on the canvas clutching his groin while O'Sullivan counts.

What seems clear is that seeing the referee about to intervene, Sharkey attempted to take advantage of the situation and claim a foul. Exactly what was in O'Sullivan's mind we do not know. Possibly, he meant to lecture both contestants. As he had not actually ordered them to stop boxing, Dempsey was within his rights to hit Sharkey. Sharkey certainly could have gotten up. Instead, he went through his foul routine, and on this occasion it turned out to be a fateful miscalculation. Sharkey's own words after the fight are possibly a tacit acceptance of this. He told his manager, Johnny Buckley, 'Stop complaining — it's all part of the game.' The plain fact is that he lost a fight he should have won.

For Dempsey, it was a highly unsatisfactory victory, but it was the win itself which mattered. Tunney–Dempsey part two was now a reality.

With the Wills saga out of the way, New York was eager for the contest. They did not get it. The main reason was that the Commission had imposed a $27.50 ceiling on tickets. Chicago, on the other hand, would allow Rickard to charge a top price of $40, and was home to a huge open air arena called Soldiers Field. So Chicago got the nod for September 22nd.

Dempsey's preparation for this fight was far better than for the first. Tunney — 'Gene the Machine' — was a natural trainer. A few days before the contest the Dempsey camp made a clumsy attempt to unsettle the champion, publishing an open letter which accused Tunney of conspiring with Max 'Bo Bo' Hoff, a well known gangster, and former featherweight champ Abe Attell*,

* After retiring Attell became a figure in organised crime.

in an attempt to fix their first fight. Ironically, the mob *had* tried to muscle in on Tunney. Underworld leader Owney Madden once visited his home for this purpose. Tunney threw him out, but it was an unhappy foretaste of things to come.

Dempsey's 'open letter' never bothered Tunney who recognised it as a psychological ploy. It was, without doubt, the concoction of Leo Flynn. One feels that Kearns would have done it better.

Although Jack was fitter, the distance was again set for 10 rounds. The contest attracted world-wide attention. In America interest was at fever pitch. On September 22nd over 105,000 people crammed Soldiers Field to capacity. They paid $2,658,660, the first two million dollar gate. Tunney received $990,445, Dempsey $425,000 plus $25,000 from the film rights. Rickard later announced his net profit as over $550,000.

Just before they entered the ring, referee Dave Barry visited the fighters in their dressing rooms to go over the rules with them. This is routine. But on this occasion it was to assume massive importance. Barry carefully explained one comparatively recent rule change to Dempsey. If a fighter went down then his count would not begin until the other fighter went to a neutral corner. Dempsey himself had been responsible for this rule because of the way he had stood over Firpo when the Argentinian was on the canvas.

The atmosphere at Chicago was supercharged with expectancy. Tension gathered and congealed in the early autumn air. Those who were there saw a good fight and the single most controversial round in boxing history.

Tunney opened fast, outpunching Jack in a heated first round in which they both gave and took hard punches. Gene knew that Dempsey would be a sterner proposition than a year ago.

To emphasise it Jack came out and took the 2nd. He had the crowd roaring as he tore open Gene's mouth with a left hook and then outpunched him in a vicious exchange. Although Gene sent a string of jabs into Jack's face during the last minute, it had been Dempsey's round by a shade.

But back came Tunney in the 3rd and the crowd's eager roar died away into a solemn whisper. He split Jack's lips with a right uppercut and then made his nose bleed with a right hook. Gene outboxed and outpunched Jack throughout the round.

The pendulum swung again in the 4th as Dempsey set up a frenetic attack and clubbed his way through Tunney's guard on sheer aggression. A jarring right uppercut hurt Tunney, then another chilling right cut his ear, and although Gene was bombarding Jack at the bell, splitting his right eye with a hard left hook, it had been Dempsey's round by a shade.

Again, in the 5th, the fight swayed. This time Tunney turned on the fire hose and swept Dempsey before him, outspeeding and outpunching him. Jack was hurt by sharp punishing attacks which Gene varied to head and body and at the bell Jack was hanging on.

Yet just to demonstrate the way in which fortunes changed from round to round, Dempsey, after looking on the verge of defeat, now staged a dramatic recovery in the 6th and won the round by driving Gene around the ring. Jack gritted his teeth and walked through pain and punishment to slam punches to Gene's body. Tunney's superb defence kept him out of real trouble but during the final minute he had to weather heavy pressure.

Now the 7th; and destiny beckoned its most controversial finger at Jack Dempsey.

Dempsey was chasing; Tunney elusive. Suddenly Jack found a chink in that iron defence and smashed home a vicious right to the head. Tunney reeled. Jack followed up with a peach of a left hook to the head and Tunney, stunned, staggered back against one of the corner posts. Dempsey was on him like a tiger, volleying five punches to Gene's unprotected jaw. Gene went down in a heap. Referee Barry stepped forward to take up the count but found Jack hovering over his fallen opponent. Barry did not count. Instead he ordered Jack to go to the farthest neutral corner. For several crucial seconds Jack stared at him uncomprehendingly. Finally Barry got through to him. Jack turned and walked away. Only then did Barry begin his count. He began it at 'one'. When he reached 'nine' Gene was up and on his bicycle, frustrating all Jack's attempts to catch him again. Come in and fight, Dempsey motioned, but Gene was too wily.

Jack tried all he knew to corner Gene in the 8th. Try as he did he could not cut the ring off, and Tunney speared him time and again with left jabs. Towards the end of the round Dempsey thought he saw an opening. Cruel illusion! As he lashed out Tunney stepped inside the punch perfectly, and bombed him with a lightning right to the jaw. Dazed, Jack slumped briefly to one knee for a count of 'one'.

All that really remained was for Tunney to set the seal on a fight that Dempsey had lost in the 7th round. Jack had nothing left and in the last two rounds Gene tied up the loose ends. He did it brilliantly, feeding Jack jab after jab, and belting him with whiplash rights whilst the old champion stumbled blindly forward, all hope gone, fighting now on memory alone. His face was a red mask of blood and pain. Had the fight gone on longer than 10 rounds then Dempsey would have been stopped.

Referee Dave Barry raised Gene's hand in triumph. It was a unanimous verdict in Gene's favour. But the controversy had already begun.

No other single issue in the history of boxing has generated so much argument as the long count in the second Tunney–Dempsey fight. Was Dempsey the victim of a referee's error; was he himself at fault; could Tunney have beaten a normal count, and if so, would Dempsey have finished him off anyway? Let us examine the issues one by one.

Was referee Dave Barry at fault? Yes, he was. But it is difficult to judge him too harshly. The rule had been in force in New York for some while, but was only adopted in Illinois a few days before the fight. Barry, an Illinois referee, was given the contest just hours before it took place. He hardly had time to familiarise himself with the new regulation and consequently misinterpreted it. Here is what it stipulated:

> *'When a knockdown occurs, the Timekeeper shall immediately rise and announce the seconds audibly as they elapse. The referee shall first see that the opponent retires to the farthest corner and then... shall pick up the count in unison with the Timekeeper.*
>
> *'Should the boxer... fail to remain in the neutral corner, the referee and timekeeper shall cease counting until he has so retired.'*

What Barry therefore should have done was pick the count up level with the Timekeeper after Dempsey reached the corner. The Timekeeper had then reached 'five'. Instead, Barry began his count at 'one'.

In retrospect it seems clear that Barry was misled by the second part of the rule.

This referred to a boxer coming out of a corner while the count was in progress. If that happened then *both* the referee and the timekeeper were supposed to stop counting.

Dave Barry obviously believed that this applied to both situations; that neither he or the Timekeeper was supposed to start counting in the first place until Dempsey had gone to the corner.

This was incorrect, but it is not difficult to see why the mistake occurred. Unless one had studied the ruling closely then it was ambiguous.

Was Dempsey at fault? Absolutely, and he admitted so at the press conference afterwards:

'I was told of the rule and should have obeyed it. I suppose a jungle fighter cannot change.'

He not only knew that the rule was now in force in Illinois, he was conversant with it from New York. This is evidenced by the *Sharkey* fight. After knocking Sharkey down Dempsey went immediately to a neutral corner.

But, as he candidly admitted, in the heat of battle he was at times prone to forget the rule and revert to type. Years later he boxed an unofficial grudge fight with a wrestler named 'Cowboy' Luttrell, knocking him down three times. After the first and third knockdowns Dempsey remembered to go to the corner. After the second he forgot and hovered over Luttrell.

Clearly then, Dempsey forgot all about the rule when Tunney hit the canvas. He was not alone; Dave Barry also had difficulty remembering it!

When Gene went down, Barry instinctively raised his arm as if to start counting (some ringsiders wrongly believed he had tolled 'one') before going to Dempsey. In the next round Barry forgot again and counted 'one' over Jack without making Tunney go to a neutral corner.

What it all amounts to is that both Barry and Dempsey made errors in that historic seventh round. Both men provide a classic example of human fallibility when faced with new or alien situations.

But did their mistakes cost Dempsey the title?

Estimates of the time Tunney was down range from 14 to 19 seconds. My watch timed it at 17. But, concentrating purely on Tunney, from the time he hit the floor to the time he got to one knee, only seven seconds elapsed. He certainly could have gotten up at this point. But had he gotten up then, or two seconds later, would he have been an easy target for Dempsey? In my view, no. As soon as Tunney is on one knee he is listening closely to the count and appears fully alert again.

At the end of the day, I do not think Barry and Dempsey's errors mattered very much. Tunney would still have gotten up and gone on to victory.

The famous 'long count' controversy has tended to obscure the scoring of the contest. The scorecards were not announced, but ringside consensus gave it to Tunney by seven rounds to three.

Dempsey obviously took the 7th and there can be no doubt that Tunney won the last three. But the fight fluctuated over the first six. Here, Tunney won his rounds more clearly than Dempsey, but the ex-champion certainly had the better of at least two and probably three. What it means is that at the end of the 7th, Dempsey still technically had a chance of winning on points. Most historians have maintained that Dempsey could only have won by a knockout, but in reality the position was ambivalent. He *did* need a kayo because he was not as young and as fit as Gene over the last third. But a younger Dempsey would have had the option of winning on points.

In the end however it is all academic. Whether by 6–4 or 7–3 Tunney deservedly won.

The controversy over the long count raged (it still does). The public wanted a rubber match to settle it once and for all. Rickard and Tunney — who stood to make absolute fortunes — most definitely wanted it. So too did Dempsey who was also guaranteed a sizeable pot of gold. But his marriage was breaking up and a doctor warned Jack that if he fought again then he risked permanent damage to his eyes. It meant that there would be no three million dollar gate, and no Tunney–Dempsey III. Dempsey never fought seriously again.

Just how much Tunney's fortunes — and Rickard's — were dependent on Jack can be seen from Gene's next — and last — fight.

With Dempsey's retirement the five top heavyweight contenders were Sharkey, Risko, Uzcudun, Heeney and Jack Delaney, a French-Canadian who had given up the light heavyweight title to try and emulate Tunney. Throughout 1927 up to mid 1928, they played pass the parcel with the No. 1 spot. Sharkey kayoed Delaney, but drew with Heeney and lost to Risko. Risko beat Sharkey,

Uzcudun and Delaney, but also lost to Delaney and had already been well thrashed by Tunney. Uzcudun finished off Harry Wills but lost to Risko and Delaney. Delaney beat Uzcudun and Risko but lost a return to the rubber man and was positively blasted out by Sharkey. Heeney beat Risko and Delaney, but was held by Sharkey and Uzcudun and beaten by Uzcudun. As Rickard was already wandering around in the dark with this bunch, he metaphorically closed his eyes and stuck a pin in his rankings. It pricked Tom Heeney's name.

Heeney, nicknamed 'The hard rock from down under', was a durable, swarming fighter who threw punches as though he wanted to say goodbye to his arms. However, his whirlwind style disguised the fact that he was neither a good boxer nor a particularly hard hitter.

On July 26th, 1928, Rickard matched Heeney with Tunney for the championship at the Yankee Stadium, New York. Tunney was guaranteed 525,000 dollars, Heeney, 100,000. But only 45,890 fans were interested and the gate receipts of 691,000 dollars ensured that all-in-all Tex made a substantial loss on the promotion.

The fight was no better than the gate. Heeney surprised Gene by hurting him with a stiff right in the 1st round but that was as far as he got. Having tamed Greb and Risko, Gene was used to dealing with hurricanes. Punch by punch he methodically reduced Heeney to a battered hulk. In the 10th the 'hard rock' splintered under an accumulation of blows and sank to the canvas for '8'. In the next round Tom was in such a bad way that the referee stopped it.

Tunney now stunned the world of sport by announcing his retirement. He resisted all temptations to lure him back, married an heiress and went into business. His son John became a U.S. Senator (Dempsey went on the stump for him). When Gene Tunney died on November 7th, 1978, he was the richest ex-fighter in history.

There is not really much more that you can say about this very private man. Gene Tunney is the anonymous great of the heavyweight division; a natural achiever but never really a champion in his own right.

Dempsey, the man in whose shadow Tunney lived, had a long and varied life. He and Estelle divorced in 1931 and Jack went on to marry twice more.

In common with many other Americans, Dempsey suffered badly during the Wall Street collapse, badly enough to necessitate a long string of exhibition matches, followed by tours as a wrestling referee. He earned money and opened a popular New York restaurant.

During the Second World War Dempsey laid the ghost of the draft dodging accusation. He enlisted in the U.S. Coastguard and served in the Pacific.

Those are the bare bones of it. The flesh is the charisma that this man had. Charisma can never be acquired. It is there or it is not. Dempsey, once the man you loved to hate, became the man you loved to love. Charisma is the personal métier of intellectualism; if you can define it then you haven't got it. You can't define Dempsey's; it was just there. He was the second most popular ex-fighter of all time; one of the most popular sportsmen who has ever lived.

On the morning of June 1st, 1983 I got up and listened to the radio while I swallowed a cup of coffee and prepared to go to work. The hours of darkness had passed in thunder and lightning, the rain pounding down like thousands of boxing gloves in the night. The radio crackled out the news that Dempsey was dead. That turbulent night marked his passing.

While I was writing this book an acquaintance said — 'I hope you're not going to write anything bad about Dempsey.' I replied: 'As a fighter no, but as a champion, yes.'

From the Autumn of 1917 to the Autumn of 1920, Jack Dempsey was one of the greatest fighters in history. After 1920 he was not. Although at only 25 he should have been at his peak he was past it. The reason for this is that Dempsey left too much of himself in the slug filled rings of the mid-west. The knock 'em down and drag 'em out brawls with the likes of Sudenberg and, later, Anderson and Kenny, took a lot of years off the back part of his career.

His championship years were cynical exercises in making money along with Kearns and Rickard. Hobo jungles did not teach Dempsey to be a philanthropist. Vast numbers of people were willing to pay vast amounts of money to watch Dempsey destroy light heavyweights and amateurs because he epitomised the savagery within us all. Because we do not like that side of ourselves, reasons were found to boo him. When he lost the title it was as if the dangerous part had been tamed and conquered. In Greek mythology, Hercules was cast out after slaughtering his family, and then restored and elevated to legend when he had completed his labours. Jack Dempsey was a Herculean legend of the 20th century.

In 1950 sports writers voted Dempsey the greatest fighter of the half century. His rehabilitation was complete.

Round Fourteen: Interregnum

Jack Dempsey had been involved in five million dollar gates. Eight years were to pass before the next one, and the young man who generated it was at this time still a wide eyed schoolboy.

In the aftermath of Tunney's retirement Tex Rickard put together a proposed elimination tournament to find a new heavyweight champion. It was a depressing prospect because there was not a lot of talent around.

To disguise this paucity Rickard brought in a crop of foreign heavyweights, 1924 Olympic champion Otto Von Porat from Norway, Vittorio Campolo an Argentinian, and Germany's Max Schmeling, to join Uzcudun who was already campaigning in America. Linking up with them would be an equal number of Americans, Sharkey, Risko, 'K.O.' Christner, and a colourful young Georgian, William L. 'Young' Stribling.

The eliminators were designed to eventually pit Sharkey against Risko for the vacant title; and, of course, to make money.

Sharkey's half of the draw matched him with Stribling, and Von Porat and Campolo against each other. It figured to be an easy ride to the final for Sharkey. In fact, it was anything but.

The scenario was somewhat marred from the start. First, Rickard died suddenly on January 6th, 1929 of pneumonia. His promotional team took over the reins with Dempsey as their front man.

Next, Sharkey, never the most consistent performer in the world, almost got himself eliminated by Stribling. On February 27th, 1929 the pair clashed at Miami. Sharkey survived a rocky 4th round to win the referee's decision. Few agreed with it.

Von Porat–Campolo never happened. Wanting a warm up, the Argentinian took on British champ Phil Scott. It should have been easy. Two years earlier Scott had made his American debut. It was somewhat akin to a penguin jumping off the Sears-Roebuck building convinced it can fly. Knute Hansen knocked Scott out in the 1st with a straight left (!), and then Risko crawled all over him. The Brit's problem was that a punch anywhere in the vicinity of his body immediately brought forth a mayday call. Unfortunately for Campolo, he hadn't learnt the art of body punching (perhaps he took lessons from Firpo), and Scott succeeded in ouboxing him. Back to the corned beef factory.

This unexpected victory put Scott in the opposite corner against Von Porat. Not for long. In the 2nd Scott took a body punch and collapsed, groaning. Dempsey, who was refereeing, after some hesitation disqualified the Norwegian. Not that it mattered very much anyway as both were supposed to be patsies for Sharkey.

Sharkey faced Scott — now dubbed 'Phainting Phil' and the 'swooning swan' by the American press — in Miami on February 27th, 1930. It was an horrendous farce.

Much to Sharkey's annoyance, Scott used superior reach to outbox him in the 1st. Things were continuing in the same vein in the 2nd until Sharkey started to whale away to the body. He was warned to keep his punches up before digging in a left hook which had Scott down for '6'. The 3rd was a lulu.

Sharkey dropped Scott with what was unquestionably a low blow. How serious it was is another matter because Scott got up protesting. Another body blow sent him down again, clutching his groin and whinging for a foul. The doctor was summoned, a chair brought into the ring for Scott, and the place began to look like a casualty ward. The doctor was not overly impressed and decided that 'Phainting Phil' should be restored to combat after a minute's rest, at the end of which period the referee told Scott to get on with it or get out. Our wounded hero limped to the centre of the ring, took another body shot and ran up the white flag. That some of Sharkey's blows were low is beyond doubt, but this was par for the course in American rings. Scott's performance led to the term 'horizontal' being coined for British heavyweights.

Sharkey, who at one point had feared that Scott's histrionics might get him disqualified, was now in the final.

The other half of the draw matched Uzcudun with Christner and Risko against Schmeling. Risko was supposed to come through, but the best laid plans...

Uzcudun was a squatly-built fighter from Spain's Basque country. He was not much on technique, but immensely strong and had never been floored. Uzcudun had a permanently crooked left arm from a childhood accident, but utilised it as a powerful hook. He outpointed Christner to set up a meeting with Risko or Schmeling.

On the surface Schmeling, the German champion, looked ideal for Risko. He was not the European heavyweight champion (a hard hitting Swede named Harry Persson), but the European *light*-heavyweight king, and a year earlier had been knocked out in one round by 'Gypsey' Daniels, a nondescript Briton who had twice lost to Scott. Schmeling was however good publicity value because of a distinctive facial resemblance to Dempsey. On February 1st, 1929, he also proved to have a similar right hand, using it to bludgeon Risko to defeat in nine rounds and thereby erasing the rubber man as a contender.

In June, Schmeling fought Uzcudun and won on points. It was more of a psychological than a physical victory. The Spaniard was inordinately proud of his strength. According to the late Tex Rickard's publicity machine, Paulino had once killed a wild boar with his bare hands (there may even have been some who believed it). Schmeling shrewdly challenged Uzcudun to a discus throwing contest and demoralised Paulino by consistently out-throwing him.

Uzcudun did not know that Max had been a German junior discus champion. When they met in the ring Uzcudun lacked confidence and allowed Schmeling to dictate.

On June 12th, 1930, not far short of two years since Tunney's final defence, Sharkey and Schmeling faced each other for the vacant title at the Yankee Stadium. They drew a healthy gate of 72,000, but the receipts, $750,000, reflected in the ticket prices the fact that there was no Dempsey or Tunney; also America's deepening depression.

It was one of Sharkey's good nights. His left hand was a whipping, darting, rapier, that turned into a scything hook at close quarters. For three rounds he jabbed and hooked Schmeling almost at will. A yard faster in speed and thought than Max, he dominated and bemused the German. In the interval between the 3rd and 4th Max needed smelling salts in his corner. At the outset of the 4th both men exchanged good rights. Then Sharkey went downstairs, digging a powerful left hook into Schmeling's body. Max went down on his face and lay writhing on the canvas.

The referee seemed about to start the count when Schmeling's U.S. manager, Joe Jacobs, leapt into the ring and started screaming 'foul'. What happened next is not definitely attested to, but the story goes that Arthur Brisbane, Editor of the Hearst Newspaper chain, leaned through the ropes and threatened to start an anti-boxing crusade if Sharkey was not disqualified. Whether or not that is true, the referee did disqualify Sharkey.

Whether the punch was low or not is a matter of opinion. I have to say that it seems to me to have been marginally above the belt. But whatever the fact of it Max Schmeling had become the only man in history to win the heavyweight championship of the world on a foul.

☛☛☛☛☛

The new champion was 6′ 1½″ and weighed an approximate 190 lbs. He was the first champion born this century — Brandenburg, Germany, September 28th, 1905 — and the first whose death I do not have to record. Age 90, Max Schmeling is happily still alive as I write these words.

Known in fistic circles as the 'Black Uhlan' because of his swarthy, Dempseyish looks, Schmeling became a professional boxer in 1924. Up to the time of the Risko fight his record read won 40 (28 kayos), drew 4 and lost 4. He had been stopped three times but the only real blot was the Daniels kayo. As Max had outpointed Daniels three months earlier it seems that the 'Uhlan' was over confident and paid the price.

The other stoppage losses were early on in his career to Max Dickmann, a good light heavy whom Schmeling later stopped inside a round to retain his European title, and Canada's Larry Gains, a heavyweight of quality who along with a useful American, George Godfrey, was excluded from Rickard's whites only tournament. They were black*.

Nat Fleischer, who was instrumental in arranging for both Schmeling and Uzcudun to fight in America, described the German as a powerful hitter and expert boxer. He rated him as having the poorest jab amongst the heavyweight champions he saw, but at the other pole one of the best rights. Like his predecessor, Tunney, Schmeling was a smart fighter who analysed his opponents shrewdly. Max was also ice cool. When one of his handlers dropped dead in the dressing room just before his first fight with Joe Louis, Schmeling did not turn a hair.

Schmeling held the title for two years but defended it only once, against 'Young' Stribling, the 'Georgia Peach'.

Stribling's 'record' is the greatest fraud in boxing history. He knocked out his chauffeur in virtually every small town in the southern States. By dint of this tactic he compiled the second highest number of 'kayos' ever. It would have been the record but for his early death following a road accident in 1933.

Even so, the Georgian could fight and was a guaranteed crowd puller. He gave Sharkey oodles of trouble in their eliminator, and genuinely licked Von Porat, Christner, Scott and Risko. Amongst the light-heavies — which was Stribling's real division — he faced five out of the six men** to hold the title between 1923 and 1933, outpointing Tommy Loughran, Jimmy Slattery and Maxie Rosenbloom and drawing with Mike McTigue and Paul Berlenbach. Alas though; Stribling could never win the big ones. When the title was at stake Berlenbach and Loughran defeated him. So too did Schmeling on July 3rd, 1931 in Cleveland.

Stribling had a well practised manoeuvre which he called 'the buckshot punch'. Coming out of a clinch the Georgian would make a double feint to unbalance his opponent, draw his left hand and then counter with a right cross. 'Buck' had outdrawn and shot down many genuine opponents. But not Schmeling!

As was expected, Stribling set a fast pace from the beginning, and over the first nine rounds he built up a points lead, keeping a lightning left jab in Schmeling's face. In the 4th Max had his right eye closed. But when Schmeling did get to grips with his man, notably in the 5th and 7th, he crashed heavy rights to Stribling's chin and hurt him.

In the 9th glory came, saw, and passed Stribling by. The challenger went into his buckshot routine, but instead of punching to the jaw, he took Max by surprise, slamming home a vicious one-two to the body. The champion was badly hurt and went reeling into the ropes. But amazingly Stribling stood off.

* My father, then a young policeman, had to summons Gains following a car crash in England. He took an instant liking to Gains and always described him as 'a gentleman'.

** Jack Delaney was the exception.

Then to compound his error, he allowed Schmeling to turn away and speak to his manager at the ringside! A ruthless fighter, given either chance, would have taken his man out.

From here on it was all Schmeling. He dug short rights to Stribling's body and followed up with booming overarm rights to his head. In the 14th Stribling was in a bad way and Max stepped back and looked at the referee. But no. The bout went into the 15th and final round, and Schmeling, opening up with both hands, dropped Stribling for '9'. When he arose the referee at last heeded both Schmeling's imploring looks, and the shouts of ringsiders, and halted the carnage. There was just 14 seconds of the fight left. It was the only time Stribling was ever stopped.

12 months later, on June 21st, 1932, Schmeling defended the title against Sharkey at the Long Island Bowl, New York.

Since losing to Schmeling the first time around life had been somewhat chequered for the temperamental Bay Stater. In fact, in his last two fights Sharkey had gone from the sublime to the ridiculous. He had thoroughly trounced the giant Italian Primo Carnera who outweighed him by 60 lbs and towered six inches over him, but was held to a draw by Mickey Walker, the ex-middleweight champion. Sharkey was ten inches taller and 50 lbs heavier than Walker, but Mickey, nicknamed 'The Toy Bulldog' and managed by 'Doc' Kearns, battled Jack right the way down the wire in one of the most amazing displays of courage and tenacity seen in a boxing ring.

The second instalment of Schmeling–Sharkey ran its full scheduled course of 15 rounds, most of them tedious. Sharkey, pawing rather than snapping his left jab, held the edge over the first few rounds. Then Schmeling, judging the pace and his opponent shrewdly as always, seemed to take over. At the end of the 9th most ringsiders had it about even, but as in the Stribling fight Max came on to really dominate the last six rounds, jarring Sharkey time and again with precision rights. He closed Sharkey's left eye and bruised his mouth and nose. At the final bell the decision for Schmeling seemed to be a formality. But there was a shock in store for the 70,000 crowd. Gunboat Smith was the referee and amidst shocked disbelief he called it in Sharkey's favour. Then the two judges, one for Schmeling amidst cheers, but the other casting the deciding vote for Sharkey. The crowd set up a storm of booing, ringsiders sat aghast, and Schmeling's manager, Joe Jacobs, raced across to the M.C., grabbed the microphone, and screamed into it:

'We wuz robbed. We shoulda stood in bed.' (The first three words have become an important part of any fight manager's vocabulary.)

Robbery or not, Jack Sharkey was the new world heavyweight champion. It was the first time that the title had changed hands on a points decision over 15 rounds.

Fighting out of Boston in the 1920s, it was almost inevitable that Joseph Paul Zukauskas would adopt an Irish ring name. In fact, Jack Sharkey was of Lithuanian origin and was born in Binghamton, N.Y. on October 6th, 1902. When he passed away age 92 in 1995, he set a longevity record for heavyweight champions.

Joe Zukauskas started to box while serving in the U.S. Navy. On discharge he decided to try his luck in the professional ring. The manager he approached — Johnny Buckley who would handle him throughout his career — was not exactly enamoured with the idea of managing a Lithuanian (heard of Mars but where the hell's Lithuania?) named Zu... — what? Well now, old Tom Sharkey was an ex-sailor — Irish too — and the champ's name is Jack, so 'Jack Sharkey' sounds good. And so Jack Sharkey it was.

Zukauskas — sorry, Sharkey — did not exactly set any rings alight at first. One, Eddie Record, outpointed him, and a Romero Rojas, later kayoed by Stribling, halted him in eight. In his 11th fight, Jimmy Maloney, Sharkey's great Boston rival, decisioned him. The fans were not greatly enthralled with Sharkey either. He called himself 'The Boston Gob' (a term for sailor); they preferred the more derisive 'Weeping Lithuanian' because of his habit of bursting into tears at the end of a fight.

Sharkey was also not bowling anybody over. He stopped just five of his first twenty-two opponents. In 1925 only one of his ten fights failed to go the distance and that ended on a disqualification. On one occasion the New York Commission summoned him to explain why he had not finished off an allegedly outclassed opponent, the implication being that Sharkey had deliberately toyed with him. Nobody seems to have asked the referee why he did not stop it.

That year also saw Sharkey drop decisions to two very average trial horses, Charlie Weinert and Bud Gorman. But he was getting better, twice outpointing Maloney and receiving the nod over Risko. Sharkey's real problem was one of temperament. When in the wrong mood, he appeared mediocre and disinterested. But when he was up for it he was a very different proposition indeed. He could punch — as Dempsey attested — and possessed a very sound boxing technique, good defence, good jab, and fast, accurate hooks. Jack has sometimes been described as a dirty fighter but the evidence does not sustain this. It was a rough, tough ring in the Twenties. Sharkey was no better nor worse than anyone else. He lost only one fight on a foul — to Schmeling — and that was probably a miscarriage of justice. What made the fans grumble was his tendency to call fouls against his opponents.

Following the German set-back, Sharkey did not lose again until he faced Dempsey, 13 fights later. Included amongst his victims were revenge over Gorman (albeit a foul), Maloney, ex-light-heavyweight champion Mike McTigue, George Godfrey and Harry Wills. After Dempsey, Sharkey's morale slumped at first. Heeney held him to a draw and Risko avenged his earlier loss.

But the mood changed again. Jack Delaney went in the 1st, Christner oupointed, and Tommy Loughran, who had relinquished the 175 lbs crown to campaign as a heavy, learnt the folly of his ways when Sharkey took him out in three, Tommy walking to his corner in a daze after getting up from a sizzling right to the head.

The eliminators took Sharkey to his first fight with Schmeling which he was expected to win. After it, New York changed their rules, very stupidly in my opinion. A 'no foul' regulation was introduced meaning that a boxer could not be disqualified for fouling an opponent; he merely lost the round, or a point. The defect is obvious. It doesn't matter if you lose points on fouls if they enable you to win in the long run. It is a dirty fighter's charter.

Sharkey lost the title on his first defence, to Primo Carnera whom he had thrashed twenty-one months earlier. On June 29th, 1933 Carnera knocked Sharkey out in six rounds at the Long Island Bowl. For fifty years it was accepted that this fight was fixed — even Sharkey's wife believed it in spite of his denials. The version which passed into boxing demonology was that Jack boxed Primo's ears off for five rounds and then succumbed to a phantom right uppercut in the 6th. However, the film of the bout became available on video in the Eighties and it compares very badly with what past writers would have us believe.

Carnera was certainly not outclassed over the first five rounds. Sharkey probably had an edge, but the fight film shows Carnera countering well, particularly with left uppercuts to the jaw, exactly the punch to use against a much smaller man when he is on the attack. Sharkey had considerable difficulty penetrating the Italian's defence. Clearly, Carnera had learnt a lot from their first fight.

In the 6th Sharkey looks frustrated. His boxing is ragged. He does connect with a haymaker which rocks Carnera, but then goes 'right hand crazy', looking for a knockout. When one wild swing misses, Carnera drives him to the ropes and connects with a tremendous right uppercut to the chin. End of story. How anybody could describe it as a phantom punch is inexplicable. It was perfectly delivered and — unusually for Carnera — he really got his body weight behind it.

The charge of 'fix' is not sustainable. But I am afraid that it is not difficult to see why it came about.

☛☛☛☛☛

The Primo Carnera story is ugly. It begins not in Italy but with a moment of madness in American history called prohibition. Prohibition led to crime on an unheard of scale. America is still paying the price today.

One man who made a fortune from the bootlegging industry in the 1920s was English born Owney Madden, who we last heard of being ejected from the Tunney residence. Madden was seeking to diversify into boxing. His leading henchman, night-club owner Bill Duffy, had connections with the fight game and claimed to be a friend of Jack Dempsey. Exactly how much Dempsey knew about Duffy's activities is unclear, but Dempsey later gave some measure of support to Carnera. On the eve of the Sharkey fight the betting odds swung from 6–5 on Sharkey to 6–5 Carnera, further evidence, some would say, of a fix. However, it may have been due to Dempsey's enthusiastic endorsement of Carnera as having 'made considerable progress, and now, hitting with precision, especially his right.' It is not suggested that Dempsey had any actual part in the great Carnera swindle.

In 1929, while the elimination series was in progress, Duffy heard stories of a giant Italian who was knocking everybody over in France and Britain. Primo Carnera was indeed a giant; 6′ 6″* and 270 lbs (123 kilos). He was born in the mountain village of Sequals, Northern Italy, on October 26th, 1906.

Most accounts of Carnera claim that he was discovered by a French journalist, Leon See, who found him working as a circus strongman. This is incorrect. He was actually working in a sporting booth billed as 'Juan, the invincible Spaniard', and it was not See but an ex-boxer named Paul Journee. Carnera was then 21.

Journee taught Carnera the rudiments of boxing and signed him to a contract. Leon See, editor of a French boxing magazine, had been Journee's manager. Journee encouraged See to have a look at his protégé and in due course See took over his management. Carnera embarked on his career in 1928 with nine straight kayos. See later admitted they were all fixed. In fact, according to See, of Primo's first 28 fights, 25 were definitely fixed and one was 'doubtful'. The only opponent definitely on the level was Franz Diener** from whom Schmeling had won the German title. Carnera stopped Diener in six, which is actually an interesting result because 20 months earlier Diener had gone the distance with Schmeling. It suggests that despite all the phoney contests Carnera had developed into a passable imitation of a fighter.

Carnera's two proceeding fights were definitely bent. He was up against that other great master of deception, 'Young' Stribling. Stribling was disqualified at London's Royal Albert Hall; Carnera in Paris three weeks later. At this stage both men's antics merit more of a chuckle than outright condemnation. Stribling's knock-about fun (literally) in the deep south gave the folks some thrills and sent them home happy. Carnera was making money by giving the fans a giant to gawp at, and nobody was getting hurt except for the reputations of certain gullible British journalists who claimed that he was too big to fight normal men. The Carnera situation, however, turned nasty the following year when he crossed the Atlantic, straight into the arms of Bill Duffy.***

* Sources vary between 6 ft 5¼ ins and 6ft 8½ i

** They fought twice, the first a 'No Contest'.

*** Madden was now in prison, but continued to have part of the action.

Duffy and his 'associates', i.e., the mob, lured Carnera and See to the U.S. at the beginning of 1930. Not that they needed a lot of enticement. There was money to be made.

The usual Carnera story runs that as soon as he and See got off the boat, Duffy made See an offer he couldn't refuse; take the next ship back across the big pond otherwise you'll end up in a little one; the East river for example! That in fact is not true. Shifty little Leon did not get the infamous 'Bandleader' treatment until 1932, and like the Bandleader he did not depart empty handed. But from the time Carnera set foot in the States, Duffy, with Madden's bar patterned shadow lurking behind him, was effectively calling the shots — almost literally, according to opponents who didn't want to lie down. However, at this point See was still along for the ride, rather than being taken for one. And he was earning out of it. How much Carnera knew is problematic, but you must have some inkling about things when opponents get disqualified for hitting you on the shoulder!

Of Carnera's long list of fights in America in 1930 only three were genuine. Leon Chevalier in Oakland on April 14th was a gem. Chevalier refused all inducements to take a dive. His corner were not quite so brave, especially when they had guns shoved under their noses. In order to make Leon see sense his handlers rubbed resin in his eyes. That didn't convince him either so they threw in the towel in the 6th, just *after* Carnera had risen from a knockdown!

George Godfrey was another who couldn't be bought or intimidated. He allegedly lost on a foul. Although Carnera's biographer maintains that Godfrey genuinely did hit Carnera low, others recorded the punch as landing on the shoulder. What is not in dispute is that before the fight Duffy beat up the local Boxing Commissioner and locked him in an empty dressing room!

Jim Maloney, still doing the rounds, was likewise unbribeable, particularly in his native Boston. By 1930 however he had faded into the second rank and seemed ready to be taken on the square. But at the end of ten rounds Maloney received a hotly disputed decision. If it was a robbery then it comes under the heading of poetic justice.

Carnera rounded out the year back in Europe with two legitimate victories. He narrowly outpointed Paulino Uzcudun in Spain. Uzcudun also lost to Risko that year, but was still a credible performer, good enough still to beat Von Porat, and the fight shows that Carnera had learnt some boxing skills. He did, as time went on, develop a decent left and learnt how to defend himself. His problem, paradoxically, was that he was too big. His muscles lacked suppleness. Because of it he was an 'arm puncher'; he rarely got leverage and body weight behind his punches. When he did, more by accident than design, his punches were genuinely dangerous. But most of the time he failed to connect powerfully. A lack of 'killer instinct' did not help. 'De Preem', or 'The Ambling Alp' as he was known, was by nature more a lover than a fighter, as the long list of women claiming law suits against him testifies!

Rounding out 1930 he knocked out Britain's future champion Reggie Meen in two rounds, a feat which required no ability whatsoever.

The fights were harder in 1931. The long list of set ups meant that Carnera was now a ranked contender. According to Leon See most of the 'Alp's' successes that year were genuine. He outpointed Maloney and the emergent 'King' Levinsky, and stopped Hansen and Campolo. But Jack Sharkey whipped him handily over 15, flooring him in the process.

Duffy went back to the drawing board and sketched up a few more fakes. Larry Gains was not one of them. On May 30th, 1932 Gains trounced Carnera in London. Needless to say, he did not get a title shot when Primo became champion.

Whether Carnera's victory over Art Lasky that year was on the level we do not know. Leon See was no longer around to tell us, having wisely accepted the mob's offer and returned permanently to Europe. But Lasky was a good young fighter who would go on to become the No. 1 contender.

At the beginning of 1933 that position was held by Schmeling. Next to him was Max Baer, a Californian who quite literally possessed a man killing right hand. Sharkey was not about to fight either of them. Instead, Sharkey had designs on defending the title against his friend, Ernie Shaaf, who despite being only 24 was a 93 fight veteran with some good names in his win column. However, there was a slight conflict of interest; Sharkey and Buckley actually co-managed Shaaf! (Few boxers have fought their own managers; many would like to!)

The fight would be rather more palatable all round if Shaaf could win an eliminator. Carnera was a leading contender. He and Shaaf hooked up at Madison Square Garden on February 10th, 1933.

It was not an especially good fight. Shaaf looked like a middleweight compared to the giant Italian. He had difficulty getting past Carnera's long left which was now a useful weapon. In the 13th Carnera put together some jarring punches, topped with a short left hook to the jaw. The punch sent Shaaf hurtling backwards and onto the canvas where he was counted out. From the cheaper seats there were boos, and cries of 'fake' were heard. But looking at the film it is obvious that there is something horribly wrong with Shaaf. He never regained consciousness and died five days later from a blood clot on the brain.

Today, it is generally supposed that the real damage was done six months earlier when Shaaf took a battering from Baer, being knocked senseless seconds before the final bell. But Shaaf had boxed three times since without mishap, including a win over another ranked contender, Stanley Poreda. We really don't know who or what was to blame. But 94 bouts in just over seven years including 13 ten rounders while still a teenager would not be regarded as very safety conscious today.

Carnera was, like any boxer, upset by the tragedy, but it had happened and there was nothing he could do to undo it. In June he knocked Sharkey out to win the title.

His reign, like his career as a whole, was undistinguished. On October 22nd he defended in Rome against Uzcudun. The occasion was turned into a propaganda exercise by Mussolini and his fascists. Duffy would doubtless have felt right at home had he been there, but two of his underlings, Luigi Soresi and Billy Defoe, enjoyed the gangster jamboree instead. Uzcudun later became chauffeur to the Spanish dictator Franco and Carnera was accused of collaborating with Germans in World War II. As for the fight itself, Primo used his long left to spear Uzcudun for 15 unexciting rounds. Carnera made no attempt at a stoppage after damaging his right hand in the 9th.

Carnera's second defence bordered on the farcical. Tommy Loughran was seven inches shorter and 86 lbs lighter than the champion, the greatest disparity in championship history. Loughran had had a good year in 1933 beating Sharkey, 'King' Levinsky, Steve Hamas — who turned right around and licked Schmeling — and a man even bigger than Carnera, 6′ 7½″ Ray Impellitiere. But anybody who knew anything gave Miami a wide berth on March 1st, 1934. Loughran simply could not punch. The fans kept away in prodigious numbers, and the contest generated the smallest gate receipts in heavyweight title history.

Loughran, a superb boxer, started off well and seemed to rock Carnera on a couple of occasions. Actually hurting somebody with his powder puff punches must have been a new experience for Tommy. But Carnera was never in serious trouble, and as the bout wore on he took the speed out of Loughran by trampling on his toes with his gigantic feet. Down the stretch the 'Alp' made his huge bulk tell and merited his points victory. The stay-aways got it right.

It was time to face the top contender. That was Max Baer who had slammed Schmeling to defeat the previous year. Coincidentally, Carnera and Baer had just made a movie together, 'The Prizefighter and the Lady'* (Dempsey also appeared in it). It is said that Baer teased Carnera mercilessly on the set and established a psychological ascendancy over him. At a physical examination a few days before the fight, Baer playfully plucked hairs out of the Italian's chest.

The playacting stopped on the night of June 14th, 1934, although to the uneducated Carnera it didn't seem that way. On one occasion Baer turned his back on the bewildered Italian and walked back to his corner to rub his shoes in the resin; on another, when they fell entangled, Baer whispered 'Last one up's a cissy'. Again, Baer was seen to blow kisses to women at the ringside. These tactics were cunning and calculated. Baer treated Carnera with indifference bordering

* A.K.A. 'Every Woman's Man'.

on contempt. The more abler boxer, Primo was made to look and feel inferior.

The bare facts record that Carnera was floored eleven times in eleven rounds, twice in the 1st, three times in the 2nd, No. six came in the 3rd, there were three more knockdowns in the 10th, and finally two in the 11th, after which referee Arthur Donovan called a halt to the proceedings. But the statistics do not tell the whole of the story.

Baer floored Carnera with almost his first punch of the fight, a superbly timed and delivered right cross. It was the best punch he threw that night, and Carnera — who had received a telegram from Mussolini more-or-less ordering him to win — got up far too quickly for his own good. After that Baer's punches were far less clinically executed. His blows were extremely powerful — particularly with the right — but were mainly swings and overarms. In the 2nd, Carnera dragged Baer down with him on each of the three occasions he was floored.

Time and again Carnera persisted on getting up in the briefest possible time, sometimes even without a count. Pride comes before a fall. On this occasion it was as much nationalistic as personal. Carnera's courage cannot be questioned;— his brain certainly can. Yet after the 3rd he began to steal the rounds with neat left handed boxing. Never the best conditioned of fighters, Baer fought only in very short spurts. He broke Primo's nose and fouled him repeatedly, but by the end of the 9th Carnera was actually ahead.

Baer was sent out to attack again in the 10th. It was a bad round for Carnera. At one point Donovan clearly wanted to stop it but Carnera dissuaded him. He also prevented his corner from throwing in the towel.

The end came in the next session. If Carnera thought that Baer's attack might peter out again then he was wrong. Max's assault was crude but relentless. Finally, shortly after rising from a knockdown, Carnera turned and spoke to Donovan and the referee stopped it. The 'Alp' had done far more than courage and dignity demanded.

Maximillian Adalbert Baer, the 'Livermore Larruper' was never going to be more than an interim champion. He simply hadn't the skills for the job.

The physique was perfect. Baer stood 6′ 2½″ and weighed 220 lbs of rock hewn muscle. Unfortunately, he abused it with drink, late nights and women. Or perhaps he didn't, because when your natural gifts are not high then you might as well use them to get as much fun out of life as possible. And who is to say that Baer was not the one who got it right?

Nat Fleischer thought that if Baer had paid more attention to conditioning and learnt to box then he might have been one of the heavyweight greats. I doubt it. Just as some master boxers cannot punch, so Baer lacked their natural fluency and brain to make him even a halfway decent boxer. He had an iron jaw, an oak of a body and possibly the most powerful right in heavyweight history, but virtually nothing else. Technically he was not so much a zero as a minus, a caveman born out of his time.

The setting for this fistic neanderthal was Omaha, Nebraska, on February 11th, 1909. Max was a mixture of German-Jewish (father Jacob) and Scotch-Irish (mother Dora). Jacob originally worked as a butcher and his claim to fame in life was winning a national meat trimming contest in Chicago. Max and his younger brother, 'Buddy', inherited the muscular development which Jacob gained from this trade.

The Baers moved to Livermore, California, where Max grew up. After a rudimentary education he went to work as a ranchhand for his father.

Details are sketchy as to how Baer got into boxing. Hype says that he discovered his prodigious hitting power one night when knocking out a hulk of a man from whom he and his friends had stolen some wine. Well, maybe, but I distrust such stories. What is fact is that Baer made his Pro debut in 1929. He was managed throughout his career by Ancil Hoffman, but by the time Max won the title Dempsey also seems to have had part of the action (did Baer perhaps remind him of somebody?).

In 1929 Baer had sixteen fights winning fifteen and scoring twelve knock-outs. His only loss was on a foul. In the next two years he had a further twenty-two and won sixteen, including thirteen kayos. One fight, in 1930, was tragic. Baer knocked out Frankie Campbell in San Francisco. A few hours later Campbell died of brain concussion.

The Inquest exonerated Baer; the California Boxing Commission didn't! After any tragedy there is a feeling that something must be done, irrespective of whether or not it fits the case. In this instance Baer was suspended from boxing in California for a year. There was no evidence whatsoever that any illegal punches had caused Campbell's death. Another facet of this syndrome is that an authority figure must never be held responsible. No blame was attached to the referee for not stopping it earlier. Some ringsiders thought he should have done. It seems that the Commission allowed itself to be stampeded by adverse press coverage, i.e., let's all panic in unison. Contrary to the newspaper image of Baer as a gruesome ring killer, he considered quitting the sport after Campbell's death.

He did not. He went on in his own inimitable way which can best be described as — 'you box rings round me or I punch your lights out'. Ernie Shaaf and Tommy Loughran gave Max boxing lessons. Afterwards Loughran was hired to polish up his ringcraft. He did not succeed, although he did manage to improve Baer's timing and delivery. However, Risko swarmed all over Max and Paulino Uzcudun outlasted him in a 20 rounder*. It was a gloomy period relieved

* Baer was the last heavyweight champion to go the twenty round distance (twice).

only by flattening Tom Heeney.

Baer seemed to perk up once California restored his licence. Back again in the golden State he beat Risko, and in 1932 made a big move; seven fights, seven wins. 'King' Levinsky twice, Heeney again, and Shaaf who ended the contest flat on his back. Later Baer was blamed for his death too. Max's brutal punching was a convenient peg on which to hang a fatality.

His 1932 record set Baer up for a fight with Max Schmeling. After 'losing' to Sharkey, Schmeling replicated him by taking a fight with little Mickey Walker, the 'Toy Bulldog'. For three rounds the cool, calm German seemed to toy with Walker. But from the 4th Walker came on, chasing, chivvying, firing in body shots. He had battled Harry Greb inside and outside the ring (he claimed to have won on the cobbles), fought Sharkey to a standstill and feared no man. Incredibly, after seven, David led Goliath.

The 8th saw Schmeling firing on all cylinders. Right after right pounded into the little middleweight. He was on the canvas three times, the last a punch which left him rolled up into a rubber ball. Fearing that Walker's neck was broken, Kearns threw in the towel.

On June 8th, 1933, Baer faced Schmeling at the Bronx Ball Park. 53,000 people turned up, not many less than later saw Baer wrest the title from Carnera*. Hitler came to power that year in Germany; Baer wore the star of David on his trunks. That night Baer, the clown prince of boxing, was replaced by a man with a fierce devouring hatred, the flame of which would first engulf Schmeling, and then burn him to a crisp.

Baer, a raging, rampant demon, tore into Schmeling with terrifying ferocity. One searing wallop almost swept the German off his feet. In the 2nd Schmeling caught Baer coming in with a terrific right to the chin. Baer merely grinned, a smile which changed into a sneer as he saw Schmeling's eyes pop out in disbelief. He had hit Baer with his best punch; nothing!

For the next three rounds Baer launched attack after attack, shaking Schmeling time after time, sometimes holding the German with his left hand whilst he cascaded rights off his head. But Schmeling was neither a coward or a weakling. He must have known by now that he was badly outgunned, a cruiser facing a battleship, but he fought on gamely, and in the 6th and 7th moved inside Baer's punches and punished him with short, sharp, rights to the head. But back came Baer in the 8th, teeth gritted, eyes blazing. He slugged Schmeling all round the ring, and the beating went on throughout the 9th. As they came up for the 10th, Schmeling was in a bad way.

Baer smashed home eviscerating rights to the head, crude but deadly, and

* 56,000 at Madison Square Garden.

Schmeling reeled into the ropes. There, Baer blasted him from his senses with a wicked right flush on the jaw. Courage forced Schmeling to his feet at '9'. Almost immediately a venomous right exploded behind his ear, and hurled him defenceless into the ropes.

Baer closed in for the kill. Then suddenly he stopped. It was not Schmeling's face he was looking at: it was Campbell's. Then the image faded only to come again as Shaaf's battered features. The hate went, replaced by sick dread that one more punch might kill Schmeling. Baer glanced imploringly at the referee, Arthur Donovan, who looked long and hard at Schmeling swaying drunkenly against the ropes. Then Donovan held up his hands to signify that it was over. Baer would never fight as well again. Schmeling's greatest moment was still to come.

James Joseph Braddock was born in New York City on December 6th, 1905. So what, you ask? Apart from Boston, Irish Americans were increasingly less a factor in boxing. According to one source Braddock only just qualified as an American anyway. His father was Manchester Irish, his mother a Dubliner. James J. was conceived on the boat which took the newly wed couple to the U.S.A.

He began to box professionally in 1926. Nothing special. A lot better than a club fighter; above trial horse status; an outside contender for the light heavyweight title. He got his shot in 1929 and blew it when Loughran soundly outboxed him. Boy's come up from the sticks, and now's going back there.

Slippage into trial horse standard, 175 lbs and above. Decent name on Maxie Rosenbloom, John Henry Lewis and Ernie Shaaf's records. End 1933, 79 fights losing 21 of them. Not a champion's compilation — one which bespoke of a limited technique. 25 knockouts said a good, damaging right hand, but with a tendency to suffering damage as the opposition toughened up. Only one 'kayo by' in the loss column. Yes, sound chin. But stop there. There's nothing more. Or at least there wasn't until June 14th, 1934.

We're at Madison Square Garden where Baer is about to rip the crown off Carnera's head. The main support is Corn Griffin, a red hot comer in the heavyweight ranks. The Corn Griffin policy board wants somebody with a decent name who will make their man look good. Jimmy Braddock? Why not? He's been on relief recently. Be glad of the eating money.

What they didn't know was that the relief clerk was a friend of Braddock's. Numb with shame, Braddock stumbled through the interview and got a temporary job on the docks. Someone once wrote that fairies only exist if you believe in them hard enough. Corn Griffin was no fairy. Unless you believed hard enough.

So they brought Braddock out of virtual retirement, took him out of the docks, and put him in the ring with young, ambitious, Corn Griffin. Down and almost out in the 1st round Braddock came back fighting like a man possessed. Which he was. Possessed of despair, of humiliation, by the pinched, white faces of his wife and young children. He destroyed Corn Griffin, walking through punches that would have downed any other man, seemingly impervious to punishment and pain, apparently made of something more than flesh and blood. He walked through the punishment and he cut Corn Griffin to pieces, reduced him to a chopping block, and finally smashed him down and out in the third round.

After being buried in the graveyard of forgotten men James J. Braddock had begun the most astonishing climb in boxing history — from obscurity to fame, fortune — and the heavyweight championship of the world! They dubbed him 'The Cinderella Man' and this was exactly what he was.

In November he fought John Henry Lewis, a brilliant light-heavy who was soon to become one of the division's finest champions. Two years before Lewis had whipped Braddock. Now it was a different story. They were even after six rounds, and then Braddock made his big effort, bringing the punches screaming up from his boot-tops as he waded in, a man on fire with determination. Lewis hit the deck twice for long counts and barely survived the round. The last three stanzas were even-steven, but Braddock's big effort in the seventh had shaded him the fight.

This win propelled Braddock in to a fifteen rounder with the new number one heavyweight contender, Art Lasky. Lasky was an aggressive, hard-hitting toughie whom everybody took for granted as Baer's next opponent. Everybody except Braddock that is. Once again he confounded the experts, revealing a brand of skilful left handed boxing that nobody — perhaps not even he — knew he possessed. At the end of the fight Braddock — the Cinderella man — had done it again.

Incredibly he was now the number one contender for the world heavyweight title. The pauper had become the Crown Prince: a magic wand had turned the rags into an ermine ball gown.

But surely it would end tonight, June 13th, 1935, at the Long Island Bowl. So too would the Bowl's reputation of being a graveyard of defending champions. Braddock was just no match for Baer. The crowd were expecting a massacre. After five rounds they were still expecting one, after ten they were getting impatient, after thirteen they were still waiting, after fourteen... Hey, wait a minute! This guy Braddock's going to win! The unthinkable, the upset that could not happen, was happening, and right before their eyes!

At the start Baer bulled into Braddock, threatening to decapitate him with his mighty swings. But Braddock moved inside them, tied Maxie up, and kept out of his way as much as possible. He boxed on the retreat, whipping the left jab into Baer's handsome features whenever he found the opportunity. By common consent Baer's aggression won him five of the first seven rounds, with one to Braddock, and the other even.

But now it is the 8th, and Max is bored. He has not trained as hard as he ought to have done. But mainly he is bored. He knows he is winning but he cannot catch this fellow and put him away. So he forgets about Braddock and starts to play the fool. He screws his face up and makes terrifying grimaces at the challenger and Braddock continues to retreat. He laughs and turns away from Braddock to smile and wave at his friends at the ringside, and Braddock moves in swiftly with raking left jabs to remind him that he is still in a fight. Then Max chases after him, but Jim has scuttled off again. So Max goes back into his clowning routine.

As round succeeds round Baer chases, grimaces, clowns, and plays to the gallery. But Jim is deadly serious as he moves anti-clockwise away from that deadly right and coolly, undemonstrably, jabs away with his left.

At the end of the 10th, although few notice it, Max's lead had been cut to one round. At the end of the 11th they are even. After the 12th Braddock has actually gone into the lead. Now it is the end of the 13th, ad ringsiders realise with a shock that on their cards Max needs to take the last two rounds to keep his title with a draw. But in the 14th there is no move from the champion. Once again it falls to this quiet, methodical New Yorker, and now there is utter consternation around the ringside. People are sitting mouths agape because unless Max can knock Braddock out in the last round then Braddock will be the new champion.

Ancil Hoffman's arithmetic is adding up the same way. Curtly, he tells Max that he needs a knockout, or he's an ex-champion. Throughout the 15th Max attacks continuously in a desperate bid to save his title. He wins the round but Braddock coolly keeps out of the way of the big ones, and as each precious second ticks away so time becomes Max's enemy and points its rigid finger of doom at him. And now finally that time has run out. The last bell cuts through the night air and there is a new champion.

Braddock champion? It is unbelievable, a fairy tale come true. But it has happened.

James J. Braddock was 6′ 2″ and weighed a muscular 192 lbs when he won the title. Late in his career he had suddenly found a dramatic spur which had taken him all the way to the top. He was destined to hold on to the title for two years. Unfortunately they were stale years for Braddock did not defend the crown until June 22nd, 1937, at Chicago's Comiskey Park. When he did so he faced almost certain defeat. His opponent? — one Joseph Louis Barrow, better known as Joe Louis, a brilliant young black who had enjoyed a meteoric rise to fame.

Louis was the odds on favourite to win. He had nearly decimated the heavyweight division blasting in turn, Carnera, Baer, and Sharkey. But despite being once again the underdog Braddock, who had pulled off so many shocks, still had one ripple of surprise left in his locker. It came in the shape of a piercing straight right which sped like an arrow through Louis's defence and crashed high against his cheekbone. Joe rose uncertainly at '2', betraying the fact that he was still relatively inexperienced. Braddock laced him methodically throughout the rest of the round, but although Louis was hurt and confused, Jim never came close to repeating his success and that round — the 1st — proved to be his swan song. From the 2nd onwards defeat was only a matter of time.

Braddock's last stand. As round succeeded round Louis lanced him with jolting jabs and swift, sure hooks and crosses. Braddock's only answer was his courage. He stood erect beneath the tattered banner of his pride and guts, whilst the forces at his disposal were systematically wiped out. Louis was a ruthless predator, circling and circling again, stripping Braddock of everything but the raw courage that flowed from his heart, raining home a ceaseless bombardment of red tipped arrows and war clubs.

By the end of the 7th the massacre was complete. Only a shell named Braddock still stood, defenceless, helpless, a white ghost smeared in red. At the end of the round Braddock's manager Joe Gould told him that he was going to surrender. 'If you do, then I will never speak to you again,' mumbled Jim through torn lips. Gould swallowed hard. He had managed and suffered with Braddock through eleven long years. How could he deny him the right to die a hero's death?

The 8th, and Braddock walked steadily to his execution. The firing squad was ready although Louis had no heart for this grim finale. He measured Braddock and then utilised every ounce of power in his rippling shoulder muscles to rip home a blazing right cross to the chin. Almost in slow motion, Braddock sunk to the floor, and then keeled over on his back. Whilst the referee tolled off the count blood streamed from Jim's mouth, cheek and nose, billowing out across the canvas.

Afterwards Louis said that the right cross was the hardest punch he ever threw, and that James J. Braddock the fighting Irishman, was the bravest man he ever fought.

Meanwhile boxing had a superb new champion. It was the end of the lean years.

Round Fifteen: The Ascent of the Bomber

He was a wizened little man with a kindly face who worked out of an office no bigger than a broom cupboard at Tex Rickard promotions. Appearances can be deceptive. It is recorded that Joseph Merrick, 'The Elephant Man', once tried his hand at door-to-door selling; with predictable results. 'Uncle' Mick Jacobs would have made a superb doorstep salesman. And he would have departed with the family heirlooms and the shirt off your back!

In 1935 'Uncle' Mike was in his mid-fifties. He never boxed, but muscled in on the fight game in the early 'Twenties as a ticket 'scalper'*. Rickard was quick to see that Jacobs was the sort of man it was better to have inside the tent pissing out rather than the other way round. Jacobs became his right hand man.

When Rickard died insiders expected 'Uncle' Mike to take over his empire. Instead it fell to the flamboyant 'Boy Bandit', Jimmy Johnston — he of the 'Boer' Rodel heart flimflam. Jacobs' ego wasn't bruised. His wallet?; — well, that was a different thing. He set up his own fight promotion business and like any good shark waited for the right fish to swim by.

Three came along all at once, Bill Farnsworth, Ed Frayne and Damon Runyan, all journalists for the Hearst Newspaper syndicate. Wouldn't it be nice, said the three herrings, if we could get a piece of the boxing action. So they set up the 'Twentieth Century Sporting Club' with Jacobs as their promoter. 'Uncle' Mike devoured them, tipping off the Hearst Chain about its employees' conflict of interest. Farnsworth and Frayne sold their interests to Jacobs for a pittance and stuck to journalism. Runyan stayed in both camps. He was a big herring and everybody read his columns.

Mike Jacobs' contacts extended a lot further than greedy reporters. As Frankie Carbo found out. Carbo was a 'made man'** in the Mafia; possibly one of the stone killers used to create 'Luca the Hun' in 'The Godfather'. He tried the 'Bandleader' treatment on 'Uncle' Mike. Jacobs called Frank Costello, the 'Prime Minister of the mob'. Carbo got told to put his gun away and treat Jacobs with respect.

What Costello could not do for Jacobs was provide him with a heavyweight champion. Rickard had made a fortune out of Dempsey. Jacobs wanted a champion and a fortune too. By 1935 reports were beginning to percolate through about a young black fighter out of Detroit.

Jimmy Johnston got first crack. The telephone call with John Roxborough,

* Tout.
** Killer.

the prospect's co-manager, went something like this:

Johnston: 'We'll take him, but he can't win all the time because he's a nigger.'

Roxborough: 'So am I,' and slammed the phone down.

By contrast, 'Uncle' Mike was a Greek bearing gifts. Unlike Johnston, he understood the way it really worked. Business is colour blind save for green. And when Mike Jacobs looked at Joe Louis Barrow, green was what he saw, vast great bundles of it.

Joe Louis Barrow. He was the seventh child of an Alabama sharecropper. Two years after Joe's birth on May 13th, 1914, Munroe Barrow went insane and was committed to an asylum. Lillie Barrow, Joe's mother, was told that Munroe had died* and re-married, a widower named Pat Brooks. The total number of children in the household was thirteen. Pat, Lillie, and their respective broods uprooted to Detroit where Pat got a job on the Ford production line. But by the early Thirties he had been laid off due to the Depression and the family was on relief. According to the Jacobs publicity department, Joe's mother paid for her now teenage son to have violin lessons to keep him off the streets. Given the family circumstances, I do not find this credible of belief. What we do know is that by the age of 18 Joe was working at the Briggs car body plant** and was boxing as an amateur for grocery cheques to supplement the family income.

Joe's first amateur bout would have put paid to most youngsters. He was grotesquely over-matched against Johnny Miler, who had represented America in the 1932 Olympics, and was stopped in two rounds after being decked seven times. Joe didn't quit. He went on to win 51 of 54 amateur bouts and amongst his pewter pots were two Golden Gloves titles***.

His decision to turn professional was of course a financial one. Exactly how he and John Roxborough met is unclear. Roxborough was, in East London parlance, a 'ducker and diver', a sort of sophisticated black version of Del Trotter. He was heavily involved in the numbers racket**** and liked to promote an image of himself as a benevolent man who doled out largesse to poor blacks. The image was not bad for business either. Although Roxborough knew nothing about the fight game, he became Joe Louis Barrow's manager. On Roxborough's advice, 'Barrow' was dropped, leaving 'Louis' as Joe's surname.

* In fact he lived for another 20 years in the asylum.
** They were taken over by Ford in the 1950s.
*** Light-heavyweight..
**** Illegal lottery.

Roxborough turned to another black entrepreneur for assistance. Julian Black is a somewhat shadowy figure. Unusually for a black in the Thirties, he was respected in mob circles. Julian Black joined Roxborough as Louis's co-manager. When the Detroit 'purple gang' attempted to move in on Louis, word came down from the higher echelons of the syndicate to 'lay off'. In view of the fact that Roxborough, Black and Mike Jacobs all had gangland connections, it should be made absolutely clear that there was never a hint of a fix about any of Louis's fights. Nobody in the Thirties would have fixed a fight *in favour* of a black anyway.

Of necessity, Roxborough and Black needed to hire a good trainer for their very amateurish protégé. Jack 'Chappie' Blackburn, a fifty-one year old ex-fighter, proved an ideal choice. Although never a champion, Blackburn had four times held Sam Langford to a draw. He was not a man to cross outside the ring either. Blackburn engaged in gunfights and knife-fights and had served a prison sentence for manslaughter. He was a long term alcoholic but still functioned well at his job, and by 1934 had trained two world champions, Lightweight Sammy Mandell and Bantam 'Bud' Taylor. Although black himself, Blackburn didn't really cotton to training black fighters, cynically holding that they would not be allowed to amount to much, an echo of his own experiences. He was also not overly impressed by Joe Louis at first sight. But if Roxborough and Black were willing to pay him good wages then he would do his best. Blackburn and Louis quickly bonded well together.

The twenty year old whose training 'Chappie' took on was still growing into a fully fledged heavyweight. At his peak Louis would stand 6′ 1½″ and weigh 200 lbs.

Under Blackburn's tutelage Louis became an outstanding fighting machine; a superb attacking boxer. He had one of the best jabs in heavyweight history and possessed tremendous punching power in both hands. Hands. They were what Joe Louis was all about. His hand speed was phenomenal. He was the first heavyweight to really put his punches together in multi-punch combinations, the modern school of boxing. Combinations had existed for a long time in the shape of the 'one-two', but Louis strung his together in clusters of four or five at a time. And he had all the punches to make them count, mixing up hooks, crosses and uppercuts, a veritable witches' brew of power and precision.

On the debit side his footwork was always poor. Blackburn turned this to advantage by ensuring that Joe always had his feet firmly planted on the canvas to maximise his power. Louis's balance too left much to be desired. He was knocked down several times while off balance. Joe also had a significant defensive flaw, a tendency to drop his left hand after delivering a punch which made him open to a right hand counter. Joe learnt by rote, but never completely overcame this problem.

When I first became interested in boxing I found Joe Louis difficult to warm to. He seemed to have all the charisma of a frozen haddock. Only later did I realise that Joe was forced to submerge his personality because of his colour. Roxborough and Black, who understood the way of things in the Thirties, laid down certain precepts. Joe must never be seen to exalt in victory, or be photographed with a white woman, and must at all times be seen to walk humbly with his God. The result was a sullen nonentity who was nothing like the real Louis. Behind the scenes he was a rutting hog where women were concerned — black and white. Relaxed, he was an affable man and possessed a comedian's gift of one liners. Bob Pastor, who retreated at high speed for ten rounds, he compared to Rin-Tin-Tin. On Billy Conn, before their second fight: 'He can run, but he can't hide.' Told that Dempsey would be in Max Baer's corner for their contest, Louis responded: 'The rules say Dempsey can't hit me, don't they?'

The reason why Joe Louis had to keep his personality under wraps was one of image. In this context it has always been fashionable to blame Jack Johnson, banned from the Louis training camp much to his chagrin. But the sports writers who built the Louis legend hardly needed a scapegoat for their racism. Later, when the Second World War revealed all the horrors of racialism, they turned around 360 degrees and wrote Joe Louis into folk hero status. But, as Chris Mead has carefully documented in *Champion Joe Louis*, earlier on they created an ugly, simian image of Louis as some ape-like creature from the jungle. Examples: 'Something sly and sinister and perhaps not quite human came out of the African jungle last night... Joe Louis, the strange, wall-eyed unblinking Negro' (Davis Walsh — *International News Service*): 'A mean man, a truly savage person... on whom civilisation rested no more securely than a shawl thrown over one's shoulders' (Paul Gallico — *New York Daily News*) 'In Africa there are tens of thousands of powerful young savages that... could annihilate Joe Louis' (*New York Daily Mirror*), and 'the sensational Negro was eyeing him (Baer) with an impassive face, eyes filled with blood lust' (Bill McCormick, *Washington Post*). The imagery here is of a bloodthirsty, sub-human more wedded to the wild hinterlands of Africa than civilisation. 'Wedded' is the operative word. Paul Gallico, who posed as a 'liberal', even dragged in the newly-wed Louis's young wife, Marla: 'He went from tenderness to terror... I wonder if his new bride's heart beat a little with fear that this terrible thing was hers.'

It is fair to say that not all of the reportage was of this ilk; some of it was patronising but well meaning. But the reality was that Joe dared not depart from the script. One fall off the wagon and he would have been cast in the muck racked image of Jack Johnson.

Louis could however express his personality in the ring and from Independence Day 1934 he did just that. His first nine fights — all victories — reaped seven kayos. Number ten was against Stanley Poreda. In the 1st, Louis twice floored him for '9' counts. Then he knocked Stanley clean out of the ring.

Bizarrely, the referee kept counting until Poreda got back in again at '21' before stopping it. The result, and the manner of it, caused consternation. Although going back, Poreda was a useful fighter who two years earlier had outpointed Carnera. Joe's next fight did nothing to quell his burgeoning reputation; Charlie Massera — the 8th ranked contender according to Fleischer's 'Ring' — went in three.

By the time 'Uncle' Mike turned up with smiles, handshakes and a trainload of well fed and liquored up reporters, Joe had sixteen straight victories under his belt (13 kayos). Louis was disappointed that Natie Brown went the distance in no. 17. Jacobs patted him on the shoulder and said 'don't worry'. He had seen enough to know that his little pot of gold was on the horizon.

Nonetheless, in best American tradition, Jacobs sent him to see how it played in Peoria. It played very well, Willie Davis exiting quickly for the second time. By June of 1935 Louis had racked up 18 knock-outs in 22 wins. Time for the first really big one, literally: Primo Carnera.

Jimmy Johnston and Co. had Madison Square Garden, so Jacobs put the fight on at Yankee Stadium. It was a warm summer's evening; a bit too warm for Primo who was methodically reduced to a battered, bleeding hulk and finished off by a left hook in the 6th. Joe Louis had arrived — big time.

There wasn't much left for Carnera after that. Leroy Haynes twice knocked him out. The second time the mob said 'thanks very much — been nice', and sent him back to Italy semi-paralysed on a cattle boat. Primo never won another fight, and retired permanently in 1945 after being knocked out again. But there is a decent sequel to the Carnera story. He returned to the U.S. and made a good living as a professional wrestler. He died on June 29th, 1967 back in his native village of Sequals.

In his next three fights Joe Louis established himself as the number one contender. 'King' Levinsky first. Levinsky is reported as being in such a state of terror before the contest that Jacobs had it brought forward half-an-hour to make sure he got into the ring at all. He wasn't there very long. After two minutes and two knock-downs, Levinsky sat down on the bottom rope and pleaded with the referee: 'Don't let him hit me again.' Goodbye 'King'.

September 24th, 1935. Max Baer. Boxing's sixth million dollar gate, 86,000 people paying $1,000,832. Christian believer Louis faced Max in his Star of David trunks, and Jacobs sang 'What a friend we have in Jesus' when Baer went down and out in the 4th. As a fight it was more organised murder. Louis's jab dominated the first two rounds. Towards he end of the 3rd a right hook sent Baer to one knee for '7'. A barrage of left hooks floored him again on the bell. A swinging right hook followed by a much shorter left allowed Max to sign off in the next. Afterwards he told the Press: 'Sure I could have gotten up one more time, but you'll have to pay more than $25 to see my execution.' Baer also had a nice repertoire of one-liners.

Paulino Uzcudun completed the tripod. For three rounds the Basque buried his head in his gloves. In the 4th he took a peek out. The right which came screaming through virtually lifted him off his feet and cleaved his face apart. When they cleaned away the blood it was found that two of Paulino's teeth had been driven up through his top lip.

The newspapers vied with each other to invent lurid nicknames for Louis. The one which stuck was 'The Brown Bomber'.

Sometimes the storm clouds gather and we don't recognise them. The spring of 1936 brought Max Schmeling from Germany to do battle with the 'Bomber'. It seemed a sure thing. Baer had taken Schmeling apart — Louis had massacred Baer. Uzcudun had recently drawn with Schmeling — Louis had almost decapitated Uzcudun. But while form books are obviously a very useful guide, they sometimes give a false picture. Contests are moulded by styles — not lines in record books. The fascination of boxing is that A can beat B and B lick C, but then C turns around and defeats A. Different styles breed different results.

Schmeling was 30 and seemed washed up. After Baer, a college boy named Steve Hamas outpointed him in Philadelphia, and then Uzcudun levelled with him in Barcelona. But back in Germany Max started to methodically put it back together again. Walter Neusel, a holy terror to British heavyweight champions, was stopped in eight; ditto Hamas in a Hamburg return in front of local Nazi party hacks. Forced to give the Nazi salute, Joe Jacobs* later told friends: 'Sure, but I kept my fingers crossed: I'm 560% Jewish.' Uzcudun was lured northwards for revenge and outpointed. Max Schmeling was far from finished. And, he saw something, something that Jack Johnson had spotted too; Joe's propensity to drop his left hand.

In training things did not go well for Louis. 'Chappie' Blackburn disliked Marla Louis being around. Sex, he opined, was bad for a fighter before a contest. Then there was a young fellow named Cream who gave Joe so much trouble in sparring that they fired him. They had not heard the last of Arnold Cream A.K.A. 'Jersey' Joe Walcott.

Two days before the fight Pat Brooks, whom Louis looked on as his real father, suffered a stroke.

June 19th at the Yankee Stadium. 'Uncle' Mike had hoped for another million dollar gate. Louis and Schmeling would make it happen, but not for another two years. This time Jacobs had to be content with just over half of it and a crowd of 45,000.

For the first three rounds Louis clearly outboxed the German. The fight

* No relation to Mike.

film bears out what Fleischer said about Max's jab; he has a tendency to paw with it rather than snap. The film also shows how light skinned Louis was*. This emphasises just how deeply ingrained was the racial prejudice.

By the 4th Schmeling's left eye was closing. But this was a different fight to Carnera and Baer. Schmeling was cool and composed. Unlike the free swinging Baer, the 'Uhlan' did not give Louis the chance to unlimber his heavy guns. In fact the two hardest punches of the opening rounds, crisp rights out of defence which made Louis blink, came from Schmeling. Now he made his move. Joe jabbed, forgot to bring his left back to guard, and Schmeling really bombed him with a right cross to the head. That punch changed the fight. Louis went down and got up almost immediately. Louis's admirers have always held that the punch which really did the damage was a right delivered after the bell which ended round five. It didn't help, but Joe was clearly hurt and befuddled by that piercing right in the 4th, and from then on was always coming second. Even in the 8th, which he won, Louis made little impact; Schmeling was taking a breather.

Excepting the 8th, Schmeling lanced Louis time and time again with surgical rights from the 4th round on. Joe several times hit him low. Schmeling wondered whether Louis was trying to take advantage of New York's 'no foul' rule. It is unlikely. Joe was not an in-fighter. He head-hunted, and never developed a good body punching technique. The fouls were probably the result of trying to do something he was not good at. Watching the film you can see his boxing visibly deteriorating. Even his vaunted jab loses its snap.

The end came in the 12th when a street procession of rights, one following another, left Joe on the canvas for the count. Afterwards Schmeling was the first to go to his aid.

Reaction to Schmeling's victory was mixed. Some writers showed sympathy for Louis (but were relieved that the next heavyweight title fight seemingly was going to be between whites); others made it clear that they preferred a white German to a black American. In Germany Dr Goebbels propaganda machine elevated Schmeling to the status of heroic representative of the master race. Hitler himself granted Max an interview. Nazi euphoria did not last long. A few weeks later Jessie Owens took the Berlin Olympics by storm with four gold medals. Hitler stomped out of his box rather than congratulate him.

Louis wept after the fight. He felt he had let everybody down. Some wrote him off: '...Blackburn's rearing tiger was just a cinnamon tabby cat', sneered reporter Jack Miley. Miley should have remembered what Mark Twain said

* He possibly had Cherokee blood, and some thought there was a strain of white ancestry.

about obituaries. A more feeling, although irrational view, was that Louis might have been doped. Joe's fertile sense of humour took care of this one: 'Sure I was doped; by right hand punches.' A champion doesn't need excuses.

The best recuperative strategy was to get Louis back in action again. Jack Sharkey was ideal. Seen in overview, Jack's last quality performance was the first Carnera fight. After that he wasn't much good. Following his loss of the title, 'King' Levinsky and Tommy Loughran whipped him and he went into semi-retirement. He re-emerged late in 1935 beating 'unknown' Winston, a name seen a lot on the record books of that era. Then Sharkey lost and drew against a Tony Shucco. Outpointing Phil Brubaker, and the fact that he was an ex-champion, gave him the credentials to go in against Louis on August 18th, 1936. It was hopelessly one-sided. Sharkey managed to stay upright in the 1st; not in the 2nd — he was floored twice. Three more trips to the canvas followed in round three. On the last occasion Sharkey did not beat the count. He never fought again.

The Louis rehabilitation programmed took in four more kayos. Eddie Sims in Cleveland was one for the scrapbook. It lasted 20 seconds and one punch, a hand grenade of a left hook to the jaw. Sims actually did beat the count at '8', but the referee took one look into his blank, staring eyes and gave him the rest of the night off.

Bob Pastor was a good heavyweight controlled by Jimmy Johnston's combine. At Madison Square Garden on January 29th, 1937, he gave Louis all sorts of trouble in a ten rounder. Joe got the decision (Pastor always disputed it), but not much praise. Pastor boxed cannily on the retreat. Louis in fact always had problems against good defensive boxers; most attacking fighters do. He liked men to come to him and give him room to punch. He was not at home picking defensive locks. But Joe always learnt from fights and was better the second time around. Bob Pastor was to find this out; Natie Brown did so earlier. In 1935 he had gone the distance by staying in close. In February, 1937, Joe straightened him up with uppercuts and wished him goodnight in the 4th.

James J. Braddock really ought to have been defending the title against Schmeling. Max certainly thought so, and he was the No. 1 contender. When fair play first came into contact with boxing, it was put into an 'iron maiden', i.e., one of those spiked medieval torture chambers. The pair have never spoken since. Braddock's manager was Joe Gould, who had been up and down the avenue a great many times, often passing the time of day with the likes of Owney Madden. In fairness to Gould, he was genuinely fond of Braddock and had lent him money when Jim seemed to be on no better track than a one way ride to Palockaville. In Joe Gould's eyes Louis was the 'Cinderella Man's' Prince Charming; Max one of the ugly sisters. Behind the scenes, Mike Jacobs did absolutely everything to encourage this view. Braddock and Gould could earn a lot more money against Louis than Schmeling.

Jimmy Johnston and Co. saw things from a different perspective. Gould had signed a contract with them for Braddock to meet Schmeling at Madison Square Garden.

Contracts? Yes; they're those bits of paper which lawyers have a lot of fun with, but you only honour them when it's in your interests.

One day, so the story goes, John Roxborough got taken for a ride, sort of Chicago style, sort of not. More a sight seeing tour of New York with a bit of menace thrown in. Eventually the goon squad deposited him at a Manhattan night-club. Roxborough expected Owney Madden to be waiting for him; instead he beheld the cheerful countenance of Joe Gould.

Gould was willing to give them a title shot but at a price: 50% of Louis. Roxborough did not allow the veiled threat of the car ride to cower him. 'Not fifty cents.' Eventually they agreed to let 'Uncle' Mike settle things.

The deal was 10% of Louis's ring earnings for 10 years. It was not honoured. Jacobs later paid Gould and Braddock a lump sum. Whether the 're-negotiations' involved horses' heads or the like is unknown. Probably not. If you like your perfidy subtle then Machiavelli's *The Prince* and the campaigns of Mike Jacobs are recommended reading.

There still remained the little problem of the Schmeling contract. A New Jersey court, presided over by a judge named Fake, obligingly set it aside. Even so, New York staged a ghostly weigh in for the fight on the afternoon of its proposed date, June 3rd, 1937. Schmeling even attended. Presumably, he also thought the earth was flat.

It is hard to avoid the conclusion that Jimmy Johnston's image as a sharp faced chiseller was rather exaggerated. Also known sometimes as 'little larceny', he was little league alongside Mike Jacobs. Johnston began in centre field and ended up in the bleecher seats, a spectator whilst Jacobs won it all.

Louis and Jacobs emerged from Comiskey park with the title and many riches to come. Later, Jacobs would also add the greatest of them all, 'Sugar' Ray Robinson, to his money making machine.

Jim Braddock? He boxed again only once, British champion Tommy Farr on January 21st, 1938, at Madison Square Garden. After eight rounds Farr believed that he was so far in front that he could afford to sit out the last two rounds. He did, and Braddock got the decision. But by the 1960s Jim's luck had deserted him. Cinderella's ball gown turned back into rags and he found himself working on the docks again. He died on November 29th, 1974.

Round Sixteen: Bomb Blasts

Remember our two aspiring boxing magnates, Farnsworth and Frayne? Let us imagine a fictional conversation between them in the late summer of 1937. It might have gone something like this.

'Who in hell's Tommy Farr?'

'British champion, so they tell me.'

'Who'd he beat?'

'Baer.'

'Probably shacked up with a broad the night before.'

'Loughran-Olin.'

'Pair of over-fed light heavies — and washed up at that.'

'Nuesel.'

'Who?'

'Some kraut who's whipped all hell out the rest of the Limies.'

'So could my granny — big deal.'

'Yeah; sure sounds like Uncle Mike's feeding the Bomber a patsy this time out.'

During the first third of the twentieth century Britain was a conveyer belt of outstanding fighters under the 175 lbs limit. Four are numbered amongst the ranks of the all time greats. Ted 'Kid' Lewis, the 'smashing, bashing, dashing kid', twice world welterweight champion*. Benny Lynch, in 1937 the reigning world flyweight champion, who despite prodigious intakes of whiskey made a ploughed field of the eight stone division. Beyond Lynch glowed the legend of Jimmy Wilde, the tiny 'ghost with the hammer in his hand'. Another Welshman; featherweight Jim Driscoll, who after Wells' second kayo by Carpentier screamed at him 'Coward...coward...coward' until Wells burst into tears. Driscoll's nickname, 'Peerless', says it all. He was the greatest exponent of the straight left in boxing history.

But British heavyweight champions almost defied coherent description. Even in Palookaville, this sad bunch were staring out of the poorhouse windows. Amongst their innumerable flaws, 'Iron' Hague had no fitness, Wells no chin, Beckett no confidence, Frank Goddard no defence, Scott no heart, Ben Foord no Technique, and 'Gunner' Moir no nothing. And where these nightmares ended, Reggie Meen took over. The chubby 'Desborough Giant' spent more time asleep on the canvas than in bed.

* He fought the main supporting bout on the Willard–Johnson undercard.

Nobody noticed Tommy Farr, a lack of recognition which always made him justifiably bitter. Because Farr could fight. Had he been born a few years earlier and gotten the chances which fell to Schmeling, Sharkey, Carnera, Baer or Braddock then he would have been a world champion. As it was, Farr actually had his first recorded contest at the age of twelve! By August, 1937, he was 23 years old and had 791 completed rounds of boxing under his belt without ever having been floored. In addition to this Farr had fought hundreds of fights in the boxing booths.

But perhaps more impressive than Farr the boxer was Farr the man. As well as the hard, grinding regime of the boxing ring and booth, Farr laboured deep in the bowels of the earth as a coal miner. Aneurin Bevan, later a Labour Cabinet Minister, recalled that in his own young days as a miner he would arrive home too exhausted even to eat his dinner. Tommy Farr also worked the rubbish boats for a time, kneeling amidst the filth and the garbage while jets of scalding hot water burnt the skin off his back. These experiences moulded an exceptional man, one who even found time to educate himself with the great works of literature. Farr's memoirs, published from a hand written manuscript discovered after his death, display a writer's fluency with words.[1]

Between 1926 and 36 Farr advanced methodically up the lists to choruses of deafening silence. To the average fan he was a bore, not exciting, just dully effective. Farr's 79″ reach gave him left-handed mastery at long range, and in close he was a superb in-fighter with a chain and padlock defence. His excellence as a boxer compensated for his one great limitation, he was not a heavy puncher, only 23 stoppages in a career total of 104 fights. But he could pitch in two-handed when necessary, and if his salvos didn't blast, they punished.

Another problem for Tommy from Tonypandy was that he was constantly overshadowed by his fellow Welshman, Jack Petersen, a dashing firebrand hussar who could both box and punch. Like Farr, Petersen was the genuine article, and had he elected to stay in his natural division — light-heavyweight — then he might have become world champion. Instead, Petersen wanted heavyweight glory. In 1932 he caused a sensation by signing to fight for both the British light-heavy and heavyweight crowns within two months of each other. It is perhaps symptomatic of the state of British heavyweight boxing that whereas Petersen had to travel the distance in winning the 175 lbs crown, he annihilated Reggie Meen inside two rounds. Unfortunately Jack — who never genuinely weighed more than 180 lbs — was just not big enough for dreadnoughts like Walter Nuesel who ground him down three times despite being a much inferior fighter. Ditto, Ben Foord, who copied Nuesel's tactics to gain a revenge win over Petersen and take his heavyweight crown.

1 'Thus Farr'.

While all this passion and energy was being expended, Farr was stuck firmly in the background. Not even faint praise damned him. At the beginning of 1936 Farr outpointed Tommy Loughran. According to the pundits, Loughran was washed up; in fact he had lost only one of ten contests the previous year. What few noticed was the manner of Farr's victory, he *out boxed* one of the finest ring masters in history. Another former 175 lbs monarch, Bob Olin, who had surrendered his crown five months earlier, was similarly outscored. Olin was also a good boxer, but found Farr's technique superior. However, the Olin victory caused no eyebrows to raise. Even when Tommy boxed Foord's ears off to win the heavyweight title, the public blew it a raspberry. They preferred Ben's roundhouse swipes to Tommy's neat skills.

But people did finally sit up and take notice on the night of April 15th, 1937. Max Baer came to Harringay, North London. Farr rammed his head back with jabs moved inside with staccato bursts of punches. Then he either tied Baer up or glided smoothly out of distance. It is doubtful whether Max won a round. Afterwards, he sat in his dressing room, blood seeping from cuts over both eyes, and mumbled: 'They told me the limey couldn't fight.'

After Baer, the teutonic destroyer of British heavies, Walter Neusel. Farr moved in and out confidently for two rounds. In the 3rd, he set up a big attack, pelting Neusel with both hands until he slumped to the canvas. An injured knee hindered the German from beating the count, but he no longer fancied the job anyway. Tommy Farr was now a player in the heavyweight stakes.

His next fight should have been against Schmeling. It was actually arranged. Now 'Uncle' Mike normally spent his hols going south to plunder a village. This time out he looked east and lured Farr from under Schmeling's nose to grapple with Louis for the world title.

The contest was arranged for the Yankee Stadium on August 30th, 1937. After years of being overlooked and ignored Farr was in the limelight. Not for long, said the American Press, noting that his training seemed to consist of eating rather large meals. After all, Jim Braddock had promised them a revolutionary strategy for beating Louis (he had one, but they wouldn't let him take the machine gun into the ring); Farr offered nothing but bombast. To mask his fear, said reporters. They didn't understand that when you've waded knee deep in excrement and risked your life in subterranean tunnels, then you lose your fear of other men. They also failed to realise — and here Jacobs was equally unseeing — that different styles made different fights. Farr, a smart defender and in-fighter with good upper body movement, was not the static sort of target who Louis easily disposed of. 36,000 turned up for Joe's first defence: they saw one of the best fights in heavyweight championship history.

Farr had injured his right eye in training, but was supremely confident. Not for him a steady retreat from the opening bell. Instead Farr attacked Louis, jolted his head back with solid jabs, pounded him around the body, and then, switching his attack to the head, raised a lump over Joe's right eye. Never had Louis been attacked so vigorously.

Having knocked Louis off balance, Farr then went into a crouching, weaving style which confused Louis. But gradually the champion got to grips with the situation and he painted Tommy's features with left jabs thrown with unerring accuracy. By the end of the 3rd blood streamed from wounds under both Farr's eyes and his face was a blood red mask. In the 4th Louis ripped home a succession of right crosses to the head, and the bombardment continued in the 5th. But now back came Farr, pulling Louis up in his tracks with a whistling left hook to the jaw and cleverly making him miss with his ducking and weaving. Farr went on to share the round.

The 6th was a tremendous round. Farr scored with a battery of left hooks and went on to outscore Louis in a thrilling toe-to-toe slugging session. The crowd came to its feet cheering. Farr had taken Joe's best punches and was not merely still there, but fighting back strongly. Right at the bell Farr ducked under a wild left hook and came up with a tremendous right to the jaw. Louis's knees buckled.

In the 7th Louis attacked non-stop, firing a ceaseless barrage of punches at Farr. The Welshman reeled, blood began to seep from his mouth, and a triple left hook gunned him into the ropes. But from the verge of defeat Farr roared back, eyes gleaming to fight head-to-head with the champion whilst the crowd lifted the roof off.

They had patched Farr's eyes up, but in the 8th Louis ripped them open again, and the blood ran down Farr's chest. But he hurled Louis back on his heels with a corking right, waded in, outpunched Louis, and drove him back. Teeth gritted, fighting mad, Farr continued his relentless two-fisted bombardment in the 9th and Louis had to cover up and retreat. Incredibly, it was now all even with everything to fight for.

Louis refused to be drawn into a slugging session in the 10th. He stood off, firing jabs that seemed to come from a machine gun set at rapid fire, so fast and vicious were they, and now Farr was walking through a maelstrom of pain and punishment. As the round ended Louis hit Farr flush on the chin with a wicked left hook, but Tommy still stood. There was just time for Joe to unleash a savage left-right but again Tommy took the punches and stayed upright, and in the 11th the Briton steamed back firing away with both hands. He kept up the assault in the 12th and ringsiders thought that Tommy had just edged this round and evened the 11th.

But there could be no doubt that Louis won the next two rounds. The champion outpunched Farr and put his punches together beautifully. He punished the challenger ruthlessly, but even so he still could not put him down.

At the end of the 14th Farr thought the fight might hang in the balance: that the last round could decide it. He went out to win it, and he did, battling it out with Louis and outpunching him in a magnificent rally. When the last bell rung referee Donovan started to walk towards Farr, and for a split second Tommy, forgetting that in New York title fights were scored by the referee and two judges, thought he had won.

In fact, Donovan's scorecard read 13–1–1 in favour of Louis. Well, he was Jacobs' house referee. Nobody else agreed with him and some believed Tommy had just edged it. Looking back in his memoirs, Farr himself thought it about 8–7 to Louis, which was in line with the two judges, 9–6–0 and 8–5–2, for Joe.

But forget the scoring. Tommy Farr had made Britain throb with pride. And, although few have noticed it, he buried the horizontal British heavyweight. Many of Tommy's successors have been just honest triers, but none were as awful as his predecessors.

Louis had really wanted a face-off with Schmeling rather than Farr. Tommy was business; Max pleasure. But that would not come until the following June. Meanwhile Joe kept in trim with Nathan Mann and Harry 'Shotgun' Thomas. Neither was a leading contender. Mann, gangster controlled, became an unmade Mann in three, while Harry's shotgun did not have the spread to prevent it being doused in five*. But it was Schmeling, Schmeling, Schmeling, whom Louis wanted. For the first and only time in his career he felt hate. Partly it was the stigma of defeat. But the racial aspect bit deeply as well. German newspapers had sneeringly referred to Louis as 'Der Neger', and the Nazis had lauded Schmeling as an example of white supremacy over black. With the Mann and Thomas warm ups out of the way, Jacobs at last beckoned to Schmeling to come on. The contest would be held at the Yankee Stadium on June 22nd, 1938.

Schmeling was unprepared for the reception he got in America. He had always been popular there. But public opinion was beginning to harden against Nazi Germany, and Americans now identified Max with Hitler's Aryan superman theories. To some extent this was Schmeling's own fault; he had made no attempt to distance himself from the Nazi's propaganda. To be fair, he was not politically minded and was being used. But his behaviour nevertheless compared badly alongside that of Luz Long, Germany's great hope for the Long Jump in the Berlin Olympics. Long made a point of sitting alongside Jessie Owens during the competition, and when the black American was having trouble with his run-up, Long's advice helped him correct it**. What Luz Long was saying could

* Or 4. The Illinois Boxing Commission insisted on it continuing after the referee had actually stopped it.

** It was the start of a lasting friendship. During the final Long broke the previous world record but still had to settle for the silver behind Owens.)

not have been clearer: political and racial bigotry had no place in sport.

Although there was a measure of sympathy for the way in which Schmeling had been elbowed aside from the Braddock fight, there was distaste for Nazi beliefs. Gould and Braddock had in fact floated their spectre in Judge Fake's courtroom as a means of wheedling out of their contract with Schmeling. In another New Jersey courtroom two years beforehand, State Attorney General David Wilentz had tainted the alleged Lindbergh baby killer, Bruno Hauptmann, with Aryan supremacy ideals. Schmeling now found himself subject to hostile interrogation, rather as though he too was in an American Court of Law. Some of the questions were unfairly slanted. Asked whether he supported the Nazi system, Schmeling praised its economic aspects and was thus cast in a bad light by appearing to endorse Nazism as a whole. In fact, the American President, Franklin Roosevelt, had been trying to introduce some of Hitler's economic policies.

Schmeling himself seems to have been perturbed by the racial aspects of the fight. After the Second World War, he made a point of seeking Louis out and apologising. The two men became friendly.

But that emphatically was not the case on June 22nd. It was the seventh million dollar gate, 70,000 people paying $1,015,012. Some observers believed it was higher, the attendance more like 80,000; Jacobs deliberately underestimating the gate to scalp the boxers and the taxman.

On his way to the stadium Louis was asked how he felt. His reply is illuminating. 'I'm scared: scared I might kill him.'

Yet it began cautiously enough. Schmeling sparred as if to say 'Does this hurt?' — and Louis flicked out two light left jabs. But his eyes glittered with hatred and suddenly it welled up irresistibly inside him and came bursting out through the floodgates. He hooked a savage left to Schmeling's body, rushed him to the ropes and gunned him with a right cross to the jaw. Schmeling reeled, and the crowd, sensing a quick kill, leapt to their feet roaring Joe on.

Louis responded with a thundering barrage to the body and as Max doubled up he switched to the head. White faced, Max lashed a desperation right to the jaw but Joe did not even feel it, so intent was he on smashing this man into pulp, this man whose people had derided him — this man who had humiliated him in this very ring two years before. A vicious left-right combination left Schmeling sagging at the knees, and then Joe closed in on him, fighting like a berserk tiger, smashing left and right to the jaw and watching as Schmeling crashed dull-eyed to the canvas.

The German came up at '3' and Louis tore into him. Two searing left hooks to the jaw — red tipped barbs of steel — and Max jerked crazily, a broken marionette worked by a deranged puppeteer, before the black ebony executioner raised his axe again and crossed a murderous right to the chin. Schmeling gave way under the onslaught. He went down, and then arose at '2', a corpse like figure beaten into and beyond the grave.

Now Louis finished it, raw hate flowing outward from his heart as he unleashed a withering bombardment. Seeking to escape from the waves of pain and shock that engulfed him, Max turned his back on Louis and the Brown Bomber smashed vicious punches into his kidneys. Schmeling let out a terrible, unearthly shriek as the punches cut into him, a cry from the depths of hell which chilled the blood of all who heard it and remained indelibly burnt into their minds forever. Then it was finally over: a left hook, right cross combination to the head left Max helpless and hopeless, face down on the canvas, and the white towel came fluttering into the ring. Referee Donovan accepted its token of grim surrender at 2:04 of the 1st round.

Schmeling was in hospital for two weeks with injuries to the lumbar region of his back. No Nazi fanfare of trumpets greeted him on his return to Germany. Two years earlier another invincible German hero, Tennis star Gottfried Von Cramm, had been ditched after losing the Wimbledon final. Now Schmeling suffered the same fate.

He came back quietly in 1939 and won the European title by knocking out Adolph Heuser inside a round. Then the war intervened. Schmeling joined the German Parachute Regiment with the rank of Sergeant and was wounded in the battle for Crete. After the war he attempted another comeback, beginning on his 42nd birthday. He retired for good in 1948 when a Richard Vogt outpointed him. Later Schmeling became a successful businessman representing an American soft drinks company.

The agreement which Louis's management worked out with Mike Jacobs called for Joe to defend the title a minimum of four times a year. In 1938 they let him off number four following the Schmeling fight. After that, business resumed as normal. The record shows that Louis made the stipulated number in both 1939 and '40, and then seven (plus exhibitions) in 1941. Perhaps 'Uncle' Mike had a premonition about Pearl Harbour. After all, he was very good at sneak attacks himself. He still managed to extract a further two defences out of Louis in 1942 before Joe joined the Army. The rash of title bouts between 1938 and '42 prompted one journalist (Bill Miley) to describe it as Louis's 'bum of the month' club.

On the surface everything appeared hunky dory. The Jacobs, Louis combine were making money, and if the quality of the opposition wasn't much, at least it was the best around, and regular too. Below the surface things were less than fine. Jack Blackburn died from heart trouble in 1942. Roxborough was imprisoned for numbers racketeering and thereafter faded into the background to protect Louis's image. Later, Louis quarrelled and split with Julian Black*.

* One, Marshall Miles, became his manager of record; in reality it was Jacobs.

Joe's womanising caused Marla to divorce him. He took up golf, a game for which he displayed a spectacular lack of talent. One writer has estimated that golf hustlers may have taken Louis for as much as $1,000,000! Worst of all were Joe's finances. He never had a tax lawyer; only his good old Uncle Mike. Jacobs regularly lent Louis money to keep him happy and then retrieved the loans from his purses, illegally listing them, as business expenses on Joe's tax returns. Jacobs also continually deferred legitimate taxes against future earnings. It was never made clear to Louis that he would one day have to pay taxes on all these amounts. Nor did he receive advice about genuine tax shelters. In the long term the effect was disastrous.

Only the fighting really went well. Between 1937 and his retirement as champion in 1949, Joe Louis defended the heavyweight title a record 25 times. Muhammad Ali successfully defended 9 times from 1964–7 and 10, 1974–7. He had a similar period of inactivity to Louis, and had he held the title between 1970–4 would, in my opinion, have surpassed Joe. Larry Holmes made 20 winning defences between 1978–85, and but for what many regard as a bad decision he might also have overtaken Louis, although Holmes did not have four years on the sidelines. But Ali and Holmes are surmises; Joe's achievement is fact.

On January 25th, Louis opened his 1939 campaign against John Henry Lewis, the world light heavyweight champion. John Henry was one of history's more gifted 175 pounders, and no slouch at demolishing heavyweight trial horses either. Louis and he were friends and up to the end of 1938 a fight between them appeared unthinkable, particularly as both were black and unlikely to draw a good gate. But Lewis was now having serious eye problems and knew he would have to retire. He needed a good pay-day and Louis reluctantly obliged him. It was the first all black heavyweight title bout in America, and Joe did not let it go on too long, the referee intervening after John Henry had been down three times in the 1st.

On April 17th, long, lean Jack Roper made it three consecutive 1st round title defences for Joe, a record.

June 28th brought Louis face to face with Roper's physical opposite, a short, fat, balding Italian-American named Tony Galento. Galento had 'colour'. An ex-bouncer, now a saloon keeper, fighting out of Newark, New Jersey, he claimed to train on beer and cigars and probably did. Some of his 'victories' were rather dubious. But fans and sports-writers liked his left hook and his boasts of 'I'll moider da bum', and 'two-ton' Tony got his title shot. 75,000 turned up at the Yankee Stadium to see it too.

Galento had some surprises in store for the champion. In the 1st he staggered Joe with a left hook to the chin. In the 2nd Louis got his jab working and soon Galento's mouth was badly cut inside. His nose began to stream blood, and his right eye was split. Then Louis triggered off a right cross which dropped 'two-ton', although the game little fat man bounced right back up off the canvas without taking a count.

Louis continued to methodically cut him to pieces in the 3rd, but then came a sensation. Galento caught Joe in his gunsights and fired home a left hook to his head. Louis went down on his behind and took a count of '2'. Surely this was no upset in the making? It wasn't. Joe fenced Tony off for the remainder of the round, and then took him apart in the 4th, raining punches on the Italian non-stop until he went down under the ruthless onslaught. The referee had seen enough and Galento's gallant attempt to haul himself up by using the ropes was just a gesture of futile heroism.

Joe went home to Detroit to face Bob Pastor, on September 20th, the first time that a heavyweight title bout was put on in the motor city. And the next but last to be scheduled for 20 rounds. By 1939 this distance had more-or-less been consigned to the history books. The Louis strategy committee apparently wanted him to have plenty of time to track 'Rin-Tin-Tin' down.

It took 11, although things seemed to be heading for an early night at the start, Joe flooring Pastor three times in the opening round. Thereafter, he couldn't pin him down again until the 11th, when murderous rights scythed Bob to the canvas twice more, and left him in no fit state to continue.

Afterwards Pastor, who always managed to see a slightly different fight to everyone else, told Jim Braddock that he would have won if Louis had not split his right eye. Braddock eyed him cynically and observed: 'Yeah; he sure hits hard don't he.'

The Louis machine rolled on inexorably. The highlights of 1940 — and I use the word very loosely — were two defences against the Chilean, Arturo Godoy, whose main claim to fame lay in ruining the 'comeback' of Luis Firpo.

Godoy couldn't fight either. At Yankee Stadium on February 9th, he spent 15 rounds performing a creditable impersonation of Quasimodo, complete with bells. About the only thing missing was a few cries of 'sanctuary' (although the audience perhaps uttered some). Louis was bewildered at fighting a man who seemed to have no head or shoulders. Afterwards he rated it his worst performance.

Professional pride demanded that he get the job done more efficiently, so on June 20th, he gave Godoy a return. It really wasn't that much better, but at least Joe stopped him, the referee intervening after the Chilean had been floored twice in the 8th.

Boxing is an order of interlocking circles. Contenders fight each other and then meet champions, the customers pay to see whether the contender can knock the champion off his perch, and then it all starts to go round again. But by 1940 the circular motions had ground to a halt. Louis, the champion, was widely perceived as unbeatable, anybody who even looked like a contender was getting his chance anyway, and fewer and fewer people were paying to see the 'bums' get their rushes. Only 42,000 watched the two Godoy fights. So Louis the tour-de-force, was forced to tour. In addition to the increasingly blasé fight mecca of New York, Boston, Philadelphia, Detroit, St Louis and Washington saw him over the next twelve months. Few of the defences were of significance. Al McCoy (cuts, six), Gus Dorazio (two) and Tony Musto (nine) certainly don't merit any attention. Johnny Paychek (two) apparently did not even land a blow in return.

Red Burman's most noteworthy feat was a win over Tommy Farr, but it was one of those 'what fight were the judges watching?' verdicts, and Tommy reversed it three months later*. The most interesting thing about Burman's tilt at Louis was that Joe knocked him out (five) with a body punch.

Abe Simon, a behemoth at 250 lbs (114 kilos), did give Louis an interesting evening in Detroit on March 21st, 1941**. Simon had a good left jab and made a lot of the rounds close (one Judge had eight even) before Joe dragged up the heavy artillery in the 13th. Simon hauled himself up twice, but was taking a hammering on the ropes when the third man decided enough was enough.

Two months later in Washington, Louis resumed his acquaintance with the Baer family, only this time it was Max's younger (and bigger) brother, Buddy, who stood 6′ 6½″ and weighed 245 lbs. The fight was a controversial one. Wrongly believing the match would be postponed, referee Donovan got drunk and had not sobered up by the time it started. Baer took Louis by surprise in the opening stanza and knocked him halfway through the ropes for a '4' count. Thereafter Joe laced him methodically, but Buddy continued to be argumentative about it and marked Louis up around the eyes.

In round six Joe floored the big man with a right. Baer looked to be on the way out, but the bell rang. Louis did not hear it and floored Buddy for a second time. Baer was still out when the gong went for the 7th.

Donovan had four options: count Baer out on his stool *à la* Ruhlin, disqualify him, give him time to recover, or disqualify Louis. Cynics might argue that the latter was a non-starter: 'Uncle' Mike would have had Donovan on the breadline the following morning. In the end the still befuddled official decided to disqualify Baer. It may have been the wrong decision, but it would have been unfair to disqualify Louis for what was certainly an unintentional foul. And Arthur Donovan still had his job.

But now, as the countdown to America's entry into the war began, came two contenders of merit, Billy Conn the fast moving former light heavyweight champion, and Lou Nova, No. 1 heavyweight challenger, who had rung down the curtain on Max Baer.

* Farr retired in 1940 but attempted a disastrous comeback ten years later.

** This was the last heavyweight title fight scheduled for 20 rounds.

There are some who rate Conn the finest light heavyweight of all time. Debatable. He held the title less than a year and across the Atlantic Britain's Len Harvey had an equal claim to it. Like most 12½ stone men, Conn was afflicted by heavyweight-itis and gave up his version of the crown to go after Louis's. Conn also suffered from another common light-heavy ailment; lightus punchingus, (14 stoppages in 74 bouts). But he was a brilliant boxer; a veritable treat for connoisseurs of the arts and crafts of the game.

Few gave Conn much of a chance at the Polo Grounds on June 18th, 1941. They were not looking at it deeply enough. Louis was always vulnerable where ringmasters were concerned.

The fight fluctuated over the first six rounds. Louis won the first two sessions, stalking Conn. Billy got into his boxing in the next two, showing hand speed superior even to Louis's. Power wise, a pop gun was fighting a howitzer, but Conn relied on movement, not power. Joe won five and six but was being made to look ponderous.

The 7th was very close. One judge gave it to Louis on aggression, the referee (not Donovan for a change) and the second judge thought Conn's ringcraft had prevailed.

But from the beginning of the 8th Conn started to kick for home. His left hand was a whipping, darting rapier that flickered like a ghost into Louis's face. He used every inch of the ring, dancing on twinkling toes, making Joe look like a carthorse. At close range he tied Louis up and pounded short hooks and uppercuts into his body. Billy fully exploited Joe's vulnerability to rights too, cracking them across time and again. Louis was confused, outboxed, outthought, outsped.

In the 10th Joe made a dramatic bid to turn the tide and took the round on sheer aggression. But Conn moved even faster to come right back at him in the 11th, and in the next round Billy fired a non-stop stream of leather at the champion, cutting loose with both hands. At the bell Louis was hurt and rubber legged.

Most historians have written that at this point Conn only had to stand up to win. Not exactly. The referee and one judge had it 7–5–0 and 7–4–1 to Conn, the other judge all square at 6–6. The scoring meant that Louis could still win on points by taking all three rounds on the referee's card and two on the last judge's. But the advantage was clearly Conn's; he needed only one more round from the first two officials.

What Conn elected to do was inexplicable then and just as inexplicable today. He decided to try for a knock-out.

It was the chance Louis had waited and hoped for. His eyes gleamed and he met Billy head on. A right cross shook the challenger. He tried to hold on but Louis nailed him with a barrage of right uppercuts. Conn crumpled to the canvas and was counted out in the act of rising. There were just two seconds left in the round.

There is a curious, little known postscript to this fight. At the beginning of the 1970s, a boxing magazine published a series of sketches said to have been made by Conn before the fight. They depict a dream he is said to have had in which he has the title in his grasp only to be knocked out. As far as I know Conn never authenticated the sketches, so their provenance may be doubtful. But if he did make them, and at that time, they indicate a lack of real confidence. Before the contest Conn tried to upset Louis by insulting him on the telephone. Joe just laughed. Perhaps then, the ploy backfired on Billy and he became a victim of his own anxieties, the dream a self fulfilling prophecy.

By contrast to the battle with Conn, the Nova fight was a much less dramatic affair.

Lou Nova had come to prominence with a victory over Farr, a verdict hotly disputed by the Welshman who at that time was neglecting training and cavorting with the Hollywood set.

Max Baer also gained revenge over Tommy in America, a close decision but accepted by Farr who found himself on the canvas for the first time.

It was logical for Baer and Nova to meet. When they did Nova opened cuts inside Baer's mouth. By the end of the 11th, Max had swallowed too much blood and the referee called a halt.

At the age of 30 it looked like the end for boxing's greatest playboy, too much of himself left in bedrooms and night-clubs across America. Not quite. Max knocked out Galento, and was then put in with Pat Comiskey, an unbeaten young heavyweight who had risen as spectacularly as Louis and was being groomed for a million dollar gate title fight. Baer was supposed to be a stepping stone. Instead the fight ended in the 1st round with Comiskey draped across the top rope and out on his feet.

This sensational victory set up a return with Nova which sold out Madison Square Garden. For five rounds it was the Baer of yore, prancing twixt thunder and tomfoolery. He shook Nova from head to toe in the 3rd, laughed and walked away; floored him momentarily in the 4th, stepped back and put his tongue out. In the 5th he cascaded rights off Lou's jaw, causing a ringsider to die of heart of heart failure. Nova hung on and Max had shot his bolt. From the 6th onwards it was last stand stuff. Nova jabbed Baer to perdition, and the unleashed what he called his 'cosmic punch' — a fast right cross — in the 8th. Arthur Donovan put his arms around Max after he rose from the second knockdown.

Baer retired now, but not from life. He did some acting and performed a night-club routine with ex-light heavyweight champ 'Slapsy Maxey' Rosenbloom, another of boxing's fabled seekers after pleasure. On the night of November 21st, 1959, Baer called the receptionist from his hotel room and asked for a doctor. Did he want the House Doctor, she enquired? There was time for one last quip — 'Hell no, I want a man doctor' and then he died, of heart failure, in the ambulance on the way to hospital. He was a funny, outrageous, mad-cap of a man. I still think he got life right.

After thrilling victories in their previous fights, Louis–Nova, in New York on September 29th, 1941, was a distinct anti-climax. Nova, a student of yoga thirty years before it became popular, had the tools to provide an exciting challenge, a good jab, solid chin and a powerful right. However, the two men cancelled each other out, circling warily and jabbing for five rounds with an edge to Louis. In the next, Louis saw his opportunity, took it and here endeth the lesson. Then weeks later America was at war and life would never be the same again for Joe Louis; or for millions of others, many thousands of whom lost their lives.

Louis was inducted into the army in June, 1942. Before that he crammed in his 20th and 21st title defences, donating his purses to the Army and Navy relief funds. Here too one has to be fair to Mike Jacobs who gave substantial portions of his profits from the contests to the same organisations. The two challenges were rematches with Abe Simon — stopped in six — and Buddy Baer. Jack Blackburn had suffered a heart attack not long before the Baer fight and really should not have been in Louis's corner. Knowing how ill Blackburn was, Joe told him: 'You won't have to climb those steps but once Chappie.'* He knocked Baer out in the 1st round.

And there I wish we could leave Joe Louis, invincible, king of all he surveyed; Buddy Baer's awe-stricken tribute dinning in our ears: 'The only way I could have beaten Joe tonight was with a baseball bat.' But we can't.

Louis served in the Army for three and a half years, and did not defend the title again until June 19th, 1946. He did not serve in a combat role. His job was to visit the troops and raise morale. As part of this programme, Louis fought a series of exhibition bouts in both 1944 and '45.

The man who went into the Army was a lithe 28 year old; the man who came out of it was a pudgy, slightly balding 32 year old. His greatness had disappeared.

Attitudes towards race changed for the better. The war was after all a conflict which featured racial genocide. The victors did learn lessons from it. Their own past histories provoked guilty consciences. Germany was not the only country before the war where anti-Semitism existed. The Nazis and Fascists were not the only ones to believe in white supremacy. The horrors of the war bred a reaction against such beliefs. Also, the allied cause was a multi-racial effort. For example, the 'British' Army which won the battle of El-Alamein was

* Sources differ on the exact words.

half made up of Australians, New Zealanders, Indians, Pakistanis, South Africans, French, Poles and Greeks. Slim's 14th Army, which liberated Burma, consisted of 70% Asian troops.

As a representative of his race, patronising though it now sounds, Louis made an important contribution to the change in attitudes. As heavyweight champion he had gained grudging acceptance. It is doubtful whether it would have had any lasting impact. But when the war came along he seen as a prominent black man playing a patriotic role for his country, and it helped to break down barriers. In a memorable speech Jimmy Walker, the former Mayor of New York*, said of Louis that he had laid a rose on Abraham Lincoln's grave. Louis himself spoke a sentence which touched the hearts of Americans: 'We'll win; we're on God's side.'

But the patriot suffered as patriots often do. Rust and neglect entered his limbs; the Tax people were catching up with him. It is often said that the first casualty of war is the truth. The first casualty of peace is the soldier. By 1946 Louis owed the Inland Revenue a sum he would never be able to pay off during his lifetime.

Louis was effectively fighting to pay his debts when he met Billy Conn in a rematch. Tax debts and Mike Jacobs debts. Conn had also served in the Army during the war and had gone back a long way. Ticket prices were high at Yankee Stadium that June. 45,266 people paid $1,925,564** making it then the second richest fight in history, but by far the lowest attendance for any of the authentic million dollar gates. American living standards had gone up by 500% because of the war, the Depression was over, the public was hungry for major sporting events and Louis–Conn II was a fight people wanted to see, but it seems that for once 'Uncle' Mike miscalculated. Had he pitched the ticket prices lower*** then he would probably have had a full house paying well over two million.

Unhappily, those who baulked at the prices were right. The Louis–Conn sequel was a great occasion marred by the fight.

For seven pacific rounds Louis plodded after Conn who retreated at high speed. Billy's swift, slashing sword of a left hand had turned into a blunt paper knife, and the right which had hurt and befuddled Louis five years earlier had gone completely. In the 8th Joe finally caught up with Conn. A right hook dazed the challenger, and then a left hook-right cross combination put him down and out.

Conn had two more fights and then retired. At his peak his fighting style was very much that of Gene Tunney. Boxing breeds endless speculation. Would

* As Mayor, Walker played an important part in legalising boxing in New York.
** Without movie and radio rights.
*** Ringside seats were $100.

a Louis–Tunney fight have developed on the same lines as Louis–Conn I? My own view is yes, but without the same ending. Gene would never have lost his cool as Conn did, and was a bigger, stronger fighter anyway. However, it is, of course, all speculation.

There is another similarity between Conn and Tunney. After retiring, Conn sank his money into oil and made a fortune becoming the second richest ex-boxer in history, behind Tunney.

Louis made his 23rd defence on September 18th, 1946. His opponent was Tami Mauriello, a big hitter, but not really the man Jacobs wanted in the other corner. That should have been the new British champion, Bruce Woodcock, who was unbeaten, a good puncher, and would give the contest an international flavour. Unfortunately for Woodcock, Mauriello spoiled his U.S. debut by coming from behind to knock him out.

Mauriello also had a mild shock in store for Louis at the Yankee Stadium. They had been boxing only for a minute when Mauriello tagged Joe with an overarm right which almost floored him. Alas for Tami, he then threw caution to the winds and paid the price. Louis caught him coming in with a left hook which put him down. When he got up a combination finished Mauriello off. Louis said afterwards that he felt his old self again. He overlooked the fact that Tami had a deformed foot which prevented him boxing off his back foot.

Louis was busy with exhibition bouts for the next 15 months. Another one was lined up for the night of December 5th, 1947 at Madison Square Garden. But the fans were getting restless. The New York Commission wanted to know when Louis was going to defend the title again. Advance ticket sales were poor and Mike Jacobs was receptive to the arguments of Louis's opponent's manager, one Felix Bocchiccio. His man had won 17 of his last 20 so why not make it a proper fight? Jacobs went for the idea: he almost wished he hadn't.

Irrespective of whether Louis remembered 'Jersey' Joe Walcott from all those years ago at the training camp for the first Schmeling fight, he had no reason to be apprehensive. The years had not been kind to Walcott. Nothing much had gone right for him and despite his recent record the trade considered him strictly an 'opponent'.

The Press panned the contest. A few years earlier nobody would have considered it because Walcott too was black (although Louis–Lewis had filled the Garden). Now the mood had changed, almost without anybody noticing it, because neither Press nor public had a problem with Walcott's colour. They simply felt he just wasn't up to it.

The story of the fight can be summarised in one sentence by the British sports writer, Peter Wilson: 'Did you ever see the condemned man turn round and shoot the firing squad.'

Walcott planned to concentrate on Joe's ineradicable weakness — his vulnerability to right hand punches, and before a minute had elapsed he had fired the opening salvo. Louis threw a right; Walcott turned his chin away from the blow and countered viciously with his own right. The punch dropped Louis on his haunches but he was up without a count. Even so, he was hurt and began to lash out wildly. Sharpshooting with chillingly accurate precision, Walcott whipped in another right and then a left-right combination, and Louis was nearly dropped again. But just when it seemed that he could score the most sensational victory in boxing history, Walcott withdrew his heavy artillery and opened up instead with his secondary armaments, laying back and jabbing.

Walcott continued to box coolly in the 2nd and Louis made little headway with a frenzied attack. But the champion's pressure pulled back some of the lost ground in the 3rd, and coming up for the 4th Joe felt better.

But Walcott had been waiting patiently for a lull in order to fire the right again, and the chance now came. Louis hit the floor for the second time and took '7'. But yet again Walcott refused to try for the kill and was content to go back to fencing with his left.

The next four rounds were ultra-close. Louis applied the pressure but Walcott counter punched excellently and seemed to ringsiders to hold his own when they joined together in a punching rally.

The 9th was a thrilling round with Walcott winging home a right that almost closed Louis's left eye. Desperate now, Joe attacked relentlessly. But although he was rocked by a right and punished along the ropes Jersey Joe kept moving and just edged the round.

Louis again attacked non-stop throughout the next two and shaded both of them with Walcott content to box on the retreat, picking the champion off with neat jabs and hooks. In the 11th they rocked each other in a fierce exchange of rights and for a split second it looked as though Walcott might be in trouble. But the moment passed and Louis never again looked as though he might floor the challenger.

In the 12th Walcott spat whiplash rights at Joe's damaged left eye and the injury progressively worsened. When Louis tried to put on the pressure Walcott stepped quickly inside with a right uppercut and as Louis reeled he almost dropped him again with a whistling right cross. But now for the third time Walcott let his man off the hook and danced away, taking the battle off to long range again.

Down the home stretch Walcott was content to slip and ride, jab and move, whilst Louis churned forward. There was desperation in the champion's eyes over those closing rounds.

When the final bell went Louis congratulated Walcott and ducked through the ropes, but his handlers called him back for the official verdict. It was a shock. Judge Frank Forbes, 8–6–1 — Louis. Disbelief gave way to a torrent of boos.

Referee Ruby Goldstein 7–6–2 — Walcott, to cheers. Judge Marty Monroe, as everybody held their breath, 9–6–0 — Louis. The crowd didn't much like that one either. Even Louis thought he had lost and apologised to Walcott.

Ironically, on New York's supplementary points system (utilised in the event of a draw), the verdict was in *Walcott's* favour: Goldstein 15–11 and Forbes 12–9, with Monroe 11–10 to Louis. Basically, the disparity in scoring centred on three rounds 7 and 11, which the two judges gave to Louis against Goldstein's vote for Walcott, and 13 which Forbes and Goldstein decided in Louis's favour, Monroe opting for Walcott. What it meant was that if Forbes had seen either two of these rounds even, or one of them for Walcott, then his points score would have come into play and Walcott would have won. So near and yet so far.

But did Walcott actually deserve it? Three times he had victory in his grasp, and three times he spurned it. And with just a little more aggression in some of the other rounds he would have put the issue beyond doubt.

The controversy set up the return, at Yankee Stadium on June 25th, 1948. For 10 rounds Walcott boxed cunningly and was ahead on points. In the 3rd he again exploited Joe's defensive flaw and produced a right that registered another knockdown against the champion. Louis was up at '1' but he was dazed. Yet for the fourth time Walcott refused to pitch in and try for the knockout. As Jersey Joe was to prove, he was a slow learner!

When Walcott did open up it was at the wrong time. A worried Louis was pressing hard in the 11th, and it should have been bike time for Walcott. Instead he opted to slug it out. Louis sent him reeling with a left hook and then exploded a right under the heart. 'Jersey' Joe sagged, and Louis tore in with both hands. Walcott slithered down the ropes and just failed to beat the count.

Louis announced from the ring that this would be his last fight. However, he delayed formal announcement of his retirement until March 1st, 1949. Interim, he engaged in a long series of exhibition bouts He was also involved in a series of complex manoeuvres outside the ring. Mike Jacobs was old and ill and the 20th Century Sporting Club was sliding into oblivion. Louis, under the aegis of his own company, Joe Louis Enterprises, was keen to promote a tournament to find his successor, and had signed the four leading contenders. But he needed financing. To obtain it he approached two wealthy businessmen, Jim Norris and Arthur Wirtz. Norris was a sports entrepreneur who owned the Chicago Stadium and two Ice Hockey teams. Some sources put his personal fortune as high as $400 million. Norris and Wirtz were keen to get into boxing*, but they wanted to control it themselves. They formed the International Boxing

* Norris already owned a chunk of Madison Square Garden.

Club and made Louis an offer which he genuinely couldn't refuse: $200,000 for his contracts with the contenders, plus $20,000 a year and a slab of IBC stock. In addition, $150,000 to officially retire*. So Louis sold his title in the end.

The proposed elimination tournament never happened. The overall crop of contenders were a poor bunch anyway. Jimmy Bivins had been recognised as the best for a while during Louis's time in the Army, but by 1949 had faded from view. Elmer Ray flickered on and off occasionally, but never solidly established himself. Joe Baksi, an ex-miner, had ruined Bruce Woodcock, but refused to fight Louis. Woodcock himself was potentially a good fighter. He had the basics; courage, a good left and a hefty right. But he never had a top flight trainer and remained very amateurish in style. Lee Oma was useful, but flopped badly against Woodcock. Freddy Mills, light-heavyweight champion when Louis retired, was irresistibly game, but too small to be a real heavyweight, and like his fellow countryman Woodcock, received a dreadful beating from Baksi.

Which left the top four, who were actually supposed to box off for the title. Gus Lesnevitch was the ex-175 lbs holder but had been beaten by Bivins, Woodcock, Mills and Lee Oma. Lee Savold later defeated Woodcock in a fight recognised by the British Board of Control as being for the 'vacant' world title. However, in 1949 he was coming off a loss to Woodcock. The I.B.C. decided that neither Lesnevitch or Savold would draw diddly squat and axed them. Interestingly, they were the two white fighters. Boxing — in line with American sport as a whole — had changed drastically.

The vacant heavyweight championship of the world, so the I.B.C. decided, would be picked over by two blacks. 'Jersey' Joe Walcott selected himself. In the other corner would be a 27 year old from Georgia, fighting out of Cincinnati: Ezzard Charles.

* Mike Jacobs was also paid $150,000 to retire.

Volume Five

Ezzard Charles to Sonny Liston

Round Seventeen: Joe and the Cobra

In the summer of 1949 Jersey Joe Walcott was 35 years old, an age at which most fighters have settled for a rocking chair. He was born, Arnold Raymond Cream* in Merchantville, New Jersey, on January 31st, 1914 and became a professional fighter young in life, possibly around 1929 because his early record is not available.

The only manager listed for Walcott is Felix Bocchicichio, an Italian-American with more than a passing connection with the mob. It is not clear who managed Walcott prior to Bocchicichio, or precisely when the latter took him over. The story goes that Walcott had quit the ring in disappointment and that Bocchicichio found Joe and his family starving in a cellar in Camden, New Jersey. Bocchicichio bought them a hamper of food and persuaded Walcott to give boxing another try. It may be true; Bocchicichio and Walcott seem to have developed a genuine father and son relationship.

Up to his first contest with Louis, Walcott had had 53 recorded contests winning 42 (25 kayos) against 10 losses (3 by kayo) and a draw. This is by no means as bad a record as some have maintained. However, it is certainly not that of a champion or leading contender, although most of Joe's defeats were sustained before Bocchicichio took over. Prior to that Walcott's career was going nowhere and fighters tended to avoid him because he made them look bad even in winning. Jersey Joe was the archetypal cagey pro, solid technique based on defence, hard, sharp-shooting counter punching, and a great round zero where any form of entertainment was concerned. But Joe's safety first tactics did ensure that he stayed around for a long time.

By contrast, Ezzard Mack Charles was an exciting fighter to watch, at least up to February, 1948.

Charles was born in Laurenceville, Georgia on July 7th, 1921. Like many other black families from the deep south the Charles's migrated northwards and settled in Cincinnati, Ohio.

Ezzard Charles had a brilliant amateur career winning all his bouts, and the national middleweight title twice. When he turned professional in 1940 he won his first 20 on the trot, scoring 14 kayos. By the time he contested the vacant title with Walcott, Ezzard had been to the post 69 times, despite three years war service in the Army**, winning 63 (and 1 draw) with 40 stoppages. He had been

* He took his ring name from the great turn of the century welterweight champion, Joe Walcott.

** He won a series of inter-service tournaments.

stopped only once himself, Lloyd Marshall, an outstanding light-heavyweight contender whom Ezzard later halted twice.

Charles was a fast moving raider with a good jab and swift hands who put his punches together in rapid-fire combinations topped by plenty of venom. He was known, appropriately, as the 'Cincinnati Cobra'. Add to his other attributes a sound defence and supple body movement and you have a picture of a very good all round fighter indeed.

He started out as a middleweight but grew into a light-heavy and then a heavy, although it is accurate to say that at 13 stone and 6ft Charles was really a big 175 pounder. By 1948 there were important names on his record in all three divisions. At middle he twice outscored Charley Burley. A forgotten name today, Burley was rated by Archie Moore as the best he ever fought. At light-heavy Ezz beat Marshall, 'Broadwalk' Billy Smith, ex-champion Anton Christoforidis, and future champs Joey Maxim and Moore. Campaigning amongst the heavies, Charles had lost to Elmer Ray and Jimmy Bivins, but twice thrashed Bivins in return.

In January, 1948, Ezzard scored what was probably his finest victory. Matched with Archie Moore in Cleveland, Charles crossed a perfect right to Moore's chin in the 8th and left him cold pie on canvas. Supercharged by this performance, Ezzard tore into Sam Baroudi in Chicago five weeks later and knocked him out in the 10th. Baroudi never regained consciousness.

Distraught, Charles decided to quit boxing. Only a touching and memorable gesture by Baroudi's father, who cabled him that he was not responsible for the tragedy, persuaded Ezzard to continue. On paper the next twelve months appeared to be the most impressive of Charles' career. He outpointed Bivins and Maxim again, stopped Elmer Ray and forced the referee to rescue Joe Baksi. But in fact the blazing 'Cincinnati Cobra' had gone to be replaced by an ultra cautious defensive fighter who was frightened to unload on an opponent. The Maxim fight was recalled by those who saw it as just about the dreariest bout they had ever witnessed. Even so, it spoke volumes for Charles' ability that he was able to change his style so effectively.

Jersey Joe Walcott and Ezzard Charles were matched for the vacant title in Chicago on June 22nd, 1949. It was the first time since Louis–Braddock that a really important heavyweight title bout had been venued outside New York and for the same reason; America's fistic capital refused to sanction it as a championship contest.

Titular disputes wee not new in boxing. They harked back even to the eighteenth century when Mendoza and Belcher both claimed the vacant championship. More recently, no less than four men had disputed the middleweight title after Ketchel's death. This was anarchic: boxing needed champions, not pretenders.

By the Twenties America's 48 States* each had its own boxing commission. 46 formed a loose knit organisation to represent them; the National Boxing Association. Later on the N.B.A. would be supported by the South and Central American countries, and the Orient Boxing Federation representing Asia.

New York and California remained aloof from the N.B.A. New York was by this time well established as the fight mecca of the world and the Commission (actually the New York Athletic Association) regarded itself as the law giver of American boxing. Internationally, it was generally supported by the European Boxing Union (then called the International Boxing Union).

In terms of resolving title disputes the N.B.A. and N.Y.A.A.C. proved to be about as useful as one legged men in arse kicking competitions. The anarchy simply became more organised.

Disputes began to flare up in the late Twenties. Sometimes all out confrontations were avoided. When Max Rosenbloom won New York's light-heavyweight championship, the N.B.A. refused to go along with it but did not recognise anyone else. It worked in reverse when Freddie Miller gained the N.B.A. featherweight crown; New York initially withheld recognition but did not nominate other candidates. Miller and Rosenbloom ultimately secured universal recognition.

Unfortunately, the very presence of two competing bodies ensured that they would end up eventually in direct opposition to each other. The middleweight division was hopelessly split between N.Y.A.A.C. and N.B.A. champions throughout most of the Thirties, and the situation repeated itself amongst the lightweights in the Forties.

When Louis retired New York, backed by the E.B.U., refused to recognise Charles-Walcott as being for the vacant heavyweight crown. Only Britain wandered out of their camp, later endorsing Savold–Woodcock. The opposition was not directed at Charles and Walcott. Louis had sold the title to I.B.C. Norris and Wirtz quickly found Frankie Carbo and his mafioso chum 'Blinky' Palermo, previously silent associates of Jacobs, muscling in on them. But that was not the main objection. The I.B.C.–Carbo–N.B.A. axis threatened New York's jealously guarded privilege of being the arbiter of the heavyweight title. In short, it was a power play. Endemic in this situation was what is happening in boxing today.

While New York and its acolytes sat on their hands, Walcott and Charles contested the N.B.A. title. It proved to be a dull battle of jabs in which Charles held the upper hand. There were few highlights. In the 7th, Ezzard rocked

* Hawaii and Alaska became States in 1959.

Walcott with a right to the head and followed up with a couple of whiplash flurries. In the 10th he split Joe's lips. Well behind on points, Walcott finally attempted to do something in the 15th, throwing a series of rights, which Charles easily avoided. The decision for Ezzard was unanimous, 77–73, and a brace of 78–72s (a rather curious points scoring system for 15 rounds).

The main bit of interest was the behaviour of Charles' manager, Jake Mintz. Mintz was an obtuse character who shared Mrs Malaprop's gift for fracturing the English language. Once asked by an exasperated reporter: 'Do you know the President's "English"?' Jake replied cheerfully: 'Can't be; you've got to be an American.' After the decision was announced in his man's favour, Mintz became so excited that he fainted, much to the amusement of the press corps.

Not being recognised by New York State did not prevent Charles from fighting there. On August 10th he defended against light heavyweight Gus Lesnevitch. At 34, Gus was almost as old as Walcott. He seemed to have based his career on beating Tami Mauriello (four times), but Billy Conn, Bob Pastor, Jimmy Bivins, Bruce Woodcock and Lee Oma had all whipped him. By 1949 he was not even the 175 lbs champion, Freddie Mills having relieved him of the crown, and in his previous fight Lesnevitch had failed against Joey Maxim for the American light heavyweight title. How he made Louis's top four and rated a title fight is inexplicable even in the labyrinth world of professional boxing. The fight was stopped in the 7th with both Gus's eyes crying rivers of blood.

Even more mysterious was Ezzard's second defence against an opponent named Pat Valentino in San Francisco on October 14th. At the end of the 4th a U.F.O. turned up and aliens abducted the audience. Well, that's as good an explanation as any for the fact that hardly anybody seems to have either watched or written about the contest. Charles–Valentino is the most forgotten fight in heavyweight history. For the record, Ezzard kayoed Pat in the 8th.

A third undistinguished defence followed in Buffalo on August 15th, 1950. Freddie Beshore was really a light heavyweight. Charles stopped him in 14 very forgettable rounds.

Effectively, Beshore was just a tune up for the biggest fight of Ezzard's career, September 27th, 1950 at the Yankee Stadium: Joe Louis.

Louis's return was hardly voluntary. He had to do it because of his tax debt which by 1950 was $500,000 and rising. It has been suggested that the Federal Government should have written it off*. It is quite impossible to justify this argument. While one can sympathise with the fact that Louis lost four peak years in the Army, and donated two purses to service benevolent funds, the fact is that

* They did later cancel part of the debt.

because of his status as a sports star he never saw action, a contrast to actor James Stewart who flew bombing missions over Germany. The ordinary servicemen who survived hell holes such as Bastogne and Okinawa also lost several years out of their lives; and they still had to pay their taxes.

The only wartime action Louis saw was between the bedsheets with a string of girlfriends. Nice work if you can get it, but hardly an entitlement for preferential treatment over G.I.s who risked life and limb on the battlefield. Negotiating his retirement package, Louis told a lawyer: 'I want to play golf, I don't want to work.' Whilst it was never pointed out to him that he would eventually have to pay his deferred taxes and 'expenses', Joe was a willing partner in the avoidance. He plainly wanted the best of all worlds: no taxes and a luxurious lifestyle without working. Of course, nobody likes paying tax but without it the armed forces which defended America in World War II could not have existed.

Television was prepared to pay a substantial sum for Charles–Louis. The fans were not. Although ticket prices were cheap, only 13,500 turned up at the Yankee Stadium. The gate receipts of $205,000 were eye-openingly down on the $264,000 returns for the Willie Pep–Sandy Saddler featherweight title bout at the same venue three weeks earlier. The live gate reflected both disillusionment with Charles and the fact that Louis's best days were well behind him. Joe's last fight, with Walcott, had hardly been entertaining. At one point the referee had told them to: 'Get the lead out of your arses and do some fighting.' After their first encounter a reporter had described Louis as: 'Slower than a peg-legged man crossing a swamp', a neat piece of imagery.

Charles–Louis is one to draw the veil over. For nine tedious rounds Charles kept his jab in Joe's face and built up an unassailable lead. Louis was nothing now. The legs wouldn't respond to the mind's promptings; the pulverising pistons, once his fists, were now motionless and steamless.

Just once there was a chance. It came in the 10th, a left hook out of memory which had Charles hurt and hanging on. But the moment passed, and Joe's chances turned to ashes which blew gently away on the night air.

In the 14th the sparse crowd sat in mourning as they watched the funeral cortege of the Louis legend. Ezzard drove him to the ropes and lashed him there with both hands. Peter Wilson wrote:

> *'It was tragic to see Louis looking like a child who has been thrashed with a belt buckle...and then getting a right uppercut which splashed blood from his nose and mouth clear out of the ring, and which nearly tore his left eye from its socket.'*[1]

1 'More Ringside Seats' p.20.

Charles eased off. Later he recalled it was like hitting his father. The decision was a formality. Some nostalgic ringsiders thought Louis might have shaded five rounds. In reality it was no more than one with perhaps a couple even.

Afterwards, the ex-champion held sad court in his dressing room. Wilson asked if there had been a turning point:

'Sure — the first round.'

The one liners were still in place even if the rest of it had gone.

Louis got up and told the journalists:

'Thank you all very much. I done my best.'

Outside were just the memories of happier times.

Ezzard Charles' victory made him the undisputed champion, New York having reluctantly agreed to recognise the winner. The other malcontents fell into line, save Britain where Savold was now officially champion. Three months earlier he had cut up and stopped Woodcock. But even in Britain nobody took Lee seriously. (Nor did he.) The consensus was that the bout should have been staged on April Fool's Day. Woodcock was anyway a busted flush and would lose his British title (to Jack Gardner) and retire by the end of the year.

On December 5th, Charles made his fifth defence, another light heavyweight hand picked for him by the I.B.C. Nick Barone had done no more than Lesnevitch, Valentino and Beshore to justify a title shot. He went in 11 unremarkable rounds at Cincinnati.

Six weeks later Lee Oma had his chance in New York. Oma at least was a heavyweight. But not much of one. He had been disinterestedly counted out against Woodcock, and beaten by Walcott. January 12th, 1951 saw another long range display of boredom from Ezzard. In the 10th he finally opened up and when Oma went down after taking a hiding on the ropes, the referee saw it as an excuse to put everybody out of their misery.

Meanwhile, Jersey Joe Walcott was, like 'Ole Man River', still rolling along. After losing to Charles he crossed the Atlantic and stopped Ollie Tandberg, a Swede who had surprisingly beaten Baksi. After losing to Walcott, Tandberg paid him a unique compliment: 'I have never known a man who could hit and be hit so hard.'

Back in America Joe knocked out top light heavy Harold Johnson, thus completing a family double. In 1936 he had kayoed Harold's father!* He

* Both in the 3rd round.

followed up with three more victories, but in November, 1950 was surprisingly outpointed by an iron-jawed young slugger from Utah named Rex Layne.

However, defeat or not, it was Jersey Joe who once again received the call to share the ring with Charles. The fight took place in Detroit on March 7th, 1951.

Nobody expected it to be a good fight and it wasn't. Charles was his usual cautious self and Joe his usual negative self. The bout went 15 rounds of jabs, tactics, and manoeuvres, all very nice for the connoisseurs, but hardly calculated to appeal to the traditional genre of boxing fan who likes to see blood, gore, and death at high noon. (Figuratively speaking.) For them the only highlight was the right hook to the jaw with which Ezzard floored Walcott for '8' in the 9th. Charles ran out a clear winner.

On May 30th Ezzard featured in an even more boring opus with Joey Maxim at Chicago. Maxim was now the world 175 lb champion, and was under the astute management of Jack 'Doc' Kearns. But Joey was the antithesis of the 'Doc's' previous champions, Dempsey and Walker. He was purely a percentage fighter who scorned attack and made a religion of defence. Maxim had a fast left jab, and a strong body and chin, but his style was entirely devoid of any excitement. As Charles had whipped him three times already, and as both were ultra-cautious fighters, anybody who knew anything about the fight game avoided this one like a leper's loin cloth. Predictably, Ezzard won an uninspired waltz on points.

Immediately after this victory Ezzard stunned the boxing world by announcing that his next opponent would be... Jersey Joe Walcott!

What?...again?... screamed the fans. Were they expected to sit through another 45 minutes of 'Come Dancing'? Alas, yes. But Jersey Joe thought: 'Wouldn't it be nice to have a different ending this time?' Whether he let his mind run all the way back through history to that long ago day on the barge when Corbett knocked out Choynski, we do not know. Probably not. What we do know is that Walcott was fed up with being an all the way loser, and at 37 he had precious little time left to do something about it.

What do you do when you're pushing 40 and up against a man younger, faster and more able than you are? Answer: fall back on cunning!

Surprisingly, 28,272 turned out at Forbes Field, Pittsburgh on July 18th, 1951. Jake Mintz was as usual the centre of attention, complaining so vehemently about the officials that he was ordered from the ring and had to watch the fight from a ringside seat. Afterwards the Pennsylvania Boxing Commission banned him indefinitely.

For four rounds the fight was dull and uninteresting. Charles boxed warily behind his left jab and piled up the points. Jersey Joe seemed to be waiting for something. But what?

In the 5th Walcott went on the attack and began to whirl rights around

Charles' head. One grazed his jaw and the champion felt a shiver run down his spine. But he came back and whaled away at Joe's body. Walcott stood his ground and kept throwing rights. One of them crashed against Charles' jaw and hurt him.

The 6th, and Walcott continued to attack with the right, hurling it like a club at the champion. But now Charles was cool and calm, stepping methodically to his right and watching Joe's big bombs whistle past his ear.

The 7th: Walcott came out aggressively again, tossing rights for all he was worth. Charles kept moving to his right to avoid them.

Then it happened. Nobody could have foreseen it, not Charles, not Mintz, not the audience. Nobody but Walcott who had planned it and now executed it. Charles moved to his right one last time, and Joe pulled the pin out of the hand grenade and threw it. It exploded on the side of Charles' jaw, a left hook that carried every ounce of power that Walcott possessed, a left hook filled with every iota of frustration, bitterness and misery which had built up inside him down through the long years.

Charles pitched forward on his knees, resting his gloves on the canvas to prevent himself from falling forward on his face. At '8' he levered himself back on his haunches, and as the referee tolled off the last second he reeled to his feet, only to fall over backwards and lie spread-eagled on the canvas.

Ezzard Charles had fallen off a mountain on which he had never perched securely in the first place. Although a genuinely gifted fighter, he was a cheese champion. His eight successful defences embraced four light-heavies (one washed up), a nonentity, a trial horse and two old men. To be fair, the heavyweight ranks were not exactly creaking under the weight of talent. But the likes of Savold and Woodcock, and the emergent Rex Layne and Roland La Starza, would have been preferable to the Valentinos and Lesnevitches. None would have beaten Charles, but Messrs Carbo and Norris ensured that they did not get the opportunity. When the title went it was to another fighter whom the I.B.C. could control.

Control of the heavyweight title was crucial. By the early Fifties over 16 million homes in America had television. Boxing was the ideal television sport and the heavyweights were what the armchair public wanted to see. In his book *Sonny Boy*, Rob Steen records that televised fights even topped 'I Love Lucy' in the ratings. Boxing delivered the big numbers in the financial jackpot.

Return bout clauses dogged boxing up to the Seventies. They meant that Joe Bloggs and Fred Nerd could play volleyball with the title while everybody else looked on. Nobody really wanted a fourth helping of Walcott-Charles (save Charles and Mintz), but the return clause ensured there would be one.

Interim, Charles did what he should have done as champion; went in with Rex Layne and stopped him. He then returned to boring normality, he and Maxim performing their traditional dance routine — slow, slow, very very slow. It was their fifth and thankfully, last waltz.

Walcott–Charles IV was not a marked improvement. It went 15 rounds to a decision on June 5th, 1952, in Philadelphia. After nine dour rounds Charles was in front, but over the final six Walcott pulled out all the old pro's tricks, in particular, cocking the left hook with which he had destroyed Charles in Pittsburgh, and feinting to throw it. Gun-shy, Charles drew back warily and allowed Joe to seize the initiative. At the end of the 14th both ringside judges had it dead even on their cards and it was Walcott who staged the grandstand finish to win a close but unanimous decision. The scoring was 9–6–0, 8–7–0, and 7–6–2.

On September 23rd Walcott returned to Philadelphia to put his title on the line against a dynamic, hard-slugging, Italian American, Rocky Marciano. Rocky had no knowledge whatsoever of the science of boxing, but he had won 42 out of 42, 37 by knockout. Before the fight Walcott told reporters: 'This guy's crude. If I can't beat him then you can take my name out of the record books.'

Marciano was small for a heavyweight, only 5′ 11″ and 184 lbs. He had short arms, the shortest of any man who ever held the world heavyweight title. But at 6′ and 194 lbs Walcott was not a giant either, and Marciano's punching power was already legendary, so terrifying that one opponent groaned that even his jabs were like hammer blows. He was immensely strong and his chin seemed to be made of concrete. Nobody, it was said, could put him down.

Walcott promptly dispelled that notion. They had been fighting for only 60 seconds when he hit Marciano with a magnificent left hook flush on the jaw. Rocky literally walked into the punch and Joe placed it perfectly, the blow travelling a mere six inches. It carried every ounce of power he possessed, a punch even more stunning than the one that had disintegrated Charles. Walcott watched Rocky go pitching forwards to the floor and circled away grinning. He had destroyed this crude young novice... but wait... he half turned and then gaped in disbelief. Marciano was on his feet again with the referee's arm coming down for only the fourth time. Not only was he up, but charging too, an enraged bull, horns open, seeking to gore the matador.

Walcott met him with a venomous, dazzling, array of punches, jabs, hooks, crosses, uppercuts, ripping them into Marciano with precision savagery. But Rocky took them all and whaled back, missing six for every one he landed, but hurting the champion every time he did land. Walcott returned to his corner at the end of the round wondering what this man was made of!

Throughout the next three rounds Walcott dealt out a vicious boxing lesson. Steely jabs and hooks — red tipped darts barbed with cutting power — fired straight and true into Marciano's face tearing open his mouth, ripping his nose, and bringing up lumps under both eyes. Crosses and uppercuts were rifled home with power and accuracy. Yet Marciano took them and kept coming on, spitting out the blood. It was a brutal, thrilling, spectacle. Walcott's strategy now was to cut Rocky down punch by punch, whilst he protected himself against the bombs the challenger hurled at him, either blocking or slipping and riding them.

In the 5th Jersey Joe moved inside a wild, swinging, punch, and exploded a devastating right hook on Rocky's cheek. The challenger's knees buckled, but by a supreme effort he stayed upright and then he roared back into the fray. However, Walcott was the sharpshooter supreme, landing everything he threw, making Marciano look crude and raw with a wonderful display of ringcraft.

But now in the 6th Marciano was at last reaching Walcott. They whaled away savagely, ripping and tearing at one another, and the crowd roared as Walcott broke off the exchange with blood streaming from a gash over his left eye. Then battle was joined again, heads met with a savage crack, and when they broke away blood was pouring from a cut high on Rocky's forehead.

In the 7th Marciano kept coming, literally unstoppable, and Walcott began to wilt. Marciano harpooned savage punches into his body and then thudded away at his head. The tide of battle had begun to turn, and Rocky kept up the pressure throughout the next three rounds. Walcott called on every atom of knowledge that he had accumulated through 22 hard years of ring warfare and continued to fight a heroic rearguard action. But Marciano would not be denied. Seemingly, no power on earth could stop him. He had not taken a backward step since the opening bell.

But in the 11th Walcott dredged up new reserves from deep within himself and mounted a thunderous body attack. A fusillade of punches played around Rocky's ribs and heart causing him to shudder and gasp. Then the champion switched his attack back to the head. A left hook ripped open another cut under Marciano's right eye, and then another to the jaw had him sagging at the knees, before yet another leather bound bomb exploded against his chin and rocked him back on his heels.

It was a big round for Walcott. So too was the 12th in which he continued his savage body attack, pounding Rocky all through the round. One murderous right hook to the stomach nearly dropped Marciano and as he doubled up Walcott fired in a left hook on the damaged eye. Marciano lurched and shuddered. Badly stricken, he reeled away from the ceaseless barrage of punishment. His face was now a crimson mask, and his body was sore and red, yet he was still trying to fight back, still trying to fix one of those bone crushing swings on target.

At the end of the 12th the referee had it 7–4–1, and the judges 7–5–0 and 8–4–0, all for Walcott, which meant that even if Rocky took all the last three rounds Walcott would retain his title on a draw. Joe knew that he was ahead on points and when he came out for the 13th he was full of confidence — too full!

Throughout the fight the champion had stayed away from the ropes, beating out his dramatic fistic symphony from centre stage. Now he sought to invite Rocky into a position where he could counter with an explosive right to the chin. So he let Rocky bull him into the ropes.

For a split second they stood facing each other, staring deep into each other's eyes. Then simultaneously they fired mighty right hooks. But Rocky was a fraction of a second faster on the draw. His punch travelled a few short inches and hit Walcott's jaw with the force of a bullet, almost ripping his head off. Joe's punch merely stroked the challenger's chin. Walcott pitched backwards into the ropes and then slowly and painfully crumpled to the floor, his left arm entwining itself around the middle rope and he fell. He came to a halt sitting on the canvas with his head cradled against his arm, completely unconscious. A swinging left from Rocky merely brushed his hair as he went down.

The referee tolled off the count '...eight...nine...ten...', and then spread his arms out wide whilst Rocky's ravaged face broke into a grisly smile. He had stared defeat in the face and vanquished it to win the heavyweight title with the most dramatic one punch knockout in history.

It was one of the greatest fights ever and the coronation of one of boxing's most formidable champions.

Round Eighteen: The Brockton Blockbuster

When I sat down to write this chapter I was torn between calling it 'The Brockton Blockbuster' — Rocky Marciano's ring de guerre — or 'Boxing's Nietzsche', because Marciano's was truly a triumph of the will. According to his trainer, Charlie Goldman, Marciano had:

> *'Wild punches, no balance, legs too far apart, stride too long, no defence, stands up too straight, needs to get more body into punches, not enough leverage, doesn't know how to use combinations, relies too much on the right, no left hook.'*[1]

He might also have added that Marciano had virtually no jab, was only 5′ 11″ and 184 lbs, and at 68″ had the reach of a middleweight.

Based on these defects, Rocky's boxing card should have read — go directly to Palookaville, do not pass go and do not collect three million dollars.

Why then did Marciano become the only undefeated heavyweight champion in history? How did he compile the highest knock-out ratio of all the heavyweight champions, 88%?* First, he hit with terrifying force. Any sort of punch from Marciano, and in particular the overarm right which he called 'Susie Q', was painful. Most boxers need to marry up their basic power to timing and accuracy. Marciano's delivery remained crude; his natural punching power was simply awesome.

Second, he was himself almost impervious to punishment. Opponents saw punches which had flattened other heavyweights just bounce off Rocky. Not only could they not down him; when they could not stop his relentless advance they became demoralised themselves.

Last, but not least, were Marciano's inner furies. On the surface he was utterly fearless, on one occasion visiting a leper colony and to the horror of his entourage, shaking hands with the inmates. Yet inwardly he was driven by fear. Of ending up like his father who toiled much of his life in menial servitude in a shoe factory, a sad and penniless, figure. Such fears fuelled Marciano's will-power.

They also produced less attractive traits. The man who shook hands with lepers was also a mean man who misered his bucks. And a fighter not overly bothered about how he won. Rocky used his head as a third fist, and slugged

* At the time of writing Mike Tyson stands at 84% and George Foreman 87%.

1 'Rocky Marciano' p.96.

away below the belt.

He was born Rocco Marchegiano (pronounced Mark-a-jahn-o) on September 1st, 1923 in Brockton, Massachusetts, the son of Italian immigrants. Father Pierino was a First World War veteran who told his son: 'Don't ever work in a shoe factory.'

Rocco didn't. But his early jobs were almost as menial and exhausting. He worked on a coal truck, in a candy factory and as a labourer and dreamed, like his fellow Bay Stater John L. Sullivan, of being a baseball star. In 1943 he was inducted into the Army. It was there that he began to box.

Marciano's first amateur fights were at Fort Lewis, Washington. He lost to Joe DiAngelis, and, while on leave, to Henry Lester in Brockton. He was disqualified for kneeing Lester in the private parts.

Leaving the army, Rocky took his first tentative steps towards becoming a professional fighter. The outcome was hardly encouraging. A trainer told him he was too old, too slow, too short and too light; forget it kid.

Marciano decided to give it a go anyway. Under the name 'Joey Mack' he knocked out one, Lee Epperson, in three rounds. The promoter attempted to bilk him, and Rocky went back to the amateurs. During the next sixteen months he boxed in the Simon Pure Ranks in Massachusetts and tried out for the Baseball Leagues. He lost two more fights, one to Coley Wallace who later played Joe Louis in a film of Louis's life. Misunderstanding has arisen about the Wallace verdict, one writer claiming that it was in the professional ring. Incorrect. Although Rocky broke the rules by re-enlisting as an amateur, the fight was, officially at least, unpaid*.

A broken thumb prevented Marciano from representing Massachusetts in the national championships. It also cost him his job, digging ditches for the local gas company. These were two components of a treble disappointment. Part three was the discovery that he was not good enough to make the grade as a baseball player. Unlikely as it seemed, only the pro ring remained a viable option for success.

Rocco Marchegiano finally committed himself to it in the summer of 1948. He was nearing 25, old to begin a professional career. He amended his name to Rocky Marciano. It rolled more easily off Anglo-Saxon tongues, and summoned up visions of power and durability.

Management was initially a problem. While an amateur Marciano had signed an agreement with his trainer, Gene Caggiano, that Caggiano would manage him if Rocky turned pro. But Gene had two strikes against him. In the first place he wasn't a professional manager or trainer. In the second Marciano

* Unofficially, Marciano was earning more as an amateur than for the Epperson bout.

claimed that Gene owed him sixty dollars. When Caggiano telephoned to remind him of their agreement, Rocky told him: 'Wipe your arse with it.' He had already been in contact with Al Weill, a top New York fight pilot. Weill's response was something along the lines of: 'Maybe; let's see how you make out in the sticks.'

From July, 1948, to May, 1949, Marciano won 15 straight inside the distance. Nobody went beyond five; 9 didn't see out the first. In his 17th, Don Mogard lasted to the final bell. Mogard was of the jab and move school, the type who always give sluggers a hard time. So were Ted Lowry and Red Applegate, two other not particularly distinguished fighters who took Rocky the distance. Lowry in fact did it twice.

By December, when he made his Madison Square Garden debut, Rocky was firmly inside the Weill–Goldman camp. Weill was not however his manager off record. He had officially given up managing fighters to take on the position of Garden matchmaker, thus creating a conflict of interest*. That was for the record. Behind the scenes Weill was still managing his boxers, the conflict readily apparent. Singing and dancing even further in the background were Messrs Norris (whom Marciano came to loathe), Carbo and Palermo. I.B.C. owned the Garden; and Al Weill.

Marciano slaughtered an Irish fighter, Pat Richards, to get things off to a good start in the Big Apple. Four weeks later Weill matched him with unbeaten Carmine Vingo, also Italian-American, likewise a power hitting slugger, in the main supporting bout to a Garden light heavyweight clash between Nick Barone and Dick Wagner. The second billing surprised those who were not in the know. Things became more easily understood when the I.B.C. matched winner Barone with Ezzard Charles for the heavyweight title.

Those expecting a bone-crushing thriller between Marciano and Vingo were not disappointed. It was a brutal, torrid slugfest. Vingo was floored in both the first two rounds, but came back and shook Marciano. He did it again in the 5th, although by this time his face had been pounded into raw meat. Rocky roared back at him. In the 6th he dropped Carmine for keeps. Almost literally. Vingo hovered between life and death for several days. He recovered, but never fought again, and was left with a permanent limp. Given Marciano's power, it is fortunate that this was his only brush with ring tragedy, but most of the men he fought were never much good again.

Rocky finally made main event Garden status three months after the Vingo nightmare, against another Italian-American, Roland La Starza. Italian fighters were very much rule roosters in the '40s and '50s. Those decades produced a tremendous clutch of Italian origin champions, including ring immortals like

* Weill's stepson became Marciano's official manager.

Willie Pep. Only the flyweight division, which the British still largely kept under lock and key, is missing from the list of Italian successes. Boxing reflects the social upturns of American life. First the Irish had climbed out of the ghetto, then the Jews, now the Italians. Later it would be the turn of Blacks and Hispanics.

Roland La Starza was a fast moving boxer with a good left hand and a tight defence. Some regarded him as a champion in the making, but in fact he had received a similar careful build up to Bill Brennan 30 years earlier. Although La Starza had posted 37 straight victories, the only name of consequence on his record was Cesar Brion, an Argentinian who later outpointed Britain's Jack Gardner (his best victory). Brion was competent, but never championship material. La Starza's punching record was the story of a light hitter. Over half of the wannabees, trial horses and outright palookas who wrote his fight biography had succeeded in staying the distance.

It was expected that Rocky would either take him out early or lose on points. Instead, the fight see-sawed continually. La Starza had the better of three cat and mouse opening rounds. Rocky came to life in the next two, flooring La Starza in the 4th. Roland got it back in the 6th and 7th behind his jab, and then Marciano finished with a rush, but lost the 8th on a foul. The scoring could not have been closer. The judges split 5–4–1 between the two fighters and the referee had it 5–5. His supplementary points score now came into effect and showed 9–6 to Rocky. This was the closest Marciano ever came to defeat.

However, he had another scare six fights later when Keene Simmons cut his left eye badly. Marciano was, in trade terminology, a 'bleeder'. His eyes and nose were prone to becoming technicolour productions. Against Simmons, the referee and doctor wanted to stop it, but were reluctant because Marciano was winning. When the referee finally did step between them it was to save Simmons who was being pounded without reply.

On July 12th, 1951, there was another acid test, Rex Layne at the Garden. Layne was a powerhouse fighter with an impressive record. He had chased and chivvied his way through Walcott's defences, whipped Cesar Brion and kayoed Bob Satterfield, a light-heavy-cum-heavy who possessed all the tools bar the ability to take a punch.

Marciano–Layne was a battle of iron fists, iron jaws and iron wills. Layne's broke; Rocky's didn't. The writing was on the wall in the 3rd when a barrage from Marciano had Layne hurt and hanging on. He stayed upright then but finally cracked wide open in the 6th when 'Susie Q' left him face down on the canvas. It was said afterwards that the punch tore out all Rex's front teeth.

Victory over Layne, and in his next fight Freddie Beshore who had contested Charles for the title, made Rocky the number one contender. But there was a sad, bloody bit of business to come. Joe Louis.

Louis' tax problems forced him to fight on after the Charles defeat. His plight is aptly illustrated by an anecdote in Peter Wilson's *More Ringside Seats.* Hearing that British sports writer Frank McGhee had to visit the tax office, Louis said, with more than a touch of pathos: 'While you're there would you leave a couple of million dollars for me.'[1]

Since Charles, Joe had won eight fights against fair to middling opposition. Brion (twice), Beshore and Lee Savold were three of his victims. Omelio Agramonte, who around this time also dropped a decision to Britain's next champ, Johnny Williams, twice stayed the distance, as did worn out and washed up Jimmy Bivins. The power base was still there but the timer had gone. A kayo ratio of 83% on retirement had now dipped to 77%.

To make matters worse Louis was also liable for taxes on the bouts he was fighting to actually pay off taxes. But he was still high in the ratings and a fight with Marciano would be a final eliminator for another title contest.

And so to Madison Square Garden on the night of October 26th, 1951. Louis is the sentimental choice, but wherever heads rule hearts, Marciano is — and must be — the favourite.

In the 1st the Rock is his usual crude self, throwing great roundhouse swings that are way off target. Louis jabs and jabs again, his left hand pinpointing Rocky's face and battening onto it like a leech. But at the end of the round there is a portent of what is to come when Marciano at last makes contact, swinging a right against Louis' temple. Louis reels back but the bell goes before Rocky can follow up.

Rounds two, three, four, and five: Louis' left jab pounds like a hammer into Rocky's craggy features. He hits Marciano with everything he throws, following the jab with hooks and crosses. But the old snap and stopping power simply aren't there any longer. The Rock lumbers forward, a human river working itself up into a torrent that no dam built by this ageing Joe Louis is going to contain. Rocky's punches are still wild and he is taking 3 for every 1 he lands. But whenever he does Louis is shaken to the core.

The 6th — and now Marciano is getting through. Louis is tired. He cannot blast this white rock from his path, and Rocky's non-stop aggression is grinding him down minute by minute. In particular, Marciano's body punches are taking a heavy toll. This round is just about even but in the next the fight shifts decisively away from Joe. He is tired now, an old man, his balding head glistening with sweat under the arc lights. Now Marciano is a grim human tank, and he snarls as he pounds clubbing blows to the body and then batters Louis around the head. Several times, Louis is almost dropped. To those at ringside it is obvious that his course has not much longer to run.

The sands of time have run from the top into the bottom of the hour glass.

1 'More Ringside Seats' p.22

When the eighth bell rings Louis is as empty as the top of that glass.

The 8th — this is where the legends die — Marciano surges forward blasting away without mercy. Louis has given up the ghost now. His jab is feeble, and like some old battered warship, his heavy guns have all been silenced and reduced to pitiful impotence. Quite literally he has nothing left except courage. And in the ring with Marciano that is never enough.

Rocky slams a left to the stomach and Joe sinks slowly to the canvas. There is no roar from the crowd — just a hush in the black night. At '8' Joe struggles to his feet. Rocky moves in and crashes a pulverising right swing against Joe's chin. The ex-champion goes sprawling through the ropes and comes to rest with his head lolling on the ring apron. The referee stares down at him. Neither he nor anyone else wants to see Louis counted out. So he raises his arms aloft and then walks over to Rocky whilst Joe's handlers clamber into the ring.

Joe Louis should never have had to return to the ring, although when we strip away all the maudlin sentimentality we find that it was largely his own doing.

He did not prosper in retirement. He wrestled for a living, refereed occasionally and acted as a front man for casinos. The I.R.S. agreed to limit his back taxes to $20,000 p.a. It made little difference and he died owing the Government millions.

When Jessie Owens returned from Berlin wearing his laurel wreaths he found that he was a two week hero. Only janitor's jobs were open to him, and he ended up racing against horses for a few bucks. His fate presaged Louis'.

In 1970 things caught up with Joe and he was hospitalised for paranoia. He recovered and in 1974 refereed the second Frazier–Quarry fight. In 1977 he suffered a stroke which left him chair-bound. He died on April 12th, 1981 and received the sort of funeral normally reserved for political Presidents. Like Jessie Owens, now that Joe was gone they could safely eulogise his memory.

Many good judges regard Joe Louis as the greatest of all the heavyweight champions. That we shall never know. Different styles breed different results. I have already intimated that Gene Tunney had the right style to beat Louis. Larry Holmes, a champion whose status I believe will grow as the years go by, also had a style which Joe would have had difficulty with. In my view Johnson would have been too clever and Ali too fast for Louis. On the other hand, Dempsey, Tyson, and Marciano when Louis was at his peak, would probably have been right for him. Joe was always at his best against fighters he did not have to go looking for. But there are as many different opinions as there are boxing fans.

Lee Savold had been Louis' victim four months before Joe had succumbed to Marciano. Now it was Lee's turn in the meat grinder. The British had given him a fool's cap to wear, rather reminiscent of the cardboard crown once handed out to Lady Jane Grey, the 'nine days Queen of England'. Savold himself treated his laurel as no more than a passing amusement. But there was nothing amusing about his fight with Marciano. Thirty-six and past his best, Savold took a hideous beating. After the referee rescued him in the 6th, the N.B.A. barred Lee from fighting again for his own good. He ended up working as a Longshoreman. At least he fared better than Lady Jane: she was executed!

Rocky knocked out Gino Buonvino and Bernie Reynolds and fretted for his title shot, held up because of the Walcott–Charles return. But he himself had one more river left to cross.

Strange tales had begun to leak out of Palookaville, about a black clad figure, gaunt of visage and baleful of eye, who stalked the streets at night en-route to the Palookaville home for terminally decayed fighters. In the morning there was always one inmate missing.

Some said that the 'Palookaville Vampire' was none other than Jack Hurley, a West Coast manager who guided Harry 'Kid' Matthews, a light heavyweight, out of Seattle. Matthews had a 77–3–7 record, and a decision over 175 lbs contender Bob Murphy suggested he could box a bit. But how had he acquired those 57 kayos on his scoresheet?

Palookaville vampire or not, Hurley knew his way around. When he began to complain that Harry the kid couldn't get a title shot because the I.B.C. had boxing sewn up, people listened and some of them were politicians. Boxing was a high profile sport and 1952 was an election year.

Running scared, Norris and Co. offered Matthews a tilt at Joey Maxim's crown. Thanks, but no thanks. Maxim had acquired the reputation in some quarters of being the most boring fighter in history, and you couldn't give him away in a soup kitchen. Instead, Hurley wanted Walcott.

The I.B.C. now pressurised Weill into fixing up a bout between Marciano and Matthews, winner to go against Walcott in the fall. Marciano didn't want it; neither did Weill. But the latter was in an invidious position. He was also the I.B.C.'s employee.

Marciano–Matthews was arranged for the Yankee Stadium on July 28th. The fight itself is not of much significance: the fall out was.

On Hurley's orders, Matthews stayed in close and jabbed Rocky's head back to win the 1st round. In the 2nd he threw away the blueprint, zigged when he should have zagged, and was counted out. 'Did ya see them left hooks,' exalted Goldman; 'who said Rocky didn't have no left?' Actually, you did Charlie.

The real drama went on backstage. Matthews was late for the weigh-in. When matchmaker Weill was asked where he was, manager Weill answered. 'How should I know...*my* fighter's here.' Four days later Weill was forced to resign as the I.B.C.'s matchmaker. Whether his slip of the tongue was intentional is an interesting question. I.B.C. was not exactly a blue chip employer, and Weill was known to be unhappy with the situation.

Ditto Marciano. He was the most exciting heavyweight for years and had drawn 31,000 people to Yankee Stadium, a massive live non title gate in the television era. Yet it was only the third time he had top lined in New York, and most of his bouts had been in the lesser fight centres of New England with purses to match. *Clarence beware; thou keepst me from the light.'*

Weill's job as matchmaker meant getting the fights as cheaply as possible, but in his dual role as Marciano's undercover manager he was losing money too, and he wanted out from being Norris and Carbo's puppet. Weill now resumed as Marciano's manager of record. It all left I.B.C. under close scrutiny. In 1957 they were forced to disband by America's anti-trust laws when it was proved that I.B.C. controlled 80% of world title fights staged in America. They had overstretched themselves.

The irritating return bout clause ensured that the Rock's first defence would have to be against Walcott. Despite the splendour of their first fight, only 16,000 turned up to see the rematch in Chicago on May 15th, 1953. They didn't exactly get their money's worth. At 2.15 of the 1st round Marciano knocked Joe down with a right uppercut. At 2.25 Walcott was counted out, and at 2.26 he got up and shuffled back to his corner complaining that the count had been fast. The fans felt that it was he who had pulled the fast one. They took the somewhat jaundiced view that Joe was simply along for one last pay-day and had exited at the first opportunity. The scribes were a little kinder; Walcott had misjudged the count, or his elderly limbs had not responded in time. I'm with the fans on this one, but in fairness it has to be said that Everett Skehan in his excellent biography of Marciano takes an opposite view.[1]

Marciano's main complaint was that he had been stiffed on the money: Walcott got more than him!

Next up was another rematch: Roland La Starza. On paper, La Starza had done well since losing to Rocky. He had put together another long list of wins. Trouble was they were more cannon fodder, and a pair of light-heavies had actually beaten him.

On September 24th at the Polo Grounds Marciano and La Starza re-enacted their first fight. La Starza began breezily, stepping fast out of danger and working his jab well. Marciano continually fouled him and it is difficult to avoid the conclusion that he was taking advantage of New York's no foul rule.

After the 6th (which he lost on a foul), Marciano began to drive for home. He simply battered his way through La Starza's defences, breaking a blood

1 See 'Rocky Marciano' pp. 223–4

vessel in his arm in the process. Roland withstood it until the 11th when 'Susie' compounded the damage by knocking him out onto the ring apron. La Starza made it up at '9', but was gone and a few punches later referee Ruby Goldstein declared it over.

There was not a lot of drama about Rocky's life outside the ring. He doesn't sway on a sea of emotion with Ali, take reluctant arms against racism (Louis), cavort around Hollywood (Dempsey), or stand in the eye of a great Shakespearean tragedy like Johnson. He was a fighting man who expressed it all inside the ropes. Problem. He had trailed havoc through the division; who was there left to fight?

At the beginning of 1954 it really boiled down to Ezzard Charles or Bob Satterfield. Ezz was still out there pitching, but not so adroitly as before. In the first flush of disappointment after the Walcott fight he was bested by Layne but got it back later. There were eight other victories, including Brion and Bivins, but then rising Nino Valdes and light heavyweight contender Harold Johnson proved that Layne wasn't just a blip by outscoring him. He returned to winning ways against Coley Wallace (now a pro), but found Satterfield in his path.

Bob Satterfield could box like an angel and punch like the devil, but when hit solidly on the chin the sound of breaking glass was to be heard all over the arena. He had floored Ezzard's old adversary Archie Moore four times in the 1st only to be bombed out himself two rounds later. Charles played strictly to Bob's weaknesses and destroyed his dream in two.

So it was Charles whom the I.B.C. summoned to appear as Rocky's next opponent. The pundits gave Ezzard little chance, but sometimes the public has a better inkling than the Press or the bookies. 47,500 turned up at Yankee Stadium on June 17th, 1954, giving Marciano his biggest purse to date, almost a quarter of a million dollars including TV rights. For once the public was right. Charles fought the fight of his life. The plodding bore disappeared; the Cincinnati Cobra re-appeared. If there was one man in the world who was not going to die under Ezzard's punches then it was Rocky Marciano.

At the end of 15 rounds — the only time Rocky had to travel this distance — the scorecards read, 9–5–1, 8–6–1 and 8–5–2, all for Marciano. Bare bones without flesh, but there was plenty of that in evidence, mostly coloured red. Marciano's left eye and nose were badly cut; Charles' right eye was gashed, his face a relief map of cuts and bruises.

Over the first five rounds Ezzard boxed brilliantly at long range, making his speed, his jab, and his combinations tell. In the 4th he split Rocky's eye, pounded rights to the damage zone, and whipped left hooks to the body when Marciano tried to come in close. It was a big round for the ex-king.

Things began to change in the 6th, Marciano's first winning round. Rights almost dropped Charles. The next three sessions were toe to toe, but as the fight turned for home so it also turned in the Rock's favour. Charles hardly won anything in the last six. He took a continuous beating. Marciano's eye gushed blood like a geyser, but Charles was too tired, too punch ridden, to take advantage. Several times he almost went down, several times it seemed that he must be stopped. But he stayed up and he kept going. Afterwards, referee Goldstein praised Ezzard's bravery but added, with the remorseless logic of the prize ring, that you win rounds on punches, not courage. He had seen all the last six rounds for Marciano; his fellow judges agreed.

Charles gained lustre in defeat. It had been a superb fight and he had taken the Blockbuster's best shots for 15 rounds, good enough for a return, at Yankee Stadium again on September 17th.

Generally speaking, sequels are never as good as the original, and this was not one of the exceptions. The fans sensed it too. 13,000 less turned up than for the first fight.

Charles was nowhere near the same force. Yet paradoxically he came closer to winning.

Marciano made the running from the opening bell. In the 2nd a landslide of punches put Charles down. In reality, it was the 17th round of their first fight.

Ezzard took only a short count, but now went into his defensive shell. He came out of it in the 6th; and almost became the first man to regain the title. A counter-tide of punches hit Rocky as he surged in, almost ripping his nose off his face. This was the 21st round of the first fight; Marciano should have had longer to let the damage heal properly.

Now began a grim race against time. That injury couldn't be carried for nine more rounds. Had it been a non-title fight it would have been stopped now.

Marciano chased and chased. The Cobra slithered and oscillated, trying to zero in on the injury while staying out of trouble himself. At the end of the 7th the doctor told Rocky: 'One more round.'

One of the tests of a champion is to stare the black imp of defeat in the face and vanquish it. In round eight they traded left hooks, then rights, and the blood again began to cascade down Rocky's face. The position was desperate now. Sensing victory Charles ripped home a right hook to the head but Rocky tore back and pounded home a left-right which shook Ezzard from head to toe. For a split second he stood hurt and defenceless and that was all Rocky needed.

Like a tiger, he pounced and exploded a savage right on Charles' jaw. Ezzard hit the canvas with electric shock waves rippling through his brain. At '4' he stumbled blindly to his feet, eyes blank and staring, darkness closing in and settling over his mind. Rocky leapt at him, smashed him into the ropes, and put everything he had behind a crushing left hook to the chin. Charles pitched forward on his knees and remained there, as though paying mute homage to his conqueror, whilst the referee counted him out.

The stories of Jersey Joe Walcott and Ezzard Charles are so intertwined that it is fitting to recount together their subsequent lives.

Jersey Joe never boxed again after the Chicago debacle. His was an amiable retirement. He served as a parole officer and later sheriff of Camden, New Jersey. He kept in touch with boxing as a referee. Indeed, we shall meet him again in that capacity.

Walcott's story is one of the romances of the ring. If at first you don't succeed and you're 37 years old then imitate the action not of the tiger but the spider! Boxing's 'Robert the Bruce' passed away on February 26th, 1994. At that time he was still the oldest man ever to win the heavyweight crown.

Ezzard Charles' story is a much sadder one. He carried on boxing until 1959, but was never the same after tangling with the Marciano wrecking machine. He just went down and down. London saw him on the most pitiful night of his career, disqualified for persistent holding against the young Welsh heavyweight, Dick Richardson. After Ezzard finally gave up he contracted multiple sclerosis and spent his last years in a wheelchair. He died on May 27th, 1975.

In sport there is often a thin dividing line between being remembered for success or failure. Sam Snead was one of the greatest golfers in history, he is chiefly remembered for the occasions on which he blew the U.S. Open. Had Sam Baroudi not died, and there had been a cruiserweight division in 1949 then Ezzard Charles might today be recalled as one of boxing's greatest pound for pound fighters. Instead he has gone down as a mediocre heavyweight champion. Life was not kind to him. I hope history will be.

Britain has produced a whole tapestry of outstanding light heavyweights: Jack Petersen, Len Harvey*, Freddie Mills, Chris Finnegan, John Conteh and Denis Andries. Often forgotten amongst them is Battersea's Don Cockell. Not that Don would have minded too much; he is recalled instead as one of our best and bravest heavyweights.

It wasn't supposed to be that way. By 1951 Cockell had overcome an uncertain start to become British and European light-heavyweight champion and stand high in the world rankings. Nick Barone and Lloyd Marshall perished inside the distance at his fists, and Freddie Beshore was clearly outpointed. A box-fighter with a penchant for body punching, Cockell was expected to get a crack at Maxim in 1952 and was not without chances. Then it all went wrong.

Cockell was hit by a bad bout of rheumatic fever which left him with a

* Like Fitzsimmons, born at Helston, Cornwall.

serious, and permanent, weight problem. Dehydrated by making 12 stone 7 lbs, he lost his titles to ex-world middleweight champion Randolph Turpin. It looked as if a brief but luminous career was over. Don Cockell had other ideas.

He came back as a heavyweight. Fans gaped, and then laughed at, the rolls of fat which hung off his body. But the boxing skill, the speed of punch and some of the power were still there. He cut up and stopped sad, comebacking Tommy Farr in a title eliminator and then narrowly wrested the British crown from Johnny Williams, an erratic though skilful performer.

Jack Hurley thought this now semi-obese Briton would be a suitable stepping stone for 'Harry the Kid' to rebuild on. Cockell won Harry outright, stopping him twice in Seattle and also besting him in England. A similar mistake was made by Roland La Starza's management team. Cockell outpointed him in London. Afterwards, La Starza's people gave it the 'we wuz robbed' treatment. More significantly they whined about Don's 'roughhouse' tactics which translated means: 'Yeah, we did get licked.'

Improbably, by 1955 Don Cockell was a contender for the world heavyweight title. It has to be said, in all frankness, that there were more deserving cases, in particular the now world light heavyweight champion, Archie Moore, and Nino Valdes, a giant Cuban who would later stop Cockell. However, boxing is not the world chess championship with its series of careful eliminators to find the best contender. The chess is played outside the ropes. Neither I.B.C., nor Al Weill, wanted Valdes or Moore at this particular moment. There was Rocky's face and his age, almost 32, to consider. The state of both meant that the once impregnable Marciano really only had about one top money spinning defence left. Moore and Valdes were therefore shunted off to Las Vegas to fight an eliminator, whilst Rocky went through a warm up defence against somebody who didn't figure to take too much out of him, or mark his features too badly. Don Cockell got the call.

Derision in the American press, when Don's corpulent glands hove into view, kept the attendance down. The British camp also rather shot themselves in the foot with their choice of P.R. man, a garrulous American named Harry Mendel. Swift though Don's punches were, comparing his hand speed to Louis', was decidedly over the top. Mendel in fact rather resembled the 'Viz' character 'Roger Irrelevant'. His press conferences consisted mainly of anecdotes about the Brown Bomber.

Cockell was 'known' on the West Coast so the Keyser Stadium, San Francisco, was as good a place as any for the contest. Only 15,000 paid to see it on May 16th, 1955, which was a pity because what was on display was a remarkable piece of courage.

Al Weill took no chances. First he had a 16½ square foot ring put in instead of the usual 20 footer. Marciano's natural style was ideally suited to a telephone box. Then, Weill insisted on 8 oz gloves instead of the usual championship 6 oz. This reduced the likelihood of Marciano suffering facial damage.

Rocky was never more ruthless than the night he fought Cockell. In the 8⅓ rounds it lasted he four times hit Don after the bell, three times struck him below the belt, butted him twice, punched him in the kidneys, elbowed him, and finally hit him when he was down.

Throughout the first three rounds the British champion made all the running, giving a classy exhibition of left handed boxing and turning hooks off the jab at close range. He was still boxing well and piling up the points in the 4th until Marciano suddenly butted him so savagely that he almost floored him. A gash several inches long opened up on Don's forehead and blood began to seep down into his eyes. Sensing victory, Marciano tore in and he nearly downed him with a left hook. Cockell had to weather heavy pressure until the bell.

In the 5th Rocky smashed one in low, then blasted another to Don's jaw after the bell had rung, again almost dropping him. Like the three allegedly wise monkeys, the referee saw nothing, heard nothing, and said nothing!

From here on Cockell absorbed a murderous beating. Time after time he reeled under the impact of Marciano's savage clubbing blows but with a desperate grim courage he refused to go down, and even tried to slug it out with the champion. At the end of the 7th Rocky planted another low blow into Cockell, a double sin because he did it after the bell had gone. Yet Cockell still came out fighting in the 8th.

Outgunned, outfought, and shot to pieces he was fighting a personal Alamo. He made it through the 8th, but it couldn't last.

At the beginning of the 9th a siege gun right blasted Cockell down for '7'. After Don hit the canvas Rocky whacked another one in for good measure!

Some unbelievable inner courage made Cockell get up and walk right back in throwing punches; a kamikaze pilot in boxing trunks. It was totally hopeless and a volley of clubbing punches drove him back down again. Incredibly game, he was up at '5', but the referee had now seen enough.

Before the fight Cockell had made his corner promise not to throw in the towel. After it, he was never much good again and soon retired. But he had stood bravely, and not without skill in the early rounds.

Time to lighten the mood with a couple of anecdotes. There is an old British music hall joke about a burglar who is asked by the police: 'Have you got an alibi? No, but I have got Marshall-Hall.'* Of more recent origin Don King is

* An English barrister famed for winning impossible acquittals.

alleged to have stepped over one of his inert fighters (Michael Dokes) in order to congratulate a new champion. Now, what have these two apparently unrelated stories got to do with the world heavyweight championship? Well, back in 1952, if somebody had asked Joey Maxim have you got a punch then quite possibly he would have replied: 'No, but I have got Jack 'Doc' Kearns.' But after Joey dropped his title to Archie Moore, 'Doc' pivoted around him waving an option for a part of Moore's contract. Together these two ancient gadflies set out to play hunt the heavyweight!

Moore is one of the great charades of ring history. He even taught Muhamad Ali something about repartee. Today, as Kennedy said of Churchill, his ship is anchored in tranquil waters. But for 30 years the waters were anything but calm. Archie Moore lived several lives all rolled into one.

Moore was born into a poor black family in Mississippi. 1916 according to him; 1913 said his mother whose date is generally preferred to Archie's. Beginning in 1936 he boxed everybody who was anybody up through the weights from welter to heavy. He globetrotted, became a friend of the Perons in Argentina, and claimed to have been given a secret weight reducing diet by the Aborigines in Australia. In 1954 he was said by the California Boxing Commission to have a heart murmur. Boxing columnist Arch Ward urged him to retire. Moore was still fighting ten years later; Ward died of a heart attack within a year.

For a long, long time nobody would give Archie a title shot. Basically, he was too good. An example was 'Broadwalk' Billy Smith, a very useful light heavy who in round seven simply shook his head, ducked through the ropes and walked out of the arena. Your average world champion didn't figure to even get in the ring with Moore in the first place. Archie was four days past his thirty-ninth birthday when he finally took the 175 lbs crown off Maxim and found 'the Doc' leering over his shoulder.

Moore had already beaten many heavyweights over the years. Kearns and he now campaigned in earnest. Nino Valdes was outpointed. Bob Baker, definitely a coming man said the reviews, was stopped in nine. Baker's face looked as though he had gone the full distance; with a bacon slicer! On May 2nd, 1955, Moore and Valdes met again, this time winner to shake hands with Marciano. It was a close one. Moore performed the old pro's trick of constantly manoeuvring Valdes so that the afternoon sun was in his eyes.* Despite this, Britain's Peter Wilson thought Valdes had won. The officials said otherwise. 'Doc' Kearns was the co-promoter, and Al Weill certainly preferred Moore. Valdes was young, strong and very big. He could fight too. Nino boxed well off his jab and was a powerful hitter. He later became a scourge of British heavy-

* The fight was in an open air stadium in late afternoon.

weights mowing down Cockell, Joe Erskine, Brian London and Dick Richardson, all champions.

There was no talk of retirement from Marciano while he trained to meet Moore that September. It was however in his mind. His wife, who had recently given birth to their second child, wanted him to quit; so did his mother who had never liked him fighting. Rocky himself may have begun to question his own invulnerability. There was the recurrent facial damage, and in training for the Cockell fight a sparring partner had knocked him down. Cynics might imply that this was to help a slow moving gate, but the knockdown appears to have been genuine. Above all, boxing had begun to hurt. 'Hurt', was exactly the word Marciano used after the Charles fights. Ezzard had taken him to pain barriers where he had not been before.

There were also financial considerations. He was beginning to fight too much for the taxman. And for Al Weill and the I.B.C. Rocky detested Weill and Norris; believed that both men had cheated him. Oddly enough — then again perhaps not because they were fellow Italians — Marciano liked Carbo and socialised with him. It is unlikely that Rocky discussed retirement with Frankie. Nobody seems to have known what was in his mind until after the Moore fight.

This was a swan song of merit. There were predictions of a live million dollar gate. In the event, it just failed, but 61,500 paying customers filed into the Yankee Stadium on September 21st, 1955. Receipts were $948,117. Marciano's share, including TV rights, amounted to $463,000.

Although few believed that 'Ancient Archie' could pickaxe 'the Rock', it was an intriguing challenge. And on a starlit night, Moore came as close to it as was humanely possible.

They began warily, each respecting the other, Moore's left jab a flickering ebony dart under shimmering arc lights; Marciano's twin war clubs asking questions about the strength of that 41 year old body.

The wariness continued into round two with Moore — as was expected — beginning to pile up the points in these early rounds. But now the Rock picked up the pace and charged forward head down. He presented Moore with a perfect target and Archie zeroed in on it, putting everything into an explosive right uppercut that landed with shattering force on Rocky's chin. Marciano shuddered convulsively, and then he pitched forward onto his face.

Against any other boxer it would have been a perfect knockout punch. But not Marciano. At '4' he had climbed uncertainly to his feet. But his eyes were blank and empty and he was oblivious to everything and everybody; a man suddenly plunged into an endlessly dark labyrinth. He staggered to the ropes and stared at the crowd, neither seeing them nor hearing the tumult that seethed around the ringside.

Another punch and Archie Moore would be the heavyweight champion of the world!

Then luck — and bad refereeing — intervened on Rocky's side. Normally under New York rules a floored boxer received a mandatory eight count, but this was then waived in title fights. However referee Harry Kessler now proceeded to give Rocky the mandatory count. Moore's seconds screamed at him to go in for the kill. Archie was in a dilemma. What should he do? The crowd was also screeching at him. But Archie stood off and waited whilst the referee tolled off four unnecessary seconds. Life was now beginning to flicker again in Marciano's eyes. Then, infuriatingly, the referee wiped Rocky's gloves very precisely and slowly, taking up another two to three vital seconds. Finally, Kessler jerked Rocky forward as he ordered 'box on'. Many ringsiders felt that that sudden jerk helped clear Marciano's head.

When Moore was finally allowed to move in on Marciano the chance of a lifetime had gone. Rocky was still groggy but he had recovered sufficiently to weather two searing right hooks that Moore flashed home on his chin.

In the 3rd Marciano did the only thing he knew — attack. Moore's whiplash left jabs split open his nose and he had to walk through a battery of rights to the head, but Rocky took them all and kept coming. In the 4th he mowed his way through Archie's defence by sheer strength, powered him to the ropes, and clubbed away savagely at his body.

Round five found Moore calling on every ounce of ringcraft he possessed to dance away from the champion's bull-like rushes and turn him on the ropes. A succession of left jabs and hooks spat into Rocky's face and Moore pounded home the right at every opportunity. But Marciano only seemed to get stronger as he absorbed the punishment and in the 6th he drove through Archie's defence again and floored him for '2' with a right swing. Then another right put Archie down again, this time for '3'.

It was the beginning of the end. Throughout the 7th and 8th Marciano kept up his relentless non-stop attack raining home a torrent of brutal, clubbing punches on every part of Moore's anatomy. Archie fought back. He kept punching. But with every second and every punch he was getting weaker. Time and again Rocky pressed him back on the ropes, planted his head on his chest, and pumped murderous short arm punches into his body. At the end of the 8th Archie was down again but the bell saved him for another minute.

The 9th saw the end. It was merely one way traffic now as Rocky belted Moore into the ropes, and then, with Archie too battered and exhausted to get away and too weak to fight back, Marciano simply clubbed him down punch by punch. The final blow was a battering ram of a left hook to the jaw and Moore collapsed into a sitting position against the ropes. At '7' he used them to try and pull himself erect, and he was still trying, caught suspended in a weird limbo halfway up from the canvas, when Kessler tolled off the final second.

Afterwards in the dressing room Marciano discussed retirement for the first time. Weill didn't believe it. Rocky, he opined, would be back defending the title next year. Rocky wouldn't, and Weill was part of the problem. Years later, Boston promoter Sam Silverman said that Marciano had offered to fight once more, for him, provided he received an extra $25,000 without Weill's knowledge. This was apparently in lieu of money Rocky believed Weill had skimmed off him over the years. Nothing came of it however, and on April 27th, 1956, Rocky Marciano officially announced his retirement. Despite tempting offers he never returned to the ring. On August 31st, 1973, the eve of his fiftieth birthday, Rocky was killed in a plane crash.

Marciano was one of the great champions. Probably, no other fighter ever achieved greatness with so many limitations. The key to it was, I believe, his tremendous willpower. But this was no will to glory. As Nietzsche himself put it, 'All idealism is falsehood in the face of necessity.' Necessity fashioned Rocky's will; his Valkyries rode in bearing sacks of gold. He was an avaricious man, tight with money. A source in boxing has told me that he died because he preferred to travel in a friend's private plane rather than pay the price of a seat on a normal passenger flight. His enmities — and he held them fiercely — were with people he believed had skimped him, no matter how small the amount.

But there was another side to Rocky Marciano, that of a man who held fast to his friendships. If he liked somebody he was loyal to them. When Mafia Don, Vito Genovese, lay dying in hospital, Marciano visited him despite warnings that his image could suffer. Peter Wilson tells of seeking Rocky's autograph for a cripple in Britain. Although tired from training, he ran a quarter of a mile and back again to fetch an autographed photo. Thus Marciano: he wouldn't give you a cent of his money, but he would give you every second of his time.

Round Nineteen: A Tale of Two Continents

The retirement of an outstanding champion always leaves a void. After a short interval two blacks, one very old — the other very young, stepped into it. After they had finished wreaking havoc on each other the void still remained.

When Marciano retired the top three contenders were Moore, Valdes and Tommy 'Hurricane' Jackson, s strong, swarming fighter who some believed was mentally backward.

Logic suggested Moore–Valdes for the vacant title. Although Archie held two verdicts over the Cuban, the second had been highly debatable. A bit too debatable for 'Doc' Kearns who showed no inclination to let his man get into the ring with Valdes again. Valdes — who never seemed to have the right connections — was frozen out. He spent a good part of the next few years commuting back and forth between Britain and America. Mad dogs and Englishmen, they say, go out in the mid-day sun, and several Britons were mad enough to risk their reputations against big Nino. He eclipsed them one by one.

The next obvious match was Moore–Jackson. The 'Hurricane' had beaten Charles, Baker, Layne and Dan Bucceroni, one of La Starza's conquerors. But the I.B.C., who controlled him, wanted Jackson to first win an eliminator against a young light-heavyweight, Floyd Patterson.

Ostensibly, Patterson had done little to merit such an opportunity. The 1952 Olympic middleweight champion, he had fought 30 professional fights, chiefly against light-heavyweights such as Dick Wagner and Yvon Durelle, who was later to fight a classic title bout with Moore. Patterson had lost, at least on paper, to Joey Maxim in his fourteenth pro fight. The I.B.C. however, had a specific reason for wanting to involve Patterson in the king making process.

Floyd's manager was a highly controversial character named Cus D'Amato. D'Amato liked to portray himself as boxing's 'Mr Clean', hater of everything crooked in the sport. This crystallised into a paranoid dislike of the I.B.C. By the spring of 1956 the I.B.C. was under intense pressure. The Federal authorities were about to commence the court action which would ultimately break up their organisation. Crucial to I.B.C.'s defence was its need to show that non-I.B.C. fighters did get the opportunity to fight for titles. Who better then than a 'heavyweight' managed by its most vocal critic? In effect, they were pulling the Matthews stunt over again.

Jackson was of course expected to win. But when the roof beams start to crack it is not unusual, under Murphy's Law, for the basement to flood as well. On June 8th, 1956, Patterson gained a split decision over Jackson. A reluctant I.B.C. had no choice other than go with Moore–Patterson.

Once again, Patterson was the underdog*. Moore appeared to have survived the Rocky demolition crew intact. In a seven month spell in 1956 he had eleven fights winning them all, eight by kayos. Included were a defence of his 175 lbs laurel and a victory over an aspiring Canadian giant, James J. Parker. As a gimmick, the audience wore white dinner jackets, some of which ended up splattered with Parker's blood.

But in training for Patterson, Archie appeared listless and jaded. On the day of the fight, November 30th, he promised to teach Floyd a lesson. It did not materialise in Chicago that night.

Instead, after an even first round, Patterson took over, moving in confidently behind his left jab and hooking swiftly to Moore's head and body. On this night Archie looked his age plus a few years more! By the end of the 4th he had taken a hammering and was bleeding from a cut eye. In the 5th Patterson opened up with combinations and Moore, looking utterly weary, went down for '9'. It was obvious that he could not survive the round and Patterson, following up swiftly, chopped him down again with two fast left hooks to the jaw. The ancient one was counted out lying face down on the canvas.

It was an unsatisfactory victory. People just could not understand how a fighter of Moore's stature had been so inept.

Archie himself said that he had over-trained, which hardly seems conducive to the facts (ringsiders thought the opposite). He was involved in a dispute with I.B.C. over money, had a court case pending against him and claimed to have felt dejected during the fight. None of this was very convincing, and until now his performance has remained one of boxing's great mysteries.

The answer lies in his schedule for 1956. Eleven fights between late February and early September is astonishing for a man of 42; and potentially self-destructive.

It was the most intensely active spell of his entire career.

Only in his very first year as a pro, 1936, did Moore box more frequently, once every two weeks, as opposed to two weeks and four days in the 1956 period. But even in 1936 he fought on average only 2.81 completed rounds per contest as compared to *5.45* in '56. In flesh and blood terms this was a killing schedule for a man of Moore's age.

A corollary of this was the weight he had to lose in June when defending the light-heavyweight title, 1½ stone. Forget nonsensical ballyhoo about aborigine diets; Moore went through hell every time he defended the 175 lbs title.

The fight itself, against British Empire champion Yolande Pompey in

* He was not actually the leading contender for the light-heavyweight crown, Harold Johnson was.

London, is an important guide to what happened in Chicago. Moore won in the 10th. But for the first nine rounds he did nothing. Peter Wilson describes him as: 'old, sagging, bloodstained and ring-worn'[1]. At one stage the referee threatened to disqualify Moore for not fighting.

When boxing Patterson, Moore was a middle-aged shell who had crammed too many fights into too short a time, compounded by a spell of rigorous weight reducing. He got away with it against an over-awed Pompey. Patterson was far superior opposition. He ran Archie into the canvas.

The new heavyweight champion was, at that time, the youngest ever, just 21 years old, from Waco, North Carolina where he was born on January 4th, 1935, the son of a railroad labourer. He grew up in the Bedford/Stuyvesant area of New York where the family moved to when he was one.

Floyd Patterson was a lonely, introspective boy, deeply sensitive. He recalled his father coming home too tired to eat, and of running away because it pained him so much. He hid in tube tunnels and was teased at school. Eventually, he landed himself in reformatory for vehicle theft. Although of normal intelligence, he was illiterate until the age of ten.

He took his first boxing steps at reformatory. After leaving it he began to work out at the Gramercy gym in New York. The owner of the gym was 39 year old Cus D'Amato who slept on the premises with a vicious Alsatian for company. D'Amato took Patterson over completely. Cus was Svengali; Floyd his Trilby. If Cus said: 'wipe your nose'; Floyd wiped it.

D'Amato's feud with the I.B.C. is well documented by historians. But some believed that he was simply a new robber baron trying to push out the old. Jimmy Cannon, a sportswriter respected for his integrity, wrote:

> *'The manager of Floyd Patterson is as phoney as snow on a Hollywood Christmas Tree and his methods are as dirty as a coalman's fingernails.'*

For all his strictures against the I.B.C., D'Amato was not above borrowing money from them, which he refused to pay back. Disturbingly, he later became involved with Mafia figures himself.

However, the young and naive Patterson initially had no reason to be anything other than grateful to Cus who guided him first to Golden Gloves titles, and then to the 1952 Olympic middleweight title which he won by knocking out a Romanian in 20 seconds. He was the first Olympic champion, at any weight, to even fight for the heavyweight title, let alone win it.

The newly garlanded Patterson swiftly turned professional. D'Amato brought him along very carefully; too carefully according to the scribes. In the main they were right, although it has to be noted that in his sixth pro fight Floyd

1 'More Ringside Stats' p.102

was put in with Dick Wagner, who had headlined at the Garden four years earlier and was still useful. Patterson won a tough fight on a split decision after taking some stick to the body. Floyd also outpointed and stopped Yvon Durelle, a powerful French-Canadian fisherman who later came desperately close to removing Archie Moore's crown. Meanwhile, Cus slept outside his protégé's bedroom door in case the mob, i.e., I.B.C., got at him!

Joey Maxim, at the Eastern Parkway arena in New York, was a sticky one. After eight not very exhilarating rounds, Maxim got the decision, 4–3–1, 5–3 and 7–1. By contrast, eleven of twelve reporters present had it in Floyd's favour. Maybe Joey the Jab put one set or t'other to sleep.

Floyd's friend Jimmy Slade was supposed to give him trouble. He didn't. Patterson chased him all round the ring and decked him five times. Afterwards, Slade's manager slapped him for not trying and the N.Y.A.A.C. temporarily withheld Slade's purse. The crowd summed up their feelings by singing 'Let Me Call You Sweetheart'.

The man who won the title was not a fully-fledged heavyweight and never would be. He stood an even 6′. Against Jackson he weighed only 179 lbs, and for Moore 182 which was to be his approximate fighting weight during his prime. In reality, Patterson was a natural cruiserweight. Had that division existed then and he had fought in it, Floyd would have gone down as a boxing great. His supreme strength was his hand speed, the best of any fighter to hold the premier title. He put punches together in clusters of sometimes up to ten. In *Sting Like a Bee* Jose Torres* shows how Cus D'Amato developed his fighter's speed and precision.

> *'We would put numbers in the vulnerable spots (jaws, ribs, solar plexus, stomach). D'Amato would call numbers. I would throw the punch. There was a time when I threw six punches to predetermined areas in two-fifths of a second... It sounded like one big punch.'*[1]

Specifically, Patterson had a fine jab, and executed his punches well. Henry Cooper thought him technically superior to Ali. Floyd was also fast on his feet, and his often derided 'peek-a-boo' defence — boxing out of a semi-crouch with both arms drawn up so he could touch his ears — was none-the-less effective.

He was not especially well balanced in attack and at times jumped forward to deliver his left hook — his 'kangaroo' punch — a defect acquired at reformatory which D'Amato was never able to quite rid him of. His worst

* Light-heavyweight champion 1965/6.

1 'Sting Like a Bee' p.39

deficiencies, said the critics, were that he did not get his bodyweight behind his punches, and that he had a glass jaw. I beg to differ on both counts.

I go part of the way with the first criticism. At time Patterson did punch so fast that it was with arm weight only. But I believe that he basically lacked power at heavyweight because he simply was not a real heavyweight.

The same problem was, I believe, behind his alleged susceptibility to punches. In title fights Patterson was knocked down seventeen times. Three of these, plus an early career knockdown by French middleweight Jacques Royer-Crecy, can be attributed to balance. Nine came against one man, Ingemar Johansson. I was tempted to call this chapter 'The War of the China Chins'. I desisted because it was not really appropriate. Patterson got up from eight of the Johansson knockdowns, and as a right-hand puncher the Swede was almost on a par with Baer. Leading contender Eddie Machen found this out the hard way, and nobody ever accused Machen of being weak jawed. Another of Floyd's knockdowns was against Ali when he was crippled with a back injury. The other four were to Sonny Liston, and it is these which I feel make my point. Sonny was just too big. Patterson lacked the size to take his punches.

Cus D'Amato seems to have reached the same conclusion. Over the next few years he kept Patterson away from Liston. And four other genuine heavyweight — Valdes, Machen, Zora Folley and Cleveland Williams. It made for a depressingly empty reign.

The first hint of 'Careful Cus's' strategy came with Patterson's proposed defence against Willie Pastrano, who a few years later won the 175 lbs crown. Pastrano sported a 27–4–4 record, but with only eight stoppages was a notoriously light hitter. His best win had been over Rex Layne who these days was fighting out of Palookaville. In the end the fight fell through. Meanwhile, Patterson gave 'Hurricane' Jackson a rematch.

In New York on July 29th, 1957, Patterson won every round, flooring Jackson in the 1st, 2nd and 9th, and forcing the referee to stop the slaughter in the 10th.

Tommy had gone back, Floyd forward, but the bout was justified because of the earlier close decision. The next one, at Seattle on August 22nd, was most emphatically not.

Pete Rademacher was a prematurely balding white heavyweight who the previous year had won the Olympic title at Melbourne. Pete was possessed of a somewhat strange notion. All that guff about learning how to fight in the pro ranks was a lot of nonsense. The (unofficial) world amateur champion* could win the professional diadem on his debut!

* Official world amateur titles did not then exist.

Had it been an exhibition bout then nobody would have complained. But Rademacher's backers dangled a cheque for a quarter of a million dollars in front of Cus and he snatched it. Vampire Jack was called in as promoter. Afterwards Hurley admitted: 'We should all have been put in gaol.' Come to think of it, Seattle isn't all that far from Shelby!.

While the world looked on in astonishment, Patterson took on the amateur. Rademacher enjoyed four seconds of glory in round two when a right to the temple put Floyd on the seat of his trunks, but after that it was all one way traffic. Rademacher went down for '9' in the 3rd, four times in the 5th, '9' again in the 6th, and was then finished off by a barrage of body punches.

Poor Pete started at the top and systematically worked his way down. After Patterson, he fought number one contender Zora Folley and was counted out in the 4th having spent even more time on the canvas than against Floyd. Rumour had it that he ended up in the Palooka home for distressed Olympic gentlefolk. In fact he became a promoter!

But there was really nothing very funny about Floyd's so-called defences. The next was on August 18th, 1958, in Los Angeles, against Roy Harris from Cut 'n' Shoot, Texas.

Harris was rated in some boxing magazines — the ones D'Amato read — as the No. 3 contender, behind Folley and Machen. In April Cus watched these two box a dreary draw in San Francisco and chortled: 'This eliminates both of them.' Discerning observers took the view that Folley and Machen — both skilled boxer-punchers — were too good and too big. Harris had won 22 straight. His best scalps were Pastrano, Baker, long finished as a contender, and Willie Besmanoff who was never more than a decent journeyman. One name absent from Harris's record was fellow Texan, Cleveland Williams. Well, I wouldn't want to fight someone who had knocked out 34 opponents either! Good judges thought that Roy was some way from maturity as a fighter.

But he was colourful, a white schoolteacher from the Confederate heartland who claimed to wrestle alligators. Wilhelm Steinitz, a 19th century world chess champion, said that he played chess with God, so why deny Roy a couple of alligators? On a more serious note, ugly things were happening behind the scenes. Squeaky clean D'Amato was in bed with the whores.

Patterson-Harris was promoted by a young businessman named Bill Rosensohn, but in order to get it Rosensohn had to agree to give 50% of the profits to one Charlie Black a.k.a. Antonucci, a close friend of D'Amato's and also of mafioso boss 'Fat' Tony Salerno. Included in Harris's contract was a return bout clause which said that he had to take Black on as manager if he won the title. It meant that D'Amato and at least one mafia stooge were sharing part of the profits, and guaranteeing that the championship would remain in their control. Patterson was kept in the dark about manoeuvres which were hardly in his interests. The situation would get worse later.

At Wrigley Field Patterson whumped Harris. For the champion, it was mainly an exercise in callisthenics, although Harris did manage to drop him for '4' with a right uppercut in round two. Aside from that the Texan did no cutting and very little shooting. Floyd won as he pleased, flooring Harris four times. Roy's corner retired him at the end of the 12th.

Columnist Red Smith would later sum up the Patterson presidency of boxing as: 'the most superbly concealed since the birth of Jim Figg.' For the moment we leave it under concealment.

The last bout of the 1952 Olympic tournament was the heavyweight final between Ed Saunders of America and Ingemar Johansson of Sweden. In the first round neither man did anything and the referee demanded more action — or else! When the pattern continued in the second, Johansson was disqualified for not trying.

Both Saunders and Johansson turned professional after the Olympics. Saunders became a ring fatality; Johansson became heavyweight champion of the world.

He was born in Gothenburg on September 22nd, 1932, and all told won 60 out of 71 amateur bouts. On December 5th, 1952 he launched his pro career knocking out Robert Masson. Johansson managed only four more fights in the next two years, his career being interrupted by a broken hand and national service in the Swedish Navy. However, in his fourth fight he gained a rather anonymous bauble called the Scandinavian heavyweight title.

I use the word anonymous because it possibly sums Johansson up. He tells us little about himself or his background in his autobiography[1]. The impression is of an amiable, likeable, certainly well-dressed young man, but there is little clue as to what makes him tick.

Much the same could be said about his boxing. Strictly a counter-puncher in the amateurs, he adapted his style to the more aggressive demands of the pro ring, but remained essentially a cautious fighter working behind a fast left jab. But he did not have a great repertoire of punches. The most outstanding was a right which he threw virtually by instinct; and with remarkable power. It was a P.R. man's dream, and acquired a variety of nicknames — 'Ingo's bingo', 'the rubber band right hand', 'Toonder (thunder) and lightning' and 'hammer of Thor'. Yet it perhaps illustrates both the man and his boxing that all the names centre around this one weapon. In essence, Johansson was a smile and a suit looking for an identity; a right hand punch seeking a style.

1 'Seconds Out Of The Ring'

When Ingemar resumed after national service he ran up a series of victories. One was over an old amateur foe, Aldo Pellegrini of Italy. Johansson won on a foul in the 5th, but had to survive a left hook in the opening round which put him down. The punch carried a double warning about his vulnerability to left hooks, and the strength of his chin.

His thirteenth fight brought Johansson a 'name' victory, although strictly in the parochial fields of Europe and the British Commonwealth. Joe Bygraves was a rough, tough Jamaican who would go on to win the Empire title. (Johansson rated him the best British-based fighter he met.) Bygraves gave Johansson a hard fight to lose on points,

Seven months on, Johansson went in with Italy's Franco Cavicchi for the latter's European title. Cavicchi was strong but immobile. However, for 12 rounds Johansson was distinctly unimpressive. He was well behind on points when the 'Hammer of Thor' came to his assistance in the 13th. Ingemar first dug his left into Cavicchi's body, and then followed it with a right to the heart. The European heavyweight title went back to Sweden for the third time in history.

Victory over American trial horse Archie McBride and two European defences followed, both against Britons. Henry Cooper had shown great promise early in his career and would come again with some style, but 1957 was not his time. He was not British champion and had just been knocked out by Bygraves in a tilt at the Empire title. In view of a position they were to adopt two years later, the British Board of Control's acquiescence to Cooper fighting for the European crown at this stage is at best a little strange. It was not much of a contest either. Little happened in the first four rounds. In the 5th Johansson repeated the Cavicchi combination, left to the body, right this time to the chin, and Henry went down pole-axed.

Brit number two was the British champion, Joe Erskine, a picture book boxer but without anything remotely resembling a punch. Joe was trading off a first round kayo defeat by Valdes, but had comprehensively outboxed Bygraves to win the Empire title. He avoided Ingo's big right, but lacked the power to keep him out overall and was cut up and stopped in 13 rounds.

Strange things happened to the heavyweight picture in the autumn of 1958. Both Folley and Machen brought their wares to Europe, and both had their stalls overturned. Logically, Folley would have expected to meet Brian London who had just kayoed Erskine to win the British and Empire titles but London wanted too much money and Cooper — a much revitalised Cooper — secured the American instead. Henry was floored in the 3rd, but got up to box very calmly and skilfully, while Folley abandoned his boxing to try for a knockout. When it ended Cooper had pulled off a huge upset, arguably the best performance by a British heavyweight since Farr's epic stand against Louis.

Eddie Machen's downfall was even more dramatic. Matched with Johansson in Gothenburg, the American was over-confident. The hammer of Thor really did behave that night as though it was being directed by the old Teutonic gods. Again that vicious prelude, a left thudded hard into the body, and then the right blurred out under the arc lights and almost tore Machen's head off. He got up at '9' in dreamland, walked into another right, went down, got up again, and then a third paralysing right put him out for the count. The whole exercise lasted under two minutes. With just 21 fights to his credit (13 kayos), Ingemar Johansson was now a top contender for the world title.

Cus D'Amato was anything but unhappy. This time Folley and Machen really had been eliminated, at least for the present. Nobody could quarrel with Patterson versus either Johansson or Cooper, especially as Cooper now proceeded to relieve London of his title via a lop-sided points decision. 1959 appeared to have all the makings of a very good year for Patterson; appearances can be deceptive.

D'Amato wanted Patterson to meet both Cooper and Johansson. The Cooper fight fell through because terms could not be agreed. Johansson signed to meet Floyd in New York in June. But the champion wanted a warm-up defence. Otherwise, by the time he faced the Swede, he would have boxed only once in almost two years.

Cus decided on Brian London. The British Board of Control forbade it on the grounds that London was not the British champion, and later fined him £1,000 for going through with the contest. The ban seems to me to have been a trifle unfair. London had won 22 of 26 fights with 19 kayos. Only Cooper (twice), who always had the Indian sign on him, Germany's Heinz Neuhaus and Pastrano, had beaten London. In his autobiography Cooper (who 'drew' with Neuhaus) claims that the Germans had their own unique version of the five point 'must' system. The visitor must be five rounds in front to get the decision! As for Pastrano, London had avenged that loss. Cooper had effectively turned down Patterson, and as the London fight was meant as a warm up, the Board's decision was, to say the least, stuffy.

Patterson has since written that he disliked everything surrounding this fight. Things were beginning to come to light. For example, London later alleged that D'Amato promised him another shot at Floyd if he took Cus on as his manager*. In Indianapolis on May 1st, 1959, Floyd boxed without conviction. Fortunately for him, so did London. Known as a head down, wade in fighter, the Briton stood off like a bumboat and tried to emulate Patterson's peek-a-boo

* D'Amato denied it.

defence. A right from London in the 3rd may possibly have levelled that stanza, but it was the limit of his achievement. Patterson, who described the bout as his worst performance, did not get his body behind his punches. He failed to impress Johansson who was at ringside. A right to the head finally dropped London in the 10th. The bell saved him at '5'. In the next he went down from body blows, and on rising was sent home by a left hook to the jaw.

Patterson–London whetted no appetites for the Johansson fight on June 26th at the Yankee Stadium. Despite the Machen kayo, the American press thought that the Swede was on an awayday from Palookaville. His training methods did not meet with approval. Ingemar seemed to spend more time in night-clubs with his fiancee than in the gym.

Johansson's training methods kept the press away from the skulduggery going on in the background. To explain it as simply as possible, Bill Rosensohn wanted the fight and had put up $10,000 of his own money to secure the option. D'Amato, however, refused to sign with him. Black now re-entered the picture apropos Salerno who agreed to cover the cost of the promotion, in return for which Rosensohn signed over to Salerno and Black 67% of his promotional company. D'Amato then agreed to negotiate. Rosensohn Enterprises Inc. could have had the fight, and also the exclusive rights to any return bout, but Cus wanted 50% of the live gate profits and all the television revenue for Patterson and himself. He got it. In the event there were no profits from the live gate, but plenty from TV. Whether Cus cut Salerno and Black in for a share of the latter was never determined. We can be sure that Rosensohn never made anything.

The fight itself was at first a gentlemanly affair. Leisurely, anyway. For two rounds Ingemar sashayed the odd jab, and Floyd peek-a-boo'd out at him.

Patterson opened the 3rd aggressively; Johansson continued to flick with the left. Then suddenly Ingo saw an opening and exploded the right on Patterson's jaw. The champion came apart. His legs turned to jelly, and a second right hurled him to the floor. At '9' he was up and staggering groggily away from the challenger. Johansson chased him, spun him round with a left hook to the ear, and then crashed home the right again. Patterson took another '9' count. It was a miracle he got up at all. Another right to the head and he was straight back down. Up he reeled, completely oblivious, merely carrying on on instinct alone, and he was soon down for the fourth time from a further right to the head, this time for '7'. Up yet again; and then down yet again; another seven seconds. Johansson was wielding his right like a broadsword. A sixth knockdown, part blow-part push, and it was becoming repetitious. The crowd screamed at the referee to intervene, but Ruby Goldstein hovered uncertainly on the fringe of the massacre. Finally, Patterson tottered towards his corner. Johansson came up behind him and cleaved him down for the seventh time with a stroke to the back of the head. At last Goldstein had seen enough.

The new champion, fourteen stone and over six foot of Teutonic embodiment, seemed like a breath of fresh air. There was a feeling that the void had been filled.

It was difficult to feel sympathy for Patterson. A nice man, yes — even his opponents went out of their way to praise him as an individual — but sadly a cardboard champion. Now night descended upon him. Day would be a long time coming.

At first Floyd retreated from the world. He brooded at home, a sad, reclusive figure. Hours crept into days, and days merged into weeks, darkened rooms taking the place of the subterranean tunnels of his childhood. He was repeating the pattern now, and for the same reason. His ego had been crushed.

It took some time before he was even able to watch television again. When he did the world seemed full of Ingemar Johansson. Floyd watched him on chat shows. What he saw he did not like. Johansson denigrated him; in effect treated him as a figure of no significance whatsoever. That hurt in a special kind of way because significance is what Floyd Patterson is all about.

It explains the man. The sensitive boy who fled from home and school, and who later indulged in petty crime, did so because his poverty and his troubles made him feel insignificant, caused him to doubt his worth.

Then came the man. The psychologist Abraham Manslow theorised that mankind has levels of significance. The basic need is for food and shelter, i.e., a secure job and a home. The next level is sexual; a mate in life. Then self esteem — social acceptance. When these three levels have been attained 95% of the population is satisfied. But 5% have an inborn need to go beyond ordinariness; to become significant individuals. They need an outlet to express this. Floyd Patterson found boxing. It was his means of expression, something he was very good at. Paradoxically, the significance it gave him allowed the gentler side of his nature to flourish.

Sometimes that nature was too gentle. Floyd always lacked what is termed 'killer instinct'. Subconsciously he felt he didn't need it; his talent was enough. The story is told that in his fifth professional fight he knocked Chester Mieszala's gumshield out of his mouth. When Mieszala bent down to pick it up Floyd, instead of pitching in, stopped boxing to assist him. It illustrates the point perfectly.

Now Johansson had not only taken his title, denigrated his talent, but made him feel insignificant — a little man. Never make the significant feel insignificant. There is first an implosion, a force of hate mushrooming inside. Then the blockage inside explodes.

Patterson began to feel hate for the first time. It grew inside him like some cold malevolence. Eventually, he forced himself to watch the film of the fight. Hate and professionalism coagulated. Johansson, Floyd saw, was not a particularly good fighter. He had been beaten by his own mistakes. Revenge became paramount.

Contractually, there had to be a return bout. Which takes us back to New York, and to the Polo Grounds on the night of June 20th, 1960, one year less one week since Patterson had surrendered his crown. None had ever regained it in the modern era. Floyd Patterson wouldn't, said the experts. Ingemar Johansson, who had enjoyed his fifty-one weeks as champion, agreed with them. He trained and took the fight lightly. He would have done better to study *Revelations*:

> *'Behold a pale horse, and the man who sat on him was death. And hell followed with him.'*

From the opening bell, Ingemar was sluggish; slow of hand, foot and mind. Patterson, by contrast, was swift, darting, sure; a man on fire within himself yet keeping the flames carefully under control.

In the 1st he kept the Swede off balance with a lightning jab. Ominously, a left hook rocked Johansson back on his heels.

Patterson continued to box smoothly in the 2nd until he came within range of Ingo's 'bingo'. For the first and only time during the fight this venomous weapon of destruction came flashing out and crashed against Floyd's temple. The blow hurled him into the ropes but Johansson was slow to follow up and Patterson, keeping ice cool under pressure, moved swiftly out of danger.

In the 3rd and 4th Patterson moved further and further ahead, yards faster in every way as he flicked neat jabs into Johansson's face and turned fast hooks off the jab in close. The audience waited patiently for the Swede to erupt again, but Ingo was befuddled and bemused, and when the explosion did come it was not from the champion.

At the beginning of the 5th Patterson moved swiftly across the ring while Johansson was slow in coming out. For a fraction of a second Ingo's jaw was exposed. It was enough. Floyd unleashed a dynamic left hook which sent the Swede sprawling on his back. He was up at '8' but badly hurt, and Patterson moved in and cut loose with a sustained, eviscerating, barrage of punches. Johansson reeled and lurched, a storm-tossed ketch caught in a red tidal wave of leather, desperately seeking a port from the storm that had exploded on him. But there was none, and finally Patterson beat aside the pathetic remnants of his defence and drove a perfect left hook against his jaw, almost lifting him off his feet. There was never the remotest glimmer of a chance of Johansson beating the count. His left leg twitched convulsively throughout the count. They counted ten; it could have been five hundred because Ingemar was out cold for eight minutes. Peter Wilson wrote:

> *'Johansson lay like a dead man.'*

There was a universal hope that Patterson would now become a 'real' champion. He had never fought better. The modern championship had been regained for the first time.

Cus also seemed to be on the way out. Bill Rosensohn had not promoted the second fight. Sick of being ripped off by sniggering gangsters, he sold his third to a New York lawyer named Roy Cohn. The mob stopped sniggering in a hurry. The same Roy Cohn had been Senator Joe McCarthy's right hand man in the anti-Communist witch hunts of the Fifties. If Salerno and Co. were sharks, then Roy Cohn was a sabre toothed shark. He instigated the N.Y.A.A.C. to set up an inquiry into the way the first fight had been run. It concluded that D'Amato had promoted it, in contravention of the rules, behind Black and Salerno. Cus, who did not attend the hearings (probably wisely), had his manager's licence revoked*.

Alas, Floyd never boxed that well again. And, if not in name, D'Amato remained his manager for another three years.

New York did not get to stage the final bout in the Patterson-Johansson trilogy (I wonder why!). The carnival moved on to Miami Beach, Florida, on March 13th, 1961. For those who like 'firsts', this fight had a cluster of them: for the first time in heavyweight title history the mandatory eight count; the three knockdowns rule; and a '20' count (mandatory '18') if a boxer was knocked out of the ring.

In their other two contests the victor had played to his strengths. At Miami both displayed their weaknesses.

The fight was hardly a minute old when Johansson got through with one of his big rights and Patterson was down. He got up at '5', took the mandatory '8', and then another right bounced him back down again. Once more the compulsory count came to Floyd's aid. Many ringsiders thought the extra seconds saved him from disaster, because another knockdown and it would have been all over. As it was, there was pandemonium amongst the spectators who thought they were in for a re-run of the first fight.

There was a third knockdown in the round but it came from Patterson, not Johansson. Trying to end it, the Swede ran into a left hook and it was his turn on the canvas. When the bell rang they had shared three knockdowns and left the audience gasping with excitement.

Alas, what followed was anti-climactic. Both men were wary in the next two rounds. It livened up a little in the 4th and 5th, but the exchanges were scrappy. Neither man boxed well.

Johansson was aggressive in the 6th, jabbing Patterson around the ring. Then, at the two minute mark, the fight ended with dramatic suddenness. Patterson caught the Swede coming in with a left hook to the jaw. Johansson

* A court later overturned the ruling on the technicality that the licence had expired anyway, but Cus never re-applied.

stood open and stunned. Following up, Patterson launched a brace of rights, the second to the back of the head. Johansson pitched forward onto his face and was counted out whilst rising.

Neither the fight or its conclusion were fulfilling. Had Johansson beaten the count? I thought so then and I am still of that opinion. He was conscious, and on one knee from '5'. He started up at '9' and had both knees off the canvas when the referee said '10'. Was the final punch a rabbit punch? Once again, my view is affirmative, but it was not intentional. Basically, Ingemar lurched into it head down.

Both fighters interpreted the 6th round differently. Johansson said he was setting Patterson up for his right and got tagged; Patterson claimed to be retreating deliberately to lure Johansson on to his left hook. Patterson's account is generally favoured. It would have been unusual for Johansson to persistently beat him to the jab, but on the other hand this was not one of Patterson's better fights, and he was never particularly effective off his back foot.

Who was actually ahead is strictly a matter of opinion. Ingemar has to be credited with the opening round by two knockdowns to one. I thought the Swede won the 2nd and 4th, Patterson the 3rd with the 5th even. Others had Floyd out in front.

It was not a conclusive ending to the series. Technically, both men were below par and made mistakes. The ending left question marks. However, there was not to be another fight. The battle of the two continents was over.

Johansson was out of the ring for almost a year. He returned to action against Joe Bygraves and stopped him in seven. The drums then started to beat for a shot at his old European title, now held by Britain's Dick Richardson. It almost never happened. Ingemar took a warm up bout with Wim Snoek, an undistinguished Dutch light-heavyweight in his mid-thirties. Snoek dropped Johansson with a left hook in the opening round. Johansson barely beat the count at '9', and ringsiders thought it was slow. Some estimates had the Swede down for 13 seconds. But he recovered to knock Snoek out in the 5th.

This performance did not bode well against Richardson, a tough, strong fighter with a good right hand punch himself. Richardson was riding the crest of a sensational first round kayo of Karl Mildenberger, a highly touted young German.

But in Gothenburg's Ullevi Stadium on the night of June 17th, 1962, Richardson was much too cautious. For six rounds Johansson gave him a lesson in using the jab. Richardson glimpsed hope in the 7th when his first decent punch, a left hook, split Johansson's right eye so badly that it seemed he would have to retire. But he came out for the 8th and produced two of the most devastating rights I have ever seen. The first left Richardson flat on his back — how he beat the count is a mystery — and the second flat on his face. Ingemar Johansson was European champion again.

The cut kept him out of the ring until the following April. His opponent then, in a Stockholm 12 rounder, was Brian London. Johansson only needed him for a clean sweep of championship-holding Britons since 1956. Watching London against Patterson, Ingemar had sneered that his sister could beat the Englishman. Perhaps he should have sent her along instead. For 11 rounds and 174 seconds it was a messy, brawling fight. Then London pounded a right to Johansson's jaw and down he went. The final bell saved Ingo at '6'. He was awarded a points decision sitting groggily in his corner. Many thought London had done enough to merit a draw.

This performance convinced Ingemar that he was past his best. At the age of 30 he retired. London, the moral victor, went on to box for the world title again.

Round Twenty: The 'Rabbit' and the 'Bear'

Charles 'Sonny' Liston is dead; in Dickens' words 'as dead as a door nail'. His rotting corpse was found on January 5th, 1971, at his home in Reno, Nevada. The autopsy concluded that he died of natural causes but some believe Sonny Liston was murdered by the mob.

While Patterson and Johansson were playing tennis with the title, Liston was waiting to come on court. His fight credentials were impeccable: a 32–1 record with 22 kayos. Almost every contender was on the list. Williams, Valdes, Harris, Folley and Machen. Henry Cooper's manager, Jim Wicks, turned Sonny down as an opponent on the grounds that he was an animalistic fighter whom Henry needed like a hole in the head.

This was a view very wholeheartedly endorsed by Cus D'Amato. Whenever Liston's name was mentioned, Cus found an excuse for Patterson not to fight him. Liston was an ex-con: Floyd himself had started to box in reformatory. Liston was controlled by the mob: coming from a man who was chorusing 'good old pal: jolly old pals' with Tony Salerno and Charlie Black this was rich indeed.

Real reasons. Liston was 6′ 1″ and weighed 214 lbs (97 kilos). He had a 15″fist, the largest of any heavyweight champion, and a prodigious 84″ reach. Patterson's was 71″. Only Carrera's was longer than Liston's; only Marciano's was shorter than Patterson's. They shared only one opponent. Roy Harris had lasted 12 unimpressive rounds with Patterson and floored him. In with Liston, Harris failed to last out the first session.

Charles Liston came from a background of appalling poverty. He was the last but one of twenty-five children fathered by Tobe Liston, a black sharecropper from Arkansas. His birth is as mysterious as his death. Charles, or 'Sonny' as he became known, claimed May 8th, 1932, as his birthday. Mother Helen originally supported the year, but recalled January as the month. Later she changed her mind to July, 1927. The latter is generally thought to be closer to the truth.

Sonny grew up illiterate in St. Louis, Missouri, and went to the bad on the city streets there. He was, to use a well worn phrase, a product of his environment. The progeny records of both parents, in bleakly impoverished circumstances, suggests that neither had heard of birth control or restraint. Helen Liston claims to have made some attempt to control her 24th offspring, but it was not successful. The teenage Sonny was a hulking, scowling thug with more chips on his shoulder than a carpenter's bench. He ran with the street gangs, mugged violently, and seems to have inherited his father's sexual appetite. Later, he exhibited signs of paranoia; the police were always out to get him wherever he went.

Get him they did in the spring of 1950. Liston was sentenced to five years for armed robbery. While in prison he came under the auspices of Father Alois Stevens, a Roman Catholic priest who ran the penitentiary's boxing team. Alois Stevens was later portrayed as Sonny's guide, philosopher and father figure in a P.R. exercise designed to show Liston as a reformed character. Cynics might contend that taking up boxing and getting into the Reverend Stevens good books was a useful device to obtain the early parole which Sonny received in 1952.

However, he stayed with the boxing and in 1953 won the National Golden Gloves heavyweight title. One of his victories along the way was over the tragically destined Ed Saunders. Late summer, 1953, Sonny turned pro under the management of Frank Mitchell, who guaranteed him a salary of $35 a week outside of what he earned from fighting. Although said to be a money man, Mitchell soon claimed that this paltry wage was beyond him. Instead, he found Sonny a job with John Vitale. Vitale was the crime boss of St. Louis. Ostensibly, Liston was employed by Vitale's concrete manufacturing company. Highly appropriate or gruesomely ironic — take your pick — because Vitale had a history of providing concrete overcoats for union officials, and Sonny's real 'job' was as a strike-breaking labour goon.

Mitchell's behaviour was at best redolent of the set up pimps use for turning women into prostitutes; at worst, a possible future heavyweight champion was being turned over to the mob because Vitale was an associate of boxing's Burke and Hare, Carbo and Palermo. Not that Mr Mitchell actually mixed with any of these gentlemen. It was pure coincidence that like Vitale he had a history of being arrested for crimes which nobody was prepared to testify against him for. Vitale? Nah; Frank had met him only once on a golf course, don't really know him at all, squire.

Liston's career got underway against this excremental background. He won his first seven fights. At this stage the record does not indicate a heavy hitter, just two kayos. But he was still very much on a learning curve, adapting his style to the pro ring. That he was good nobody could doubt. His sixth and seventh victories were over Johnny Summerlin, a 'dangerman' fighter who most avoided, and who the following year (1955) snapped Zora Folley's unbeaten skein.

In his eighth fight Liston was outpointed and had his jaw broken by Marty Marshall. The way Sonny recalled it, Marshall's antics amused him, and he had his mouth open, laughing, when Marty hit him and caused the injury.

Liston gained his revenge, one of six victories, in 1955, knocking Marshall out in six rounds. Marshall claims that he floored Sonny in the 4th, taking advantage of his carrying his right hand too low (Liston said it was a slip).

The following year he met Marshall a third time and won on points. This was his only fight in 1956 and there were none in 1957. The record book baldly states 'inactive'. In fact he was back in the slammer, this time for beating up a policeman and stealing his gun.

On Sonny's release, Frank Mitchell's pumping duties were dispensed with. Frank of course knew nothing about anything: 'Some of the boys in the fight mob came up to me and said they were taking Sonny east.' Natch. 'East' meant Philadelphia where Joe Barone became Liston's 'manager'. Sonny's contract entitled him to an expense-free 50% of his purses. The other 50% was split: Frankie Carbo 26%, Barone 12% and Palermo and Vitale each 6%.

1958 was trial horse time. Not Palookas, but average fighters who didn't have it at the highest level. Wayne Bethea and Bert Whitehurst were the best. Only Whitehurst (twice) went the distance out of eight fights in all.

Contender class came in 1959. First Mike de John, a strong white heavyweight with a potent left hook, was despatched in six but not before wobbling Sonny first. Cleveland Williams also staggered him. This was a real battle of punches. Cleve had previously lost once inside the distance, Bob Satterfield on a night when Bob succeeded in keeping his chin out of the way. Liston made it two, cleaving Williams in the 3rd. August saw the finish of Nino Valdes as a contender. Valdes was curving downwards, but Sony still looked awesome in taking him apart in three*. Willie Besmanoff, a smallish German-American, lasted into the 7th in December and demonstrated that for all his power Sonny was not really at ease against retreating boxers. Liston couldn't reach him with any big ones, but his long left jab cut Besmanoff up.

House cleaning continued in 1960. While Floyd was still brooding over Johansson, Liston stopped Howard King, Williams again in two, and disintegrated Harris. After Patterson regained the title, Sonny told him loudly and clearly who the number one contender now was. First Folley. Following the Cooper defeat Zora had gotten back most of his lustre with ten straight victories including Machen, Besmanoff, King and Bygraves. But as with Cooper, Folley fought a stupid fight, electing to trade with Liston. He was chilled in the 3rd. Machen came on at summer's end and went the 12 round distance in an eliminator. It was a bout which emphasised Liston's problems with ring mechanics. He won clearly enough, but Eddie went backwards and sideways and held in close. Sonny made his power tell only once with an 11th round knockdown, but Machen was still there at the final bell. Another knockout of Howard King, in Miami five days before Patterson–Johannson III, brings Liston's story up to date with Floyd's.

The next eighteen months are probably best described as the gangster wars. At stake was the heavyweight title, although overall the mob already controlled both the champion and the No.1 contender.

* Valdes degenerated into drug addiction.

In one corner was the D'Amato–Salerno–Black axis. Patterson has always said that he was unaware of the true picture and in my view he should be believed. In the other, Carbo, Palermo and Vitale. Liston, without any doubt, did know what was going on.

Refereeing was Estes Kefauver, a pugnacious Senator from Tennessee with aspirations to the White House. Kefauver had tried for the Democratic nomination in both 1952 and '56 and had been Adlai Stevenson's running mate in the latter contest. Throughout the '50s the Tennessean chaired a number of well publicised Senate investigations into organised crime. In 1960 he began to probe its links with boxing.

Kefauver's kerfuffles originated from a very nasty can of worms involving the welterweight title, won in 1958 by Don Jordan, a foul-mouthed Central American who claims to have been a 'hit man' at the age of ten! Jordan was not one of the division's more significant champions which is probably why Carbo did not have a piece of him. This seems to have offended Frankie's pride. Revealingly, in a telephone call threatening wooden overcoats galore, the Murder Inc. boss said: 'I have had that title 25 years and no punks are going to take it way from me.' Carbo attempted to muscle in on Jordan, but found his way blocked by Jordan's co-manager, Don Nesseth. Eventually, Carbo was charged under federal law with extortion. Simultaneously, he was under indictment in New York for tax evasion and matters arising out of I.B.C. Hoping to get out from under his federal problems (he didn't), Carbo pleaded guilty in New York (a bit like Jack the Ripper admitting common assault!), and was sent to prison for two years. Ironically, Don Jordan went to pieces after Carbo's conviction.

This, and the imbroglio over the Patterson-Johannson fight, led to the Senate hearings. They lasted well into 1961. One of the centrepieces, inevitably, was Carbo's control of Liston, who stonewalled his testimony. Light comic relief was provided by Frank Mitchell, deliciously reminiscent of Monty Python's 'Ethel the Frog' sketch. 'Frankie? Nah, he's a lovely bloke — and I don't know him anyway.' As for Carbo's 26% of Liston, Mitchell claimed he was still drawing that!

During the hearings Carbo was tried for the Federal offences, along with Blinky Palermo. They were sentenced to 25 and 15 years respectively. Carbo later died in prison*. Shaking his head, Senator Kefauver opined that if Liston became champion, the heavyweight title would revert to the control of the mob.

Which all appeared to have turned out nicely for D'Amato and friends, who escaped investigation by the Senate Committee. Why is unclear. The

* Palermo was paroled in 1971.

N.Y.A.A.C.'s inquiry had unearthed plenty to look into. Charlie Black, for example, was described as: 'the type of personality whose presence would inure to the best interest of boxing.' One possible answer lies, unintentionally, in Patterson himself. He had become very acceptable to the U.S. establishment (black militants would later denigrate him as an 'Uncle Tom') and was *personae grata* at the Kennedy White House; along with Martin Luther King a symbol of Camelot's commitment to blacks; as long as they were the right sort of blacks which Liston most assuredly wasn't.

Sonny, D'Amato unctioned piously, must rid himself of the mob influences surrounding him in order to get a title shot. Well, evil though Carbo and his henchmen were, they gunned down other killers and dominated a sport which has always had its seamy side to balance the heroic. Cus's pal 'Fat Tony' was a heroin trafficker on a vast scale. How many lives this degraded creature had wrecked by the time he finally went to gaol in 1988 cannot be estimated.

But in the summer of 1961, Liston was doing his own cause no good at all. He was arrested in Philadelphia for an incident involving a woman. Sonny contended it was all a joke and the charges were dismissed. The exact truth can only be guessed at. Despite the case being dropped, the Pennsylvania Boxing Commission stripped him of his licence, and the other N.B.A. affiliated States followed suit. His new manager, George Katz, appeared to be free of mob connections but Katz's share of Liston's purses, 10%, was suspiciously low. All in all the D'Amato faction appeared triumphant.

In fact they were not. Cus's public refusal to allow Floyd to fight Sonny — 'He (Liston) is not included in (Patterson's) future plans — eventually generated a backlash of sympathy in Liston's favour. The behaviour of the Pennsylvania Boxing Commission smacked of witch hunting and most concluded that Patterson was just plain scared of Liston. Estes Kefauver put into words what many felt about Sonny:

> *'I have nothing but goodwill towards this unfortunate man. Those who heard him must carry with them the haunting memory of a tragic man... Mr Liston's new management, if cleared, [then] he should obtain a championship bout.'*

Liston also took steps to clean up his image. There was a much publicised friendship with another Catholic priest, Father Edward Murphy, who converted him to Catholicism, and the renewal of his old acquaintance with Father Stevens.

The events of December 4th, 1961, were a harbinger of how much things had begun to move in Liston's favour.

With Sonny's suspension Henry Cooper was installed as the top contender by the N.B.A. and should have been Floyd's next challenger. This time the problem was not with terms; D'Amato simply ignored Cooper and chose instead Tom McNeely, a white American heavyweight somewhat optimistically rated the number nine contender. Even leaving Cooper and Liston aside, there were other more deserving opponents, among then two iron-jawed Canadians, Robert Cleroux (28–2–1–23 kayos) and George Chuvals (20–7–1–15 kayos), who were engaged in a private war for the Canadian title. The irony was that Patterson-McNeely would go on at the Maple Leaf Gardens, Toronto, the first heavyweight championship bout to be held in Canada in the modern era, and the first outside America since 1933.

Tom McNeely was unbeaten; in every sense. He had won all his fights but never beaten anyone of consequence. The kindest comment made about him was that he was some distance from fistic maturity.

Basically, the only way this turkey figured to make money was if Liston fought too, so that comparisons could be made. But Sonny was suspended. Amazing what happens when there's money in the pot. Liston was reinstated and signed to fight in Philadelphia, an hour before Patterson boxed, so that both bouts could go out on closed circuit.

Sonny's opponent was even more ludicrous than Floyd's, a 5′ 7½″ baker from Germany named Albert Westphal. He was certainly not the best his country had to offer; promising Karl Mildenberger then stood 29–1, although whether Karl would have wanted Sonny at this point is another matter. Predictably, Liston knocked Westphal colder than last night's coffee in the 1st round. Afterwards the German was asked if he fancied a rematch! The little baker stared at the reporter as if he were mad, and then scuttled back across the Atlantic with the epithet 'Quickfall' dinning in his ears.

Tom McNeely didn't 'phal' quite so early, but a lot more often. Ten times he made the acquaintance of the white ring awning. The last was in round four, when he finally failed to beat referee Jersey Joe Walcott's count. Like Varro at Cannae, Tom enjoyed one tiny success amidst the massacre, momentarily dropping Floyd with a left swing to the body.

Although both 'fights' devalued boxing, it was Floyd who took the flack. Liston was credited with having shown enormous power. And within 24 hours he was the No. 1 contender again. Cooper unwisely took a rematch with Folley ('enery's folly) and was flattened in the 2nd.

According to Patterson, D'Amato always refused to give him a reason for ducking Liston. Cus simply stuck to the mob angle. When, in 1962, Sonny got himself another new manager, Jack Nilon, D'Amato quipped: 'there's no change — whether it's Nilon, Rayon, Cotton or Silk.' He was right: Nilon was an associate of Sam Margolis, a business partner of Blinky Palermo. Liston agreed to fight exclusively for a corporation owned by himself and Nilon's brothers. 27.5% of said company found its way back to Margolis who in turn transferred half of it to his lawyer. Business doesn't stop for prison sentences.

D'Amato however misjudged public opinion. He was singing the same old song and, on the surface, Jack Nilon seemed respectable. Finally Patterson took matters into his own hands and announced that Liston would be his next defence.

His decision caused a permanent split with D'Amato, one which Floyd always regretted.

Patterson had won the title in Chicago and he went back there to defend it against Liston on September 25th, 1962. This was not inspired by nostalgia or good luck omens. New York was supposed to be the venue, but Liston, who had not previously boxed there and never would*, was refused a licence.

Liston and Patterson clashed twice, but in reality it was one fight consisting of two separate rounds. Patterson was in some quarters a slight favourite to win at Comiskey Park. Having at last overruled Cus, he found himself popular. Floyd was, after all, a symbol of the 'good nigger'. The public, having championed Liston's cause to get the title shot, really didn't want 'Old Stoneface', the 'bad arse nigger', to actually win the title.

Sentiment was banished in 126 seconds. Liston, who looked ginormous by comparison with the champion, thudded hooks to the body, trapped Floyd against the ropes, and then despatched him with a left hook to the side of the head. The camera angle makes it appear more of a cuff, but ringsiders immediately below the action saw it as a very powerful blow.

Afterwards Patterson slipped out of Comiskey Park in a false beard which he had secreted in his dressing room *before* the fight. All the many months of Cus refusing to let him in the ring with Liston had destroyed Floyd's confidence. A significant man had been rendered insignificant.

Round two took place on July 22nd, 1963, at Las Vegas. Interest centred on whether Patterson could recapture the messianic fervour of the Johansson rematch. The answer was no; Liston-Patterson II lasted just four seconds longer than the first offering.

Patterson opened with a kangaroo leap and then rushed in wildly, catching Liston on the shoulder with a frenetic left hook. Liston's right arm swept downwards and Floyd promptly followed it. He was up at '8', Liston measured him for a three punch combination and Floyd was back down again for another '8'. Then the champion ended it, topping a whiplash combination with a perfect left hook to the point of the jaw which dropped Floyd for the full count.

The two quick victories over Patterson turned Sonny into a gothic figure. He was awarded a pedestal with three steps leading up. On the podium was placed Liston himself. The first step below was occupied by the men around him, assuring everyone that Sonny Boy was invincible. Nilon predicted that he would hold the title for at least five years. On the middle step stood the press, filling their columns with images of a Frankestein monster *sans* bolt. From the bottom step gazed a perplexed public, not knowing whether they were looking

* The only modern heavyweight champion never to do so.

up at a sporting giant or an ogre. They wanted a kindly colossus, a substitute role model for their children, just like good old Floyd and good old Rocky. But could this gaolbird with his *open* mob connections provide the illusion? What if the bad guy in the black hat had actually won? In the early Sixties Liston, and after him Mohammed Ali, presaged the spaghetti western craze, the era of the anti-hero who on celluloid is permitted to win because he has a few crumbs of decency and the baddies do not. One such western which bleakly ended with the good bad guy being killed by the bad bad guys bombed at the box office and was swiftly pulled by the distributors. Such was the frightening dilemma posed by Charles 'Sonny' Liston. Good bad guy — or bad bad guy?

The question was never really answered. The unbeatable hulk who stood comparison with the greats of the past did not actually exist. Oh yes; Sonny Liston was good. A pro golfer once observed that you don't shoot 63 by hitting the ball sideways, and you don't decimate the heavyweight division by not being able to fight. But Liston was very much mortal. He had a long, accurate jab and could hit with tremendous power. But he had flaws and his technique was defective. Predominantly, he was slow both of hand and foot. Watching him on tape, Ingemar Johansson asked whether the film had been slowed down! Marty Marshall called attention to Liston 'dragging' his right hand which left him exposed to fast counters. Rocky Marciano thought Sonny's stance was too upright and criticised his punches as too long and looping; rather like Rommel performing a flanking movement in the desert (my metaphor — not Rocky's). The man who Liston made his second defence against, at Miami Beach on February 25th, 1964, was ideally suited to exploit these weaknesses.

To a large extent Liston had put himself out of business. He had made mincemeat of all the contenders save Cooper, whose manager wanted no part of Sonny, and Johansson, who had fistically demised even before the second round with Patterson. The only man who could draw a gate was a brash young Kentuckian then going by the name of Cassius Clay.

In terms of achievement Clay hardly merited a title shot at this stage. He had stopped Archie Moore, but Moore was then either 45 or 48, depending on which year of his birth you believe. Henry Cooper had fallen in five, as predicted by Cassius, but only after coming desperately close to knocking Clay out. Doug Jones was outpointed, but Doug was really a blown up light-heavy. However, the heavyweight scene was distinctly impoverished, and the extraordinary way in which Clay had captured the public's attention actually meant that Liston needed him more than he needed Liston.

The story of Mohammed Ali a.k.a. Cassius Clay, will be told in the succeeding chapters. At the moment what needs to be said is that he displayed an overweening confidence and arrogance to the extent that some thought at the time that his elevator did not go all the way to the top! Prospective opponents were derided in phantasmagorical style. Liston, for example, was 'the Bear',

Patterson 'the rabbit'. His many, many antics were the height of bad taste and poor decorum. But they put bums on seats.

Few actually gave Clay a chance against Liston. An eve of fight poll amongst reporters went 43–3 to the champion. Clay's demented behaviour at the most bizarre weigh-in in boxing history convinced many that he was terrified of Liston — too frightened, said some, even to turn up!

In fact the press were victims of their own mythology about Liston the titan. Like the 'Titanic' — and its sister ships — he was not unsinkable.

The opening round of the fight was a revelation. Gone was the hysteria of the weigh-in. In its place, an icy calmness prevailed. Clay was on his toes spearing Liston with long, razor sharp jabs. Liston looked bemused and shocked almost. The difference in speed was eye opening, as if a marathon runner were trying to sprint with Carl Lewis.

But the champion did better in the 2nd, cutting the ring down and reaching Clay's body with long rights. Clay however was unperturbed. He had felt the bear's claws and he was not impressed.

But now it is the 3rd. Ringside hummed with a mixture of anticipation and incredulity. Clay moves up through the gearbox and suddenly Liston looks like an old man; old and vulnerable. A jab slices open a cut beneath his left eye and then a scorching right cross has Liston lurching away, hurt. The behemoth of the Patterson fights has gone. To paraphrase what Peter Wilson wrote about the Charles–Louis fight: a squinting Lear is being thrashed with a belt buckle.

Clay continues in the 4th. Curving, scimitar punches serrate Liston. The challenger is boxing masterfully. Jabs jolt, toes twinkle. Not a lot comes back and what does Clay sways his body or jerks his head away from. Liston had spent a decade learning this blood-soaked business and now he is being made to look ordinary.

But in the 5th there is sensation. Clay is pawing at his eyes and shouting that there is something in them. Only a slap across the rump by trainer Angelo Dundee gets him out of the corner. He runs and runs, Liston lumbering after him throwing punches for all he is worth. Occasionally Clay sticks out his left to measure the distance between Sonny and himself. But he is, to all intents and purposes, one of the blind mice running from the chopper. Liston however is slow; oh, so slow, and the opportunity to save his title vanishes before him. The bell ends one of the most bizarre rounds in history and Cassius Clay still stands.

All is transformed in the 6th. Clay's corner have washed his eyes out. It is almost schizophrenic to see the way in which the panic-ridden figure of the previous round has returned to the precise fighter of the first four. It is Liston who is now in trouble. He is no longer punching with his left. Clay dominates. Jabs, hooks, crosses. A scattergun of punches at close enough range that none miss.

When he comes out for the 7th, Clay is momentarily surprised to find himself alone. Then he throws his arms in the air and begins a wild dance of joy.

The bear sits huddled in his corner, Jack Nilon shaking his head at the referee's query. American record books will say 'ko by 7', British, 'Ret 6'. It matters not. It is as academic as the question of whether Liston would have been a reputable champion now is.

Volume Six

Cassius Clay to Muhammad Ali

Round Twenty-One: The Making of a King

Cassius Clay celebrated winning the title by changing his name to Muhammad Ali and announcing his membership of the Black Muslim religious-politico sect. In doing so he sparked a controversy which ended his first period as champion and drove him into boxing's wilderness.

On the face of it there was hardly anything to object to. Any individual has a legal right to change his or her name, religious freedom is guaranteed by the American Constitution, and the Muslim faith is as old and respected as Christianity.

The problem lay with the Black Muslim's extremist political philosophy which in the early sixties held that whites were the children of the Devil — a teaching not expounded anywhere in the Koran — and preached separation of the races. That the heavyweight champion of the world should be a spokesman of such views, many found dangerous and obnoxious. Liberals, black and white, felt that it undermined their efforts to end prejudice, while white bigots fed on racism in reverse. It was an unhappy situation which was to rob Ali of his greatest years, and indirectly lead to the onset of Parkinson's syndrome which has left him a sad shadow of his former self.

Ali was born in Louisville, Kentucky on January 17th, 1942, the son of Cassius Marcellus Clay Senior, an extrovert sign writer not above getting into scrapes with the law. A tender point with Ali is the fact that there is a strain of white blood on either side of his family. His younger brother, christened Rudolph, later followed Muhammad both into the boxing ring and the Black Muslims, changing his name to Rahaman Ali.

Muhammad Ali began to box at the age of twelve. Somebody stole his bicycle and he wanted to 'whup' the culprit and get it back, so he went along to a gymnasium run by a local policeman named Joe Martin. Ali never did get the bike back but he did start whupping other boys in the boxing ring under Martin's tutelage.

By 1959 Ali had made good progress. That year he won both the National Amateur and Golden Gloves light heavyweight titles. The following year he retained the National A.A.U. championship and won the Golden Gloves heavyweight class, knocking out an opponent who outweighed him by 40 lbs in the final. In August he went to the Rome Olympics as America's light heavyweight representative.

It was a march of triumph, fought four, won four, gold medal. And against distinguished opposition, Russia's Gennadi Schatkov, winner of the 1956 Olympic middleweight title, Australia's Tony Madigan, the Empire Games champion and pre-tournament favourite, and in the final a Pole, Zbiegniew Pietrzyzkowksi (pity the poor commentators!), thrice European champion. In the shadow of the Coliseum Ali staged a grandstand finish to make sure of the decision.

He slept with the gold medal around his neck, allegedly fell in love with the Women's Sprint champion, Wilma Rudolph, and on returning to America turned professional. Here the first sour note of his career was struck: he discarded Joe Martin who had looked forward to earning money with his protegé. However, in retrospect it was the right, hard-headed decision. Martin had only ever trained amateurs and Ali needed professional guidance.

Outstanding amateurs do not necessarily make successful pros. Britain's finest trio of amateurs, Harry Mallin, Dick McTaggert and John Lyons always resisted the pro ring because they felt their styles were not suited to it. Many good judges were actually derisive of the eighteen year old Muhammad Ali's chances. They felt his style was, to say the least, too unorthodox.

Unorthodoxy did not begin with Ali. Britain's Jimmy Wilde and Pedlar Palmer, America's Maxie Rosenbloom, and the Australian Young Griffo had all been highly unconventional world champions in their day. But Ali was something else.

He simply tore up the boxing manuals. Technically, Ali had no defence, sometimes led off his right foot, often punched from hip level, missed a lot, and appeared to be flicking his punches rather than getting his weight behind them. Body punching and in-fighting were excluded from his arsenal. According to professional coaches, Ali should have been dumped on his behind in his first pro fight and remained there. But they were wrong. Why?

Everything Ali did was related to phenomenal reflexes and leg speed, at least in the first, youthful phase of his career. Bouncing around the ring like a human pogo stick with his hands held low might seem like an invitation to the Palookaville general hospital. In fact, Ali's speed of foot generally enabled him to be somewhere else when his opponent threw punches, and if they did arrive his superb reflexes and upper body movement combined to enable him to avoid contact by jerking his head aside or arcing his torso backwards. Like Palmer and Griffo, who employed similar tactics, the young Ali scorned conventional defence. Think of a soccer team without an orthodox back four but a midfield packed with Olympic sprint champions and there you have it.

Flyweight legend Jimmy Wilde often led off his right foot, and 'Slapsie Maxie' Rosenbloom appeared to cuff more than punch. In Ali's case, his hand speed almost matched Patterson's. He missed some, but then he threw a lot more than other fighters. They might not appear hard but this was deceptive. Ali hit so fast and so often that it was the cumulative effect which did the damage. And, whilst never a power hitter like Louis or Marciano, Muhammad could time individual shots with devastating effect. As Jose Torres remarks: 'In boxing the punch which knocks you out is not the hard punch. It's the punch you don't see coming. And Ali was a master at that.'[1] Ali also had the knack of twisting his

1 'Muhammad Ali: His Life and Times' p.128.

knuckles on impact to hurt and cut opponents. The purists conceded that a slugger like Marciano could throw away the textbook; they never imagined that a master boxer could also do it until Ali came along.

Muhammad Ali was big business from the start. He was managed by a consortium of eleven Louisville businessmen (seven of them millionaires) under the chairmanship of Bill Faversham, a wealthy brewer. Ali received signing on fees and initially 50% of his purses (later 60%), the other half going (after expenses) to his backers in equal shares. Faversham acted as business manager. As for a trainer, Ali knew who he wanted. He had already been in contact with Angelo Dundee prior to the Olympics. Dundee, who trained and also managed Willie Pastrano and future welterweight champion Luis Rodriguez, was a dumpy Italian American refreshingly free from mob connections. He would join the team for Muhammad's second pro fight and be with him throughout his career. Dundee did not attempt to change Ali's basic technique; he did however refine it.

On October 29th, 1960, Ali had his first pro fight, against Tunney Hunsacker, later a police chief. He boxed for a distance fight, outpointing Hunsacker over six and cutting him up in the process. After a brief but unhappy spell training with Archie Moore, Ali, now ensconced with Dundee, stopped Herb Siler to round out the year. He was on his way.

But to what? Perdition, said the textbook eaters. Most of them were also more than a little infuriated by Ali's brash publicity seeking. He was making waves. Patterson and Johansson, said Ali, I can beat right now! Johansson in fact sparred with him while preparing for his rubber match with Patterson. After Ali had thoroughly exposed what Angelo Dundee called Ingo's two left feet, the Swede growled: 'What does this kid do; ride a bike for ten hours a day?' Truth to tell, Muhammad was beginning to impress some knowledgeable fight people. Harold Johnson, Moore's successor as light heavyweight champ, summed him up as faster than Patterson and a good boxer.

The accolades were better than the results. Between December, 1960, and May, 1962, Ali sailed through eleven opponents. Of these only Alex Miteff, a tough Argentinian who Dundee did not want Ali to fight yet, figured to give him trouble. Angelo's doubts produced Ali's best performance to date and a spectacular one punch finish, a short right hook to the jaw which dropped Miteff in a heap. He beat the count but was out on his feet and the referee stopped it. Afterwards the N.B.A. middleweight champion, Gene Fullmer, declared that Ali was already too good for Patterson.

The rest were a bunch of dismal jimmies, quite literally in the case of Jim Robinson who had been knocked out in his only previous pro bout. Lucien 'Sonny' Banks, had lost two out of fourteen, but embarrassed Ali by actually knocking him down with a left hook in the 1st before exiting in round four. Pride of place however went to Lamar Clark. On paper Clark was a fearsome proposition with 47 kayos (45 straight) in 50 bouts. In reality he resembled nothing more than Ronald Reagan's famous question in 'King's Row', a punch asking 'where's the rest of me?' because that was all Lamar had. In his biggest test Rademacher had tamed him. 'The punch' did manage to find Ali's body and hurt him before a torrid burst of punches put paid to Lamar in the 2nd.

Basically these were not so much fights as product advertising. As a publicity stunt Muhammad had started to nominate the round in which an opponent would 'fall'. Fall in that round they generally did, and it captured the public's imagination. In reality, the quality of the opposition was so poor that Ali often carried them until the chosen round. Supplementing the predictions were rhymes and couplets. For instance:

'This boy likes to mix,
so he must fall in six.'

Not everything went to plan though. Duke Sabedong, a lumbering Hawaiian, and Alonzo Johnson both defied their predicted demises to lose on points and Johnson ran him close. In neither fight did Muhammad display any real power.

The lynch-pin of Ali's braggadocio was actually a professional wrestler, 'Gorgeous George' Raymond, whom writer John Cottrell describes as: 'the most outrageously ostentatious and gimmick-conscious sports entertainer of his time.'[1] Ali caught Wagner's act one night in June, 1961 and was immediately impressed by the wrestler's flair for pulling in the crowds. Wagner was the baddie, a preening, strutting peacock whom people came to see get knocked off his perch. Most importantly, they paid great wads of money to watch it. Nobody ever accused Muhammad Ali of not wanting to be rich.

Ali modelled his act on Wagner's but did not directly imitate it. Things worked because he was his own original.

In wrestling the results don't really matter. In boxing you're only as good as your last fight. All the publicity gimmicks in the world meant nothing unless Ali kept winning. In May, 1962, he faced his sternest test, Billy Daniels, a gangling 6′ 5″ heavyweight with a rangy left and a raking right who was unbeaten. Ali was lucky that night. Daniels constantly beat him to the jab, and was ahead on points when the referee stopped it because Billy had a badly cut eye. The press panned Ali, in particular the way Daniels had lanced him with long rights. However, Daniels put some perspective on it a few months afterwards when he used those same rights to skewer Mike Dejohn. Alas for Billy, he later ran into the evergreen branches of Williams and Folley, and was left mumbling his Brando impersonation: 'I couda been a contender.'

1 'Man of Destiny' p.35

Sometime earlier Folley had been surprisingly knocked out by Alejandro Lavorante, a young Argentinian. Archie Moore took the shine off it by stopping the South American in ten, but summer of '62 Alejandro was still rated a comer and when Ali chose him as his next opponent some believed he was heading for his first defeat. Ali was always at his best when his ego was challenged. For four rounds he glided in and out pasting Lavorante with jabs, hooks and combinations. In the 5th he knocked him out, the final punch a peach of a left hook which had Alejandro's head bouncing off the canvas. In his next fight Lavorante was kayoed by trial horse John Riggins. He went into a coma and never came out of it, dying two years later. He was not the only tragic figure amongst Ali's opponents. Sonny Banks also became a ring fatality, Liston died mysteriously and Zora Folley was killed in a swimming pool accident. Tunney Hunsacker's boxing career ended with a life or death brain operation. Happily, he made a full recovery.

Ali's carnival moved on to embrace Archie Moore in what was to be a battle of words rather than punches. Although still ranked the No. 6 heavyweight contender at the age of either 48 or 45, the ancient one was finally at the end of his illustrious career. In the six years since the Patterson fight Archie had lost only once on 29 contests and that defeat, later avenged, was viewed rather cynically in some quarters. He had defended his light heavyweight crown four times, and amongst the heavies knocked out Lavaronte, Rademacher, Roger Rischer, Bert Whitehurst (a feat not equalled by Liston in two fights), Besmanoff and King. Many believed that D'Amato had avoided a Moore rematch as studiously as he had ducked Liston and co.

The build up to Ali-Moore provided much genuine humour. Ali predicted Archie would go in four. Moore, a veteran of such tactics, responded: 'The only way I'll fall in four is by toppling over your prostrate body', and threatened Ali — now known as 'The Louisville lip' — with the 'lip buttoner' punch. Ali riposted with the 'pension punch'. 'Conversationally', said the *New York Times*, 'it has assumed the magnitude of the Battle of the Century'.

A battle it sadly was not. Moore's age was cruelly exposed. He did not sit down between rounds for fear that his ageing limbs might lock. It was stopped after he had been down three times in the 4th. Archie has since expressed doubts that he could ever have beaten Ali; more eye-raisingly, that Muhammad would have beaten Joe Louis four times out of five.

Moore at last retired four months later after knocking out an unknown. His final record (officially) was 193–26–8 with one 'no contest'. Archie's 140 stoppage victories is the most in boxing history and probably will never be surpassed.

In his dressing room after annihilating Moore, Ali chalked on a blackboard 'Liston in eight'. He had fired his opening salvo at Sonny four weeks earlier after watching him take the title off Patterson:

'When people left the park
You could hear them say,

Liston will stay the King
Until he meets Cassius Clay.'

Most people of course were saying nothing of the kind. Liston was now regarded as a giant ogre and the consensus went something like, 'Fi-fo-fum — Sonny will flatten the bum.' But it was good for boxing. Jack Dempsey mused: 'I don't care if this kid can't fight a lick. I'm for him. Things are live again.'

Whether Ali could actually 'fight a lick' was at this stage still a moot question. He had impressed against Miteff and Lavaronte and scored good marks from some shrewd observers. But he had not yet come of age as a fighter and was being kept away from a Daniels rematch and the likes of Folley, Williams and Machen. Even so, the latter joined the small but growing band of Muhammad's admirers. Ali, Machen averred, had speed and class, exactly the qualities needed to beat Liston. Along with Pastrano, Rademacher, and Marty Marshall, Eddie would later be one of the few to give Ali a chance of beating Liston at Miami Beach.

Charlie Powell, in Pittsburgh a week after Ali's 21st birthday, became his seventeenth straight victim. A very large white American football player, Powell had switched to boxing without noticeable success. During the weigh-in Powell and Ali were happily exchanging jibes when Powell's brother intervened in the hype and began to taunt Ali, using the word 'boy', a particular insult to Southern blacks. Ali went tight lipped. That night he destroyed Charlie Powell. A stupendous barrage of punches — some counted 40 — knocked Charlie out in the 3rd. His face was mashed into pulp and when he came round Powell vomited blood in his corner. Afterwards he commented: 'I was getting dizzier and dizzier every time he hit me... Clay throws punches so easily you don't realise how much they shock you until it's too late.'

At this point Ali was the no. 4 contender behind Patterson, Williams and Doug Jones. Doug who? The Jones boy and his rating were a classic example of the way things get turned on their head in boxing. Up to May, 1962, Jones was a light heavyweight unbeaten in 20 fights. Then he went in with Harold Johnson for the title and got himself a boxing lesson. After this Jones tried his luck amongst the big men and had his ears pinned back by Machen and Folley. In reality he was still just a decent light heavyweight and proved it by halting future 175 lbs champion Bob Foster in October. But in December he had a rematch with Folley at the Garden. It promised to be an easy night for Zora. But, just as he had done with Cooper four years previously, Folley became over confident and ended up being knocked out in the 7th, a result which put him out in the cold again, and enabled Jones to take over his No. 3 ranking. Machen also managed to get himself beaten by a light-heavy, Johnson, and began to slide*.

* Previously only Liston, Johansson and Folley had defeated him in 41 fights.

All of which left Doug Jones in the demonstrably false position of being a contender for Mr Liston's crown.

Jones should really have been easy meat for Ali. He wasn't, possibly because he was small and compact, which never quite suited Ali, possibly because he was enjoying his little moment in the sun too much to be fazed by Muhammad's confidence sapping insults. The fight, on March 13th, 1962, attracted the sort of attention usually reserved only for title bouts. There was a capacity house at the Garden; they could have sold it out several times over.

Officially Ali's record reads: 'Doug Jones w pts 10'. In actuality it was a very hard contest which some thought could have gone the other way. The referee with his 8–1–1 scorecard was not one of them, but both judges saw it more accurately as 5–4–1. Not until the last three rounds did Muhammad really take command. Early on Jones whaled away at him, particularly with punishing right hooks to the body. In the second phase of his career, as his speed diminished, Ali would be famed for his strength, but at the beginning body punches troubled him. In addition to Jones, Clark and Powell both hurt him with left hooks to the heart. These, and the Banks knock-down, also indicated a slight vulnerability to left hooks. Confirmation of it came dramatically in Muhammad's next fight.

We last left Henry Cooper shaking the resin from his thinning locks, Folley having downed him in two. Defeat never seemed to douse the spark in this amiable Briton, perhaps because 'enery' knew his strengths and his limitations. He was not a big man by heavyweight standards — a cruiserweight really — suffered from fragile eyebrows, and did all his boxing off his left hand, which, it has to be said, was a weapon of considerable erudition and well timed power. 'Enery's 'ammer was not a force to be trifled with.

Folley's revenge was the only blot on Cooper's record in four years. Since jabbing London silly to win the British and Commonwealth crowns — a befuddled London actually raised Henry's hand in victory at the end of the *fourteenth* — Cooper had won all his other nine fights. Previous nemesis Joe Erskine was banished like a Banshee three times, the first a frightening display of left hooking which left Erskine with his back arced over the bottom rope. That same left hook hammered Dick Richardson into retirement and accounted for Gawie Deklerk in the last Commonwealth title fight to feature a South African. Marciano protége Tony Hughes didn't impress his mentor, losing in five, and trial horse Wayne Bethea, Miteff and Roy Harris were all presented with their ears courtesy of the Cooper boxing academy. Whilst it didn't send shivers up spines Stateside, it was none-the-less an impressive collection and Henry was rightfully still rated in the top ten. Ideal, thought the Ali brains trust.

They escaped by the skin of their teeth; or to be more exact, a boxing glove.

The fight was venued for London's Wembley Stadium on June 18th. Ali arrived in Britain an enigma, briefly became the most hated man ever to visit these shores, and left them an idol!

British fans had to date been mesmerised from afar by the 'Louisville Lip'. Contact proved a chastening experience. Ali derided Cooper as 'a bum, a cripple and a tramp', predicted he would fall in five and in general made himself thoroughly obnoxious, on one occasion storming out of a T.V. interview after calling the interviewer a 'puny featherweight'.* British phlegm was upset. One thing to do it in your own country old chap; quite another to do it in ours. By June 18th Ali was positively loathed. Cooper was not a dissenter, at least not then. Ali's jibes had gotten to him and he was angry. The stumblebums whom Ali had destroyed early on had gone into the ring beaten men, demoralised by his constant denigration. But Cooper was a good fighter with an ego of his own and Muhammad had pricked it.

An anticipated sell out crowd of 55,000 at Wembley never materialised, only around 25,000. Partly the threat of rain kept people away and partly a feeling that Ali was indeed too good. When the fighters made their appearance, Ali was booed vociferously. Henry entered the ring to a sustained chant of 'Cooper — Cooper'. Occupying one of the cheaper seats I realised that I was probably the only person in the audience who wanted Ali to win: he was the future of boxing.

Cooper came out very determinedly, trying to cut off Ali's angles. The Briton jabbed and hooked and roughed Ali up inside. The crowd roared with every punch. Ali's people were later to say that everything was going to plan, but the way Ali was looking at referee Tommy Little when Cooper pounded his body inside indicates that he was rattled. In common with most, I awarded Cooper the opening two rounds.

Ali was much better in the 3rd, used his speed and outjabbed Cooper. Nearing the end of the round, a left-right combination tore open a dreadful cut above Henry's left eye, sending an angry red stream down his face. A great groan went up from the audience. Manager Jim Wicks wanted to pull Cooper out;— Henry dissuaded him. He had something to prove.

The eye continued to bleed in the 4th. Ali jigged around the ring flicking jabs into Cooper's face. At this point things were very clearly back in place and there can be no doubt that Ali was biding his time to fulfil his fifth round prediction. It almost blew up in his face.

Right at the end of the round Cooper backed Ali into the ropes behind a string of jabs. Muhammad possibly didn't realise how close they were until his back came up against them because he momentarily lost concentration. It was all Cooper needed. He stepped in and exploded a glorious left hook flush on Ali's jaw. Ali went down. Most would not have gotten up, but as he was to demonstrate many times in his career, Ali had a very good chin. However, he

* David Coleman

was dazed and shocked, and '4' was too soon. Ali now stood defenceless against a noted finisher. One definition of luck is being in the wrong place at the right time. Ten seconds earlier in the round and there may never have been an Ali legend. But it wasn't ten seconds earlier and the bell went before Cooper could follow up.

Pandemonium in Ali's corner. Angelo Dundee called Tommy Little over while the seconds worked furiously to revive his fighter. Smelling salts were administered, actually a breach of British rules. Dundee pointed to a split in Ali's right glove. Little sent an official for a new pair of gloves, but none could be found so he ordered Ali to box on with the damaged glove. The delay meant that the interval lasted at least 90 seconds, probably closer to two minutes. The extra time enabled Ali's head to clear completely. Fully recovered, he set about Cooper with a vengeance. A hail of combination punches had Henry's head bouncing around on his shoulders like a ping pong ball. Blood poured in torrents from Cooper's ravaged eye, and Ali's buzz-saw fists sent it showering over ringsiders. Mid-way through the 5th Tommy Little said 'that's it chum' and led Cooper back to his corner.

Henry accepted defeat philosophically. 'He said he'd do it and he did it.' He had every justification for being proud of his performance. Ali had nothing but praise for him, and Briton's now saw the other side of his character, liked it and took to him with an affection never to be relinquished. Suspicions existed that Dundee had split the glove with a razor to buy Ali precious time. Not exactly, but years later Angelo would admit to prying open an existing tiny split with his fingers. He did his job.

Five weeks on, Liston finished dismantling Patterson. His next opponent, although actually No. 2 behind Williams, had picked himself. Almost entirely through self-aggrandisement. In boxing terms Ali had achieved little. Leaving Moore aside because of his age, Muhammad had fought only one contender worthy of the name, Cooper. Good judges saw sparkling potential, but it was as 'Supermouth', 'Gassius Cassius', and 'The Louisville Lip' that Ali sat in what was now the driving seat of the heavyweight division. Around him people tended to lose themselves in hyperbole. Time magazine, which had featured him on its front cover, said:

'Cassius Clay is Hercules, struggling through the twelve labours. He is Jason, chasing the Golden Fleece. He is Galahad, Cyrano, D'Artagnon. When he scowls, strong men shudder, and when he smiles women swoon. The mysteries of the Universe are his tinker toys. He rattles the thunder and looses the lightning.'

I don't doubt the writer's knowledge of Greek Mythology, but I hardly think Damocles was guiding his pen!

In fact the Ali hype had gone too far, been too successful. Privately, he did not think he was ready for Liston. But he could not halt his own bandwagon.

Accordingly, he speeded it up!

Churchill wrote that there is a point at which policy and strategy converge. Here, the point of convergence was a psychological campaign without parallel in boxing history. Its purpose was two-fold. To destroy Liston's confidence and boost his own. Tell somebody you're better than them and they think you are;—and you think you are too. Do it over and over again until you are both certain of it. Ali screamed at Liston: 'I'm prettier than you, faster than you, I've got more class than you', time and again. And note how subtle this is. Ali is trumpeting *his* strengths and *Liston's* weaknesses. Liston will find this very easy to accept and is being steered away from thinking about his own strengths, as though they do not matter. Ali meanwhile is continually emphasising his own. That's psychological warfare at its most cunning.

Ali applied the pressure remorselessly. He turned up at Liston's home at 3 a.m. and screamed abuse at him. He interrupted the presentation of Liston's championship belt sneering: 'Watcha gonna use that for man? Hold your pants up.' He flounced into the gym where Liston was training and told the champion 'You ain't so hot.' In one celebrated incident, at the Thunderbird gambling casino, Las Vegas, the pair of them had a run in at a dice table. Ali taunted: 'Look at that big ugly bear; he can't even shoot craps.' A scuffle of some sorts followed. Ali was led away. Years later he admitted that Liston had frightened him. Then, it was not apparent. What the world saw was Ali's bombast. Sonny routinely replied with dire threats, but they were leaden, like his style, not Ali's quick, deft shafts. And Ali was always the aggressor; always got his insults off first. It was ugly and unpleasant, but it achieved its purpose. On the surface Sonny Liston was a very angry man; beneath it, he was puzzled, perplexed and beginning to doubt. There was something else too, fear of the unknown. Following the rematch with Ali, Liston told Jose Torres that when in prison he was never frightened of the hard men. It was the 'crazies' who bothered him; you never knew what they might do. Liston was one of those who believed that Ali was not playing with a full deck of cards.

Liston was able to rob Ali of one cherished ambition. The date of the fight was just over a month past Ali's 22nd birthday. He would not be able to become the youngest heavyweight champion.

The weigh-in on the morning of February 25th was Ali's piece de resistance. He turned up in a jacket with 'Bear Hunting' embroidered on it, flanked by Dundee, Sugar Ray Robinson and Drew Bundini Brown, a friend and founder member of his entourage. Ali and Brown began chanting 'Float like a Butterfly, sting like a bee', a line which was to become the most famous of all Ali's sayings, but which Brown is credited with having originated. They followed with 'Rumble young man, rumble', the twin chants echoing through the auditorium. Then Ali began banging on the floor with a walking stick and shouting 'I'm ready to rumble, I'm ready to rumble', followed by a volley of insults against

Liston. He was warned that he would be fined if he continued to behave in such a fashion.

Liston arrived shortly after eleven and now Ali went into overdrive: 'I'm ready to rumble now, I can beat you anytime, you're scared chump', and so on while in the background Bundini Brown kept up the insidious chant of 'Float like a butterfly, sting like a bee.'

'Float like a butterfly, sting like a bee'. Note again how clever this was. 'Floating' i.e., moving and boxing, and stinging, was exactly what Ali was supreme at and Liston knew it; exactly what he, Liston, was not good at. And Sonny knew that too. His only response was to mutter, 'Don't tell everybody,' a strange, inarticulate remark, the meaning of which nobody has ever been quite sure about, but which might suggest that he did not have his head together; a reflection of inner turmoil and uncertainty. And Ali was behaving just like a 'crazy'.

For his behaviour, Ali was fined $2,500. His pulse rate was measured at 110 against his normal 54. The doctor pronounced him 'scared to death'. This part was not an act. The show had been designed not only to impose his will on Liston and eat away at his confidence, but also to bolster Muhammad's own ego and draw a shroud across his fears. Ali would later admit that when he stepped into the ring that night and saw Liston in the other corner he felt twinges of fear.

Who wouldn't?

A champion had been made, the like of which boxing had not seen before. He would reign as a King for three years, be forced into exile and then come back again. His first reign and its ending are the next part of this history.

Round Twenty-Two: Abdication

The history of boxing from 1964 to 1978 is the story of one man. Others have reigned supreme in their sports, Bobby Jones in golf, Bjorn Borg in tennis, Pele in soccer, but Muhammad Ali transcended his. He became a global figure on a par with Presidents and Statesmen.

Whether this was a good thing for boxing is debatable. When one man is transcendent what can follow him? After Alexander the Great died his Empire fragmented into anarchy. When Ali retired boxing dissolved into anarchy.

The controversy over Ali's membership of the black Muslims superseded the two great talking points from the first Liston fight; how Ali came to be blinded at the end of the 4th, and why, exactly did Liston quit?

Precisely what the substance was has never been established. Black Muslims at ringside initially jumped to the conclusion that Angelo Dundee had been bribed to put something in Ali's water bucket. Dundee splashed its contents into his own eyes to ally suspicion. At the post fight press conference, Dundee absolved Liston's handlers from any mischief: 'I know the guys in his corner and they wouldn't do that.' But recent evidence suggests that Angelo was being a touch naive. According to Rob Steen, Liston's biographer, his cut man Joe Pollino* later admitted smearing a substance on Liston's gloves at the end of the 3rd, on Sonny's instructions. Whether this is the whole of the story is an *arresting* question, but there I will leave it.

As to why Liston quit, the official explanation is a torn left shoulder muscle. Many have doubted it. Let's look at the evidence. The fight film clearly shows Sonny's left arm hanging limp in the 6th. In the immediate aftermath of the fight, Liston was examined by the Boxing Commission's doctor, Alexander Robbins, who diagnosed a torn tendon in the left shoulder. This was confirmed by a panel of no less than eight doctors. Their x-rays were studied by the Florida Boxing Commission who found no argument with them. Finally, the local D.A.'s office submitted the findings to another panel of doctors who also endorsed them. Liston had a torn shoulder and that's it. The accusation that he threw the fight is not sustainable. It is true that the rights to promote any rematch were held by the Liston-Nilon-Margolis (Carbo and Palermo) combine, but you don't give away something you already have. *Nor do you try and blind the other guy if you're going to throw the fight!* The scenario is just not realistic. The mob does not always win, and they didn't this time out.

More interesting is *when* Liston incurred the injury. Jack Nilon said in

* Pollino later also functioned briefly as Sonny's manager.

training before the fight, claiming that Sonny aggravated it in round one. The latter part is not borne out by the film which shows Liston throwing lefts as hard as he can be up to and throughout almost the whole of round five. Pollino later pinpointed the fifth, which makes it poetic justice. They temporarily blinded Ali but in trying to take advantage of it Liston wrought his own downfall. Most sources agree that Sonny was heading for defeat anyway. Ali had psychologically destroyed him. The Liston camp's immoral gamble failed.

Let's move on. The contract called for a rematch. The first fight had been tainted by controversy; the second would be totally marred by it.

First and foremost was Ali's allegiance to the Black Muslims. The prevailing attitude in the fight press was that the title was better off in the hands of the mob, a concept both racist and repulsive. The Black Muslims, at that point, were certainly racist themselves, but one extreme breeds the other. In the early Sixties in the U.S.A., black students were still unwelcome on Southern university campuses, blacks continued to be refused service in restaurants and diners and still had to ride at the back of the bus. The Klan remained active, and in Washington an African leader was denied admission to a restaurant only hours before meeting President Kennedy. The logic of the Black Muslims was defective, and their views unhelpful to racial progress, but it is easy to understand why they held them. There was no legal or Constitutional debarment to the heavyweight champion of the world being part of such a movement. In a democracy an individual has the right to be wrong. Voltaire summed it up with his classic endorsement: 'I do not agree with what you say; I defend to the death your right to say it.' Unfortunately, this lofty ideal is too often booted into touch by the unthinking carp of: 'I don't like it so I want it stopped.'

It is against this background that the actions of the World Boxing Association have to be understood. The N.B.A. became the W.B.A. in 1962. Prior to Ali becoming champion, the organisation's more recent actions had been judicious and well timed. They had stripped Sugar Ray Robinson of the middleweight crown in 1959 because he had not defended it for fifteen months and was ignoring contenders like Spider Webb and Joey Giardello. The following year they voided Archie Moore's title for refusing to fight long time No. 1 contender Harold Johnson (New York and Europe later followed suit). An archaic dinosaur adage in boxing holds that titles can only be lost in the ring. If carried out then this means that champions need never defend their laurels, or at least not against genuine opposition. The W.B.A. had also taken the useful step of outlawing return bout clauses. However, this was not meant to be used to arbitrarily strip champions of their titles. Nor was it. Emile Griffith fought three bout title serials with Benny 'Kid' Paret*, Luis Rodriguez and Nino

* Paret died after the third fight becoming the first reigning champion to lose his life in a ring tragedy.

Benvenuti, and the W.B.A.'s successor to Robinson, Gene Fullmer, a similar series with Dick Tiger, all without opposition from the W.B.A. Nor had they created a fuss over the Liston–Patterson return. But on August 28th, 1964, the W.B.A. withdrew recognition from Ali for signing to meet Liston again. Their official statement made it clear that the real reason was Muhammad's political and religious beliefs: '[He is] setting a very poor example to the youth of the world.' As an eighteen year old at the time, it didn't seem that way to me; not to my contemporaries either. And none of us were exactly enthralled by the W.B.A.'s proposed elimination series to find a 'successor' to Ali, Ernie Terrell, Williams, Patterson and Doug Jones.

Decisions based not on logic but spurious moral grounds have a habit of coming apart at the seams. Doug Jones went and got his butt kicked by George Chuvalo and Billy Daniels. Exit Doug. Then Cleve Williams was shot by the police in Texas. Exit Cleve. Patterson wanted nothing to do with the fiasco. Exit Floyd. Which left Terrell, a 6′ 6″ Chicagan with a long left jab and precious little else. Ernie was sporting a 36–4 record which included wins over Williams and Folley. But Williams had earlier stopped him, and Terrell had been beaten by two ordinary fighters, Wayne Bethea and Johnny Gray (twice). 18 kayos spoke for him, an unadventurous fighter who clinched as much as he punched, and used his size to maul his way to victory over technically superior opponents. Liston had derided Terrell (an ex-sparring partner) with the comment that Ernie hugged him more than his wife.

And somebody to contest the 'title' with big Earn? Eddie Machen finally got his opportunity. Unfortunately it was all too late. Machen was now well over the fistic yard arm and just to add a note of farce to the proceedings was off a recent whipping by Patterson. When they met in Chicago on March 5th, 1965, Terrell wrestled his way to an insipid points victory. Nobody cared, and to set the seal on things the mob was found to be lurking in Terrell's chuck wagon. Apparently, the descendants of Al Capone were better examples to the youth of the world.

Meanwhile, back to the real deal. The W.B.A.'s ban on Ali–Liston II had been endorsed by New York, California, Europe and Britain, although they did not withdraw recognition from Ali. For a while it looked as if nobody would stage the fight but then Massachusetts broke ranks. The contest would go on in Boston on November 16th, 1964. Ali's behaviour towards Liston was as equally outrageous as before. On one occasion, dressed in his 'bear hunting' jacket and armed with a bear collar, he halted Liston's car in down town Boston and ranted his way through his 'big ugly bear' act. But the fight was not destined to take place there or then. Friday, November 13th, Ali collapsed vomiting in his hotel room. Rushed to hospital, he was found to be suffering from an incarcerated hernia and underwent an emergency operation. Physicians announced that he could not possibly fight again before April. Liston and his associates lost half a million dollars because of the cancellation.

A new date was set for May 25th, 1965. Everything seemed to be running to plan but then with two weeks to go the Massachusetts Commission suddenly reversed its earlier decision and banned the fight.

Exactly why has never been revealed. It was certainly not fear of expulsion from the W.B.A. That tame threat had been made months earlier and was never going to be carried out. Boston was too important a fight centre and Massachusetts had been thumbing its nose at the W.B.A. for years. The Bay State had carried on recognising Robinson as champion, endorsed his direct successors Pender and Downes, and staged four of that trio's five title fights in Boston, complete with return bout clauses. Even after the non-aligned bodies recognised W.B.A. champion Dick Tiger, Massachusetts continued to support local boy Pender right up to his retirement. Officially, Massachusetts disliked the background of the Liston Promotional Company, Intercontinental Promotions, and well it might, but it had known about their mob connections all along. There were rumours of pressure from patriotic organisations; their opposition had been ever present too. Nobody can say it with certainty, but the real pressure was probably brought to bear from high political sources — perhaps even the highest. Muhammad Ali was already paying an extortionate price for his principles.

Money talks though, and in the spring of 1965 Maine was looking to promote itself as a tourist attraction. Like Shelby over forty years earlier, what better way of doing it than staging a heavyweight title fight? Like Shelby, Maine would also come a cropper.

Approved by the State Athletic Board, the fight went to the little town of Lewiston. Closed circuit and satellite broadcasting made the size of the stadium redundant. The show was back on the road — and heading for disaster.

Ali forecast a three round victory and introduced the press to the latest member of his entourage, an elderly comedian named Stepin Fetchit who claimed to have known Jack Johnson. Fetchit, said Ali, was teaching him one of Johnson's pet punches, a blow variously described in the press as the 'anchor', 'pivot' or 'piston' punch. It cut no ice with the bookmakers; Liston was 9–5 on to regain the title. In Miami there had been a late Ali surge in the betting (thus adding to the fix rumours). This time the odds remained constant.

Two months earlier Terrell and Machen had gone through their silhouette contest. There is an old American political saying: 'As goes Maine so goes the Nation.' The Nation very decidedly went with Maine that Ali–Liston was the real title fight. Unhappily, public opinion afterwards joined Maine in condemnation.

The most controversial fight in boxing history was also the most innocuous. There was some preliminary sparring and then Liston bulled his way into Ali. Sonny took a left hook to the jaw, seemed to overbalance, and tumbled headlong into a right which was just a blur. He went down like a Canadian pine tree.

Pandemonium reigned for the next few seconds. Ali stood over Liston snarling and shouting. Spectators came to their feet in astonishment. Referee Jersey Joe Walcott, officiating in his second (and last) world heavyweight title fight, seemed completely nonplussed. Finally, he pushed Ali away and took up the count, but in his confusion he did not take it up level with the timekeeper. Instead he began at 'one'. At 'nine' Liston tottered unsteadily to his feet and Ali pitched straight into him. At this point Walcott was attracted by Nat Fleischer who was banging on the ring apron to get his attention. Fleischer informed Joe that the timekeeper had in fact counted Liston out. Walcott turned away and jumped between Ali and Liston. He was just in time for Liston was completely dazed and on the point of going down again.

At 1.42 of the 1st round Muhammad Ali had kayoed the seemingly indestructible Sonny Liston!

The official announcement was drowned in a torrent of boos, and chants of 'fake, fake, fake' which the following day would be taken up by the press. One particular remark, allegedly uttered by a ten year old boy, gained prominence in the newspapers: 'I was here the night boxing died.'

Not quite, but for a time it seemed that way. Several State legislatives proposed bills to ban boxing and abolitionists had a field day. Teddy Waltham, Secretary of the British Board of Control, said that in Britain there would have been an immediate inquiry. Tommy Farr described Liston and Ali as 'slugs'. Jack Dempsey's earlier cheerful view of Ali had undergone revision. The old champion now stated that he had kept away from Lewiston because he knew what would happen. Dempsey's old friend and foe, Gene Tunney, made comments of a similar nature. Whether Dempsey's newly found hostility towards Ali really centred around the Black Muslims is another matter. Ditto Tunney, who had unjustly described mob controlled Primo Carnera's knockout of Sharkey as 'a phantom punch'. People were seeing what they wanted to see; not what had actually happened.

Jose Torres, commentating for Puerto Rican radio, glimpsed the tidal wave of criticism at first hand. When he played back the tape of his broadcast he heard himself term the knock-out punch as: 'a perfect shot to the jaw'[1]. Amos 'big train' Lincoln, Liston's sparring partner, knocked his opponent out on the undercard with a similar right. Asked if he could have achieved the same result against Liston, Lincoln replied: 'Anytime in the last six weeks'. Patterson called Ali's knock-out blow 'perfect'. Johansson agreed: 'a terribly fast and hard right'. Walcott said it was 'a beauty' and added that Ali would have beaten the peak Joe Louis. But these comments, made by Ali's fellow professionals — four of

1 'Sting Like a Bee' p.142

them world champions — were witch hunted into the background.

Ali himself was unconcerned, describing the punch as the one Fetchit had shown him. As for Liston, it was not the hardest shot he had ever taken, but it was hard enough and he had not seen it coming. Sonny respected Ali's power more than most. After their first fight, his face swollen and lumpy, he had lamented: 'That's not the guy I was supposed to fight. That guy could punch.'

The allegations of a fake have persisted, irrespective of the evidence to the contrary. In 1995 the respected trade paper Boxing News published a major article which endorsed that conclusion. In my opinion it is wholly the wrong one: this was as genuine a knockout as has ever been seen in the ring.

Ali's right hand punch does not seem to be that hard; he himself has since termed it as a good, jarring punch, but not a knock-out one. However, the best kayo punches do not rely on power, but speed, precision and timing. Ali's punch was short, perfectly timed, delivered at tremendous speed, and, echoing what Torres told his listeners; 'right on the button'[1]. It was also delivered against a man propelling himself forward on to the punch, thus doubling its impact. Look at the film and you will see Sonny's head twist round on his shoulders, the sure sign of a knock-out blow. When Liston arose (after 'ten') he was clearly out on his feet.

This knock-out invites comparison with Sugar Ray Robinson's kayo of Gene Fullmer in 1957, probably the most perfect knock-out drop ever delivered. Fullmer moved on to a short, exquisitely timed left hook delivered at such speed that it can only really be seen in slow motion. If one was compiling a list of the ten most durable boxers in history then Gene's name would be on it; it was the only time he was ever floored in 62 pro fights. Robinson produced some spectacular one punch kayos, but always maintained that he was not a power hitter. Speed and execution were his essences.

From 1966 to December 1969, Sonny Liston won fourteen fights, thirteen inside the distance. 'Big Train' Lincoln found that he couldn't replicate Ali's feat after all and hit the buffers in two. Also exiting via the kayo route were Amos Johnson, the last man to beat Ali as an amateur*, promising Henry Clark, and Roger Rischer. But despite this Sonny never featured in the title picture again. The stigma of Lewiston was too great. Ostensibly the villain of the piece, he was banned in every U.S. State bar Nevada, Britain and Europe, save Sweden which

1 'Sting Like a Bee' p.142

* In the 1959 Pan American Games trials.

ironically a few years hence would outlaw boxing. Ring magazine temporarily dropped him from its rankings, Fleischer smugly telling Sonny: 'Frankly, you are the forgotten man', (he meant 'best forgotten'). In 1967 the W.B.A. lifted its ban, but too late for Liston to be included in their next elimination series (certainly by design).

On December 6th, 1969, Liston faced one of the former participants in that tourney, Leotis Martin from Toledo, Ohio. After eight rounds Sonny was ahead on all scorecards and had had Martin down in the 4th. In round nine Liston walked into one of the most explosive combos of the decade, right hook-left hook-right cross which spread-eagled him on the canvas without any hope of beating the count. *Persona non grata* now became contender *non grata*, though by a cruel twist it was Martin who had to retire afterwards, Liston's punches having damaged a retina.

Seven months later Charles 'Sonny' Liston had his last fight halting Chuck Wepner, 'the Bayonne Bleeder' on cuts which required 55 stitches. By the end of the year Sonny was dead.

How did he die? The coroner theorised that he had fallen and hit his head on a bench, thereafter expiring from lack of oxygen and blood to the heart. The post mortem was hampered by the decomposition of the body. It has to be said that equally credible is the solution that Sonny was knocked unconscious and then murdered by being injected with drugs. There were fresh needle marks on his arm and traces of codeine and morphine were found in the kidneys. Scuttlebut held that he had fallen out with loan sharks; alternately, Liston had certainly threatened a senior mob figure on one occasion.

Following Lewiston, Sonny was victimised for a 'crime' which never happened. But he was an unsympathetic figure, a dishonest, unpersonable man. There is no more to be said.

The victor of Lewiston had now developed both as a fighter and as a man. The confidence gained by winning the title had matured Ali fistically. The man was more complex.

The poet Carl Sandburg observed of Abraham Lincoln that he was as hard as steel and as soft as drifting fog. The same might well be said of Ali's character. he was an ambitious young man who wanted the riches and the glory of being heavyweight champion. Along the way he used people. Liston for example. Ali capitalised on Sonny's defects, his poor image, his lack of grace and charm. He projected himself at Liston's expense. Muhammad's most significant foe, Joe Frazier, would be exploited just as shamelessly. While Ali's belief in the Black Muslims was genuine — he sacrificed his best years to their cause — his views suited his convenience. Ali can accurately be described as pro black but not anti white. When the Muslim's softened their stance on whites in the late Sixties, Ali did not merely go along with it; that was where he was at right from the beginning. It enabled him to accept the backing of the Faversham combine and employ Angelo Dundee as his trainer. These tangents in his personality are hallmarks of an individual with several dimensions to his character, i.e., a highly complex man. The same tangents are evident in his relationships with women. His first two wives were expected to adhere strictly to Muslim codes, while he himself had affairs whenever it suited him. There is a rather ruthless self-centredness here denoting at the core an overweening egotism and arrogance. Yet he was also considered a warm man, capable of making and sustaining close friendships, and of inspiring genuine loyalties. The soft side of his character has been expressed in acts of generosity and simple kindness, such as his financial help to a community centre for elderly Jews faced with closure. Note here that the recipients of his benevolence were white. Many of his opponents came to admire him as a man; Ken Norton, George Chuvalo, Ernie Shavers, George Foreman*, Larry Holmes, Zora Folley, Henry Cooper, even Patterson.

However, it was the ruthless side of Muhammad Ali which was on show when he defended the title against Patterson on November 22nd, 1965, at Las Vegas. Three weeks earlier Terrell had defended his cardboard crown in Toronto by outpointing George Chuvalo in 15 dreary rounds. How that fight came about intertwines neatly with Ali's defence.

When Floyd Patterson was beaten by Liston for the second time he was still only 28 and in fistic terms nowhere near past his prime. He would in fact carry on — minus Cus — for another nine years. In 1965 he was breezing along quite nicely thank you, although his rehabilitation programme was mainly outside the U.S. In Sweden, he outpointed Machen and stopped Tod Herring and Sante Amonti, and in Puerto Rico, Charlie Powell. His one fight in the States was a points win over George Chuvalo, a bout which the W.B.A. hoped would provide the first challenger for the winner of Terrell-Machen. They again received the sex and travel answer (politely because Floyd doesn't swear), so loser Chuvalo got to fight the Mogodon man instead. Meanwhile, Patterson wanted Ali. And Ali wanted Patterson. And the whole business turned very ugly indeed.

The 1965 Ali stood 6′ 3″ and weighed in at around 210 lbs (95 kilos). The round naming game, and the 'bear' baiting tactics used against Liston, had served their purpose. Alongside being a fully fledged heavyweight, Muhammad was now a fully fledged showman, attempting to keep his act fresh from fight to fight. Stepin Fetchit, claimed Ali, had now taught him another Johnson weapon, the 'linger on' punch. Ali invaded Patterson's training camp bearing a lettuce, the right food, he said, for Floyd the 'rabbit'.

* I am relying here on Foreman's remarks in Thomas Hauser's biography of Ali, and not on Foreman's autobiography.

This was all good hype and nothing more. The genuine unpleasantness began with Patterson. Beating Ali, Floyd avowed, was a moral and religious crusade. Patterson, who had married a white woman and become a Catholic, detested the black Muslims and their extremist views. The war of words started here and got nastier and nastier. Patterson never realised he was out of his league. Ali was able to represent him as the symbol of white America, and forced him to bear its cross. Ali sometimes conveyed the impression of being boxing's mahdi looking for a white Christian General Gordon to defeat, although Ahab seeking the great white whale is probably more apposite. Muhammad never found him. Patterson was the closest he got.

This 'jehad' (holy war) psyched and fuelled Ali. It did not have the same effect on Patterson, the man who had called down the thunder. Ali began to term his jab the 'snake licker'. There was a darker hue to this than is normally appreciated. Asked once in Britain whether there were not well meaning whites, Ali replied that if a whole litter of snakes came slithering towards him then he could hardly be expected to know which meant him harm and which didn't*. Floyd Patterson became a snake to be licked. What followed has to be seen in that context.

Patterson won the 1st round because Ali never threw a punch. He simply bounced around the ring sneering 'C'mon Mr White American.' 'Snake licking' began in the 2nd and went on and on, accompanied by endless jibes. Occasionally there were hooks and combinations, but Ali did not want to end it early. Man had given offence; man had to be punished. By the end of the 4th, a bad back had added to Floyd's misfortunes. As round succeeded round he became a bent over, pain racked figure. He fell only once, to his knees in the 6th, a supplicant kneeling before his master. Ali could have finished it at any time. Instead, one is reminded of 'The Pit and the Pendulum' with Poe's black garbed inquisitor remorselessly swinging the blade ever lower, the victim consigned to a cruel, lingering fate. This, and not any particular blow, was Ali's 'linger punch'. It was finally left to referee Harry Krause to halt the pendulum in the 12th.

Before the bout, Ali (and Patterson) had posted a $50,000 bond to meet Terrell. But that fight would not yet take place. Muhammad was about to sign, or rather voice, his abdication document.

It ill behoves an Englishman to comment on the woes of another nation, so I will merely repeat what the distinguished American historian Barbara Tuchman has said about the Vietnam War. America, wrote Tuchman, betrayed itself in South East Asia in the same way that Britain did in the American

* The Michael Parkinson Show.

Colonies two centuries earlier.[1]

Ali nee Cassius Clay, had originally been registered for National Service in 1960. Two years later he was officially classified as available to be drafted. At that time it appeared just a formality. A small handful of American soldiers were in Vietnam as 'advisors', but the Kennedy administration, unwilling to be drawn into a conflict there, intended bringing them home. Things changed after the Kennedy assassination. Lyndon Johnson was both pro-military and susceptible to the arguments of an ailing defence industry. Early in 1964 potential draftees were obliged to take induction examinations. Ali's, on January 24th — a month before the Liston fight — turned out rather humiliatingly for him. He was assessed as having an I.Q. of 78, too low for service in the armed forces. In March he was re-examined and the classification ratified. It seemed then, and has done ever since, incongruous that a man seemingly of high intelligence should flop so badly. But there are different forms of intelligence and Ali's school record suggests that he was not academically bright. Moreover, he was first tested while in training for Liston, and then re-assessed shortly after his membership of the Black Muslims had been revealed. In both instances his mind was a long way away from educational tests.

That Ali is not 'the smartest' (his own admission) was confirmed by a highly embarrassing incident in 1980 when Muhammad was asked by President Jimmy Carter to undertake a tour of Africa to explain America's withdrawal from the Moscow Olympics following the Russian invasion of Afghanistan. The trip proved a disaster. Ali had clearly not thought his own position through before departing, and was equally unable to cope with hostile questions in the countries he visited. This bears out the assessment made of him by one of his biographers, Wilfred Sheed, who found him lacking in spontaneity.[2] While I believe Ali has a far higher I.Q. than 78, the evidence suggests that he is neither academic nor analytical, and that when examined at the wrong time, would probably not fare well in tests.

That was not however the way in which his critics saw things in the spring of 1964. Ali, it was claimed, had flunked the tests deliberately. Apart from revealing a lack of sophistry in their own minds, his detractors were really assessing him on the basis of political and religious views which frightened them.

The issue then lay dormant until the Gulf of Tonkin brought America fully into the Vietnam War. By the beginning of 1966 American needed its manpower reserves. The qualification standard was lowered, and Ali and the others in his bracket were declared fit for service. Ali's response could not have been better

1 'The March of Folly'.
2 'Muhammad Ali'.

prepared by his enemies: 'I ain't got no quarrel with them Vietcong.'

Ali's admirers have since vouchsafed that he was under intense pressure from the media. His actual choice of words was certainly unfortunate and reflects the weak spontaneity noted by Sheed. But equally there can be no doubt that these sentiments accurately summed up the way Muhammad Ali felt. He put it more articulately later:

> *'I'm expected to go overseas to help free people in South Vietnam, and at the same time my people here are being brutalised and mistreated, and this is really the same thing that's happening in Vietnam.'*

The press took a somewhat different view. Jimmy Cannon, normally a perspicacious boxing writer but never an admirer of Ali, wrote:

> *'Clay [sic] is part of the Beatle movement. He fits in with the famous singers no one can hear and the Punks riding motorcycles with iron crosses pinned to their leather jackets and Batman and the Boys with their long dirty hair and the Girls with their unwashed look and the College kids dancing naked at secret proms held in apartments and the revolt of students who get a cheque from Dad every first of the month and the painters who copy the labels off soup cans and the surf bums who refuse to work and the whole pampered style making cult of the bored young.'*

At first sight Cannon's diatribe simply appears to express a paranoid dislike of anyone under fifty. But what it really denotes is fear; fear of a society which appeared to be changing. Things never remain static, but the Sixties *seemed* more raucous, more radical, because of the changes in youth lifestyle and culture. The real revolution was in marketing which at the end of the Fifties suddenly realised that youth constituted a specific market and targeted it. In substance nothing really altered, a point made very tellingly by Zeferelli in his cult film 'Blow Up'. Ali represented a generation with the same basic goals as its predecessors, but a different style, while Cannon and his contemporaries saw only the style and not that underneath it was business as usual.

Professional politicians were gripped by similar fears seeing only a challenge to established authority. Representative Frank Clark spoke for them:

'The heavyweight champion of the world turns my stomach.'

A French politician was sitting in a coffee house with a friend when he saw a crowd go rushing by. 'I must go,' he said, 'I am in charge of that mob.'

The fears and phobias of the Cannons and Clarks were expressed not only in Vietnam but the ugliness of the 1968 Democrat Convention in Chicago. By then the mood of America was changing, but in February, 1966, Ali reflected everything the establishment hated. The Terrell fight suddenly went dead in the water.

It had already been kicked out of New York, ironically nothing to do with

Ali. Terrell had been refused a license because of his association with Bernie Glickman, yet another Carbo-Palermo acolyte. The moral vigilantes of the W.B.A. had tumbled head first into a tureen of egg yolk. They were still wiping it off their faces when Ali's Vietcong pronouncement came to their aid. Illinois, which after New York had agreed to the bout for March 29th, was forced to withdraw by the State's political bosses. it was the same story in Kentucky, Florida and Pennsylvania. Toronto had no such problem. Vietnam was none of Canada's business; they just wanted to see a boxing match. But now Terrell withdrew, unhappy about the size of his purse owing to closed circuit cancellations in America. George Chuvalo substituted (again) and the W.B.A. withdrew their recognition.

Right. That's enough of politics. Let's get back to the boxing. It has been said of George Chuvalo that if contests were of 100 rounds duration then the likeable Canadian Croat would have become world champion. Durability was his stock in trade. He was never floored in 97 fights. That aside, he was not more than an average fighter, deficient in both technique and real punching power. His record showed losses to Howard King, Bob Baker, Joe Erskine, Pat McMurty, and Rademacher. Robert Cleroux had beaten George two out of three for the Canadian title, and in contender-town Zora Folley had exposed his limitations alongside Patterson and Terrell. Only two months before getting into the ring with Ali, Argentinian Eduardo Corletti bamboozled George in London. Corletti was never more than second echelon.

Ali–Chuvalo, at the Maple Leaf Gardens on March 29th, 1966, was strictly 12 rounds of watching Ali working on the speed ball, followed by a three round fight as the maestro tired. George edged the 13th, working away to Muhammad's body. This temerity stirred Ali to try for a stoppage in the 14th, but Chuvalo took it all and came back smiling to shade the final round with more body punches. The judges had it 73–65 (10–2–3), 74–63 (12–1–2) and 74–62 (13–1–1).

No cigar for George, but an excellent demonstration of Ali's skills. And the whole atmosphere surrounding the fight had been a stark contrast to the ugliness of the Patterson miasma. When Ali refereed to Chuvalo as a 'washer woman' before the contest, Chuvalo turned up at his training camp dressed as one, complete with mop and pail. Everybody, Ali included, joined in the laughter.

If America didn't want Ali then Britain certainly did. Vietnam was not our affair, and there was a feeling that Ali was being persecuted. He arrived in London to a warm reception. Henry Cooper got his shot at the crown on May 21st, at the Arsenal soccer stadium.

In the spring of 1966 Cooper was moving towards a level of popularity which few other British sports stars have enjoyed. It had as much to do with his personality as anything else. In actual fistic terms he was just about clinging on to a rating in the bottom half of the top ten. Since the first Ali fight, 'enery had successfully lauded his domestic rights over London and Johnny Prestcott. Against a procession of minor Americans he enjoyed mixed fortunes. Roger Rischer and Amos Johnson, basically decent trial horses, outpointed him on nights when he seemed to go to sleep. But like 'Drake's Drum', Cooper's left hook awoke with a vengeance at the gates of contender-town when Hubert Hilton, Chip Johnson, Dick Wipperman and Jefferson Davis came calling. Could the 'ammer do what it had done to Ali before, only this time a bit earlier in the round? 42,000 people paid to find out the answer.

It was not a bout which Ali took lightly. Knowing he would need his speed, he came in at his lightest championship weight to date, 201 lbs. Cooper's left hook perturbed him, also the Englishman's penchant for hitting on the break, a tactic still then legal in British rings. Cooper planned to make more effective use of his right, hoping to surprise Ali, and manoeuvre him on to the left.

Britain's first world heavyweight title fight for 58 years was absorbing rather than spectacular. George Whiting of the London *Evening Standard* summed up the Ali style with a flurry of imagery:

> *'Undulate like a cork on the ocean swell, sway like a reed in the wind, and move in and out like a cuckoo in a clock.'*[1]

Cooper was the aggressor over the five completed rounds, always trying to cut the ring off, jabbing and hooking when the opportunities came. Ali boxed on the retreat, making his reach and his speed tell. Henry did surprise him with a few rights, but eschewed his best opportunity when in the 4th Ali stopped boxing to complain about a low blow. Shades of Sharkey: but Cooper hadn't ridden hobo rails like Dempsey!

In round five Ali began to unwind and in the next he started to let the punches go. One of them, a superb right cross, tore across Cooper's left eyelid like a razor blade, and the blood began to cascade down his gaunt features. He attacked desperately, Ali countered with precision combinations, and after his second inspection of the injured eye referee George Smith called a halt. Question put; question answered.

Perspective about who was leading at the time varied, and shows how, when the rounds are close, opinions about them will differ. Cooper judged the first three about even and thought he won four and five. George Whiting scored 1 and 2 Cooper, 3 even, 4 and 5 to Ali, Peter Wilson the opening two to Cooper, the next three to Ali, and John Cottrell 1st and 3rd even, Cooper the 2nd and, going along with Whiting and Wilson, the 4th and 5th to Ali. I watched the film again in preparation for this book. Ali I thought took the 1st by dint of a good

1 'Great Fights of the Sixties' p.222

left-right combination, Cooper reversed it in the 2nd with a left-right of his own, and for me just shaded 3 and 4 on aggression, with Ali unwrapping his wares in the 5th. Ali himself estimated Cooper ahead 3-2. If one accepts Muhammad and Henry's judgements, then Cooper has the unique distinction of being the only man ahead of Ali twice at the finish.

Ali's next bout was with the draft board. He appealed against military service on the grounds that it would cause financial hardship to his family. This was turned down so he sought instead exemption as a conscientious defector because of his religious beliefs. A decision on this was still pending when he returned to Britain to fight Brian London. While Ali was preparing for London, Terrell defended the W.B.A. diadem, in Houston on June 28th.

What Doug Jones had achieved since his narrow loss to Ali to merit a title shot is a secret the W.B.A.'s executive board will take to their graves. However, Terrell–Jones turned out to be the greatest fight in boxing history. Both men boxed off this planet and shared a record number of knock-downs. At least that is the fight you might have seen if you were hallucinating on that well known '60's substance, marijuana. In reality Big 'Earn and Little Doug comatosed the tiny handful of spectators who bothered to turn out. True to form, Terrell won on points and nobody cared.

Not that Ali–London was exactly a mouth watering prospect either. Since convincing Johansson to retire, Beefy Brian had gone to the post 10 times. Cooper had clinically outboxed him, ditto Thad Spencer, a rising young American. There was a third loss on the record too, but 'L pts 10' to Johnny Prescott had been followed by the Board of Control temporarily downgrading the referee. On the credit side London had beaten Sixties 'golden boy' Billy Walker, outslugged Amos Johnson to win on a foul and crawled all over Roger Rischer in 50 seconds. These last two wins, over Cooper's conquerors of the period, put London in the opposite corner at Earl's Court on August 6th.

It really should have been an exhibition and it turned out that way anyhow. Titually, London had no right being in the same ring as Ali. In the 1st the champion staggered him twice with whiplash rights to the head, and in the 2nd he painted London's ample features with fast left jabs whilst the burly Briton stood hopelessly bewildered by his speed. The fight lasted one hundred seconds into the 3rd, at which point Ali ended it with an unbelievably vast volley of left and right hooks to the head that left London sitting stunned and shattered against the ropes to be counted out.

From London Ali moved on to Frankfurt, Germany, to meet the European champion Karl Mildenberger at the Frankfurt Walstadion on September 21st. Mildenberger had won the European title by blasting out Italy's Sante Amonti in the 1st round — seven rounds quicker than Patterson had managed to stow away the same opponent. But nobody seriously gave the German a chance. A southpaw, he boxed adequately and hit reasonably hard, but he was at best only a competent performer, certainly far removed from the Ali league.

But on the night Ali was well below par and gave a jaded performance. As an amateur, he had been uncomfortable against Southpaws. After the champion had opened well, Mildenberger stormed through to take the 2nd with a battery of right jabs to the head. At this point Ali was making a hash of things, but he got to grips with Mildenberger in the 3rd and throughout the next three rounds pounded a steady stream of rights to the German's head, cutting his left cheek and flooring him for 'one' in the 5th. At the end of the 6th British referee Teddy Waltham asked Mildenberger if he wanted to retire.

The answer was no and Karl fully justified his refusal by taking the 7th and then running Ali close in the 8th. The champion only just jerked his head away from a series of lunging left hooks, and Mildenberger went on to do even better in the 9th, pressing Ali strongly and clearly winning the round.

Not until the 10th did Ali really move into a higher gear, and then he freely punished the German with fast clusters to the head. At the end of the round Ali hit him with a double left hook followed by a right cross. Mildenberger spun round, did a half somersault, and hit the canvas with a thud. He was up at 'five' and the bell rang to prevent Ali finishing him off.

Ali more-or-less toyed with his game opponent in the 11th, but he opened up with hard combinations again in the 12th. The challenger's face was now a bloody mess; left eye and cheek cut, nose bleeding, and right cheekbone badly swollen. Ali finished it with a series of hooks and crosses which sent Mildenberger lurching headlong into the ropes where referee Waltham rescued him from further punishment.

Ali had triumphed over a brave, efficient performer who was ranked in the bottom half of the world ratings, but his form had been disappointing. He had been stale, occasionally flummoxed by Mildenberger's southpaw style, and at times even appeared disinterested.

There was good news from the States where Muhammad's deferment from the draft had been recommended. But this was subject to ratification. The road was still littered with thorns.

In October, his contract with the Faversham group expired and was not renewed. Herbert Muhammad, son of Black Muslim leader Elijah, took over the managerial reins. A company called Main Bout Inc. was formed to market ancillary rights to Ali's bouts. Although controlled by the Muslims, included on Main Bout's board was a sharp witted Jewish lawyer named Bob Arum who would go on to become one of boxing's top promoters. Meanwhile, it was important to keep Ali fighting and Texas agreed to sanction his next contest.

Question: What do you call a police officer holding a gun? Answer: Sir! In the early hours of November 29th, 1964, Cleveland 'Big Cat' Williams ignored this fundamental logic and ended up being shot in a scuffle with the Highway Patrol. He was taken to hospital with a bullet in the stomach, underwent four operations — one to have a kidney removed — and survived only through his magnificent physique. But his weight dropped from 215 lbs to 155, and it was fourteen months before he put it back on and returned to the ring. He was not the old force and never would be again, but he won four fights, in the last poignantly kayoing Tod Herring who had provided him with an emergency blood transfusion on the night he was shot. Only in boxing.

On November 14th, Williams went in with Ali at the Houston Astrodome, the culmination for Ali of a good year inside the ropes, despite all the troubles outside them, and it produced one of his most memorable displays. This fight saw the introduction of the famous Ali shuffle, Muhammad's jig time dance routine.

He used it to mesmerise Williams in the opening round, the beginning of an Ali super show. In the 2nd he unleashed a white hot attack, a ruthless molten lava of punches that erupted around Williams head like an angry Vesuvius. Blood began to pour from the challenger's nose before Ali bounced a straight right off his jaw which put him down for 'six'. Williams completed the mandatory 'eight' count swaying groggily against the ropes. Almost immediately a combination flopped him back down again, this time for 'three'. Five seconds later he lurched back into the maelstrom and Ali — a gleaming, whirling, black Dervish, fired home cluster after cluster until the Big Cat collapsed on his back. Ali raised his arms in victory, but the bell saved Williams and a minute later he gamely came up for the 3rd.

Within seconds he was on his back again following another machine gun volley to the head. The same courage that had sustained Williams through those four operations forced him to climb back up, but he was as utterly beaten as any man in history and Ali was merely hitting him how and when he liked when the referee halted the carnage midway through the round.

Ali's display against a faded but still dangerous opponent had been sheer magic. He displayed speed, skill, precision power, and venom in what seemed like one long, dazzling cluster of punches. A brew mixed with exquisite variety and timeliness.

Ali went back to the Houston Astrodome for his next outing, February 6th, 1967, Ernie Terrell at last. This was to be as ugly as the Patterson fight.

It had nothing to do with Ernie's phoney title. Terrell was perceived as a long armed* joke, the front end of the W.B.A.'s pantomime horse. In truth, he had maximised his limited assets to become a legitimate contender, but no more.

The unpleasantness arose from Terrell's refusal to call Ali by his adopted name. Ernie would only use 'Clay'. Later, he was to say that he did so as part

* His reach was 85 inches.

of the promotion to help sell the fight. Terrell had once been Ali's sparring partner; had stayed at his home. He assumed they were friends. But he was also aware of how seriously Ali took his religion, and his black consciousness. Ali genuinely felt slighted. His pre-fight insults labelling Terrell as an 'Uncle Tom' were a foretaste of what was to come in the ring.

It was not a good fight. Ali was simply too fast, too clever and too varied for Terrell's pedestrian style to cope with. Muhammad could have stopped the lumbering giant. He chose not to.

For four rounds Ali mainly performed the shuffle, interspersed with the occasional punch. Terrell, bulling in and clinching to wear his man down, took the 2nd and 4th, but that was the limit of his achievement.

In the 5th and 6th Ali began to slip Terrell's long lefts and score heavily with his own. He used right uppercuts to open up Ernie's tight defence and then followed through with swift combinations. This set the pattern for the rest of the fight, but Ali refused to launch an all out attack. In the 7th he knocked most of the fight out of Terrell with two power laden right hooks to the jaw that left Ernie stunned and helpless. But Ali deliberately refrained from following up. By the end of this round it was obvious that Ali intended to torture Terrell. The Houston Astrodome had been designated a Babylon of Hatred!

The 8th was the worst round. Ali jabbed and hooked his man at will, and as he drove in the punches he demanded: 'What's my name — what's my name?' The verbal and fistic punishment lasted the full three minutes.

The rest of the fight was hopelessly one sided. Ali carried out a cruel, systematic campaign of dissecting Terrell's face with his scalpel of a left hand. Long before the end Ernie's visage had become a grim, crimson, ruin. He peered dimly at Ali through two slits of eyes and could only cover up and ship more and more calculated punishment. Many thought the referee ought to have stopped it.

The decision was a formality. The referee and one judge — 148–137: — the other judge, 148–133. This meant that each official gave Ali 13 rounds and Terrell 2. The second judge had given Ali 4 rounds by enormous two point margins.

He was again the undisputed champion. Not for long though. The prelude to abdication came on March 6th when the Selective Services Board turned down his recommended deferment. April 28th was fixed for Ali's induction into the Army.

There was time for one more defence: Zora Folley, at Madison Square Garden on March 22nd. Folley has deservedly been mentioned a lot in these pages. Half black, half Indian, he was a master ring mechanic liked and respected throughout the fight game. A decade earlier he might have become champion but now, at almost 35, his best days were gone. Zora still held a world ranking. However, he was by this time more a gatekeeper barring the way into contender town. As such he had denied entry to Henry Clark, Jefferson Davis (along with Cooper), Oscar Bonavena (who would come again), Billy Daniels and Bob Foster. Only Terrell had gotten past him since the Jones debacle, whilst Cleroux and Chuvalo were on his list of recent victories. But in 1967 Zora never figured to have a chance against the peak Ali.

Ali and Folley had nothing but mutual respect and liking for each other. Muhammad merely shuffled and ziz-zagged around the ring for the first two rounds. Folley won them purely because he was trying to land a punch, although not very successfully. Nothing happened in the 3rd except that Ali raised his arms in the air and bounced around in front of Folley inviting him to try and land a big one. Zora was too old in the tooth to fall for such a baited hook. Then, in the 4th, Ali at last went to work, flooring the Arizonan with a swift burst of punches to the head. Folley got up at 'nine' and to the crowd's delight he attacked and sent Ali scurrying into retreat. But it was only a token gesture.

Ali had simply made a tactical retreat. In the 5th and the 6th he sallied forth again, whipping home left jabs to Folley's face. In the 7th he suddenly stepped in and finished it with two short, stunning right hooks to the side of Folley's head. Zora pitched forward on his face and was counted out. Ali had demonstrated yet again his flair for the dramatic, producing an explosive finish to a rather tame waltz.

Afterwards, Folley assessed Ali the fighter for the press.

> *'Louis wouldn't have a chance; he was too slow. Marciano couldn't get to him and would never get away from Ali's jab... The moves, the speed, the punches, and the way he changes style every time you think you got him figured. The right hands Ali hit me with had no business landing, but they did... Many times he was in the wrong position but he hit me anyway. I've never seen anyone who could do that.'*[1]

Folley went on to call Ali the greatest fighter of all time. Zora's career spanned Marciano, Patterson, Johansson and Liston's championship reigns and he was himself an excellent craftsman. His words have weight.

Unhappily though, Zora Folley was to be Muhammad Ali's last opponent for three and a half years. On April 28th, Ali refused induction. In June he was tried for draft evasion and sentenced to five years in prison. He was granted bail to appeal. But his first tenure as champion was over. New York, California and the W.B.A. stripped him both of his licence and his title. Britain and Europe continued to recognise him but his passport was taken away. Boxing's voice, The Ring, withheld its 'Fighter of the Year' award for 1966 because, said Nat

1 'Sports Illustrated'

Fleischer, it would have gone to Ali, a man who: 'most emphatically is not to be held up as an example to the youngsters of the United States.' Thus wrote Fleischer, a man who steadfastly refused to see the mob influence in boxing — he presumably thought Franky and Blinky were a cabaret act — and always refused to give Ali his worth*. As for so called 'role models', a youth's character is shaped by his environment and the influence of those around him. It was sad that because boxing refused to admit that it had a gangster problem, it gave no credit to the man who had taken the heavyweight championship away from the mob. Instead it pilloried him for his religious and political views, views that led him to turn down a Government compromise which meant that he would be in the Army only in name. Principles are apparently not part of a role model's job description.

But that is to wander into the domains of political and social history. This work is primarily a boxing history. Its king had been forced to abdicate. Effectively the title was now in a void again.

* Ironically, 'The Ring' continued to recognise 'Cassius Clay' as champion up to 1969.

Round Twenty-Three: The Wars of the Three Roses

Shortly before his death, the boxing historian Jim Jacobs said:

> *'In some ways the exile from Boxing was the best thing that could have happened to Ali. In terms of his skills, it was a tragedy. But in terms of his earning power, it was a plus. If you go back to the Folley fight he was no longer commanding large amounts of money. A substantial proportion of the American public disliked him, and worse, they were getting tired of hearing what he was about.'* [1]

Today's hero/villain/tragedian is tomorrow's ennui. The Space programme lost impetus because the public wearied of it. Before he was forced to abdication, Ali was stuck on a similar plateau. Even credible opponents were running out. Thad Spencer had been mooted as his next challenger. Spencer was regarded as a stylish boxer, but short on hitting power and with a spotty record. It would have been difficult to sell a fight between Ali and a man who had once lost to a boxer with the unlikely name of Shirley Pembleton!

Ali's biographer Thomas Hauser has written that before his exile Muhammad's fights were more performances than contests.[2] In 1967 it is difficult to see anyone who might have extended him. The man who was to become his greatest rival, Joe Frazier, was then still comparatively raw and two years away from his peak.

Frazier and Spencer, along with Patterson, Mildenberger and Terrell, were nominated by the W.B.A. to take part in an elimination tournament to find a new champion. They were joined by three newcomers, Oscar Bonavena, Jimmy Ellis and Jerry Quarry. The way in which boxing's racial mix had changed in the past twenty years was reflected in the fact that of the six Americans only Quarry was white.

At first, it appeared that the proposed tournament might become a farce like its predecessor. Frazier, who at the time of Ali's conviction had had only sixteen pro fights, withdrew and was replaced by Leotis Martin, ranked ninth by the W.B.A. However, things solidified after that.

August 5th at the Houston Astrodome saw Ellis pitted against Martin, and Spencer taking on Terrell. Ellis, a stablemate of Ali's, convincingly mastered Martin, forcing the referee to stop it in the 9th. Spencer produced a career best performance to smoothly outbox Terrell and remove him from contention.

1 Hauser: 'Muhammad Ali' p.209.
2 'Muhammad Ali: His Life & Times' p.161.

The show moved on to Frankfurt where the two non-Americans, Bonavena and Mildenberger, fought each other on September 16th. Bonavena is the best heavyweight to come out of South America to date. A rough-hewn Argentinian nicknamed 'Ringo' because of his Beatles haircut, Oscar had lost legitimately only to Folley and Frazier in 33 bouts, scoring 25 kayos which included Tom McNeely and Billy Daniels. His power was too much for Mildenberger. Karl made the distance but had to pick himself up off the canvas four times to do it.

The last quarter-final was a rematch between Quarry and Patterson, at Los Angeles on October 28th. In July they had boxed a draw, Patterson twice coming off the floor to win the later rounds as Quarry tired. But Jerry had gone to school in that fight and this time went one judge better, winning a split decision.*

The first semi saw Ellis meet Bonavena in his native Louisville on December 2nd. Jimmy boxed crisply at long range, dropped Oscar twice with rights, and won going away.

The second semi-final, at Oakland, California on February 3rd, 1968, was a more explosive affair. Spencer employed exactly the wrong strategy against Quarry. At 6′ 4″ Thad ought to have taken the bout off to long distance. Instead he attacked. Quarry, a puncher with either hand, decked him several times and finally stopped him a few seconds from the final bell. The last knock-down, a wicked left hook which had Spencer turning a double somersault across the ring, lives in the memory.

On April 27th Quarry and Ellis met for the vacant title in Oakland. Irish-American Quarry's record stood at 26–1–4 with 15 kayos. He was short for a heavyweight and his reach was not very long, yet his natural bent was to counter-punch. Ellis was taller, 6′ 1″, with a longer reach. A crafty, hit and run boxer with a sound defence and a good jab, Jimmy had no hesitation with his tactics. Spencer had shown what *not* to do against Quarry, whereas Eddie Machen, the only man to beat him, had capitalised on Jerry's limitations and boxed out of defence. It made for a dull fight. Quarry never really got untracked. When Ellis did not come to him, he should have attacked, but he was perhaps too mindful of a sneak right hand which Ellis could use to malevolent effect. After 15 uneventful rounds one judge scored it a draw but the other two had Ellis deservedly out in front.

The new W.B.A. camp was managed and trained by Angelo Dundee. Born on February 24th, 1940, in Louisville, he had beaten Ali as an amateur and was his friend and sparring partner. He turned professional as a middleweight and on one occasion defeated two men on the same night, the only claimant to the heavyweight crown to have done so, professionally. This notwithstanding, Ellis did not make much progress in the 160 lbs division. He lost to feared hitters like

* The referee voted a draw.

Henry Hank and Rubin Carter — who floored him — and craftsmen such as Holly Mims, Don Fullmer and George Benton. But Ellis put on poundage and developed into a heavyweight*, and as he did so he matured as a fighter. Even so, his best victory prior to Leotis Martin was probably top light-heavyweight contender Johnny Persol whom he axed inside a round. Which brings me to a minor statistical distinction which Ellis holds. When he won the title 67% of his 12 kayos had been in the first round, the highest such *percentage* in heavyweight championship history. (Runner up Dempsey had 59%.)

New York threw a spanner into the works by refusing to recognise Ellis. Their argument was that any new champion should beat Frazier before receiving recognition. As Frazier had been the W.B.A's No. 1 contender this seemed logical and fair. In fact New York was playing politics again. While the W.B.A. tournament was still underway they approved a fight between Frazier and Buster Mathis as being for the vacant title.

Joe Frazier, born William Joseph, on January 12th, 1944, at Beaufort, South Carolina, would become the first man to win both the Olympic and professional heavyweight titles.

Frazier married young, fifteen, and was a father before his seventeenth birthday. He moved his family first to New York and then Philadelphia where he worked in a slaughterhouse. As an amateur he lost only twice, both to Buster Mathis who outpointed him in the 1964 Olympic trials. Mathis however broke a finger in an exhibition bout with Frazier, and Joe substituted in the Olympics. He stopped a Ugandan, an Australian and a Russian to reach the final. Ironically, in the semi he broke his left thumb, but went ahead with the final against Germany's Hans Huber and won a majority decision and America's only boxing Gold of the Tokyo games.

Back home though, nobody queued up to offer the 5′ 11½″ 209 lbs Frazier a professional contract. His height and reach** were considered too short, his legs too thick-set, and he relied on his left hook too much. So he turned pro with Yank Durham who had latterly trained him as an amateur. By contrast, Buster Mathis had several offers and turned pro amidst a blaze of publicity. Almost nobody noticed Frazier. They soon would.

'Smokin' Joe, as he liked to be called, won his first eleven inside the distance. Included were Dick Wipperman, Billy Daniels and Chuck Leslie, one of Thad Spencer's early conquerors. Along the way Durham secured the backing of fourteen Philadelphia businessmen — Cloverlay Inc. — in a deal similar to Ali's with the Faversham syndicate. Its shares started out valued at $250 and each ended up worth 14,000.

* He weighed 197 lbs in beating Quarry.
** 71 inches.

Fight number twelve was against Bonavena, and saw the Cloverlay stock market wobble and almost crash. Bonavena ripped a right cross to the jaw in round two which sent Frazier hurtling to the canvas. At '5' he scrambled to his feet and stood dazed whilst the referee tolled off the other three seconds of the mandatory eight count. Then Bonavena, blood seeping from a cut left eye, bulled his way in and unleashed a murderous left hook to the temple that deposited Joe on the floor again. He crawled to his feet knowing that another knockdown and he was finished, for three knockdowns in one round automatically terminated the contest.

There was a minute of the round left: a minute in which Joe Frazier's career could disintegrate into the night air; a minute in which he could be washed up on the failed prize-fighters' beach. But although Bonavena thudded home punch after punch, and Frazier reeled and staggered, somehow he reached deep into the reserves of his courage and will-power and stayed upright, gritting his teeth as the tornado swirled around him. At the end of the round Joe walked unsteadily back to his corner. But he had survived. He took a buffeting throughout the 3rd but from the 4th onwards he was back in the fight, and winning it. He was unable to drop the rugged Argentinian but he pounded his face into raw meat down the stretch to win an ultra close decision.

Eddie Machen was brought on next. Some questioned Durham's wisdom: Machen was over the hill but massively experienced, and only four months previously had licked Quarry. In the early rounds it looked as though he might do the same to Joe. But Frazier smoked him out and put paid to him in the 10th. Afterwards, Machen told the press:

> *'He's awful good. The boy has no defence, but the way he stays on top of you, he don't need one.'*

Pressure was what Joe Frazier was all about. He would never be able to box off his backfoot, jab somebody silly, or move silkily around a ring. And he always favoured his left hook too much. But it was an awesome weapon, one of the best in heavyweight history. Frazier powered it like a steam hammer driven by a piston. He used attack as the best form of defence, his upper body movement startlingly similar to Dempsey's in the way he continually bobbed and weaved and slipped punches. His legs looked ungainly — or to be more exact too gainly — but he moved with deceptive speed, cutting the ring down and staying right on top of an opponent, never giving him room and pounding away to head and body.

Doug Jones fell; then Jefferson Davis. George 'Scrapiron' Johnson, noted for his toughness (but not much else) went the distance. Sixteen straight and came there now a man of even more iron, George Chuvalo. In the 3rd Joe unleashed a thunderous barrage of hooks which almost drove the Canuck through the ropes. It was halted in the next with George's face gushing blood like a burst water main. He had never been stopped before. A pair of trial horse kayos rounded out 1967 and made it 19–0–0. Mathis came on March 4th, 1968, eight weeks before Ellis and Quarry met.

The photograph of Buster Mathis which stares out of the Ring Record Book has the sad-eyed look of a man who seems to know that he is never quite going to make it. He had not been fated to go to the Olympics, and now Frazier, starting quietly, had eclipsed him in public attention. He stood 23–0–0 with 17 kayos, but most of the opposition were what used to be called Palookas, now renamed 'opponents' to give them more credibility. Buster's best victory had been over Ron Marsh who had himself cut a swathe through a field of 'opponents'. Mathis won a battle of gilt edged prospects in the 4th. He was 6′ 3″ and weighed a very blubbery 243 lbs (110 kilos). Despite his bulk — he may have had a glandular condition — Mathis was fast on his feet, and a good boxer with a stern right uppercut.

On the night of March 4th Mathis took the first four rounds in a row, jabbing superbly and spinning hooks off the jab at close quarters. For such a fat man his footwork was eye-opening.

Frazier began to get on terms in the 5th, barrelling his way through Buster's defence and hooking fiercely to the body. But he had to endure a rough ride in the next round where Mathis made his big effort. Midway through the stanza he hit Frazier with the right uppercut that had scorched 17 opponents. Frazier halted in his tracks, momentarily hurt, but then shaking his head he came on again, grinning as if to say, 'Now let me show you something about punching.' Shaken, Mathis began to lose heart. From this point on ringsiders could see his confidence almost visibly evaporating.

The corner had been reached and turned. Frazier took over, sinking vicious hooks into Mathis's body throughout the next four rounds. In the 7th a battery of left hooks split open Buster's nose, and slowly but surely Joe reduced him to a sitting target. By the end of the 10th Mathis was a battered, bleeding hulk. In the next round Frazier finished it.

A searing right hook exploded on Buster's temple and the big man reeled backwards into the ropes. Following up, Joe bombed him with a vicious left hook to the chin, and Mathis went sprawling across the bottom rope, his head and shoulders resting on the ring apron. He was still in the act of rising when the referee tolled off the final second of the count.

Frazier's accession to their 'title' worked out better than New York could have hoped. It effectively split the W.B.A. Five breakaway states decided not to recognise Ellis–Quarry: Texas, Maine, Massachusetts, Illinois and Pennsylvania. They were followed by the W.B.A.'s Latin American allies. The renegades went with Joe. But hanging over all of them was the shadow of Ali, the king in exile. Muhammad's courtroom battles are not part of this book: they have been documented in numerous biographies. But as casualties began to mount in Vietnam and more and more young Americans chanted 'Hell no, we won't go' outside the White House, so the mood of America perceptibly altered. At the same time as Frazier and Ellis were basking in their split titles, Lyndon Johnson was announcing his withdrawal from the 1968 Presidential race and his party was turning in great numbers to anti-war candidates Bobby Kennedy and Eugene McCarthy. On the Republican side eventual winner Richard Nixon was also promising to end the war. Muhammad Ali though could only watch and wait.

Frazier made his first defence in New York on June 24th. It is memorable purely because Manuel Ramos is the only Mexican to have boxed for the heavyweight title. His challenge did not last long. Stung by a right uppercut in the first round, 'Smokin' Joe overwhelmed Ramos in the 2nd.

Ellis also made a defence, outpointing Floyd Patterson in Stockholm on September 14th. It was an indifferent bout and almost everybody bar the officials thought Patterson had won. Ringsiders credited him with nine of the fifteen rounds.

But a new player was about to emerge on the scene that autumn, George Foreman a 6′ 3″, 220 lbs, black Texan who in October went to Mexico City and came back with the Olympic heavyweight crown. Foreman stopped a Russian to win the gold and afterwards paraded around the ring waving a little American flag. In a Games riven by Black Power demonstrations, his gesture went down well in the U.S. Foreman turned professional the following year.

Frazier ended 1968 by giving Oscar Bonavena a return, in Philadelphia on December 10th. It was a pounding fight, but Joe had matured since the first one and dominated the first ten rounds. He tired over the last five and Bonavena, a fighter who wore his heart on his sleeve, took over. But he couldn't claw back the deficit and Frazier was a unanimous winner.

1969 was not a vintage year for boxing. The throne was occupied by two pretenders. Who was the better man? 1969 would not tell us.

Things reached a particularly low ebb during the first few months of the year. Frazier took his half of the title to Houston and put it on the line to a white heavyweight named Dave Zyglewicz. Zyglewicz had won 28 out of 29 (14 kayos) against opposition which left almost everything to be desired. The loss on his form sheet was to one, Sam Wyatt, a 15 fight 'veteran' who had managed to lose seven of them. All too predictably, Zyglewicz fell apart in 96 seconds against Frazier, at that time the second shortest heavyweight title fight on record.

Jimmy Ellis was supposed to defend against Henry Cooper in London in June. After losing to Ali Cooper was very comprehensively knocked out by Floyd Patterson, but still had a couple of tingles left for his adoring public. He took the European crown from Mildenberger, and then defended it in Rome where Piero Tomasoni repeatedly hit him low until the 'ammer came to the rescue for one last glorious finale. Alas, it never tested Ellis's chin. Cooper injured a knee and the fight was cancelled. The W.B.A. had twice stripped Ali at the earliest possible moment, but did nothing when Ellis remained inactive all year*.

Joe Frazier and Jerry Quarry did liven things up in New York on June 23rd. They went to war. Quarry got his tactics wrong again. This time he should have used his counter-punching skills. Instead he went in and slugged it out. Bone-crushing wallops exploded on iron jaws and spectators shouted themselves hoarse. Late in the 4th Quarry hit Frazier flush on the chin with the left hook which had had ringsiders fearing that Spencer's neck was broken. Frazier took it and rasped: 'You through? Because it's my turn now.' It was. Frazier battered him throughout the 5th and 6th. Next round the referee stopped it with Quarry's face looking as though it had been torn off and then grafted back on again inside out.

However, the thrills and spills could not mask the fact that the public really did not care. Neither Frazier nor Ellis was a dazzling personality in the Ali mode. People still called Muhammad the real champion. Outside the ropes, his stand for his principles had made him a hero to many.

The situation is best summed up by an experience I had in Belgium in February 1970. Frazier and Ellis finally met at Madison Square Garden on the 16th of that month. In Brussels I tried, and failed, to get the B.B.C.'s radio broadcast in my hotel room. Later that morning I asked staff: 'Who won the fight?' My question was met with blank stares and shrugged shoulders. 'Fight — what fight?' Nobody knew who the heavyweight champion was, or even that the championship had been decided a few hours earlier. Basically, nobody cared.

The winner turned out to be Frazier. Had they met in 1967–8, before Joe reached his peak, then the outcome would possibly have been different. Then, Yank Durham was wise to pull Frazier out of the eliminators. But by 1970 Joe had come of age.

Ellis began confidently, stabbing long lefts into Frazier's face and twice sneaking over hard rights. But the blow that had carved out many first round knockouts had no effect on Frazier. From then on it was merely a matter of time.

Throughout the 2nd and 3rd Joe walked through Ellis's punches, trapped him on the ropes, and hooked viciously to the body. At the end of the 3rd Frazier spun him round full circle with a left hook to the chin. Only the bell saved Ellis. The end was in sight.

The 4th round was the last. An explosive double left hook — one to the body, one to the head — left Ellis in dire straits on the ropes. Another double left hook, both to the chin, sent electric shock waves rippling through his body and he pitched forward on his face. At '8' he scrambled to this feet. Blindly, lashing out in a vain bid to stave Frazier off. But Joe measured him and fired

* He withdrew from a proposed defence against Argentinian Gregorio Peralta.

home a bullet of a left hook to the jaw. This time Ellis went down flat on his back. The bell rang at '5' but the count continued. Somehow Ellis managed to stagger groggily to his feet at '9'. Back in his corner Angelo Dundee worked frantically to revive him. But to no avail. When the bell sounded for the 5th Ellis got off his stool but Dundee gently pushed him back on to it and signalled the referee that he was surrendering his man.

Frazier had now annexed the W.B.A. title. Europe recognised him. Only Britain remained aloof, staying loyal to Ali. So did the public. To the man in the street Joe Frazier was just a contender-pretender.

The forty-three months from March 1967 to October, 1970 were unhappy ones for Muhammad Ali. The money he had made was devoured in legal costs. Inactivity put a sheen of rust on his once marvellous reflexes. In the long term these two factors combined were to prove ruinous. He boxed on longer than he should have done and wrecked his health.

At one stage even the Black Muslims turned against Ali. Twice it looked as though he might fight again. California's Board was in favour but gave in to pressure from the state's then Governor, Ronald Reagan. Nevada's Governor took a different view to Reagan, but here the mob had its revenge, using their political tools to block the fight. However, with public opinion now shifting into Ali's corner, it only needed one ray of sunshine to pierce the clouds and he would be back. It came in Georgia.

In 1968 Georgia was on of six states to vote for George Wallace in the Presidential election. It could therefore hardly be said to be either liberal or integrationist. The state's right-of-centre outlook was reflected in its Governor, Lester Maddox, the sort of man who would sooner have had his daughter marry Jack the Ripper than a black. But times were changing in Georgia — and throughout the south as a whole — as southern blacks began to flex their political muscles, especially in Atlanta, the state's capital, where a large proportion of the city's population was black. Leroy Johnson was a black state senator who controlled a block of votes which Atlanta's mayor Sam Mansell needed to get re-elected. Leroy Johnson had a financial interest in Ali fighting in Atlanta. Leroy Johnson paid Sam Mansell a visit.

Mansell agreed, albeit reluctantly, to Ali fighting in Atlanta on October 26th. Opposition? The call went out to Jerry Quarry. At 25, Jerry would actually be Ali's first professional opponent who was younger than him, a sign of how time had quietly crept on.

Ali–Quarry was more an occasion than a fight. Atlanta's whites stayed indoors. In Jack Johnson's day, black celebrities could have shared a taxi; now they packed the ringside reflecting an emergence which sport had signposted. Ali began as though he had never been away, but was noticeably less up on his toes in round two. It was developing into a contest when in the 3rd an Ali right cut Quarry's left eye to the bone. Referee Tony Perez stopped it during the interval between the 3rd and 4th. Quarry cried, but was gracious, dismissing any suggestion that it might have been a butt. Next day Ali's return made headline news around the world.

But others had business too that fall. Up to November, 1970, George Foreman had enjoyed 23 winning outings. When Earl Grey's Cabinet was announced, the outgoing Prime Minister, the Duke of Wellington, kept asking 'Who? — Who?' Boxing writers were asking the same question when they looked at the list of George's 'opponents'. Very few seemed to have been heard of before. It was even rumoured that one 'opponent' had been hired in a bar on the night of the fight. Those with discernible records might just as well have fought out of wheelchairs given their apparent inability to stay upright for very long. There were only two useful names on big George's form chart. Gregorio Peralta was an Argentianian light-heavy who gave him all sorts of trouble. Indeed, it was whispered that George wanted to quit at the end of the 9th; that manager Dick Sadler had to push him out for the 10th. Foreman took a close decision, and was a lot more impressive against George Chuvalo, becoming only the second man to stop the Canadian punch sponge. A tremendous volley of hooks draped Chuvalo across the ropes in the 3rd, and with his wife in hysterics the referee hauled Foreman off him. But although Chuvalo had surprisingly kayoed Quarry earlier in the year, he was still considered past his best.

November 18th at Madison Square garden, Foreman faced what was supposed to be his acid test, Boone Kirkman, a white heavyweight from Seattle managed by the one and only 'Vampire Jack'. Hurley was obsessed with finding a white heavyweight champion. Kirkman had retired Machen and Doug Jones and, like 'Harry the Kid' before him, had decimated the heavyweight population of the north-west. That night Foreman trussed him up, bundled him together, and dumped him in the baggage car with a 'Palookaville' label on him. Hurley was reported to be so upset that he retired to his castle in Transylvania. But Foreman was hardly impressive. True, he carried tremendous firepower, but his accuracy and timing seemed off and he started his punches from well behind his back, like a baseball pitcher.

The main bout that night came from Detroit via closed circuit link-up with the Garden. Joe Frazier was making his first defence of the unified title against light-heavyweight kingpin Bob Foster. Foster was one of the best 175 pounders in history and probably that division's hardest single-shot hitter ever. But his power cut little ice amongst the big boys where Terrell and Folley had beaten him. His encounter with Frazier was brief, exciting and important.

Joe smoked out of his corner and targeted Foster's beanpole of a body. Foster responded with one of the rights that had made a graveyard of his own division. Frazier shrugged and came on again. The 2nd opened with a Frazier left hook to the head which left Bob gangling on the canvas. He got up on dream street. Left hook, right hook, gunned him into the ropes and then a truly awesome left hook finished it.

What the people saw that night was a very good champion in action, a fighter who didn't deserve to be in another man's shadow. But if people now sat up and took notice of Frazier — as champion and not as contender — it was because of Ali's return three weeks earlier. And the emphasis had subtly changed. Before it had been on Ali as the champion in exile. Now it was on Ali as the man who had returned to win back his laurels. A good Frazier performance against Foster had been crucial to ensuring that Ali-Frazier was a blockbusting money spinner.

Equally crucial was Ali's next fight against Oscar Bonavena at Madison Square Garden on December 7th. New York routinely turned down Ali's request for a licence and then found themselves smartly and expertly taken to court by his lawyers on the basis that the Commission's denial violated Ali's constitutional rights. They did indeed. Judge Walter Mansfield described New York's actions as: 'astonishing; an intentional, arbitrary and unreasonable discrimination... not the even-handed administration of law which the Fourteenth Amendment requires.' Ali got his licence.

Bonavena gave him a lot more trouble than the New York Boxing Commission did. The main support bout featured Britain's world lightweight champion Ken Buchanan against Canada's world-rated welterweight Donato Paduana. Buchanan's display of pure skill that night was one of the greatest — some say *the* greatest — in garden history. Listening to the thunderous ovations from their dressing rooms, Ali and Bonavena must have known they had a very hard act to follow. They didn't make it.

Ali–Bonavena was frankly boring. Not much happened in the opening three rounds. Ali fenced without sparkle. Bonavena body-punched his way to the 4th and 6th, evened 5, made Muhammad wince. Ali took 7 and 8 behind his jab; Bonavena spurted again in the next three. The Argentinian's gut busting attempt brought him the 9th and 11th with the 10th level. What excitement there was came from Oscar. Ali was showing the effects of all that time in courts instead of rings. But he finally mastered his brief. Tiredness dogged his heels, yet he hit a groove above Bonavena and stayed in it until the end of the 14th. Then came fifteen.

They had not been boxing very far into the round when Ali produced a scintillating left hook to Bonavena's jaw which caught him coming in. He crashed to the canvas, took '9', and arose on jellied legs, eyes staring blankly into space. Today it would go no further. A brief flurry dropped Oscar again for '8', and then a gentle combination pitched him onto his side. Three knockdowns terminated it.

The drama of that last round, Beelzebub suddenly woven into a nondescript tapestry, was needed. In essence it was a one punch knockout over a man who had gone 25 rounds with Frazier without being dropped. Ali still had that something extra, a little piece of meteorite moulded into the steel.

The latest 'fight of the century' was now a reality. This time not an old, toothless lion dragged out of retirement by race prejudice, not a conman's masterpiece, but a real battle between two outstanding, unbeaten fighters, one at his absolute peak, the other the more brilliant but now with flecks of sandstone amongst the hard brick.

The Garden got it for March 8th, 1971, the first of two important dates for Ali. The second, six weeks later, would hear his final appeal before the U.S,. Supreme Court.

Ali–Frazier did not need selling but still became the most hyped match in boxing history. Bud Schulberg devoted a whole book to the fight's background; not, I hasten to say, the hype, but its social and racial context.[1] Hype in itself is simply drivel, on no higher par than today's sexism of bikinied girls parading around the ring. This work can do without repeating it.

Behind the P.R., interesting things *were* happening. First Ali. The dancing master was gone, except in short, sharp bursts. A fundamental re-assessment had taken place. Dr Ferdie Pacheco, Ali's doctor and friend, explains:

> *'After the lay-off, Ali came back and his legs weren't like they'd been before... he lost his first line of defence. That was when he discovered something very good and very bad. Very bad in that it led to the physical damage he suffered later in his career... He discovered he could take a punch... He could run for a round and rest for a round, and let himself get punched against the ropes while he thought he was toughening his body.'* [2]

Dr Pacheco did not endorse this strategy, as is clear when he discusses the eventual effects on Ali's health. But robbed of his peak years, his money spent on staying out of gaol, the 1971 Ali really had nowhere else to go. He had in fact been working on coping with body shots since before the Liston return. John Cottrell:

> *'He stood still against the ropes and invited Codly to hammer him bout the body. The champion threw no punches in reply; he merely locked his forearms behind Jones's head and pressed down on the neck and shoulders until his sparring partner was bent double.'* [3]

This was a combination of will and tactics. Will, to overcome his fear of body punches; tactics, designed to lessen their effect. It would form the nucleus

1 'Loser and Still Champion'.
2 Hauser: 'Muhammad Ali' pp.213-4.
3 'Man of Destiny' p.196

of Ali's rope-a-dope strategy, lolling on the ropes to save strength, while luring the opponent in to expend his own on a body attack which he, Ali, minimised. From 1970 Ali was forced to concentrate on will, tactics, strength, and the ability to take punishment as well as give it. Ultimately, the effect was retrograde.

Now Frazier. Let him explain it himself:

> *'I never liked Ali... [his] words hurt me more than the punches... calling me the white man's champion. All that was phoniness to turn people against me... How would you like it if your kids came home from school crying because everyone was calling their daddy a gorilla?'* [1]

Dave Wolf, a sports-writer at the time, later a boxing manager, fleshes out Joe's dislike of Ali:

> *'He [Ali] isolated Joe from the black community. He constantly equated Joe with the white power structure... Ali demeaned Joe at every turn... There were moments when Joe was so hurt and which he remembers so vividly even now.'*[2]

There was not, on Ali's side, the raw hate of the Patterson fight, or even Terrell. But he used Frazier as he did Liston, despite the fact that Joe is a man of much higher character. It wasn't necessary. As Wolf says: 'It was cruel; that's all.'[3] Ali was pumping himself up as the great black hero at the expense of another black, egocentrism manifested in ethnocentrism. But as Schulberg makes clear in his book, Ali already had the idolatry of blacks. Underpinning his campaign against Frazier was insecurity, both personal and fistic. He had to ensure that he would still be their hero even if he lost; that Joe would not become a rival for black affections.

So to March 8th and a battle which lived up to expectation. Different eyes see different fights. I saw a different fight from the judges but with the same result.

For Ali the contest divided up into thirds. For Frazier it was a single fight from beginning to end. Joe only fought one way: march forward, get to grips with the foe, impose your will on him; break him. Ali, for the opening five rounds, showed, at least some of the time, how he would have boxed Frazier at his peak, up on his toes, making the angles, jabbing deftly and putting together swift, sure combinations. In the 1st I noted two good Ali left hooks against one by Joe who lunged a lot and missed a lot. Round two saw Muhammad moving so lightly that he seemed to be floating on a cushion of air. By comparison Frazier appeared to be treading water in a swamp. At the end of the session Ali put together a beautifully executed four punch cluster. There were so many good punches throughout the whole of the fight that in this vignette it is possible to report only the really choice ones.

1, 2, 3Hauser: 'Muhammad Ali' pp.219, 220, 231 and 325.

There was a really impressive left hook to the body from Frazier towards the end of the 3rd, good enough to edge him the round on the judges' cards (but not mine), and they also gave him the 4th. Once again, near the round's end Joe fired in a good left hook to the body and followed it with a double dose to the head. I was in a strict minority in giving the round to Ali. He was not moving quite so well as in the 2nd, but still boxing quite magnificently and landing the majority of the punches, making Frazier's nose bleed into the bargain.

Round five: that air cushion again. If it was an open air arena you would say Ali was dancing on a moonbeam. Boxing off it too. In the final minute, Frazier, in frustration, dropped his hands and invited Muhammad to hit him. Ali did. Bad move Joe.

With a third gone I had it 5–0 to Ali, although two were by a whisker. All three officials (referee and two judges) had scored 3–2 to Frazier! They were using what is termed 'collateral value', i.e., that one of Frazier's hard hooks was worth four or five of Ali's lighter punches. The puncher has an in-built advantage in his power and I don't see why he should enjoy it in the scoring too.

Round five was the last time we saw the old fire and movement Ali. His feet were very decidedly back on the canvas in the 6th. Frazier meanwhile was heading up steam like a tugboat pulling away from the dock. The pressure builds and so does Joe. His round, clearly. But Ali broke right back at him to take round seven with some excellent combinations. Twice Joe put in thudding left hooks to the body, grunting as he drove the punches home. Muhammad responded with strings of jabs to the head. His supporters were ecstatic: 'Ali, Ali, Ali.' But on my card this is the last round Ali will win.

The 8th was designated a rest period, complete with comic relief. Ali allowed Frazier to bull him into the ropes where he forced Joe's head down onto his, Ali's, chest and continually patted him on top of the skull. Frazier joined in the zanyness, tattooing Ali's ribcage with light blows. He wanted a break too. But every so often he winged in a hard one. Muhammad hadn't quite perfected rope-a-dope yet!

It was back to serious business in the 9th, the round in which Frazier had promised to stop Ali.* He tried. Hard. For two and a half minutes it was a big round for Joe climaxed by a left hook which threatened to break Ali in half. A huge gasp from the crowd, but Ali responded with a piece of near genius. Two searing left hooks to the temple stopped Frazier in his tracks, a brilliant five-punch cluster — scimitars worked by pulleys — rocked him back on his heels, and another scorching left hook left him stunned. There stood Frazier, just, legs turned to jelly, twenty seconds remaining in the round. But Ali, this 1971 Ali, couldn't follow it up; couldn't find the crowning touch to regain a

* Ali had nominated the sixth.

crown. He let Frazier off the hook; literally.

Joe recovered during the interval and came out to join battle again. The 10th was a surging round, ceaseless pressure by Frazier, whiplash combinations from Ali. At one point, breaking them from a clinch, referee Arthur Mercante accidentally thumbed Joe in the eye. He was not amused. The round itself was level, I thought.

They were now two-thirds of the way through this titanic clash. I gave the middle third to Frazier 3–1–1. So did judges Arty Aidala and Bill Recht, 3–2 and 4–1. But Arthur Mercante's 4–1 to Ali was a surprise.

Eleven was a big, big round for Frazier. Ali slipped and Joe closed without mercy, delivering a shattering left hook to the head. Only the ropes kept Ali on his feet. Frazier fed him a battery of left hooks — always that left hook — and it seemed as if Ali must go under. Somehow he lurched away, managed to survive. In the last seconds he even tried kiddology, feigning to sag at the knees, trying to con Frazier that he hadn't really been hurt. But he had.

The next three sessions were attrition on their dwindling reserves. Frazier came on the same old way, Ali threw him back as best he could, left hooks crossing swords with countering combinations. A savage left uppercut almost ripped Ali's head off in the 13th, more than enough to give Frazier the round. The others I judged even. But what was happening on my card was irrelevant.

It ended in the highest of dramas. Frazier backed Muhammad into a corner and fired in a sweeping left hook which took him full on the cheek. Ali went down with a thud. Pride forced him up at '3' but he was glad the mandatory eight count was in force. Frazier volleyed hooks into him, but was just that little too tired to finish Ali off. The final bell was sanctuary to them both.

The completed scorecards read: Mercante 8–6–1, Aidala 9–6 and Recht 11–4, all for Frazier. Mine said 6–6–3 on rounds, but scoring by points I had awarded Frazier 11 and 15 by 10–8 margins which meant Frazier 144; Ali 142.

Ali's right cheek was swollen like a pumpkin. He briefly went to hospital but refused to stay in overnight.

Frazier's left eye was closed, his right cut. He too later went to hospital, for a much longer stay; almost three weeks. Ali, who claimed, outlandishly, to have landed three punches to every one of Frazier's, crowed that it was the effects of the punishment he had inflicted. Frazier's camp said it was hypertension.

Both fighters received a guaranteed 2.5 million dollars each. They could have had much, much more. The original offer had been 1.25 million plus 35% each of the gross, believed, ultimately, to have been over 20 million! Instead they took the assured amounts (shades of Dempsey 50 years earlier). An option for a Los Angeles rematch in 1972 guaranteed Frazier 3.5 million, Ali 2.5. But it was not to happen.

'Oh how wrong he is,' Ali responded after Frazier said that Muhammad would not want to fight him again. However first there were more pressing matters.

On June 15th, 1970, the U.S. Supreme Court ruled that religious beliefs constituted grounds for exemption from military service. Ali appealed against his conviction for draft evasion. On June 28th, 1971, his appeal was upheld without dissent. However, just as 'L pts 15' does not tell the whole story of the Frazier fight, so 'Ali v U.S. Government W 8–0'* was not the entirety of the Court's ruling. Initially, the judges split 5–3 *against* Ali. Then one judge altered his mind and deadlocked the proceedings at 4–4. Had this remained constant then the Appeal would still have been dismissed and Ali would have gone to gaol. The history of boxing in the decade of the Seventies would then have been very different.

A compromise was suggested. As the draft board had never specified exactly why it had excluded Ali from conscientious objector status, it was possible to rule in his favour without legitimising his beliefs. The vote now changed to 7–1 in Ali's favour, only the Chief Justice remaining obdurate. He eventually decided not to split his court's ruling: 8–0.

One long struggle had ended, another was about to begin: the quest to regain the title.

During the next twenty months Ali had ten winning fights. He kept interest in boxing alive. As ever, there were exciting champions in the lower weight divisions, but like it or not it is the heavyweights who command the public's attention. Up to this point only heavyweight title bouts had warranted closed circuit coverage and of these only two, Ali–Liston and Frazier-Ali, had received such coverage abroad. Not only were Ali's non-title bouts shown on closed circuit in the U.S., but several were also piped overseas, most notably to Britain. In sharp contrast Frazier's two title defences struggled to receive ordinary television coverage.

But that was the upside of the Ali campaign. The downside was that many of Ali's performances were unimpressive, and some critics thought he was not always in the best of shape. And the campaign almost kicked off with a 'fight' which, had it taken place, might have been good for Ali's bank account, but very bad for boxing.

Wilt 'the Stilt' Chamberlain was a 7′ 2″ basketball star who had never boxed in his life. But shortly after the Frazier fight negotiations began for a contest between Ali and Chamberlain. Fortunately Chamberlain, who later appeared in Bruce Lee's last film 'The Game of Death', saw sense and pulled out.

During the second half of 1971 Muhammad had real fights with Jimmy Ellis (r.s.f. 12), Buster Mathis (pts 12) and Germany's Jurgen Bilin (ko 7).

* One judge recused himself.

There was nothing remarkable about them, aside from one of those superb single punch kayos which Ali star-spangled his career with. It came against Mathis at the end of the 11th and laid the lard mountain out cold.* Unhappily the bell rang at '5', the count did not continue and Mathis, although hopelessly groggy, was sent out to stumble through the last round, Ali refusing to land any meaningful punches.

April, 1972 found Muhammad in Tokyo fighting Mac Foster who had been a sensational prospect with 24 straight kayos before knocking on the door of contender town. Jerry Quarry answered it and ferociously counter-punched Foster out of sight. Ali won virtually all 15 rounds against Foster and practised 'rope a dope', locking his arms around Mac's head, forcing it down until he was bent double.

George Chuvalo took part in another painful (for him) training exercise in May, and the following month Ali gave Quarry a second crack. Irish Jerry was arguably the best white heavyweight since Marciano. I can testify to his punching power having watched him kayo British champ Jack Bodell in 64 seconds with one sensational right. Ali' performance against Quarry was his best between the Frazier and Foreman fights. He entered the ring in peak condition (at Chuvalo's expense) and at times rolled back the years to reveal the mid-Sixties Ali. He jabbed and danced Quarry silly, hit him with blindingly fast combinations and halted him early in the 7th.

July found Ali in Dublin doing battle with fellow American Al 'Blue' Lewis, a somewhat enigmatic figure who possessed a highly dangerous left hook, and who had been a contender for some time without apparently showing much interest in trying to land a title shot. Ali had to kayo Lewis twice. In the 5th he ostensibly notched up another one punch knockout, an exquisite right cross which spelt lights out and good night. Seemingly, the leprechauns got into the timekeeper's watch that night because although 'Blue' was adjudged to have gotten up at '9', he was in fact on the canvas for some twenty seconds. Ali finally ended it in the 11th.

New British champ Danny McAlinden was postulated as August's sacrificial goat. There was a personal element: McAlinden had beaten Ali's brother, Rahaman, on the Frazier–Ali undercard. However, McAlinden had been totally outclassed by American Larry Middleton, and the Board of Control made it clear they did not regard Danny as a suitable opponent for Ali.

Muhammad should have faced Bonavena at the Garden again in September. First Oscar had to get past 37 year old Floyd Patterson. He didn't. Floyd produced one last memorable performance, calling on all the guile he had accumulated in 20 ring years, out-thinking Bonavena, out-manoeuvring him,

* He had become obese since the Frazier fight.

drawing him on to those rapier hands. Patterson's points victory gave him the Ali return instead. In reality it was a sentimental journey. The contrast with their first fight was stark. Now, neither had a bad word to say about the other. They boxed six gentlemanly rounds, and then Floyd's career ended on one of the most bizarre notes in the sport's history. He blew his nose and his left eye swelled up like a balloon. This malady he carried throughout the 7th. With the eye now shut tight he retired at the end of that session.

Coleridge's words from *The Ancient Mariner* might have been written for Floyd:

> *'Like one, that on a lonesome road, doth walk in fear and dread,*
> *And having once turned round walks on,*
> *And turns no more his head;*
> *Because he knows, a frightful friend doth*
> *close behind him tread.'*

It trod no more. In the nine years since Las Vegas Floyd Patterson had banished the spectre of the Liston humiliation. He had been unlucky not to regain the W.B.A. title, and had become the respected elder statesman of boxing. A significant man had regained his self respect.

Ali, on the other hand, very nearly betrayed his image by fighting next in South Africa. Contracts for a bout with fellow black American Al Jones, like Lewis a once highly touted fighter who seemed to have become side-tracked, were signed, but then the promotional company went bankrupt. Just in time to save Ali's neck. The Black Muslims had approved him boxing in the home of apartheid on the grounds that the rules of South Africa were no different to those of America. That is not the way most Black Americans would have seen it. Nor Black Africa, where Ali had been a hero since his first visit in 1964.

Instead the November date pencilled in for South Africa ended up in the safety of Stateline, Nevada, with Bob Foster providing the opposition. Foster cut Ali for the first time in his career, a nick under the left eye in the fifth round, and also hurt him with a right on one occasion. Those aside, Bob did a creditable impersonation of a ring repair man looking for holes in the canvas. He finally failed to beat the count in round eight.

The roadshow cross-countried to Atlantic City, February 1973, there to feature Ali against the European champion, Britain's Joe Bugner.

Bugner was a curious performer, world class one night, a dub the next. He had taken Cooper's titles in a fascinating contest, froze to lose almost every round and his laurels to Jack Bodell, lost and had his jaw broken by Middleton, and then fought with verve to regain the European crown from Jurgen Blin. In with Ali, Joe rose to the heights. Despite nursing a badly cut eye from the 1st, he boxed with precision, and at times imagination, to be level on points at the end of the 9th. Ali, who was in tip-top condition for this one, pulled out a two point round in the 10th, and produced some imagination of his own, braiding

Bugner with a series of bolo punches; that meteor in the steel again. Eleven and twelve were also rounds of real quality from the ex-champion. He took the fight beyond argument, but Bugner's display was, to my mind, one of the best by a British heavyweight this century.

Meanwhile, Joe Frazier was no longer the champion.

While Ali was turning contender town into a desert stop-over, Frazier wasn't doing much of anything. There were persistent rumours of a kidney complaint, not given much credence by the Ali fan club who claimed Joe had no relish for a return with their hero. Whatever the truth of the matter, it was certainly Frazier who passed on the 1972 rematch and its guaranteed pot of gold.

Between March, 1971, and January, 1973, Frazier defended only twice, a pair of undistinguished white heavyweights, Terry Daniels and Ron Stander.

At New Orleans on January 15th, 1972, Frazier massacred Daniels. Although Terry edged the second — a puzzling lapse into lethargy by the champion — he spent most of the contest being repetitiously bounced up and down off the canvas until the referee put everybody out of their misery in the 4th; not before time.

May 25th found Frazier in Council Bluffs to meet home town boy Stander, the only time Iowa has ever staged a world heavyweight title fight. Once again, Joe won in the 4th. The local man gave it his best shot and did momentarily stagger Frazier with a right in the first round. But Stander had a reputation for shedding more blood than a Pekinpah western and when it was stopped he had cuts over both eyes which actually met on the bridge of his nose! The nose itself was broken and Frazier was wearying of the bloodbath. He had stopped working in slaughterhouses eight years before!

The last time we looked in on George Foreman he was 'Boonedocking' white hope Kirkman. There had not been much to look at since. In fact, the press were accusing Dick Sadler of taking everyone for a ride. There was a whole shooting gallery of 'opponents' — that wonderful word again — and by the end of 1972 big George stood at 37–0 with 34 kayos. Looked impressive but wasn't. Earlier I remarked that you don't shoot 63 by hitting the ball sideways, but you do if it's a pitch and putt course! Foreman's technique was not developing at all. He appeared crude and artless.

However, his punching power was a force to be reckoned with. The Brazilian Luis Pires adopted what might euphemistically be termed as 'deep defence', i.e., wrapping his arms around his head like a tortoiseshell. Foreman solved that Gordian style by simply breaking Pires' arm with a punch. Gregorio Peralta was brought on for an encore and went into slumberland in the 10th, three sleeping pills administered from the right.

But overall Foreman's career became a prototype for what is happening today in boxing under the regime of the Alphabet Boys. Don't fight somebody who might beat you; fight everybody you can beat. In a sport which even in 1972 was controlled by lax and supine bodies, Foreman found himself No. 2 contender without ever having beaten an authentic contender.

The scene now shifts from the rolling croplands of Iowa to the Caribbean sunshine of Kingston, Jamaica. There is an old joke about Jamaica: no, she did it of her own free will. But whether Frazier's decision to face Foreman there on January 22nd, 1973, was based on free will or fear of losing to Ali is another question.

Few gave Foreman a chance. He was held to be too technically limited. But so too was Max Baer and there were similarities. Like Baer, Foreman was big, strong and a prodigious puncher. Frazier, much smaller, would be attacking *him*; not employing the crafty hit and run tactics of a Gregorio Peralta, which had given George so much trouble in their first fight. On the eve of the contest Foreman told the British boxing writer Walter Bartleman: 'See that concrete down there?; I'd like to smear Frazier all over it.' Convinced the sentiment was genuine, Bartleman became the only reporter to tip Foreman to win.

Frazier began as though he was running from a house on fire — and blaming Foreman for setting light to it! He rushed at the challenger with two sweeping left hooks, the second of which definitely jolted him. Then suddenly it was all over; bar the courage that is. An electric ripple of a right crashed against Frazier's jaw and down he went. He arose hurt, and Foreman hit him with a series of battering ram jabs followed by two cudgel rights and then a really devastating right uppercut. That, in essence, was the killer blow. Although Joe got up from it he did not get over it. A left-right sprawled him on the canvas for the third time amid pandemonium. The bell brought relief, but not recovery.

The 2nd was just a case of let's finish up and go home to dinner. After a right hand had spun Frazier around, Foreman exploded an overarm right on the back of his head and Joe was down — and up — yet again. A snarling left hook dropped him for the fifth time, and now we were all sickening of it. Courage and pride had been satisfied, there was no way back and we wanted the end. George obliged with a thunderbolt of a right hook which actually lifted Frazier off the canvas — all two hundred and odd pounds of him — and then down on his knees paying homage to the new Numero Uno on the block. He was getting up again, with futile heroism, when the referee at last waved it over.

George Foreman looked awesome that night, and much more accomplished than was thought, but as I left the closed circuit cinema an elderly West Indian tugged at my arm and said: 'Seventeenth round, Ali.' He knew his boxing.

Just when you think everything is clear somebody comes along and screws up the picture again. After Kingston there could only be one fight: Foreman v Ali.

Of course Muhammad had a little bit of business first, an ex-marine named Ken Norton whom he criss-crossed back across America to attend to after Bugner.

Norton, born in Jacksonville, Illinois, on August 9th, 1943, weighed a splendidly proportioned 215 lbs and stood 6′ 3″. He turned pro at the comparatively late age of 24. Now pushing 30, he really hadn't gone anywhere much, except to South America where Jose Luis Garcia, whom I saw Bugner almost decapitate, knocked him out in six. Chuck Leslie had also beaten Norton. Leslie was not so much washed up; the tide had never come in in the first place. Currently resident in San Diego, Ken appeared to be just a warm up for Ali there on March 31st.

Ali thought so too. Other things were on his mind, like an acting career. He spent less than three weeks in training camp and did very little of it because he had sprained an ankle playing golf. Norton, who had been a sparring partner for both Ali and Frazier, trained like a monk under the watchful eye of Eddie Futch, a veteran handler who was now also training Frazier. The game plan was to cut the ring off to Ali and beat him on the jab. Now that Muhammad's speed had left him he was vulnerable to a good jab, a point emphasised by the Bugner fight.

The tactic worked to perfection in the 1st round, Norton following through on the jab with left hooks, a punch Ali was never comfortable against. One of them broke his jaw. For the next eleven rounds pain seared through him whenever Norton landed a punch on the chin, and there were plenty of them.

Despite the pain and discomfiture Ali got his own jab working to good effect in the next five rounds and by the end of the 6th had carved out a big lead. But now his lack of fitness came into play. From the 7th he began to wilt little by little and Norton came on and on, chasing and chivvying him with the jab, reaching him with long left hooks, revelling in the sharpness he had gained from working with Frazier and Futch. The fight took on the character of a 1,500 metre race with the man behind closing on the leader all the time. Norton was up on Ali's shoulder at the last bell. But who had gotten over the finishing line first? My card said Ali, 6–5–1. One judge scored it the same, but the other two went for Norton, a major upset.

Many believed Ali was finished after this. He wasn't but the road had become harder.

Foreman made his first title defence on September 1st. He had won the crown in Jamaica — a first for that country — and now went to Tokyo for his opening defence, another first in heavyweight title history. Unhappily George reverted to type. His opponent was Jose 'King' Roman, 'king' of nothing he surveyed outside Puerto Rico. The day before the fight I was asked who would win. I replied, 'Foreman in the first round.' Beyond being right, there is not much more to be said. Technically, Foreman should have been disqualified for hitting Roman after he went down for the first time, but it would have been a travesty.

George took another three knockdowns to finish Roman off, basically because he was back to crude swipes. For the Frazier fight he had had extra tuition from Archie Moore and ex-featherweight champion Sandy Sadler (a legendary knockout artist). Now the caveman had returned.

Nine days later Ali faced Norton for the second time. The ex-marine's victory in March made him, for a while, the most talked about and sought after fighter in the world. Could he repeat the trick?

Ali, for once, trained out of the spotlight. And he trained hard. Lose again and his dream died. Once again the contest took on the shape of a race, only this time it was decided by a sprint finish.

Ali began superbly. Over the first few rounds he outboxed Norton. But Ken had ability and determination, and he surged forward during the middle rounds. The fight was between Ali's lightning jabs and combinations and Norton's pressurising tactics. The marine kept up a steady rate of fire with long left jabs and hooks. Ali threw single right hand shots. Why, remains a mystery. It later gave rise to the theory that his right hand had 'gone'.

After eight rounds they were even. Over the next three the fight teetered and hung in the balance, swinging first one way and then the other. At the end of the 11th they were still level.

Rarely had Ali shown such determination in the ring as he did now. The chips were down, the spectre of another defeat danced hauntingly before his eyes. And so he forced his tired limbs to react: a triumph of the will. He dug deep into his past to reach and drink from the fountain of youth, again dredging up every last ounce of himself for three glittering minutes to jab, dance and throw a satin bedded diamond of punch clusters. The San Diegan tried to go with him, but there was nothing left. He had fought his heart out, but now all that remained for the final lap was the sight of Ali pulling further and further away as he galloped down the home straight.

And at the bell it was Ali. The decision was split, 6–5–1 and 7–5–0 Ali, 6–5–1 Norton.* The 'greatest' was exhausted, but he was back.

On October 20th Ali engaged in what can best be described as a sparring session. He had fought in many outlandish parts of the world but nowhere as strange as Djakarta, the capital of Indonesia. It was virgin territory for boxing. Ali's opponent was the Dutch champion Rudi Lubbers, whose main claim to fame was his durability. As usual it was an Ali carnival, an extravaganza of colour which the Indonesians lapped up. As for the fight itself Ali easily won every round, lashing Lubbers with jabs and combinations for 12 rounds. But again, he attempted few individual rights and never looked like stopping Lubbers.

* My card, for Ali, was 6–5–1 again.

Joe Frazier fought once in 1973 after losing the title, a twelve rounder at London's Earls Court with Joe Bugner. Again, Bugner distinguished himself in a losing contest. He did well in the early rounds, and then Frazier came on in the middle part of the fight. One of his pet left hooks put Bugner on the floor in the 9th, but the Briton then brought the crowd to its feet by almost dropping Frazier with a right. However Frazier had the better of the last three stanzas and was worth his points win.

A rematch with Ali was scheduled for Madison Square Garden on January 29th, 1974. A year earlier they would have split six million. Now their wages were 32.5% each of the gross with a minimum guarantee of $850,000.

Frazier's personal dislike of Ali came to the surface during the build up. An impromptu wrestling match on a TV show resulted in both men being fined by the New York Commission. Although most thought it hype at the time, it was subsequently revealed that Joe genuinely lost his temper.

The fight lacked the drama and quality of their first encounter. Ali motivated himself into excellent shape and dominated the first half of the contest. The shuffle was there, the jabs and combinations, and the allegedly missing right returned, particularly in round two when a cross shocked Frazier to the core. He might have gone but for referee Perez who jumped in between the fighters under the mistaken impression that the bell had sounded.

The second half was different. Frazier had big rounds in seven and eight, thudding in the left hooks, applying that ceaseless pressure of his. He beckoned Ali to come and fight in the 9th and regretted it. Muhammad responded with a big rally, rested in the 10th, made another big effort in eleven, and then hung on for the bell in the final round. I made him the winner by 7–5–0. The judges gave him a unanimous verdict.

Contracts were signed between Ali and Foreman. The only obstacle was that Foreman had already agreed to defend against Norton on March 26th, in Caracas, the capital of Venezuela. Perhaps George had shares in a travel agency.

If the form book was right then Norton figured to give George a very tough fight. It wasn't, and he didn't.

On paper at least Ken was as big a man all round as the champion. He was not as powerful a hitter, but a better boxer and technician. Moreover, Foreman had problems outside the ring. He was in trouble with the taxman, and had somehow succeeded in signing away 215% of himself in various contracts, another comparison with Baer who managed 113%!* Law suits buzzed around George's head, affecting his training, and only hours before the contest he developed an infected nerve in a leg.

No challenger could have had more going for him tan Ken Norton. And

* Interestingly, Foreman had bought a ranch in Livermore, Ranchhand Baer's home town.

no challenger has ever thrown it into the discard so wantonly. Before the Ali fights he had employed a hypnotist. On March 26th, he could have done with a witchdoctor, an archangel and a Centurion tank. The power of positive thinking utterly deserted Norton in the ring. Foreman looked a giant in comparison with the Californian's shrinking form.

In the 1st Norton tried a string of jabs. Foreman merely sneered at him. Then Ken banged over his left hook. Foreman's only reaction was an icy stare. Norton's was to ice-up! From that moment on what spirit he had begun with lifted up its skirts and fled! Foreman ended the round by clubbing him with vicious rights under the heart, and Norton looked hurt as the bell went.

The second round was merely a scaffold upon which the executioner liquidated the condemned man in public. First with the axe, then the garrotte, and finally by firing squad.

First the axe. A scything right hook to the head that smashed Norton to the canvas for '8'. Then the garrotte, a coil of punches that left Norton on the floor with his eyes popping out. Incredibly, the referee ruled it no knockdown. Finally the firing squad, a bullet of a left hook to the jaw, and poor, shattered, Ken Norton collapsed and slithered down the ropes. End of story.

On the face of it, the man whom Ali would be trying to wrest the title from was not a complex person. Born George Edward Foreman on January 10th, 1949 at Marshall, Texas, he had several things in common with his contemporaries, Patterson and Frazier. All three were the sons of railway workers, all originated from the South and migrated — Foreman to Hayward, California — and all had birthdays in the first half of January. In common with Patterson only, Foreman had had a troubled childhood leading to delinquency and reform school where like Floyd he began to box.

Unlike Floyd, George was ostensibly an arrogant, unpleasant young man, the violence of the streets running deep within him, manifesting itself against his opponents. But that was not the complete picture. There was more to Foreman than that. He may be likened to a wounded animal licking its hurts from inside. His environment permitted no gentler feelings, yet they existed and later found expression in his becoming a born-again Christian, and eventually, a minister of the Gospel.

Two years before George won the title a burly, middle-aged black man sat listening to the radio broadcast of Frazier-Ali in his prison cell. He was serving a sentence for the manslaughter of a friend who had betrayed him. Before that Don King had been a numbers boss in Cleveland, on one occasion defending his territory by killing a would-be robber in a Wild West style gunfight. (He was acquitted on the grounds of self-defence.) King had been briefly acquainted with Ali before ending up in gaol. When he was released he decided to get into boxing.

He promoted a number of small shows in Ohio and pestered Ali to let him have the rights to promote his bouts. Ali refused; at this stage nobody took King seriously. But then Video techniques, promoters of Foreman–Norton, hired him as a consultant. Before that fight King asked Herbert Muhammad what Ali would want to fight Foreman. $5,000,000, said Herbert.

Ali in the winter of 1974 was in the same position as almost eleven years earlier, when Liston needed him more than he needed Liston. Foreman could fight someone else, but for relative chickenfeed. Ali had torn up everybody else's scripts and was the man the public wanted to see. A contest between Foreman and newcomer Ernie Shavers had loomed as the only other viable option for a big money fight. Some were calling Foreman the hardest punching champion in history; others said that Shavers was, quite simply, the biggest hitter of all time. In fact Ernie was a latter-day Bob Satterfield. He had knocked Ellis out in the 1st round with a nuclear powered right uppercut, but only after almost adding to Jimmy's first round victims himself. Then Shavers ran into the script ruiner supreme, Jerry Quarry, and was flattened, all of which panned out perfectly for Ali.

Ali wanted five million; so did Foreman. Plus $450,000 each for training expenses. In the 1970s only governments and giant corporations had that sort of money lying around loose in their coffers. Video Techniques came up with a government: the Central African Republic of Zaire.

Zaire, in the name of Risnelia Inc., funded Ali–Foreman. The details get a bit complicated, but Risnelia employed a British company, Hemdale Leisure Corporation, to deal with Video techniques. The fight was booked for the 20th of May Stadium, Kinshasa, for September 25th.

Ali arrived in Zaire first. He charmed the Zarois; he was, after all, a hero in Africa anyway. Otherwise, he was not so charming. A television interview with David Frost for American and British TV turned into a thirty minute rant espousing religious and political bigotry. To objective observers it seemed a pity that he was not a little more circumspect about the host nation: 'twenty-eight million people run this country, and not one white man is involved,' said Ali.

In fact one man ran the country, its dictator, President Mobutu Sese Seho. And a number of white men had played a very big part in putting him there, namely 'Mad' Mike Hoare, 'Black Jack' Schramme, Bob Denard and John Peters, all prominent mercenaries who had freebooted around Zaire — then the Congo — in the '60s 'assisting' Mobutu's ramshackle army with their own forces. Mobutu himself was a political gangster who had had the country's first Prime Minister, Patrice Lumumba, taken for a ride Chicago-style, and later deposed President Moise Tshombe as soon as the U.N. forces departed. He ran Zaire as a personal fiefdom, brooking no opposition and raking in a personal fortune while his people dwelt in poverty. Four years on he would need the aid of the French Foreign Legion to survive. Zaire was hardly the beacon to

American blacks that Ali propagated it as. It was not to be his last exercise in naiveté.

But in one sense Zaire was appropriate for this fight. The Congo of the Sixties resembles portions of English history such as Stephen and Matilda's struggles with each other for the throne and, three centuries later, the Wars of the Roses which lasted over thirty years and brought five different kings to power. Art and sport imitate life. Boxing is a microcosm of larger struggles. This one, lasting five years, between Ali, Frazier and Foreman, was a sporting War of the Roses.

Foreman arrived in Kinshasa only two weeks before the fight with a spare tyre of fat corpulating around his middle. The press asked whether he would be able to lose it in time. The question proved academic. His right eye was cut in training necessitating a postponement until October 30th. It was a damaging hint of vulnerability, especially as Ali was renowned for cutting his opponents with his sharp, twisting punches. It was also a blow to the promoters and their backers who had banked on making a very great deal of money. Grosses of anywhere between 30 and 100 million dollars were being bandied about. It would certainly be the richest fight in history. But now the press left grumbling, not guaranteeing to be back again. They had not much liked Zaire, one scribe commenting tartly that the fight was being held there because the top of Mount Everest was busy! But everybody knew that they would return by October 30th. Overwhelmingly they went for Foreman. Frank McGhee of the British *Daily Mirror* spoke for the consensus: 'The Ali legend dies at dawn.'

U.S. time zones dictated holding the contest at 4 a.m. in the morning Zaire — and British — time. The mind fleeted back over the decades to a previous fight which had then been the most important in history, Sayers–Heenan in the dawn light which bathed an English meadow.

Ali was first into the ring preceded by a huge American flag, an ironically patriotic gesture. The packed stadium went wild for him.

Then, a full five minutes later, Foreman to boos. One of his handlers bawled through a megaphone, 'Oyez, oyez, here is the champion.' Ali's eyes gleamed. Leaning over the ropes he whipped the Zarois into frenzied chants of 'Ali Bomba ye — Ali bomba ye' ('kill him Ali'). George should have remembered to stick to his own territory. He was also giving Ali something to take his mind off those bone breaking punches. Inside the ropes, Ali and Drew Bundini Brown set up a rhythmic chant of hate, just as they had done all those years ago at the Liston weigh-in. And just like that time Ali could not afford to lose now. He had crossed the Rubicon.

Conventional wisdom said that the only way Ali could win was by moving and boxing. Ali never followed other people's scripts. He and Foreman briefly fenced at each other like Olympic swordsmen engaging one another's blades, and then Ali went straight into his boxing with hard, precise combinations. No dancing, no moving. Foreman bulled him into the ropes and Ali stood and traded with him. Foreman should have been wearing a kilt rather than boxing trunks; he reminded you of an ancient highland warrior whirling a claymore around. But then George switched to the body and the punches threatened to rip Ali's entrails out and spread them across the canvas. Even so, it was clearly Muhammad's round and he set his seal on it with a cloudburst of punches as the round closed.

Round two really established the pattern of the fight. Rope-a-dope . But not rest-a-round. Each stanza Ali fought in spasms. He lured Foreman in, a siren against the ropes, and let him punch himself out. Ostensibly, Ali was taking fearful punishment around the body, but in fact it was only at the outset of these encounters. As they wore on he pushed Foreman's head further and further down until he became ineffectual. Then Ali would come off the ropes and work in staccato bursts, skewering Foreman with jabs, lancing him with right crosses, rapping out combinations. Foreman was throwing a lot more punches but they were crude and roundhouse. Ali was punching inside George's arms, zeroing in on the target while Foreman swept his blows around in inelegant arcs.

It went on like this throughout rounds two, three and four, a gruelling contest testing the will and the heart. A global audience of a million people watched it live either on closed circuit or television. Few, if any, at the time understood or appreciated Ali's tactics. It *appeared* that at any moment Foreman would break him in half on the ropes. In reality the stamina was being systematically drained out of the champion. Psychologically he was being utterly defeated. Ali kept up a constant patter of conversation. Afterwards it was revealed that he had said: 'Where's your big punch George'; 'I told you you had no power'; 'C'mon George, you're the champion — show me something'. And George tried, on one occasion literally jumping into the air to throw punches at Ali's head. Air was all they did hit. Air was what Foreman's confidence was evaporating into, alongside his strength. In between rounds Ali conducted his African choir in their hymn of hate 'Ali bomba ye, Ali bomba ye'. During the interval between the 2nd and 3rd he strolled across to George's corner and peered in on him, a shock to Foreman's psyche after some of the body blows he had driven in. In the 5th, after more of them, Ali turned to ringsiders and winked!

The fight passed beyond Foreman's reach in that round. He came out of his corner with his right arm extended like a battering ram and charged Ali into the ropes. There, for the next 2½ minutes, he threw punches as though he never wanted to see his arms again. But there was little accuracy; no timing. He looked like a preliminary boy who had been told to go out and swing away; rather as though if the Titanic's band kept playing then the ship wouldn't sink! Muhammad let him flail away, parrying or avoiding most and minimising the rest. And then...

Ali broke off the ropes. For a split second they crouched facing each other. Then Foreman started a massive left uppercut from somewhere in the region of the floorboards. But Ali cut the punch off in mid-air, trapping Foreman's gloves between his own. Then in the twinkling of an eye he retaliated with a searing combination. Another combination jolted Foreman back on his heels. A right hook hurt him; another jerked his head round on his shoulders and his knees buckled. Pandemonium. Ali had the bull going!

Desperately Foreman tried to come inside. But another right hook jarred him, swiftly followed by a left hook, and his knees went again. At the bell he was hurt and in trouble.

In the 6th Foreman was open mouthed with exhaustion. He betrayed his lack of technique by simply plodding round the ring after Ali. Seemingly, nobody had taught George the skill of cutting the ring off. Ali retreated calmly, watching a succession of left swings cleave the night air, impaling Foreman on the end of his jab as he did so.

Foreman attempted a desperation ploy during the interval. He got off his stool early and waited for Ali, trying to con him that he wasn't tired. Don't kid a kidder George. Ali turned it into a nightmare, getting off his own stool and strolling around the ring joking with ringsiders. Round seven itself was a replica of the 6th, Ali's jab playing a rhapsody on Foreman's now battered features while George could only totter after him.

At the end of the round Ali fired in two whistling left hooks, and now there was blood on the sand of this bullring in Kinshasa. Ali planted the bandeleros in the exhausted bull. Now, back in his corner, he concealed under his cape the short swords with which he would slay the bull. When he came out again he was walking with destiny.

Foreman's right eye was closed. His left eye was swelling ominously. He looked a shambling, hollow wreck of a man. Somehow he dredged up the strength for one last charge. Hopeless, hopeless. His punches were now as rubbery as his legs. The final attack petered out. For Ali the supreme moment was at hand.

Ali pushed Foreman away. He lashed home a combination. Foreman lurched. Another combination. Then a whipping left hook and George stumbled sideways into a lightning right hook which exploded on the side of his jaw. Slowly his massive frame gave way. He pitched forward onto the canvas and rolled over on his side.

Everywhere — from Zaire to Alaska — Buenos Aires to Moscow — London to New York — a million people leapt from their seats with one mighty roar of acclaim. And as the count reached 'five', with Foreman still on his side, his eyes two blank empty sockets, voices screamed into the night, 'He's not going to make it', and then all hell broke loose as we realised that Ali was the champion again. Foreman reeled to his feet but it didn't matter because referee Zack Clayton's mouth had already formed the magic word 'ten'.

Champion again. Another door opened that December: President Gerald Ford invited Ali to visit the White House. Interviewed for Thomas Hauser's book, Ford recalled:

> *'I wanted to meet Muhammad, not only because of my interest in sports, but because it was part of my overall effort to heal the wounds of racial division, Vietnam, and Watergate.'* [1]

But beneath the adulation heaped on Ali lay the reality of a 32 year old athlete who was now taking a lot of punishment, particularly around the body. True, 'rope a dope' enabled Ali to either minimise or neutralise much of it, but a percentage of Foreman's shots had hit and hit hard. Ali did not really have all that much left in him. But he did have an entourage to feed. Whilst some of the people around him were genuine friends — Drew Bundini Brown for example — others were simply sucking on a meal ticket. By the beginning of 1975 it was estimated that the entourage was costing him $1.4 million annually. Which meant Ali needed to keep fighting.

On March 24th, 1975 Muhammad made the first defence of his second reign. It was a significant occasion for three people. One was Don King. This was the first title fight he promoted on his own. It has been alleged that he borrowed money from the mob to do so. Another was a struggling young actor named Sylvester Stallone who watched the fight on closed circuit. It inspired Stallone to write the screenplay for 'Rocky'. The third was a 35 year old, balding liquor salesman from Bayonne, New Jersey. He was Ali's opponent!

We first met Chuck Wepner having his face re-arranged by Sonny Liston. Afterwards Liston was asked 'Is Wepner the bravest man you've met?' Sonny responded cynically: 'No, his manager is.' Not long after this Joe Bugner made a similar bloodstained mess of Wepner in London. At best a trial horse, Chuck could never have expected to box for the championship. That he did, and it was sanctioned, is not a tribute either to Ali or the sport's governing bodies.

Unlike its cinematic reproduction, Ali-Wepner, at the Cleveland Coliseum, was a dull, pedantic fight livened only by Ali suffering the fourth (and final) knockdown of his career, a right to the ribs doing the damage in round nine. Ali claimed it was a push and arose at '3' more embarrassed than hurt. He had to go to the last round to finish it, dropping Wepner with a right to climax a four punch barrage. Chuck was up at '7', but referee Tony Perez* halted it with 19 seconds remaining on the clock.

1 'Muhammad Ali' p.28.

* Perez later unsuccessfully sued Ali for remarks made after the fight.

Ron Lyle was next, at Las Vegas on May 16th. Lyle was an aggressive, heavy fisted slugger with a 30–2–1 record (21 kayos). He turned pro late and was the same age as Ali. The fight was tame, Ali performing 'rope-a-dope', and Lyle not really having the skill to open him up. Despite this one judge had Lyle 6 points up after 10 rounds.* In the 11th Ali reached into his bag and pulled out one of those masterclass shots of his, a blistering right cross to the jaw. Lyle did not go down but he was helpless on the ropes when the referee heeded Ali's entreaties to stop it.

Then it was on to Kuala Lumpur, Malaysia, where a black American defended the world heavyweight title against a pale-skinned Englishman, Joe Bugner, in temperatures which made it seem as though they were boxing in a furnace. The bout, on July 1st, was not an exciting one. Bugner was clearly hoping Ali would perish in the heat. In fact, Ali set a torrid pace, particularly in the first half of the fight, really whipping the blows into the blond Briton. Bugner picked up a little in the middle rounds, won the 10th, but took stern correction in the later sessions as Ali piled on both the pressure and the points. The scorecards 73–67, 72–65 and 73–65 reflected the champion's superiority.

But all these bouts, Wepner, Lyle and Bugner, were build ups to the final battle in boxing's War of the Roses, Ali's *pièce de resistance*, the last great fight which he had left in him.

Joe Frazier was still out there, and against Jerry Quarry looked as good as new. Today, with all the different sanctioning bodies, Quarry would certainly have won a version of the title. In the days of single and dual champions, he lacked that something which would have brought him the belt. After the losses to Ellis, Frazier and Ali he went through a period of demoralisation. George Chuvalo kayoed him in seven. Jerry claimed he had misjudged the count; others thought he lost heart after Chuvalo took his best shots and kept coming. Jerry recovered his morale against Bodell and Mac Foster, but then Ali shipwrecked him a second time. The rugged Irishman hung in there outpointing smooth boxing Larry Middleton and giving his rendition of the 'Mountains of Mourne' to Shavers and Lyle, both of whom he stopped. Mid '74 he was ready to trade hooks with Frazier for the second time.

Sadly, he flunked the test again. It was a vintage wine performance from Joe who wielded his left hook in ceaseless combat against the Californian's head and body. After four rounds Quarry had been punched to a standstill. In the 5th Frazier harpooned a left to the body and Jerry slumped to one knee. He arose, but there was only courage left in the tank. Joe Louis was the referee. He looked on uncertainly until even Frazier appealed to him to stop it. Then he did. A fighter only has a certain number of recoveries in him, and Quarry had no more. Ken

* Another judge had Lyle one point in front and the third had it even.

Norton wrote 'end of' to Jerry's career the following March. Frazier still had his to come.

But right now Joe was training for a fight which would become a legend, the 'Thriller in Manila'.

Manila. It seemed a strange place to hold a heavyweight title fight. But then so were Council Bluffs, Kingston, Tokyo, Caracas, Kinshasa and Kuala Lumpur. Venues no longer counted. Live gates now were more for atmosphere than profit contribution. In Manila Ali received 43% of the fight's gross with $4 million guaranteed. He ended up with 6 million in total (Frazier, 3 million). It was Ali's biggest purse, but interestingly the gross was only two-thirds of Ali–Frazier I, and nowhere near that of the Foreman fight. It was not that Ali's popularity had diminished; the drop in closed circuit business was indicative of the fact that few believed Frazier could beat Ali again.

Ten days before the contest Ali and Frazier were invited to the Presidential palace to meet President Ferdinand Marcos. The fact that, as in Zaire, Ali was appearing to endorse yet another shabby political gangster eluded him. Ironically Marcos was also supported by the same U.S. establishment which the Black Muslims claimed to despise (he was seen as a bulwark against communism in the area).

The increasing poundage added by the years was reflected in the weights. 33 year old Ali was 225 lbs, Frazier, 31, 215. Yet both were in peak physical condition. They needed to be. The bout, actually staged in Quezon City just outside Manila, would be in an indoor arena with heat more intense than Ali had endured in Kuala Lumpur.

Frazier's tactics harked back to their first fight in which he had drawn Ali into throwing right uppercuts so that he could counter with left hooks and had constantly pressurised him against the ropes. Ali countered this by not throwing right uppercuts; what few uppercuts he landed came from his left, a rare punch in boxing. Since 1971 he had developed his 'rope a dope' strategy which set problems for the Frazier camp. Eddie Futch later confessed that they never worked out how to cope with it. They didn't have to. Referee Carlos Padilla, who controlled the match superbly, refused to allow Ali to perform his rope tricks. The upshot was that Frazier did his best work when he forced Ali back against the ropes.

Thus to October 1st, 1975 and one of the greatest fights in boxing history. It was a night which had emotion; an acquaintance of mine admitted afterwards that the courage of these two men made him cry. It recalled epic poems of bravery and combat, triumph and adversity. A throwback to the days of the gladiators and when knights jousted in earnest. This was two men coming close to death in a 20 foot ring, reliving the epic of Roland's last stand:

'Straight at the bundles
of the multitude of

burnished spears.
You have a battle
such as you have
never had before.'[1]

They set a searing pace in searing heat. As with their first fight, the punches were so numerous and of such quality that only the exquisite stood out from the excellent.

The first round was Ali's, up on his toes moving and boxing, while Joe chugged after him. In the 2nd Muhammad produced an unholy trinity of rights, each straight and to the point, and timed to perfection. Yet Frazier took them and came on again as though a hundred warrior Joe Fraziers stood behind him, like Scott's brave highlanders:

'Each stepping where
his comrade stood,
the instant that he
fell' [2]

In the 3rd he would not be denied. Cutting the ring off, forcing Ali to the ropes through a barrage of pain and punishment, wielding the left hook like a tomahawk and never counting the cost:

'a mighty man in
the fight...
a champion in the
charge' [3]

I made the round level, but in the 4th Ali was stepping high once more, burnishing Frazier with volleys of hooks and combinations.

Joe tried to bring it back to close quarters again, for it is written that:

'Evil is the heart
that cowers
We shall keep this
ground with swords and
spear.' [4]

The 5th saw the first of the dramatic twists and turns which lends greatness to a fight. Ali was still pouring it on, straightening Frazier up with left hooks,

1 Turoldus 'La Chanson de Roland'
2 Sir Walter Scott 'Flodden
3 'Gododdin'
4 Turoldus 'La Chanson de Roland'

beaming his right over Joe's left. But Frazier just kept fighting for dear life. In Scott's imagery:

> *'But yet though*
> *thick the shafts*
> *as snow,*
> *Though charging*
> *knights like*
> *whirlwinds go,...*
> *The stubborn spear*
> *men still made*
> *good'* [1]

Keep punching... keep punching. Ignore the hell in Ali's fists. Ram him back against those ropes, welt his body, pound his head.

And win the round!

The 6th was of the same ilk, only even more savage, more intense, from Frazier. 'Smokin' Joe was aflame; Ali was not the force of the early rounds. Early on Frazier landed the best punch of the fight, a left hook to Ali's jaw which even today, when I look at the film, makes me gasp as it lands. Ali's back was constantly against the ropes. He was being hit and hurt. It continued that way throughout the 7th, a ceaseless, surging tide called Joe Frazier, roping Ali and then crunching hooks into him.

Round eight:

> *'They close in clouds*
> *of smoke and dust,*
> *With swords sway*
> *and lances thrust'* [2]

This was a magnificent session. Ali came out firing on all cylinders and set up a barrage as brutal as it was scintillating. Thunder and lightning flashed around Frazier's head. Yet he took it all, took the blows and went forward again, mounting a big attack in the second half to share the round.

> *'Recoil and rally,*
> *charge and rout,*
> *And triumph and*
> *despair'*[3]

1 Scott 'Flodden'
2 Scott 'Flodden'
3 Scott 'Flodden'

Thus Frazier winning the 9th. Driving his body beyond pain and endurance, his face marked to damnation, but his courage indomitable. Yet the triumph ended in despair because the body can only give its all and all had been given.

'Thoughts shall be
braver,
hearts shall be
bolder,
courage shall be
greater,
as our strength lessens' [1]

And so it was. They had both given everything. From hereon in it was just about will. Who wanted it the most.

We saw now the extraordinary quality of Ali, the way in which he could dig deep into his soul and bring out that something extra. Which is what he did, moving the fight along as its minutes receded into history, punishing the desperately exhausted man in front of him with combinations.

Frazier still stood and fought, still made Ali pay for the rounds he was winning. At the end of the 10th Muhammad told Angelo Dundee: 'this is the next thing to death.'

Frazier was thrashed and battered throughout the 13th. At one point a right hook turned his treetrunk legs to sap. The 14th was the last.

'Soon we will meet
our destined end.
We cannot live
beyond today' [2]

So it was. In boxing terms neither could live beyond this day. They had given their bodies as weapons of the war and were done.

The final minute of the 14th saw Frazier in hell. Herotodus' words, in which he describes the last few minutes at Thermopylae, tell the story:

'Now encircled
upon every side,
overwhelmed, and buried
the remnant which
was left,
beneath showers
of missile weapons'

1 'The Battle of Maldon'
2 Turoldus 'La Chanson de Roland'

Eddie Futch refused to let Joe come out for the 15th. He feared he might be killed!

Ali arose from his stool to take the cheers of the crowd. His legs gave way and he collapsed onto his back. A chair was brought into the ring and he sat on it for several minutes before he was able to leave the ring.

For the fourteen completed rounds the judges had it 66–60, 67–62 and 66–62, all for Ali. My unofficial scorecard read 8–4–2 to Ali in rounds, but 66–61 on points as I scored the 14th to him by a two point margin.

Frazier's face was a ruin, swollen grotesquely. His left eye had disappeared under a shelf of flesh and his right too was almost closed.

Ali's body was badly bruised. Afterwards he cajoled most of the press corps into believing that Frazier had only won rounds in which he had rested. That was nonsense. Frazier never let him rest; the rounds Joe won, he won. Ali also made most believe that he was feigning when he collapsed at the end of the contest. He wasn't. Today he acknowledges that Frazier's corner threw in the sponge just before he did. At the end of the 14th Ali asked Dundee to cut his gloves off. Dundee ignored him, but whether Muhammad could actually have fought another round is doubtful. Possibly both might have collapsed and died. The poems of heroic death, used here for imagery, may actually be too close to the truth for comfort.

When I left the closed circuit cinema I was convinced neither man should fight again. But there was something else too, something I did not see at the time. Just as somebody you love can say goodbye without your realising it, so I did not notice that an era had come to an end, that of boxing's greatest rivalries. Maybe too the whole epoch of boxing's greatness — down through the decades — ended that night as well.

Volume Seven

Larry Holmes to Mike Tyson

Round Twenty-Four:

The Rise and Rise of the Alphabet Boys

The final two chapters of this book are more epilogue than climax. Although two great champions appear the story is one of decay. But before that let us lay the warriors to rest.

Frazier went first. In June, 1976, Joe had a return with Foreman in New York. This time he lasted into the fifth round, but there is little more to be said. Frazier — who fought with a shaven head — had nothing left. He attempted to box rather than slug early on, hoping both to avoid George's big shots and wear him out as Ali had done. In the event Joe merely looked sad. He caught Foreman with a left hook in the 4th but there was now little steam powering the hammer. In the next round Foreman downed him twice. After the second knockdown referee Harold Valan heeded Eddie Futch's entreaties and stopped it. 'It's time to hang the gloves on the wall,' said Joe. He did.*

Foreman himself had been more an object of ridicule since the Ali fight. On April 26th, 1975, he fought a series of 'mini-bouts' in Toronto against Boone Kirkman, Terry Daniels, Charlie Polite, Jerry Judge and Alonzo Johnson, on a show promoted by Don King with Ali sharing the ringside commentary. These were exhibitions, not real contests, but Big George still got panned by the critics for engaging in them. Two more exhibitions followed; at this stage of his career Foreman appeared more interested in making girlfriends pregnant than in fighting.

But fight he did on January 24th, 1976, in what was one of the most brutal slugfests in heavyweight history. The opponent was Ron Lyle, and in Foreman's own words they used each other as punchbags. Neither man displayed much skill, but their courage and endurance were awe-inspiring. Mighty blows were traded without fear for the consequence, whilst the bout swung dramatically from one to the other. Lyle hurt George in the opening session, Foreman came back to edge the next two, and then in the 4th found himself looking up at the ring lights after Lyle unloaded a three punch salvo on his chin. Foreman did some exploding of his own upon rising, and it was Lyle's turn to hit the deck. Yet again it swung, Ron flooring Foreman for the second time just before the bell. Lyle was still on top at the beginning of the 5th and had George dancing a drunken sailor's reel on the end of his fists. But now the pendulum went back the other way, Foreman blasting Lyle's gumshield out. It had to end, and end it

* He made a brief comeback in 1981.

did with a supreme effort from the ex-champion. He roared after Lyle and simply slugged him into the canvas — ringsiders counted some 30 punches — where Ron lay, his will broken, to be counted out.

After Lyle came Frazier followed by previously unbeaten Dino Dennis, and Pedro Agosta, both in the fourth round. Foreman was indisputably the number one contender again and looking forward to a rematch with Ali. Many a slip George, many a slip.

Jimmy Young was a heavyweight nobody ever really noticed; and some paid the price. Young was a fine boxer with a good jab and sharp combinations. His problem was that when it mattered he failed to impose himself; and then he paid the price. Almost a year before facing Foreman in Puerto Rico on March 17th, 1977, Young had lost a title bout with Ali when a little more aggression would have seen him the winner. Foreman entered the ring a 3–1 favourite but his lack of technique militated against him round by round as Young avoided his anachronistic swipes and handed out a boxing lesson. Only in the 7th did George really look as though he might turn it around, staggering Young with a left hook. But it was not to be. By the 12th and final round Foreman's stamina had gone completely and he was floored by a right. The decision for Young was unanimous, and, on the referee's card, wide. Foreman was stretchered from the arena and spent the night in hospital suffering from cramp and dehydration. Afterwards he announced his retirement.

Had Foreman stayed retired then he would have had the highest kayo percentage of all the heavyweight champions — 89%. But then he would not have had the most extraordinary Indian summer in boxing history. That later. In 1977 George's downfall was lack of technique. It was said that he also had a stamina problem but this cannot be divorced from his technical demerits. Plodding after opponents and throwing roundhouse swings into the air is in itself exhausting and debilitating.

Between October, 1975 and February, 1978, Muhammad Ali successfully defended the title six times. Each fight was an illusion rather than an effusion of talent. In reality he was a spent force systematically damaging his health.

Belgium's Jean-Pierre Coopman was not a credible contender. Dubbed as 'The Lion of Flanders', Coopman had minimal ability and the punching power of a newt. It is alleged that he consumed a liberal quantity of champagne before getting into the ring with Ali in Puerto Rico on February 20th, 1976. Coopman and the fight were nothing. Ali kayoed him in the fifth round.

Jimmy Young, at Landover, Maryland, on April 30th, also figured to give a 230 lbs, poorly conditioned Ali an easy outing. Ali received a unanimous verdict at the end of 15 tedious rounds. However, the decision seemed more based on sentiment than logic. I had Young winning and I was not alone. In retrospect, had Jimmy been a little bolder then he would have gotten it. As it was, his tactic of ducking his head and shoulders out through the ropes when Ali attacked certainly went against him in the judges' eyes.

The British heavyweight scene was less than flourishing in the Seventies. Bugner's ability was matched by his inconsistency. Lyle, no longer a featured player, eventually ended his title aspirations via a Las Vegas split decision. Aside from Bugner, Bodell and McAlinden were wholehearted triers but definitely not world title contenders. Bunny Johnson holds the distinction of being the only man to win both the British heavy and light-heavyweight crowns by clean knockouts, but lacked the body weight of a genuine heavy. His conqueror, Richard Dunn, was an amiable Yorkshire tyke who always came to fight but was a long way short of world class. Nevertheless, he went in with Ali at the Olympic Hall, Munich, on May 25th.

The most intriguing thing about it was to compare Dunn's challenge with that of London, a similar (though better) type of fighter, nine years earlier. The comparison clearly showed the way in which the years and the punches had taken their toll of Ali. I gave Dunn the opening two rounds. Ali brought things under control in the 3rd, but was light years away from even the man who had bested Frazier just nine months ago. Right hooks chopped Richard down twice in the 4th, and later on in the round he was given a standing eight count, the first ever in a world heavyweight title contest. At the start of the 5th Ali gestured peevishly at the canvas, annoyed perhaps that Dunn was making him look bad. The Briton went down twice more, the second time for the count. He had boxed bravely but to no avail.

Ever heard of Antonio Inoki? No, Japan had not produced a heavyweight boxer. Inoki was a wrestler who on June 25th took part in an horrendous boxer-wrestler match with Ali in Tokyo. Thomas Hauser sums up this degraded farce with succinct contempt:

> *'Ali-Inoki was insufferably boring. For fifteen rounds Inoki crab-walked around the ring, horizontal to the canvas, kicking at Ali's legs. Ali threw six punches. Two of them, both jabs, landed. At the end the contest was declared a draw.'*[1]

Ali received in excess of two million dollars which was the purpose of it anyway. He paid with ruptured blood vessels in his legs for which he was later hospitalised when blood clots formed.

Rumblings of discontent. When was Ali going to fight a leading contender? The answer was, on September 28th at Yankee Stadium. The opposition was

1 'Muhammad Ali' p.337

Ken Norton. If one accepts Norton's claims, then he won three out of three against Ali but was twice robbed of the decision. Others may see it differently; that Ali actually won three close ones. But did Norton really want it badly enough, because Ali was there for the taking at Yankee Stadium?

After eight rounds Norton was ahead on all scorecards. Ali had done little. He was really a shell. Boxing International commented:

'The magic was gone; the body no longer superb. The punches lacked crispness and strategies no longer could be executed.'

The crux of Norton's strategy was a pressurised body attack. It looked to be working. Ali tried 'rope-a-dope' and that *didn't* work. But just when Ken appeared to have the fight in the bag he allowed Muhammad to come back and take it away from him, almost as though he had been waiting for this to happen. 'Do something Ken,' Ali taunted. Norton riposted: 'I am... I'm taking your title.' But he wasn't. Ali was now punishing him with rights, particularly in the 11th. As with their first two fights everything came down to the final round. After 14, referee Mercante's scorecard read 7–6–1. Ali, and the two judges were deadlocked on 7–7–0. Again Ali made a big last round effort, although Norton finished the stronger. At the bell he called out to Ali 'You don't win.' Was this a Freudian slip? 'You don't' is not the same as 'I do'. After the verdict had gone against him Norton asked: 'What do I have to do to beat him?', but subconsciously had he all along settled for crying in his beer because he thought, deep down, that Ali was still just that bit better than he? If so, then Muhammad Ali didn't win: Ken Norton lost.

Ali basically rested for a year. His May 16th 'defence' at Landover against Alfredo Evangelista, a Spanish based Uruguayan novice, was hardly worthy of the name. The contest was dreadful and does not merit description. Ali won on points. After Dunn he never stopped another opponent.

On September 29th, 1977, he took on Shavers at Madison Square Garden. Fists of granite Earnie had, but he had never developed technique apace. He was also up against the main man, a living legend. After Manila Ali boxed on his reputation as much as anything else. Shavers' punching power was astonishing. 52 of his 54 victories had come inside the distance (96%). His chin was not so powerful. Stander, Quarry and Lyle had put him on the floor, Ellis nearly. Even the post 1975 Ali could box rings around him. But Ali's speed was now equivalent to an athlete competing in a sack race. Could he survive Shavers socks on the jaw?

He did in the 2nd, three of them no less, and again in the 4th. Shavers' confidence began to wilt. He had to rely on single shots because he could not put punches together efficiently. By the end of round twelve Ali had already won on the judge's cards.* Shavers enjoyed a big 13th, hurting Ali, and he took

* Eva Shain became the first woman judge in heavyweight title history.

14 as well. Muhammad said afterwards 'When the hour is darkest I come through.' But he had help from Earnie's corner who inexplicably told him he was ahead at the end of the 14th. Instead of continuing to try and kayo a fading champion, Shavers relaxed and Ali won the 15th to cement his victory. But, as against Norton, he was working his body beyond endurable limits.

The upset which was always in the making came next time out. Ali ignored a fourth bout with Norton. Since the previous loss ken had put the skids under Duane Bobick, America's heavyweight representative in the 1972 Olympics who was being groomed as a 'white hope'. And in a W.B.C. final eliminator Norton outscored Jimmy Young on two of the judges' scorecards, a verdict which seemed a bad decision, but which Young could yet again have made sure of getting with more aggression. Ali sought leave — which was granted — to pass Norton by for a 'voluntary' defence. Gerry Coatzee of South Africa and Italy's Alfio Righetti were considered;— and rejected. The call went out instead to the 1976 Olympic light heavyweight champion Leon Spinks.

Boxing was stunned. Now campaigning in the pro ranks as a heavyweight, Spinks had had just seven professional fights, six wins (4 kayos) and a draw. A raucous scream of 'mismatch' split the air. It should have been, but wasn't. The upset which could not happen, happened.

On the night of February 18th, 1978, at Las Vegas, all the toils and labours of a once majestic career caught up with Ali. True, he was abysmally out of shape. So much so that at first I wrongly believed he had given away the title so he could become the only man to regain it twice. In reality, the lack of fitness merely compounded what we had known for some time; only the memory of greatness now remained.

I awarded Spinks eleven of the fifteen rounds. He just kept reeling off inconsequential punches which Ali could do little about. They say in golf that the young pros cannot envisage missing a short putt. Leon Spinks had not the experience to be in awe of Ali. Possibly, not the wit either. Born in St Louis on July 11th, 1953, he had often slept rough in the streets as a teenager and was not given much credence for brains. But the fact that he had overcome drug problems did suggest character, and against Ali he was no respecter of reputations. It was not a good fight but at the end of the 15 rounds two of the officials had it 145–140 (10–5–0) and 144–141 (9–6–0) in Spinks' favour. The third somewhat unbelievably went for Ali, 143–142 (8–7–0).

When they met again, on September 15th at New Orleans, only half the title was at stake. The regime of the 'Alphabet Boys' had arrived.

The World Boxing Association had existed in one form or another for fifty years. The W.B.C. — for 'World Boxing Council' — had developed from the loose-knit alliance of New York, Europe and Britain in the early Sixties. In reality it was a political rival to the W.B.A. Today the lines of demarcation have long gone. The various national and international commissions recognise the titles of all the main sanctioning bodies.

By 1978 the W.B.A. and W.B.C. had between them succeeded in splitting the titles of every weight in boxing at one time or another.* That March only Spinks, middleweight Rodrigo Valdez and lightweight Roberto Duran stood as undisputed champions of their divisions. In Spinks' case that would change on the 18th.

The W.B.C.'s official contender was Ken Norton. Not surprisingly, Spinks wanted nothing to do with Norton: a return with Ali promised to be (and was) one of the most lucrative bouts in boxing history. When Spinks and Ali signed to meet again the W.B.C. responded by taking away its version of the title from Spinks.

Whether this was fair is a matter of dispute. The match the public wanted to see was Spinks–Ali. Although the W.B.C. had a point it would not have taken much flexibility to have awaited the outcome of that contest. What the W.B.C. did next was certainly *not* fair.

Ken Norton was simply installed as W.B.C. champion! Titles can be lost outside the ring; they can never be *won* outside it, particularly when a contender is as lucky as Norton was to be the official challenger. He would be he shortest reigning heavyweight title holder in history, remembered now as a rather cruel quiz question — 'Which heavyweight champion never won a title fight?'

On June 9th he made his first 'defence'. His opponent was Larry Holmes, a 6′ 3″ 210 lbs, twenty-eight year old fighting out of Easton, Pennsylvania, but originally from Cuthbert, Georgia, where he was born on November 3rd, 1949. Holmes had compiled a 27–0 record (19 kayos) without lighting up the boxing scene. One trivia question which I could not answer was: 'Who was known as "the black cloud"?' I'm afraid that I would also have failed with his alternative ring-de-guerre, 'the Easton assassin'. There were few recognisable names on Holmes' record, Jerry Judge — one of Foreman's 'mini-bout' victims; Charley 'Devil' Green, who had been kayoed by Patterson, beaten by Coopman and ended up in prison for murder; Rodney Bobick, brother of Duane, and Roy Williams who at one time had looked a prospect. But there was one big name, Shavers, whom Norton had outpointed in a March eliminator.

Included on the undercard of Norton–Holmes at Las Vegas was Jimmy Young who fought a ten rounder with unbeaten Ossie 'Jaws' Ocasio, a Puerto Rican who was to become the W.B.A.'s inaugural cruiserweight champ four years later. Young entered the ring with a roll of fat around the middle and showed his usual lack of purpose. Poor Jimmy had slept in every deck chair on

* New York was technically under the auspices of the W.B.C. at the time of Frazier–Mathis.

the 'Titanic' and now the waves closed around him. When a split decision was announced in Ocasio's favour Young stormed angrily out of the ring. He had, alas, blown his last chance.

Norton exited by the same door, but only after a superb battle. Holmes, the underdog in the betting, displayed adroit skills and an excellent all round technique. Norton's preparations had been hindered by an arm injury in training and for the opening six rounds he found it impossible to get past Holmes' jab. Things changed in the 7th. Ken began to find the range with left and right hooks. In the 8th he opened a deep cut inside Holmes' mouth and now he was back in that old racing mode again, coming closer, ever closer, to a man who had sprinted away from him at the start. But this was over 15 laps of the track and by the end of the 12th Norton had drawn level. Shoulder to shoulder, Holmes attempted to break away again in the 13th, gritting his teeth to drive home rights which left the *de facto* champion on legs all-a-tremble. But as Larry's burst came to an end, so Norton reeled him in again on lap 14, and with the bell ringing for the last it was a dead heat. Incredibly, all three judges had it 7–7! Who had the finish?

Norton made one last great effort, a short, vicious break in the shape of a right hook which made Holmes' eyes roll. But Larry came again with his own right, an uppercut, and Norton's gumshield went spinning across the ring. Rocking and rolling, the tape in sight, they traded punches for ground and Holmes just fought his way over the line first. The judges each had it 143–142 (8–7–0), two for Holmes, one Norton. Ken had lost his last big race.

Spinks–Ali II was by comparison a wholly pedestrian affair. Ali was in much better shape than for their first fight. At 221 lbs he seemed to dwarf the 201 lbs, 6′ 0″ Spinks, whom he nicknamed 'Goofy' because of a prominent gap in his front teeth.

The rounds followed a sameness. There were no highlights and few punches of any significance. Ali smothered Spinks' attacks; Leon lacked the experience to cope with it. The outcome was a 360 degree turnaround from the previous encounter. After an even 1st, Ali took command. The verdict in his favour was unanimous and big; 10–4–1, 10–4–1, 11–4. I could not be even that generous to Spinks, giving him only the 4th.

However, what the contest did illustrate was Ali's extraordinary magnetism, the hold which he still had over *his* public. 63,500 packed the New Orleans Superdome paying 4.8 million dollars, the largest ever indoor attendance and the biggest ever live gate receipts. This despite the fact that the fight was broadcast on television. It drew the second largest T.V. audience in history, eclipsed only by the final episode of 'Roots'.

The heavyweight division was firmly saddled with another dual champion situation. The W.B.C. recognised Holmes; the W.B.A. — ironically in view of past antagonisms — endorsed Ali. There was no movement towards a unification bout. Only the most blinkered Ali supporters thought he might have Holmes' measure in his thirty-seventh year.

The fighter whom the fans wanted to see in the ring with Muhammad was actually not Holmes but Teofilo Stevenson, a giant Cuban who had won the Olympic title in both 1972 and '76. Handsome, charismatic, and with a right hand seemingly gifted to him by Zeus, a fortune was Stevenson's for the asking if he turned pro. He didn't. Instead he went on to claim a third Olympic title in 1980 and then became a member of the Cuban Parliament.

A ludicrous 'fight' was proposed between Ali and Kent Green who had stopped him as an amateur twenty years before. However, on June 26th, 1979, everything came to naught when Ali retired; five naughts to be exact because Bob Arum, who had promoted the Dunn and Spinks' fights, reputedly paid Ali $300,000. The end of the line had been reached. Unhappily though it was to take two more fights before Muhammad was fully convinced of it.

Despite the quality of his performance against Norton, Larry Holmes seemed at first to be a hollow champion. A dour man who shunned the limelight, he is the only great heavyweight champion never to be biographised. We know virtually nothing about the inner man. What we do know is that he could certainly fight. A superb boxer-puncher, Holmes had all the punches, a jab second to none, a powerful right and flowing combinations. Defensively, he had a weakness. Like Louis and others before him Holmes held his left too low and was vulnerable to fast, right hand counters. But he could take a punch when it landed.

He suffered from being in Ali's shadow and from the way in which the W.B.C. title had been acquired from Spinks. Personality wise, Holmes was also pushed into the background by his promoter, the effervescent, or effluential, — depending on your point of view — Don King, whom, Holmes claims, ripped him off to the tune of ten million dollars.

By 1979 King stood out as the emerging Czar of boxing. He owed his position to his association with Ali, although in fact he had exclusively promoted only two of Ali's fights, Wepner and Evangelista. The Ali camp, astutely piloted by Herbert Muhammad, moved away from King before the Dunn fight and allowed Arum back into the picture. Arum's alleged retirement present to Ali was widely believed to have been made because Bob had the rights to promote the bout to find Ali's successor as W.B.A. champion. This notwithstanding, King was still the dominant force. When Holmes became W.B.C. champion King not only had him sewn up but Shavers, Norton, Young and several lesser contenders as well. During the Eighties King would control the heavyweight division almost in its entirety, in some instances his stepson Carl becoming the fighters' 'manager of record'. It is also maintained that Don King virtually ran the W.B.C. through his friendship with its President, Jose Sulaiman. There are many intrigues and much mist clouds the picture. What can safely be said is that King made a lot of money and is cordially hated by many of the boxers he promoted.

To return to Holmes. His initial defence was hardly calculated to win public approval. Alfredo Evangelista was summoned forth again. Evangelista had eked out a split decision over Tod Ballard, one of Foreman's exhibition opponents, on the Holmes-Norton undercard. At least the good people of Landover were spared Alfredo this time. Holmes knocked him out in the 7th at Las Vegas on November 10th. Larry was back there the following March 24th to meet Young's conqueror, Ossie 'Jaws' Ocasio. With only 13 fights and his future at the next weight down, 'Jaws' was not so much a barracuda as a hammerhead;— and hammered around the head he was, with distressing frequency. Holmes peeled him with uppercuts, dropped him four times, and forced the referee to step in in the 7th.

These offerings were really not good enough, and nor, on paper, was the next, Mike Weaver at Madison Square Garden, June 22nd. Weaver stood 20–7 which included losing three out of his first four and being iced by such halcyon names as Howard Smith, Billy Ryan and Larry Frazier. Duane Bobick had also stopped him, Rodney outpointed him, and Mike was just hoping that he didn't run into their dad! But sometimes the record book deceives. Weaver gave Holmes a roaring fight, exposed his vulnerability to rights, and caused the champion all sorts of grief before being stopped in the 12th round. Mike would be heard from again; loudly.

Ernie Shavers, at Las Vegas on September 28th, was much more like it. Shavers had put himself slap bang into contention again by decimating Norton in 62 seconds on the Holmes-Ocasio undercard. He had a big one reserved for Larry as well. It came in the 7th after Holmes had dominated the first six rounds with his jab. Larry became over-confident and a prodigious right crashed against his jaw. Down he went. That, as they say, should have been the ball game. When Ernie hit you, you stayed hit. But not this time; not against a champion like Holmes. At '4' he was on his feet for the rest of the mandatory eight count. Then he clung on. Had Shavers been a more accomplished boxer then he might have ended things. Instead, Holmes made it through to the bell and Ernie was left incanting the loser's requiem mass — 'It might have been'. During the next four rounds a recovered Holmes reduced him punch by ruthless punch to a parlous, bleeding hulk. He was still on his feet when it was stopped in the 11th, but only just.

According to one analysis Holmes landed 378 jabs in the 32 minutes of combat. Under the bizarre judging system of Olympic boxing none of them would have scored. In the real world they had rattled up the points, cut Shavers over both eyes and exposed his technical limitations.

Meanwhile, the next door neighbours were getting up.

In its June 26th, 1981, edition the trade paper Boxing News assessed twelve heavyweights, Holmes included. Between June, 1979, and December, 1983, no less than seven of them held versions of the heavyweight championship. Not then listed as contenders were another five claimants making twelve in all. On average that is one every eight months. This is what happens when titles are split two and three ways and anarchy rules.

One man not included by Boxing News because he had by then departed the scene was John Tate, a 6′ 5″ former truck driver from Knoxville, Tennessee; although he had been born at Marion City, Arkansas on January 29th, 1955. Tate was destined to become the third W.B.A. champion in eighteen months.

His opponent, Gerrie Coatzee from Boksburg, South Africa, was just over six months younger than Tate. Coatzee too would become a W.B.A. champion.

John Tate's greatest victory came as an amateur; he decisioned Teofilo Stevenson in the final of the 1975 Pan American Games. An augury of things to come: Stevenson took him apart in the Olympic semi-final the following year and Tate went home with just a Bronze. Turning professional, he won 20 straight, including his Olympic predecessor Duane Bobick, but nobody paid Tate much attention, certainly not Don King: Big John became a Bob Arum acolyte.

Perhaps the most noticed thing about Tate were his encounters with white South Africans — in more ways than one. He defeated Kallie Knoetze, a policeman who had once shot a black demonstrator in the leg. Fighting him earned Tate no accolades amongst his fellow blacks. But the excreta really began to fly out from between the spokes when it was announced that not only would Tate meet Coatzee for the vacant W.B.A. title, but it would be in Johannesburg, October 20th, in front of an all white audience. John did however manage to cock one snook at the apartheid regime. Literally. He bedded a white South African girl on the night before the fight!

Probably that was more exciting than the contest, an ugly, mauling affair in which Tate used his strength to wear down and outpoint the more technically able Coatzee. One writer, with a somewhat defective knowledge of history, described it as 'the second bore war'. Afterwards, 81,000 disappointed springboks trekked out of the stadium leaving just one happy white. Bob Arum went home with lots of Rands jangling in his pockets.

The eminently sensible idea of a unification fight was broached. Ali was also making rumblings about coming out of retirement to meet Tate. Holmes meanwhile warmed up on Lorenzo Zanon of Italy, formerly European king, at Las Vegas on February 3rd, 1980. Possibly, Larry was under instructions to look bad in order to entice Tate because bad he looked. The undistinguished Italian even outjabbed him in the opening rounds. Not until the 4th did Holmes get out of bed. Then he bounced Zanon off the canvas twice and forced him to take a standing count. Holmes eventually knocked him out in the 6th with a right to the head.

Scene setting. Fights have to be sold and what better way to do it than a double header featuring both potential adversaries. March 31st saw both Holmes and Tate defending their 'titles' in boxing's first triple city hook-up. Holmes met Leroy Jones, unbeaten in 25 fights with a draw the only blot on his record, in (where else?) Las Vegas, whilst Tate opted for what he imagined would be an easy defence against Mike Weaver in Knoxville.*

Watching the telecast of Holmes-Jones I saw one of the best champions I had ever seen. True, Leroy Jones resembled Mathis for blubber, but his record — which included Weaver — showed he could fight. Holmes mastered him comprehensively with a display of concise and varied hitting from the 'how to do it in style' manual. Jones was still perpendicular when the referee rescued him in the 8th, but had been outclassed.

Tate-Weaver was 14 rounds of nondescript fighting with a storybook ending. Tate, long on strength — short on technique, bulled his way to a points lead. Weaver, constantly being exhorted by his corner to: 'come on Mike — don't let him get away,' appeared to lack confidence. With one round to go Tate led on the scorecards by margins of five, three and three points respectively.

John was still there and coasting now after two minutes of the 15th. Then he dropped his guard. Weaver saw it and produced one of those lifetime punches — a left hook from nowhere — which caught Tate perfectly on the chin. Tate's whole body spun to the left and went rigid. He stared out at the audience goggle-eyed — oblivious to a pair of grazing rights — and then crashed forwards onto his face. Paramedics were needed to revive him. Weaver too, almost. He fell to the canvas with joy and succeeded in cutting himself. The Herald Tribune's headline summed it up marvellously: 'Every minute counts in boxing.'

Success had never seemed likely to find Mike Weaver, a 27 year old from Gatesville, Texas. He was not a fighter of great natural gifts. The early record was very patchy indeed; misleading too. It implied that Weaver's jaw was made of less than iron. In fact durability was his stock in trade. The early stoppages were due to lack of conditioning. He was a magnificently built man, dubbed the 'black Hercules', 6′ 1″ tall and weighing 210 lbs. He learnt his trade methodically and found an extra gear when it was needed.

Weaver at this point did not feature in Holmes' plans. Holmes had wanted Tate or Ali. He got Ali.

It was the fight which should not have happened. Money of course was at the root of it, but there was also the ex-champ's titanic ego; 'titanic' in all senses of the word. He had been embarrassed — made a near laughing stock — by the failure of his diplomatic mission in Africa to dissuade countries from competing in the Moscow Olympics. Becoming champion again would win back respect.

* The third was Landover where welterweight champion Sugar Ray Leonard kayoed Britain's Dave 'Boy' Green.

His fight plan was Tate — terms were actually agreed — and then Holmes. Weaver was a gatecrasher into both their parties. But in thinking that he could even have taken Tate Muhammad was hopelessly deluding himself.

Holmes warmed up for the bout by whipping Scott LeDoux in Minneapolis on July 7th. Le Doux was capable but not in Holmes' class and his face was very marked up when the referee stopped it in the 7th.

Larry was back at Las Vegas for Ali. It was a sad fight for Holmes, a former sparring partner of Muhammad's, who liked and respected the ex-champion. Don King promoted. Holmes received three million dollars, Ali was guaranteed eight although it is alleged that King, pleading hardship, paid him just over seven.

Controversy over Ali's medical condition still lingers. In July he checked into a Minneapolis medical centre for tests. I am not qualified to assess their significance, but based on them the Nevada Commission cleared Ali to fight again. Others believe that the Commission should have studied the test results in more depth; that they indicated the condition normally referred to as 'punch drunk'.

Separately, several weeks before the fight, Herbert, Muhammad's doctor (not Pacheco), diagnosed a thyroid problem in Ali and prescribed Thyrolar, a corrective drug. However, neither the Minneapolis tests, or tests carried out after the fight, gave any indication of a thyroid condition. Whatever the truth of the matter, two things are beyond dispute: 1) It was potentially disastrous for a man to box whilst taking Thyrolar; 2) If Ali did have a thyroid complaint then he should not have been in the ring in the first place.

On October 2nd Holmes and Ali faced off in a makeshift ring pitched in the carpark of Caesar's Palace. Normally, one would be tempted to make a quip of two about this, but there is nothing about this match which lends itself to humour. Ali looked the part, a sleekly handsome 217 lbs. In reality, his hair had been dyed to cover up the grey, he was *too* light and felt listless throughout. Whether this was due to Thyrolar is a moot point, but in fistic terms it would hardly have made a difference anyway. Put in its simplest form, Ali was finished.

The fight itself was a cruel, mercenary joke. Not for one second of one minute of one round was Muhammad in with a chance. Holmes, who had no wish to hurt him, laid back and boxed. The ends of other ring legends have been played out amidst drama: Johnson attacking with the dying furies of a hurricane, Dempsey watching the seconds of the 'long count' tick by, Louis's heroic rearguard action against the all conquering Marciano. But there was no drama here; only pathos. Holmes fenced off the hits one by one until Angelo Dundee retired Muhammad at the end of the 10th. Predictably both Time and Newsweek headed their reports: 'Requiem for a Heavyweight'; perhaps Time should have sent for its Greek Tragedian again, on this occasion more appositely.

Upbeat. Twenty-three days after Holmes–Ali, Mike Weaver made the first defence of his W.B.A. crown. Like his predecessor, Weaver was lured to Southern Africa to fight Gerrie Coatzee, this time in the black homeland of Bopthutwatsana;—which, as it's as unpronounceable as 'Sesquicentennial', we will simply call Sun City.

Blacks, in one of their so called 'homelands', were not much in evidence at the ringside in Sun City. White South Africans were, having flooded across the 'border' in 10,000 cars and transits and 50 privately owned aeroplanes and helicopters. Sun City, which also hosts the world's richest golf tournament, was more aptly referred to as 'Sin City', a Mecca for rich South Africans to indulge in everything they outlawed in the Republic, gambling and interracial sex for example. The opulent lifestyles of those who turned up hoping for a Coatzee victory were a striking contrast to the slums of Soweto, whilst their hypocrisy was shamed by Mike Weaver's genuinely held religious beliefs.

Leaving aside the worth of the audience, the contest itself was meritous. Coatzee, quoted in the press as being opposed to apartheid, had earned his previous crack at the title by doing a Johansson style one round demolition job on Leon Spinks. 6′ 3″ and 220 lbs, he had a good jab and an effective right cross. His main defects were lack of stamina and variety plus a tendency to become demoralised, deficiencies tailor made for Weaver.

Watching on live television, I noted that Weaver was the sort of man who would remain unflappable even if you lit a brush fire under him. He needed to be to survive the first third of the contest; Coatzee dominated, hurting Weaver in the 1st and 5th, cutting him to in the latter round. Yet Mike seemed to get stronger as he absorbed the punches and he began to take control in the 6th, stepping up his work rate minute by minute. But he had to survive a big round by Coatzee in the 8th. A right blasted against the side of Weaver's head leaving him in dire trouble. However, Coatzee's follow up was weak and stereotyped. He ended up fumbling and mauling; crispness and adaptability would have given him the title.

After the 8th, Weaver just kept on increasing the pace and the punches, while Coatzee's suspect stamina turned against him. The end came midway through the 13th. Weaver set him up with a left hook and then powered home a right to the head. Gerrie was counted out in the act of rising. Afterwards Weaver revealed that during the fight Coatzee had told him 'You can't punch,' to which he had retorted: 'So why are you wobbling then?' It had been hard fought and worth watching. Injury though would prevent Weaver boxing again for almost a year.

The stage was therefore Holmes'. Although it passed unnoticed in the sadness of Ali's defeat, that victory equalled Tommy Burns of eight successive kayos in heavyweight title defences.* Sadly for Larry he didn't beat it. On April

* Louis had 14 consecutive inside the distance but no. 8 (Buddy Baer) was via disqualification.

11th, 1981, Trevor Berbick, a tough, brawling Canadian went the distance at Las Vegas.

Holmes gave the gambling capital a miss next time out, Leon Spinks in Detroit on June 12th. Spinks had put himself back in the picture by crawling all over the W.B.C.'s No. 1 contender, Colombian Bernardo Mercado, and stopping him in the 9th on the Holmes-Ali undercard. But both Mercado and Spinks were in false positions. Demonstrably. Holmes gained his quickest title win to date by halting Leon in three one-sided rounds.

Larry rounded out his year by stopping Renaldo Snipes in Pittsburgh on November 6th. But it was almost a shock upset. Snipes, from Texas, had won 22 out of 22 as a pro. A fast jabbing boxer with an Adonis-like physique, he would have been better advised to wait awhile. His purse of $150,000 was hardly a mega-incentive. Snipes however became the closest of Holmes' eleven challengers to dethroning him.

They boxed six skittish rounds, Holmes on top, Snipes proving an awkward, elusive challenger. Danger came out of a clear blue sky in the 7th. Snipes 'bowled' what in cricket is known as a 'beamer', a terribly fast overarm right aimed at the head. Holmes' guard was low, the punch connected with great force and down he went.

Pandemonium in Pittsburgh. Holmes arose groggily, but here Snipes' inexperience, the fact that his technique was far from matured, told against him. He didn't put his shots together, went right hand crazy, and Holmes' ringcraft enabled him to survive. The hubbub subsided. So did Snipes. From then on he took a systematic beating although there were many dissenters when the referee waved Holmes off in the 11th. Snipes' chance never came again.

Weaver had returned to duty a month earlier, defending against James 'Quick' Tillis in Chicago. Tillis had 20 straight wins and was quick, but his stamina and power were suspect. The fight was awful, played to slow hand-claps and boos from a tiny crowd who ensured that promoter Arum made a substantial loss. Things finally came alive in the 12th when Tillis stunned the W.B.A. title-holder with a right to the head. He failed to follow up and let Weaver off the hook. They gave and took hard punches in the 14th and then Tillis, near exhaustion, hung on throughout the last round. Weaver was awarded a unanimous decision, a triumph for his usual perseverance over Tillis's anaemically pretty skills. Some thought it a bad decision; most didn't care.

Logically, Holmes and Weaver's next fight should have been a unification bout. Logic counts for ought in boxing, especially when there's money in the frame, in this case a challenger who would draw mega bucks. Such a man was Gerry Cooney, a 6′ 5″, 225 lbs Irish-American larripur from Huntington, New York. Cooney was a crushing puncher, in particular with the left hook. The fact that he was white made him a huge draw. Prominent amongst 22 kayo victims out of his 25 wins were Jimmy Young, Ron Lyle and Ken Norton, the latter two inside the first round. The Norton stoppage was my first look at Cooney and I was singularly unimpressed. Norton was a completely spent force and although Cooney could certainly punch he appeared to me to be muscle-bound. But he and Holmes were what the public wanted, and the following spring they were what the public got.

Beforehand though, a sad finale at boxing's wailing wall had to be played out.

After losing to Holmes, Muhammad Ali retired again. Almost immediately he became embroiled in another affair which dented his image. Harold Smith (a.k.a. Ross Fields) had put together a company named 'Muhammad Ali Professional Sports'. In return for the use of his name Ali would receive 25% of net profits. At the end of 1980 Smith and an employee of the Wells Fargo Bank embezzled from the bank 21.3 million dollars, the largest bank fraud in history. Smith was tried and convicted.

Ali was not a party to this but suffered from having given his name to Smith's company. To compound it, he was also persuaded to attend the trial during Smith's attorney's closing argument.

Once again Ali had been played for a fool. He responded in the only way he knew, by fighting again.

On December 11th, 1981, Ali fought Trevor Berbick at Nassau in the Bahamas. A Jamaican born Canadian, Berbick had won 18 of 21 pro bouts and was a battler in the Chuvalo–Cleroux mould. He had stopped John Tate after Weaver, but had in turn been knocked out with a single punch by Mercado and outpointed by Holmes. He would have posed no problem to the Ali of yore. However, the 1981 Ali was within touching distance of his fortieth birthday, and his tools were rusted beyond repair.

The decay of a once great fighter was reflected in the organisation of the contest. The stadium was still not complete on the day of the fight, gloves had to be flown in from Miami at the last moment, some of the supporting bouts were cancelled and a cow bell was substituted for the regulation bell. Don King flew in demanding a cut; he got it from the fists and boots of a local goon squad. Berbick wisely demanded his money in advance.

The contest itself was ten rounds of tedious pawing. Berbick won six of the ten on all three judges' cards. Two of them awarded Ali only one. The referee was Zack Clayton who seven years earlier had counted Foreman out on that magical night in Zaire. We can only imagine what thoughts went through his mind.

This time Ali retired for good. The years since have been sad ones as his health deteriorated. According to medical experts he suffers not from Parkinson's disease, but Parkinson's *syndrome*, a condition which can be induced by a number of factors one of which is physical trauma i.e., blows. Those who argue that there is no evidence that boxing caused Ali's problems are therefore wrong. But it is not a common occurrence amongst boxers. The evidence points overwhelmingly to Ali having taken too many punches because he had to fight on too long after his best years were taken away from him. But we must also insert a caveat here. Muhammad — or rather his ego — was himself partially to blame. An entourage requiring over 50 hotel rooms when he travelled had to be paid for by the punches which he took.

Where he stands in the roll of champions is an endless debating point. Obviously very high. How high? That we can never know for sure; different styles breed different results. The best comparison is with Jack Johnson. My own guess — and it is worth no more than any other fight fan's — is that Jack would have beaten Ali three times out of five. They were so well-matched, Ali with greater speed, Johnson with superior guile. Johnson's in-fighting ability would just, in my view, have given him the faintest of edges. It does of course pre-suppose them starting on a level field in terms of height and weight. The Johnson of 1908 measures today as a cruiserweight, but heavyweights have gotten bigger all round as living standards progressed.

ATLANTA 1996: America's 'Dream Team' is contesting the basketball final with a Yugoslav side. Play is about to resume for the second half, the teams already on court, when suddenly the audience comes to its feet applauding. Muhammad Ali is coming on court.

The player's cluster around him, admiration mixed with respectful deference. Each wants to shake his hand, black and white, American and Slav. Ali's gait is slow, his hands shake uncontrollably, but he is pleased and warmed by his reception, and he smiles the old Ali smile as he moves amongst the players, accepting their homage.

I know of no other figure in sporting history who has this effect. Muhammad Ali is already a legend.

Boxing carried on without Ali. June 11th, 1982, saw the eagerly awaited Holmes–Cooney clash at — yet again — Las Vegas, now the fight Mecca of America. This had nothing to do with promoter wars; taxes in New York had become too high.

The white versus black angle sold the fight, generating a live gate of 32,000 and a closed circuit audience of 2.5 million. Total revenues have been estimated at $50,000,000. Who received what depends on who you listen to. Holmes was said to have earned $10,000,000. However, some believe he ended up getting less than Cooney.

It was a solid fight in terms of action but not technique. Boxing News evaluated Holmes as being only 67% of the fighter he had once been. Cooney was awkward and limited, his main weapon a long, sweeping left hook which took in the scenery before landing. In spite of this two judges actually had him ahead on rounds at the end of the 12th; their twin scorecards of 113–111 for Holmes including three points deducted from Cooney for fouls and a 10–8 Holmes round in the 2nd when he decked Cooney with a countering right. That aside, the action is not easily defined. Holmes constantly arched left to avoid Gerry's big gun, pecking away at the challenger's beak-like nose with his own beak — his left jab — while Cooney swiped away at this 32 year old body, some of the punches straying low. Cooney was penalised two points in the 9th and another in round eleven. Cooney was at his most effective early on. As the fight got older Holmes put his combinations together.

The end came in the 13th. A ruthless barrage of punches left Cooney reeling and broken. His trainer, Victor Valle, dashed into the ring to rescue him. Confusion reigned. Referee Mills Lane originally announced a technical knock-out; later this was changed to a disqualification, which under the rules of boxing Valle's action rendered it. However, rules can be bent in a charitable cause and the Nevada Commission afterwards amended the outcome to a retirement in round thirteen.

The final retirement of Ali and a battle with a white hope giant* had given Larry Holmes a stage to strut upon; command from the centre. He had not taken it: Ali's ghost hung over the feast like Banquo's. Wrote *Newsweek's* Pete Axthelm:

'Holmes would love to soar across history, command respect, burn into our consciousness... But...(he) seems to get dragged down by the excess baggage of poor timing, flat style and chip on his broad shoulder...

'"I'm sorry I can't be what you expect," he said. "I can't be Muhammad Ali or Joe Louis or Leon Spinks." Leon Spinks? When a man hangs bumbling, unlamented Leon in his personal charisma gallery, his image problem clearly runs deep. Larry is almost surely the first champ to celebrate a major victory with the words, "I'll keep my head up. I have nothing to be ashamed of."'[1]

Telling the assembled Press Corps to 'shut up and listen' was not exactly good public relations either. Nor was Larry's next fight.

Randall 'Tex' Cobb was an average white heavyweight from Texas. A personable fellow who went from the ring to gung ho movie roles. In terms of his record Cobb had done no less than some others who went in for the title (which doesn't make it right). In terms of his style he was made to order for the champion. Cobb took a horrible fifteen round beating — and I stress the word 'horrible' because this was the sickest spectacle I have witnessed in 35 years as

1 Newsweek June 21st, 1982

* Some sources list his height as 6′ 6″ and even 6′ 7″.

a boxing fan. Don King promoted; it might as well have been the 'ban boxing' lobby. I dread to think of how many punches the brave hearted, durable, but hopelessly outclassed Texan took as he walked on to Holmes' punches in a straight line, a point which certainly contributed to the awfulness of the beating. I thought then — and I still think now — that referee Steve Crossan showed poor judgement in not stopping it. The same stricture applies to Cobb's corner. Only one judge gave a single round to Cobb; and which one that was can only be guessed at. Tex's collective 43 point deficit was the largest in heavyweight history — possibly in all boxing history.

Afterwards, commentator Howard Cosell — a veteran Ali cheerleader — announced that he would never attend another boxing match. But post-fight, Cobb had his moment of glory. King had lopped a third off his purse. Cobb introduced him to the press as: 'The lying, thieving motherfucker who cut me to $500,000.' Good job you had the acting career Tex.

On December 10th — two weeks after Holmes-Cobb at Houston — there were more ructions, this time in Las Vegas. Mike Weaver defended the W.B.A. title against Mike Dokes, a 6′ 3″, 216 lbs Ohian with a record of 25 wins and a draw in 26 fights. A good boxer with extremely fast hands Dokes was managed by Carl King and promoted by Don.

Weaver had been out of the ring for over a year and was of course a slow starter. Dokes planned to start fast and — in his words — 'Instil the fear of God' in Weaver. After only 40 seconds he dropped Weaver with a left hook to the head. Weaver was up almost immediately but following the mandatory count was trapped against the ropes where Dokes poured in the punches. They seemed not very damaging and some were undoubtedly blocked, and it came as a shock when referee Joey Curtis stepped in and stopped it at the 63 second mark, a new record for heavyweight title matches.

A scuffle in Weaver's corner and a near riot amongst the spectators followed. Weaver took up their cry of 'fix' blaming Don King. Curtis, unrepentant, said that he had been influenced by the death of a South Korean boxer* in a recent lightweight title bout. In my view his explanation has to be accepted. When in doubt fights should be stopped too soon rather than too late. But there are always exceptions to every rule and given that Weaver did not appear to be 'in extremis', plus his known powers of recuperation, I think Curtis' action, while understandable, was too hasty.

Don King has a saying: 'Only in America', and it would seem that only in America could a man go from being a 'thieving motherfucker' in November to complete control of the heavyweight picture in December. Don and the Alphabet Boys were now in full flow. And they would soon have a baby!

* Duk Koo Kim.

By the beginning of 1983 Larry Holmes was becoming increasingly unhappy with Don King. That March he made his first tentative move to get out from under him. His fight on the 27th at Scranton, Pennsylvania, with European title-holder Lucien Rodriguez, a French Moroccan, was largely promoted by Holmes himself, although King helped with the arrangements.

The W.B.C. had reduced the distance of tile fights from 15 to 12 rounds following the Kim tragedy. Unhappily, the W.B.A. did not, at that time, follow suit thus creating a situation which worked against unified titles: neither body now recognised each other's distance. It was, however, in the interests of promoters, along with the proliferation of weight divisions. More title fights meant more money. In the heavyweight division Mr King-of-all-he-surveyed could do better financially promoting more fights with lesser purses, than with a single colourless champion.

The W.B.C.'s inaugural 12 round heavyweight title fight epitomised this state of affairs. Holmes — who appeared overweight at 221 lbs — boxed lethargically but easily outpaced an inept challenger down a one way street. The only knockdown came in the 6th, a right uppercut to Rodriguez's chin. Holmes did not lose a round on any card and had now won his last two fights by the astonishing plurality of 76 points. This, alas, was due to the quality of the opposition and not Holmes' abilities which were now beginning to look distinctly past their 'use by' date.

He needed them all for his next encounter, 'Terrible' Tim Witherspoon at Las Vegas on May 20th, part of a double header also featuring a Dokes-Weaver rematch, ordered by the W.B.A.

Witherspoon, age 25 from Philadelphia, matched Holmes for height at 6′ 3″ and outweighed him 219–213 lbs. A good boxer and hard hitter who did everything well fistically he is, in my opinion, the third best heavyweight behind Tyson and Holmes since Ali.*

The fight was as hard as hell. Witherspoon frequently nullified Holmes' jab, repeatedly picking it off, while hooking powerfully and concisely to head and body. Holmes had to rely on his main armaments, digging deep to hit back with hard rights. That he had slipped was apparent, and admitted by him afterwards. He took a lot of punches.

The fight kept see-sawing. Witherspoon had the better of the first quarter, for once another man's jab ascending Holmes'. Holmes picked up during rounds 4–6, but Witherspoon, calm and unfazed, broke right back at him in the third quarter. At times it resembled matchplay golf, one man having his period on top, then the other enjoying his.

Round nine was what they call a humdinger. Witherspoon set up a monumental attack battering Holmes with both hands. The champion swayed

* But see the Postscript.

like a tree in a hurricane and at one point referee Mills Lane seemed about to stop it. But champions don't give up their titles easily. The tree slugged back at the hurricane! Holmes broke Witherspoon's grip on his title by driving him back with his own hard punches.

There is a golden maxim in boxing that you don't relax because you think you've won, and you don't retreat because you think you've lost. Nobody knows what's on the judges' scorecards. Witherspoon seemed to coast in the last quarter, Holmes drove himself to the point of exhaustion to land punches. Judge one had it 118–111 for the champion (9–2–1), a card which seemed way out of line and was greeted with a torrent of boos. Judge two said 115–114 Witherspoon, (6–5–1). Twelve rounds and thirty-six minutes of bloody, murderous fighting and it was all down to one man sitting at ringside. 115–113 (7–5–0) Holmes, reaction neutral because the audience realised it was close either way. Opinion split about evenly. 'Terrible Tim' had served notice.

Dokes–Weaver was like watching the 400 metres after the 100 in 'Chariots of Fire', more thrills and drama seemingly concocted by a screenwriter. Before the 1st round was out they had brought the crowd to their feet, Dokes with a pair of rocking left hooks to the head; Weaver with a double left hook to body and head. It went on like that throughout, another matchplay situation with each man hurting the other in turn. The different styles played their part in making it a pulsating fight, Weaver's ceaselessly accumulating pressure counterpointing Dokes' nifty boxing. When it ended they couldn't be separated, 144–144 (6–6–3) and 143–143 (7–7–1) making up the drawn verdict (only the third in heavyweight title history). The third judge thought Dokes won, 145–141 (9–5–1), but this was counterbalanced by the majority ringside view favouring Weaver. It was one of those bouts which nobody deserves to lose.

At the time it seemed that Dokes, at 24 just reaching his peak, might be in for a long stay. He was clean bowled next ball! On September 23rd Gerry Coatzee knocked him out in ten rounds at Cleveland. It was after this kayo, claims Dokes, that he looked up to see his mentor, King, stepping around him to congratulate the new champion.

Coatzee's accession was rather overshadowed by other events happening in boxing. Foremost was the arrival of a third sanctioning body. Originally conceived as the United States Boxing Association by Bob Lee of the New Jersey Commission, it was a reaction to Latin American domination of the W.B.C. and W.B.A. Lee soon broadened the spectrum of his infant organisation, changing its name to the International Boxing Federation. The most important decision it made was to recognise Holmes as heavyweight champion.

After the close call with Witherspoon, Holmes defended twice against minnows in 1983. One was Scott Frank in Atlantic City on September 10th. Frank survived into the 5th before going down on one knee, claiming he had been thumbed in the eye. The referee was not impressed. Nor were ringsiders, who thought his trip to the canvas had more to do with a sharp right uppercut. On rising Frank buried his head in his gloves and it was stopped.

The second offering was Marvis Frazier, son of Joe, at Las Vegas on November 25th. Holmes speedily annihilated him in the 1st. But this routine slaughter was to have far greater significance than could be imagined. The W.B.C. refused to recognise it as a title bout on the grounds that Frazier was not a suitable opponent. They were right, although Marvis — who had spoiled a Joe Bugner comeback — was scarcely less credible than others they had sanctioned.

The upshot was that Holmes gave up the W.B.C. belt. Beneath the surface the real reason was dissatisfaction with King and the promoter's close relationship with the W.B.C. The six year old Holmes-King exclusivity came to an end.

Seen from Holmes' vantage point, he was the premier heavyweight in the world and he still had a 'title', the I.B.F.'s. The I.B.F. was delighted. It was exactly the boost they needed. Without Holmes the fledgling organisation might have remained a non-event strictly on a par with the W.A.A. (World Athletic Association) set up two years earlier. Instead the I.B.F. grew to rival the W.B.C. and W.B.A.

Although it has to be said that the I.B.F. today is often regarded as the most credible of the sanctioning bodies, it might also be held that their success not only plunged the sport deeper into anarchy, but also encouraged the scrabble minded auxiliaries of the U.B.A. (apparently now defunct), W.B.O., W.B.F., W.B.U., I.B.O., and I.B.C., to come slipstreaming along in its wake. One, the W.B.O., has even gained a measure of recognition (although not in this book — see the appendix). In case you skipped the Introduction, here is a gem.

Lester Ellis of Australia won the I.B.F.'s super-featherweight title in 1985, when most of that organisation's 'titles' were on a par with those of the I.B.O. and W.B.F. today. He lost it five months later. The years plodded on and so did Lester, going up through the divisions to light-middle. Each successive weight brought him another 'world title', three I.B.O. and one W.B.F., which in theory put Ellis on the same level as boxing greats Sugar Ray Leonard and Thomas Hearns, and above such mundane fighters as Roberto Duran and Bob Fitzsimmons! Strangely, we British, who love to regard 'Ruby Bob' as one of our own, have never laid claim to Lester despite the fact that he was born in Blackpool. I wonder why.

Great champion though he was, Larry Holmes inadvertently played his part in creating the third ring of this circus. From 1984 to 6 the heavyweight title chaotically resembles an inept juggler trying to keep three balls in the air. Every so often one of them hits the floor so he takes another ball out of his pocket and starts again. Tim Witherspoon won the now vacant W.B.C. title by decisioning Greg Page. He lost it almost immediately to Pinklon Thomas who successfully defended against Mike Weaver, but then succumbed to Berbick. Gerry Coatzee paused for over a year before venturing a defence, Greg Page, a flashy, Ali-style boxer from Muhammad's home town of Louisville. The resultant fiasco illustrates how well the W.B.A. looked after at least one of its champions.

At the start of the 2nd, Page was allowed to commence his attack while Coatzee was still in a semi-sitting position in his corner. The referee jammed his gumshield into his mouth without halting the action. In the 6th Coatzee was floored by a punch after the bell. The referee warned Page but took no other action. Nobody heard the bell at the end of the 8th and Coatzee was counted out 50 seconds after the round had ended! The W.B.A. appointed referee — who spoke no English — blamed Coatzee's handlers for the shenanigans at the start of the 2nd — although it was his responsibility to clear the ring — and quoted the W.B.A.'s Joseph Heller style rule-book to cover the 6th: Page couldn't be disqualified because of their new 'no foul' rule and he couldn't penalise him because the punch wasn't low; catch 44! As for Coatzee being knocked out when he should have been resting in his corner, it was the boxer's responsibility to defend himself at all times (catch 66?). The W.B.A. sang 'Les Miserables' Gerrie in a cable expressing their satisfaction with the bout. He didn't even get a rematch!

Page wasn't around as champion too long. He dropped the bauble to the appropriately named Tony Tubbs, a fighter who at times seemed to resemble a barrage balloon with boxing gloves. Tubbs then failed on his first defence, to Witherspoon who knocked out Britain's latest hope, Frank Bruno, in London before another Bruno conqueror, James 'Bonecrusher' Smith, stopped 'Terrible Tim' in the 1st, avenging an earlier points loss to Witherspoon. Juggle, juggle.

Witherspoon at the time was having outside the ring problems with Don King, two thirds ringmaster of the alphabet circus. Tim later sued King — the only boxer to-date with the courage to have done so — and won an out of court settlement. Witherspoon's claims make interesting reading. For the Holmes fight Witherspoon's purse was $150,000: he received $63,000, Carl King, his manager of record, $75,000. For Page it was $250,000: Tim got $41,000, Carl King $125,000. Against Thomas, Witherspoon says he held out for $400,000. Don King, he says, indicated that he would lose if it went to points. There is no supporting evidence of this, but coincidentally Thomas's margin of victory was penalty points deducted against Witherspoon. Bruno should have been his biggest pay-day. In the end Witherspoon received $90,000, Carl King $250,000. By the time the Smith fight came around — it should have been Tubbs again — Tim was thoroughly depressed. His final tally from that fight was $124,000; Carl King netted $127,000. Witherspoon was a highly talented fighter whose abilities merited much more than they received.

Meanwhile, out there in ring number three Holmes was racking up the defences in a reign which he hoped would eclipse Louis and Ali's. 'Bonecrusher' Smith, stopped 12th, David Bey, stopped 10th, and Carl 'The Truth' Williams, points. In reality the record was being padded. Smith was regarded as just a trial horse until he came from a mile behind on points to kayo Bruno, a fighter whose own record was littered with 'opponents'. Bey had an extraordinary amateur career winning 42 of his 53 bouts inside the first round, but was no more than a good prospect when he fought Holmes. Williams, with 16 straight, was another prospect whose only victory of note had been over the fading Tillis.

Twenty winning defences, five shy of Louis's. A lot nearer was Marciano's unbeaten record; Carl Williams was Larry's 48th straight victory.

Number 49 would, he hoped, be Michael Spinks at Las Vegas on September 20th, 1985. Michael, brother of Leon, was the undisputed world light heavyweight champion. Born in St. Louis on July 13th, 1956, he was younger and lighter than Leon, but incontrovertibly a better fighter. Michael was a superb boxer, a fast raider with an excellent jab who had unified the light-heavyweight division in 1983 and overall made ten successful defences. Holmes, who believed he was walking with history, seemed to have it on his side. No reigning 175 lbs champion had ever won the heavyweight crown; nor had brothers. But Spinks was a maker of history. At the Montreal Olympics he and Leon had become the first brothers to win Olympic titles.*

It was not a dramatic fight. Spinks retreated behind a high right hand guard popping out his jab. Holmes plodded after him and was the aggressor throughout. He thought he had done enough to win; the judges disagreed and Michael Spinks was the new I.B.F. champion.

When you're so close to rewriting the history books, a defeat like that really hurts. According to Holmes the judges were either bribed or drunk. Not really, although it may have been a bad decision.

What was left for Holmes now was to try and become the third man to regain the title. At Las Vegas again, on April 19th, 1986, he made his bid. Four weeks earlier a scaled down Leon had failed in a Reno bid for the W.B.A. cruiserweight crown. Would both brothers come unstuck in the Nevada desert?

In my opinion they did. The contest followed the same pattern as the first, but with more highlights. Holmes advanced, Spinks back-pedalled. In the 2nd Larry planted a triple right hook on Spinks' jaw which left him limbo dancing along the ropes. In the next he broke his right thumb on Spinks' skull, but came back to welt his body in the 4th.

There can be no doubt that Holmes won all the first four rounds. Maybe that was the problem because over the next nine the rhythm of the fight didn't change. Holmes pressed forward and for most of the time appeared to have the initiative. Spinks jabbed well and produced flashy combinations which made the pattern suddenly bulge out, but he didn't seem to be winning the rounds. Yet two of the judges gave Holmes only the 7th, and one of them tabbed the 10th even. The rest they gave to Spinks.

* Michael at middleweight.

The 14th was the best. A rippling Spinks cluster sent the sweat spraying from Holmes' head and then he came back with the best punch of the fight, a brutal right which almost dropped Spinks. Even so, it wasn't worth the 10–8 margin which judge Joe Cortez awarded to Holmes. Larry landed another good right in the last stanza. To me he appeared to have done enough. Cortez agreed with 144–141 (8–6–1), but not his compadres. One scored 144–142 (8–6–1), the other 144–141 (9–6–0), both for Spinks. *Ring* magazine spoke for the majority at ringside, 145–142 Holmes, but it didn't matter. The ex-champion was still just that.

Holmes was 36 and the sun had gone down on him. He decided to retire. Spinks stayed around to outclass Steffen Tangstad, former European champion, in four rounds at Las Vegas on September 6th. For anyone compiling a boxing quizbook, Tangstad is the only Norwegian to have boxed for the heavyweight crown. Afterwards Spinks vacated the title. His place was taken in the lists by Tony Tucker who on May 30th, 1987, stopped James 'Buster' Douglas for the vacant championship at Las Vegas.

But few took notice. Instead they were watching the smoke from a bomb blast ascend into the sky. A terrible fury was venting itself on the 'alphabet boys', their scrabble board kicked from their hands. 'Iron Mike' had arrived!

Round Twenty-Five: 'Iron' Mike

Michael Gerard Tyson is a product of mean streets. His thirty years of life have included running with the Brooklyn street gangs, reformatory, marriage to — and divorce from a young television actress, and a sensational rape trial which ended in his being convicted and sent to prison. We are primarily concerned here with Tyson the fighter. The man, to put it in its cruellest terms, seems to bear out the adage that you can take the man out of the streets, but you cannot take the streets out of the man. If that perception of him is to alter in the future then it is up to Tyson to do it.

Tyson was born in Brooklyn on June 30th, 1966, the last of three children sired by a construction worker, Jimmy Kirkpatrick, who separated from Tyson's mother Lorna when he was still small. The background was one of dire poverty and as Tyson grew older he began to hang out with the gangs who infest this sad neighbourhood. Several brushes with the law led to the Tryon reformatory in Upstate New York in 1978.

Tryon was a positive experience. Tyson went there a delinquent illiterate classified as a borderline sub-normal. He learnt to read and write, proved himself of normal ability and never ran with the street gangs again. If only everything else in his life had worked out as well.

While at Tryon he began to box. He came under the auspices of Bobby Stewart, a Tryon counsellor and former Golden Gloves light heavyweight champion who had won that title by defeating Mike Dokes. Stewart saw in Tyson a natural aptitude for fighting and an aggression satiated inside the ropes. Although only twelve Tyson already stood 5′ 8″ and weighed a muscular 200 lbs. Future championship material, Stewart thought. He decided to contact a man who could help his young lion.

Cus D'Amato.

Age 72, D'Amato was living in semi-retirement in the Catskill Mountains when Stewart contacted him in March of 1980. D'Amato liked what he saw in Tyson. There was plenty to like. The youth who only six years later would win the W.B.C. title may accurately be described as a black Jack Dempsey. Like Dempsey he has incessant aggression, bobbing and weaving his way in, drawing and slipping punches to explode inside the other man's guard with precisely lethal hooks, crosses and uppercuts. A treetrunk neck absorbs punishment, and he is cat-like on his feet. Not an artistic boxer, not a jabber, but then like Marciano and Frazier before him a fighter whose style is dictated by physique because the squatly murderous Tyson never grew beyond 5′ 11½″.

Such then was the fighter D'Amato taught and made, the house Cus built. Cus D'Amato died in 1985 without seeing his work come to fruition. Earlier in this book I outlined his proven connections with mob figures. Objectivity demands that it be made clear that no such influence permeated his relationship with Tyson. D'Amato never managed Tyson but the managers he chose, boxing historian Jim Jacobs — who was to sadly die from leukaemia in 1988 — and Bill Cayton, a businessman-cum-fight manager, were untainted by mob links. The final member of team Tyson was Kevin Rooney, a former pro fighter who found his métier as a trainer. He too was above reproach.

Tyson progressed rapidly as an amateur. In 1983 he won the U.S. national title. The blueprint called for him to turn pro as Olympic champion. 1984 saw the introduction of the super heavyweight division for fighters above 200 lbs, which was basically still Tyson's weight at that time. He would therefore compete in the heavyweight division, now the second one down and roughly equivalent to the new cruiserweight division in pro boxing. Things did not go according to plan. In the trials Tyson was twice outpointed by Henry Tillman who then went to Los Angeles and won the gold medal. The inaugural super heavyweight crown was won by fellow American Tyrell Biggs. But America failed to make a clean sweep of the heavier weights. Light heavyweight Evander Holyfield garnered only a bronze.* Not to mind. Evander would make his presence felt later.

Tyson turned professional in March, 1985. His run was devastating. He put his first nineteen opponents to sleep in a total of 38 rounds, twelve coming inside the first. His twentieth opponent was James 'Quick' Tillis. This fight showed up weaknesses both in experience and temperament. Nineteen straight knock-outs had not taught Tyson a lot. He was used to less than gifted fighters dropping like nine-pins from his terror punching. Tillis had boxed for the W.B.A. crown and been in with the daddy of all punchers — Shavers. He used his accumulated ringcraft and experience to thwart and frustrate the Brooklyner. A lot of the steam seemed to go out of Tyson when he was unable to pin Tillis down. He did not put his combinations together effectively and ringsiders thought his confidence suffered. Tyson did manage to hook Tillis to the floor in the 4th, and at the end of ten rounds this proved to be the margin of victory on the judges' scorecards.

The Tillis fight was a good learning contest. Seventeen days later he boxed Mitch 'Blood' Green, a husky, 6′ 5″heavyweight from the Bronx at Madison Square Garden. Green's attacking style was more up Tyson's street (literally: they had both led street gangs). He established a good rhythm and maintained it, working Green over to head and body and not trying for a one punch knockout. After ten he had won it handsomely.

Six straight knockouts from June to September 1986 took Tyson to the

* He was disqualified for hitting his opponent after the bell.

position of No. 1 contender for the W.B.C.'s crown. He was the most talked about, potentially exciting fighter since the young Ali, with almost unlimited money spinning potential for television and promoters if he went on to unify the title. In the Holmes era a fragmented championship had generated more money. Now the opposite was vogue. The T.V. company, Home Box Office, sponsored a unification series effectively built around Tyson. It turned into a long drawn out (and prosperous) multi-bout series of champions and contenders from which it was anticipated Tyson would emerge victorious.

Weighed in the pros and cons of their ephemeral trade the men he had to beat to become undisputed champion were: Michael Spinks — I.B.F. king. A superlative boxer but lacking the power and weight of a real heavyweight.

Tim Witherspoon — W.B.A. titleholder. No weaknesses and seemingly all strengths. But by autumn 1986 he was a depressed and demoralised fighter.

Trevor Berbick — W.B.C. ramrod. Good, but not exceptional. Berbick had a little surprisingly taken the title from Pinklon Thomas.

Tyson and Berbick took the spotlight at Las Vegas on November 22nd.

What sticks indelibly in the mind is Berbick's thigh length socks which gave the impression that he was spindly legged.* Not that we were destined to see too much of them. The Canadian had the utmost difficulty in lasting out the 1st round. Tyson closed his account out in the 2nd. A barrage of rights dropped Berbick. You knew the end was coming soon and it did. Another right — to the body — doubled Berbick up, an overarm left bounced off his cranium like a falling brick, and he was on the floor again, rising and falling twice from that same knockdown until referee Mills Lane decided it shouldn't go any further. Mike Tyson, 20 years, 4 months and 22 days old had become the youngest heavyweight champion in history. As a footnote, Cus D'Amato had taught the division's two youngest ever titleholders. Tyson had been a pro for less than twenty-one months.

Twenty days later the man who loomed as Tyson's greatest rival, Tim Witherspoon, collapsed in miserable ineptitude against 'Bonecrusher' Smith in New York. Smith was generally regarded as a punch looking for a technique. Unhappily if your mind is elsewhere then a puncher is the last person you want to face. Witherspoon shocked by exiting in the 1st. He was to spend the next few years battling Don King in the courts before coming back in 1996 at the age of 38.

Michael Spinks also vacated his championship, but not in the ring. Contracted by H.B.O. to take part in their unification series, he pulled out to fight Gerry Cooney (winning in five) and was stripped by the I.B.F. for failing to meet No. 1 contender Tony Tucker in the tourney.

* In contrast, Tyson never wears socks in the ring.

On March 7th, 1987, Tyson and Smith went to the mat in Las Vegas. The wrestling metaphor is appropriate. The bout was twelve rounds of holds and clinches. Faced with a fighter who was far superior technically and possessing much greater hand speed, Smith appears to have adopted a policy of nullifying his work and hoping for an opportunity to land one of his big wallops. It came — a right to the head — but only in the dying seconds of the contest. Shock waves rippled through Tyson and it was his turn to hang on, but hang on he did to receive a lop-sided verdict and the W.B.A. belt* to add to the W.B.C.'s.

Tony Tucker and James 'Buster' Douglas met for the vacant I.B.F. title on May 30th at Las Vegas, a fight dictated by the television money; the grand finale had to be a unification bout between champions. Tucker, a useful boxer and strong puncher, had a 35–0 record with 29 kayos. He made it 36–30 stopping Douglas in the 10th. At that time anybody predicting what would happen less than three years later would have been regarded as either a) a person who still believed the earth was flat, b) hopelessly insane or c) a suitable candidate for purchasing the Eiffel Tower — possibly a combination of all three, because on the same bill this dreadly awesome 'Iron' Mike Tyson — as he was now prefixed — ground out the impurities in Pinklon Thomas's ore.

Pinklon Thomas will be a footnote in championship history, a Tom Spring or a Harry Orme. Yet he was one of the most naturally gifted heavyweights of the last twenty years, a superb box-fighter who might have had a great career. His story is a terrible warning to the youth of the world, excellence subordinated to a frightening battle against drug addiction. He was coming back when he fought Tyson, but you don't take a narcotics-ravished talent up against one of the greats just reaching his prime.

In the opening round Thomas was rocked and rocked but forced himself to stay upright. Over the next four he showed glimpses of the fighter he might have become, breaking up Tyson's attacks with his jab. Tyson, reduced to near impotence, was displaying again the faults of the Tillis fight. In the broader context he was showing how an aggressive puncher of the Dempsey-Louis-Marciano mould is almost always uncomfortable against a smooth technician. Sadly for Thomas though, he couldn't maintain it. Tyson got his act together in the 6th. To borrow another cricketing metaphor, he began to bowl length and line, putting together concisely powerful combinations. Thomas didn't stand up to it. He went down for '9' and when he arose the referee decided against further continuance with Pinklon's trainer, Angelo Dundee, already through the ropes to rescue his stricken fighter.

Everything was now clear for Tyson to meet Tucker. But troubles began to dog Tyson's footsteps. A few weeks after the Thomas fight he was charged

* W.B.A. championship bouts were now over 12 rounds.

after an incident with a man and a woman in a car park in which it was alleged that he had molested the woman and slapped the man when he came to her aid. The couple decided not to prosecute and the charges were dropped. Tyson by this time had met and fallen in love with a young television actress, Robin Givens. It was not destined to be a happy relationship.

On August 1st Tyson and Tucker met in Las Vegas. Tucker at 6′ 5″ had considerable advantages in height and reach but was not given much chance against the W.B.C./W.B.A. champion. His injury marred career resembled an episode of 'M.A.S.H.'. Tucker picked up yet another one — to his right hand — in round four and it hampered him throughout the remainder of the fight. However, once again Tyson seemed to possess few ideas against a man who refused to stand and trade with him. Tucker fought a constant war of movement and was never in serious trouble although he was never winning many rounds either. It was a largely sterile fight, Tyson switching from body to head and then back again and always on top, but not producing any dynamite. The scores, 119–111 (9–1–2), 118–113 (7–2–3) and 116–112 (8–4–0) gave the now undisputed champion a wide margin of victory and enabled him to more comprehensively eclipse Patterson's record. Meanwhile, the Juggler had had his balls cut off in mid-air.

Tyrell Biggs on October 16th marked the first defence of the undisputed title for almost a decade. It was a sad marker. The 1984 Olympic super heavyweight champion was coming off drug problems, still boxed amateurishly and had had only 15 fights, mainly against 'opponents'. The two 'names' on his record — Snipes and Bey — were considered washed up. But it was a fight Tyson particularly wanted. He personally disliked Biggs and resented not having gone to the Olympics.

The most interesting thing about Tyson–Biggs was what was going on in the front office. The fight was promoted by Donald Trump, a mega-rich entrepreneur whose assets have been variously estimated at between $1.3 and $3.7 billion. The venue was one of Trump's gambling casinos in Atlantic City. In 1987 Atlantic City was still the run-down gangster resthome depicted in Louis Malle's film of that name. Its casinos were the poor relations of Las Vegas's. Trump hoped to change this and one way was to promote big time boxing in the same way that the Vegas casinos had. However, Tyson–Biggs was hardly an auspicious start.

Tyson gave every impression that he could have ended it whenever he chose. Instead he methodically worked Biggs over, savouring the punches as he wrecked the ex-Olympian. I once saw a cat play with a doomed vole by continually taking its head in its mouth until finally the cat wearied of the game and bit the rodent's head off. In the 7th Tyson bit Biggs' head off, thundering left hooks dropping him twice before the carnage was halted.

After this bout Cayton and the dying Jacobs signed a $26.5 million, seven fight deal with H.B.O. For a young ex-hoodlum from the ghetto slums this was an undreamed of bonanza. The only problem in-so-far as the champion's management was concerned was that H.B.O. wanted Don King to exclusively promote the fights.

The first of them was Larry Holmes on January 22nd in Atlantic City. Holmes didn't need the fight financially. He had retired a rich man. On the other hand his ego did. Boxing's remorseless logic said that that ego would be splattered all over the canvas. At 38 Larry was 17 years older than Tyson, at the time the second greatest age disparity in heavyweight title history behind Cus D'Amato's other protegé and Archie Moore. Holmes had been out of the ring for the better part of two years, ballooned up in weight, and even before retiring there had been clear evidence that his meticulous skills were on the wane. No contest.

So it proved. Holmes clung to the wreckage of a once great technique for three rounds and then succumbed to rights in the 4th. There really isn't anything more worth saying about it, except that if they had met at their peaks things might have been very different; it certainly would have been a colossal battle. That 'if' again.

Sixteen days later Tyson married Robin Givens. One year and one week later they divorced. Those 53 weeks were to have a traumatic effect on Tyson. It is that effect which this work is primarily concerned with. Who knows what goes on behind the scenes of a marriage? A boxing match takes place in a public arena and shows to a wider audience on T.V. The spectator sees what is going on. The relationship between two people largely takes place in private. The spectator is only told what has happened and hears two conflicting stories. Shakespeare wrote of his star-crossed lovers: 'A plague on both your houses.' In the event, Tyson and Givens brief union was to leave his throne in ashes.

Don King had been hovering on Tyson's coat-tails for some time. The man with the electric haircut had promoted Tyson-Green and then, as H.B.O.'s favoured promoter, the unification title fights. He was back in the saddle when the bridegroom took his show to Tokyo for the third defence of the Unified title on March 21st. The opposition was Tony Tubbs, and there is scant to be said. Nothing much happened in the first round; in the second Tyson stopped Tubbs. It seemed that people were coming to see not real contests but sudden, ferocious explosions of power, as though Tyson was a catharsis avenging every hurt in their own lives. For the chronicler it is like watching an action replay of the same round over and over again.

Jim Jacobs died two days later. Tyson, who had not been told how ill he was, was shocked and upset. Jacobs' death began the break up of team Tyson. It has been well documented by his biographers, Jose Torres, Peter Heller and Montieth Illingworth. We need only examine the salient points.

Cayton and Robin Givens clashed from the start over control of Tyson's finances. It is alleged that King manipulated this situation to his advantage, undermining Cayton and winning Tyson's confidence. King's goal was simple. He wanted control of Tyson. Cayton was a formidable obstacle. So too was the emergent Trump who had promoted Tyson's fights with Biggs and Holmes, paying King 'site fees' to run the undercards, even though King had played a major role in setting up Tyson–Holmes.

King, along with H.B.O., was also relegated to a supporting role for Tyson's next defence, Michael Spinks in Atlantic City on June 27th. It was officially then the richest fight in history.* Trump had the promotional rights. H.B.O. found themselves paying $3.1 million purely for the delayed transmission rights. King fared even worse. His $11 million site fee was to be divvied up with Cayton. In the end King got only $2 million, out of which he had to pay all the expenses of the undercard. For Cayton though it was a pyhrric victory. Three days before the fight he received a letter from Tyson effectively sacking him.

Total gross for Tyson–Spinks, the most ballyhooed non-event in history, amounted to $70 million. In addition, over the four day period preceding it Trump's casino generated a record 30 million from gambling. Of the fight gross, 22,000 'live' spectators paid $12.3 million, with the bulk revenue coming from closed circuit venues. Tyson's purse was $22 million, Spinks 13.5. The contest lasted 91 seconds. This means that each second of the fight earned almost $770,000! One can only hope that the live spectators fared better at the gaming tables.

To some ringsiders Spinks appeared overawed. He certainly looked frail beside the powerfully built champion. But nobody can take away the hugely impressive way in which Tyson ended it. On the minute mark he landed a devastating combination of left uppercut to the chin and right hook to the body. Down went Spinks. He took '2', received the mandatory '8', and then retreated to the ropes covering up behind his gloves. A desperate left missed and as he brought his glove back Tyson hit him with a right hook clean through his guard, short, beautifully timed and flush on the jaw, a perfect knockout punch. And for Spinks a retirement punch too.

Nobody could know it then but in that galvanising moment we had seen the best of 'Iron' Mike Tyson. Throughout that summer his marriage steadily broke up. In August Tyson resumed hostilities with Mitch Green, this time out of the ring, suffering a hand injury in a brawl outside a New York night club. The injury necessitated a postponement of his next title defence, Frank Bruno in London, a fight which the increasingly unhappy champion did not really want at that stage. It was on again for September but on the 4th of the month Tyson

* Although whether it actually exceeded Ali–Foreman is unclear.

drove his B.M.W. into a tree and was hospitalised. Doctors announced that Tyson would not be able to train again for two months. Meanwhile a curious story spread that the accident had in reality been a suicide bid. It was claimed that Tyson was manic depressive (a psychiatric examination found no evidence of this); also that he had begun to drink heavily. Several major companies cancelled contracts with Tyson to endorse their products.

On October 20th Robin Givens filed suit for divorce. The following day Tyson signed an exclusive promotional deal with Don King. It was the final nail in the coffin of the fighter's relationship with Cayton. What remained of it would be spent in litigation. Kevin Rooney was also fired that December.

The outstanding Bruno fight was rescheduled for February 25th, 1989, but in Las Vegas, not London.* Though little known in America, Bruno was a household name in Britain.

Franklyn Roy Bruno was born of Jamaican parents in London on November 16th, 1961. The baker's son from Wandsworth was destined to become the first out and out Briton to win a genuine version of the championship in the gloved era. He also became the most popular British sports star since Henry Cooper.

Bruno's rapport with the public built up during his early years as a pro. A magnificently muscled man with the physique of an Olympic weightlifter, he stands 6′ 3″ and has latterly weighed around 240 lbs. But outside the ring he may fairly be described as a gentle giant, much in demand for children's pantos. A role reinforced by a well deserved image of a family man. There is an infectious good humour about Frank Bruno, epitomised by his post fight 'double act' with T.V. commentator Harry Carpenter which made the question 'Know what I mean, Harry?' a national catchphrase. But more than humour, likeability and family values, there is too a deeper quality very dear to British hearts; the perseverance to succeed over limitations.

Limitations there are in plenty. First the strengths, an excellent jab and a powerful punch in either hand. The weaknesses seem mainly allied to Bruno's otherwise splendid torso; a muscular development which robs him of mobility, adaptability, suppleness and stamina. Some say durability too, but I suspect this is bound up with stamina.

Before meeting Tyson, Bruno had already had a crack at the W.B.A. title, against Witherspoon at Wembley Stadium on July 19th, 1986, the first time that the venue had been used for boxing since Ali-Cooper in June, 1963.

* For legal reasons King was unable to promote the title bout itself.

The contest was hard-hitting and at times brutal. Witherspoon was below his best, but that should take nothing away from Bruno who fought his heart out, some ringsiders having him ahead — although not the judges — going into the 11th. In that session Witherspoon ended a game challenge with a battery of powerful rights.

Bruno had frankly (no pun intended) done very little to merit the W.B.C. and W.B.A.'s No. 1 contender spots in the intervening two and a half years before meeting Tyson. Perhaps it was 'Buggins' turn. By agreement with the 'alphabet boys' Tyson would consecutively face their no. 1 contenders and all three would recognise them as title bouts.

The fight was only 12 seconds old when a right to the head dropped Bruno to one knee. When action resumed Tyson swarmed into him but was back to his old fault of trying to end it with one punch. Towards the end of the session Bruno caught him coming in with a right and then followed through with a powerful left hook to the jaw. Just for a moment Tyson's legs turned to jelly and he was there for the taking. But Frank had neither the speed nor the adaptability to take advantage of it. The moment passed.

Since that February evening a myth has grown up that Frank Bruno almost won the title and then went down to a homeric defeat. It is a myth as watery as Atlantis. In fact, Bruno more resembled a man trying to shovel water up a hill; with a fork! His challenge did not really exist. Tyson, who rated it as by far his worst performance, lacked snap and timing until the 5th when he suddenly found his length and line and bowled Bruno into the ropes with a fusillade of punches which threatened to decapitate him. Referee Richard Steele and Bruno's manager, Terry Lauless, moved simultaneously to stop it. Bruno had not won a round.

This fight has a sad little footnote. When Bruno returned to Britain he was mobbed at the airport by enthusiastic fans and reporters. A short while earlier Denis Andries had walked proudly through the same gate bearing the W.B.C.'s light heavyweight belt; proudly that is until he found nobody there to greet him. He had just become only the second British boxer in history to regain a world title.

Tyson took on his I.B.F. challenger on July 21st at Atlantic City. If Bruno's status was dubious then Carl 'The Truth' Williams' was inexplicable. In the four years since the Homes fight Williams had fought only nine times which included being belted out by Mike Weaver. Against Tyson he displayed the punch resistance of a blancmange going out in 93 seconds. Afterwards he complained that he had been capable of carrying on. Well, he thought so.

The champion was by now becoming an increasingly unpopular figure in America. There were rumours of too many women, and his behaviour seemed to some to leave much to be desired. Speeding offences, which resulted in community service, were viewed as arrogance; much as Jack Johnson and Sonny Liston's had been seen. The most disturbing reports centred on two well publicised night club incidents in which he was alleged to have sexually molested young women.

Overseas though his popularity was at its zenith. There were offers of fights in Israel ($10 million), Taiwan ($18 million), and China, $25 million, a project drowned in the gunfire at Tiananmen Square. A London consortium was said to have offered a staggering $100 million for a fight a month for twelve months. H.B.O.'s contract for seven fights had priority though with three left to fulfil. Tyson accepted an offer to meet Donovan 'Razor' Ruddock in Ruddock's native Canada which King would promote. Pencilled in for November in Edmonton, the bout fell through when Tyson became ill. Instead Tyson and King decamped to Tokyo where Tyson would face James 'Buster' Douglas on February 11th, 1990.

Seen it its wider perspective, Tyson–Douglas was a tune up bout for a mega rich defence against the undefeated world cruiserweight champion Evander Holyfield in the spring. Donald Trump had secured the rights prior to Tyson's deal with King who would nevertheless receive a $12.5 million site fee to stage the undercard. Tyson was guaranteed $22 million.

Cynics argued that Douglas was a far easier warm up than Ruddock. It wasn't that 'Buster' couldn't fight. The son of ex-middleweight contender Bill (whom I saw box at the Albert Hall), he was 29, having been born in Columbus, Ohio on April 7th, 1960. At 6′ 4″ and with a best fighting weight of around 230 lbs, he possessed a genuine aptitude for his trade, but his career had been marred by strange lapses and weight problems. Three of his four defeats had been inside the distance. The last was against Tucker in the I.B.F. bout, a fight which Douglas appeared to be winning until the 10th when he was caught by a good punch and literally quit fighting. Father Bill, his trainer, was so disgusted that he quit the job and never attended another of his son's fights. Since Tucker, Douglas had won five straight, beating a young Oliver McCall and Trevor Berbick. But he had looked poor in both fights and had recently undergone a series of personal tragedies. Odds against him topped out at 42–1, but sometimes adversity stiffens the backbone.

All was not well in the Tyson camp. Rooney had been replaced by Aaron Snowell, who had never boxed himself, and who up to 1989 had acquired a reputation as a 'gym rat' (hanger on). Claims that he had trained Witherspoon were angrily disputed by that fighter.

Tyson himself seemed mean and moody, almost to the point of sadism. There was a story that he had tried to tear the head off a live pigeon, just for the hell of it. But he looked listless in the gym and was knocked down in sparring by Greg Page.

I once sorted out a school bully by the simple expedient of hitting him in the eye with a stone. Tyson, the bully boy in gloves, was also about to get one in the eye; in more ways than one. Many of his opponents had capitulated through fear. The way to beat him, conventional wisdom said, was to box on the retreat, moving from side to side, nullifying him on the inside. That had been tried but had never succeeded. It was wrong in one vital ingredient. Tyson needed somebody to stand up to him, not just move and box but take the initiative and get his own punches off.

'Buster' Douglas, the greatest no-hoper in boxing history, did just that, not just moving laterally and boxing out of defence, but using his jab as an offensive weapon to pave the way for hooks and combinations. Nobody had ever treated Tyson like this before. When they did come to close quarters, Douglas did not just tie him up but made an 11 lbs weight advantage tell, tiring him. He forced Tyson on to his back foot — more unexplored territory — and then exploited his longer reach. Kevin Rooney might have known what to do; Snowell and Co. didn't. When Tyson's eye was swollen at the end of the 5th, this keystone corner hadn't even an ice-bag on hand. Instead cold water was applied; in a condom! Well, it wouldn't be needed for the victory party afterwards.

A few seconds before the end of round eight Douglas made his only mistake of the fight, Tyson getting inside his guard with a right uppercut which floored him. Douglas pounded his gloves together in annoyance, took the mandatory '8' calmly, and rose on '9'. Referee Octavis Meyran sent them to their corners provoking an astonishing — and perhaps revealing — outburst from King who was claiming that the count had been slow. Turning to W.B.C. President Jose Sulaiman, King screamed: 'What kind of fucking ref did you bring *me* (my italics) from Mexico? You're going to get *my* man (my italics) beat.'

Douglas was back in command in the 9th. At the end of it Tyson looked weary, demoralised, defeated. But at least the judges were right, from King's point of view, because one had Tyson a point in front and another had it level. Ringsiders saw it very differently; some had given Tyson only the 8th, a view shared by the third judge.*

At the beginning of the 10th Tyson bombed Douglas with the sort of straight right which had squelched the confidence of previous opponents and made their eyes roll with fear. The effect on Douglas was zero; instead the last vestiges of spirit slipped away from Tyson. Douglas came on again, blasting him with a right uppercut and then following through on the reeling champion with a cluster of big punches. Tyson went down on all fours and was counted out in the act of rising. The man whom we all thought was invincible was unbeaten no more.

* 88–82.

The fall out was ugly. Don King appeared flanked on either side by Sulaiman and W.B.A. president Gilberto Mendoza. Sulaiman announced that he had received a protest from Tyson's corner that Douglas had been down for longer than 10 seconds in round eight. Pending investigation, the W.B.C. and W.B.A. would withhold recognition from Douglas. King had apparently not completely regained his equilibrium because he unwittingly made another self incriminating remark: '*I'd* (my italics) have done the same for Buster Douglas.' Referee Meyran, who had been closeted with King and Sulaiman immediately after the fight, contritely admitted to having made an error. Bob Lee of the I.B.F., who was not at the fight, announced that his organisation *would* be recognising Douglas. For good measure, another of the I.B.F.'s executives commented, about the way boxing worked in Japan: 'They have a history of promoters buying judges and some of the most ludicrous decisions.'

Newspapers are not above criticism, and have been in this book. But they do sometimes articulate the feelings of the world. The storm of criticism which descended upon Sulaiman and Mendoza was exemplified by the press. Within 48 hours these two auxiliary bully boys had fled: 'All a mistake Guvnor — we never really meant it,' and Buster Douglas was the undisputed champion. Even Tyson clambered on board.

Analysis of the tape reveals that Douglas was down for 13 seconds in the 8th. No referee can possibly count seconds like a stopwatch; no count is ever exact.* Meyran's approximates to 1.44 seconds per digit. But the whole thing is irrelevant anyway. The boxer goes by the referee's count and nothing else. Douglas was alert and watching him. He rose on '9'. Had the count been faster then he would have risen accordingly.**

Shakespeare wrote: 'Mark how a plain tale will put you down.' This tale, of a shabby machination to take away another man's right, could not be plainer.

Launching personal attacks on Don King is rather like firing a cannon into the ocean. The sea opens up, swallows the projectile, and then the waves just keep on lapping in. Taking money from him? Now that, by his own admission, hurts.

Tokyo cost him his main meal ticket. In order to get the fight Douglas had had to sign a promotional deal with King, but Buster, unsurprisingly, did not want to play ball. Instead, he and his manager were very interested in a two fight, $60 million deal on offer from Las Vegas casino owner Steve Wynn. King refused to step aside from his contract with Douglas and legal manoeuvres began.

* For good measure, Tyson's '10' count is timed at 14 seconds.
** Unlike Tyson, who couldn't get up in 14 seconds.

Tyson meanwhile had to rehabilitate himself. The chosen goat was his old amateur nemesis, Henry Tillman, who had not made much of a success of his career since his gold medal triumph. On June 16th at Las Vegas Tillman exited in one from the first solid punch Tyson landed.

Don King and Steve Wynn settled out of court. Wynn had entered a $32 million bid for Douglas's defence against mandatory W.B.A. challenger Evander Holyfield. King took $4.5 million, plus Douglas's next two defences guaranteed him, to allow Wynn to promote the fight. Trump, with a partial right to Holyfield's title challenge, also wetted his beak to the tune of $2.5 million. All heart, Wynn deducted the $7 million from the $24 million purse he was paying Douglas. The fight was fixed for Wynn's Mirage Casino on October 25th.

Unhappily, Popeye had been neglecting his spinach since February. Buster had been on a binge. By October 25th the bone hard 231 lbs of Tokyo was a flabby 246. The will to win exited through the opposite door. Few champions in history have surrendered their titles as meekly as Douglas did. 'Mirage' was the appropriate venue.

Holyfield was a manufactured heavyweight in physical terms, body building his 6′ 2½″ frame from the cruiserweight limit of 190 lbs to a respectable 208. He was — and still is — an excellent boxer with a fine jab and fast, flaring combinations plus heart and will in abundance. Holyfield had won the W.B.A. cruiserweight title on his 13th pro fight and gone on to unify the division winning in all six title bouts. Before the Douglas fight Holyfield had not looked altogether comfortable against heavyweight opposition but he was unbeaten and — leaving aside Tyson — the outstanding contender. From Atmore in Alabama, Evander stepped into the ring with Douglas six days after his 28th birthday.

Little needs to be said because little there is to say. Holyfield set out to beat Douglas to the jab and did. Near the halfway point of the 3rd, Douglas attempted an uppercut, Holyfield countered firmly with a right and Douglas went down and out. 'He could have got up,' referee Mills Lane said disgustedly. Bill Douglas would have been justified in saying — 'I told you so.' No one was more sad than Don King. The new champion had an exclusive promotion deal with one of his arch rivals, Dan Duva.

That December, Tyson had his second comeback fight, British born Alex Stewart in Atlantic City. Stewart had knocked out a string of 'opponents', but lost to Holyfield. Tyson stopped him in the 1st but failed to impress.

Whilst this was happening Holyfield was savouring his first defence against...

How the hell did George Foreman get back into this!?

When George Foreman announced his comeback in 1987 he was 38 years old, weighed 300 lbs and had been out of the ring for ten years. During that time he had become a Baptist minister in Humble, Texas. Humble was appropriate. The scowling, arrogant Foreman of the Seventies had mellowed into a much more rounded, personable individual.

George looked rather different too. Although he eventually got down to around 250 lbs, he was very fleshy, particularly around the middle. And the Afro hairstyle had disappeared; completely. The Foreman of the Eighties and Nineties fought shaven headed.

Foreman's stated reason for his comeback was to raise money for a community centre. He was mocked at first, but plodded on and on to 24 consecutive victories — 23 inside including Gerry Cooney — and by the end of 1990 the public wanted to see him in with Holyfield.

Not that anybody expected him to win. The quality of Foreman's opposition was a reprise of his early days as a pro. But there was nostalgia and novelty about his challenge, and the new George had warmed hearts with a self deprecating brand of humour.

Atlantic City on April 19th, 1991, was chicken in the pot for Evander, George and Dan Duva. Gross receipts amounted to around $80 million! Holyfield was guaranteed $30 million, Foreman 12.5. At 42 he would officially become, then, the oldest man ever* to box for the heavyweight title.

Consensus maintained that to win Foreman would have to knock Holyfield out;— and early. He was too old, too fat and too slow to go the distance. In fact he did just that and exposed Holyfield as a puffed up cruiser. Evander started as though he would win early — Foreman survived a hell barrage in the 3rd — but as the fight wore on Foreman not only survived but came more into things, working his jab well and winning the odd round. He got through rough passages in the 7th and 9th and then brought the crowd to its feet in the last as he rocked Holyfield with right hand shots. Evander deserved his unanimous decision but had hardly looked like the heavyweight champion of the world. The odds shifted to Tyson regaining the title should they meet.

That was beginning to look extremely likely. On March 18th Tyson had stopped 'Razor' Ruddock in seven at Las Vegas, and on June 28th he repeated the win, this time outpointing Ruddock by a wide margin. But he did not look like the vintage Tyson. Boxing News editor Harry Mullan noted of Tyson in the second fight that he lacked any form of subtlety or variety, and that the old upper body movement had gone. He was still punching hard — four knockdowns over the two fights and he broke Ruddock's jaw — but — there are so many 'buts' — Ruddock, a poorly balanced fighter, arose from each almost immediately.

* He was to better that record later.

Their first fight ended controversially, the referee being accused of stopping it prematurely. Overall a lot of the spark seemed to have gone out of Tyson, his technique seemed to be unravelling into strands of untidy, inchoate punches, and opponents no longer feared the bully who had been bested, a point made by many commentators.

Don King was in no hurry to come to terms for Holyfield–Tyson. Tyson's contract with Cayton would finally expire the following February. There was also the fact that Holyfield was promoted by Duva, who had won the bidding for the fight with a $51 million purse offer, but couldn't stage it without King's agreement. More anarchy. In the end two things triggered an accommodation. One was Tyson's desire for the fight, and an increasing unhappiness with King. The other was the sudden appearance of the master embezzler himself, Harold Smith, who had a proposition for Tyson.

Harold never got to make it. King and Duva agreed on $15 million for Tyson with King receiving 40% of the profits *above* $48 million. The telephone numbers make the head spin.

On September 9th, two months before the contest, Tyson was charged with raping a young woman in his hotel room the previous July. The trial was set for January. Out on bail, he fully intended going through with the fight until he damaged a rib which meant a ten week postponement. What followed is difficult to fathom but the fight was cancelled amidst a welter of charges and counter charges between Duva and King. As a substitute opponent Holyfield would defend against Italy's Francesco Damiani on November 27th. Damiani had been the inaugural 'world' champion of the latest addition to the alphabet ranks, the W.B.O. (World Boxing Organisation), but lost it to Ray Mercer, the 1988 Olympic heavyweight gold medalist.

Damiani was strictly a trial horse. The same applied to 'Smoking' Bert Cooper, a blown up and not very able cruiserweight who replaced Damiani when he sprained an ankle. Las Vegas spurned it and Holyfield-Cooper was relegated to the cotton fields; Atlanta to be precise.

Predictably, it was a mismatch except for one minute in the 3rd when Cooper sent Holyfield hurtling into the ropes from a left hook. That aside, it was one way traffic and the referee stopped it in the 7th with Cooper no longer able to fight back.

On February 10th, 1992, Tyson was convicted of the rape charge and later sentenced to ten years in prison (four suspended). A surprising number of writers have protested his innocence, but I suspect their arguments will carry little weight with crime historians. Speaking as the author of two books on miscarriages of justice, I can find no fault with the Jury's verdict on this occasion.

Tyson's defence, as opposed to the facts of the case, is another matter. His Senior Counsel, arranged by King, was one of the most brilliant lawyers in America, but had only minimal experience of criminal trials. Earlier, other lawyers had made what their peers regard as a serious error of judgement in allowing Tyson to testify before the Grand Jury. Above all, Tyson's line of defence was uniquely self destructive. It can be summed up as: 'Any girl who goes out with me knows what to expect'! Why he was allowed to persist with it is inexplicable.

There is a theory about this case that legal constraints do not permit me to explore so I will cease with the matter here.

Tyson went to prison on March 26th and emerged just over three years later to find that King had lined up a $100 million deal for him. In the interim boxing went on without him.

Evander Holyfield made his next defence on June 19th at Las Vegas. So far his defences had been against an ex-champion one step removed from the antiques department and a near nonentity. No. 3 would be another elderly ex-champion. Yep. Unhappy Larry was back in town.

Some say Holmes decided to seek the championship anew when the charisma transplant failed. He was certainly still hungry for recognition. He had won six fights, the last against Ray Mercer who was stripped of the W.B.O. bauble for going through with it. Mercer lost no sleep over that; he did when Holmes trounced him with his own version of 'rope-a-dope', lounging on the ropes and jabbing Mercer's head off.

Mercer was strong but strictly one paced. Holyfield was in a different league. He held the centre of the ring and peppered Holmes with combinations. Holmes' once proud jab shaded him a few rounds but Holyfield won it wide. The problem was that Evander never came close to even dropping a tired, 42 year old man let alone stopping him. Afterwards Holmes managed a rare flash of humour. Asked what he should have done differently, he replied: 'Fought him in 1980.'

Without Tyson, the heavyweight division presented a stale and depressing picture. Holyfield seemed not to be an authentic heavyweight and while his skills were of a high order there was a certain sterility about them. Explosion appeared to have been replaced by implosion, a reflection perhaps of the champion's introverted personality.

Behind Holyfield was the old guard of Foreman, Holmes, Ruddock and Bruno. On the way up were Lennox Lewis, a British-Canadian who had won the 1988 Olympic super heavyweight title, his defeated opponent Riddick Bowe, Oliver McCall, Bruce Seldon and Michael Moorer, none of whom seemed calculated to put the colour back in the bride's cheeks.

Riddick Bowe was considered by many to be the pick of the bunch and he got his chance on November 13th at Las Vegas. Originally from New York, where he was born on August 10th, 1967, Bowe was 6′ 5″ tall and weighed around 240 lbs. He possessed a solid, all round technique, could hit hard and was unbeaten in 31 fights (27 kayos). However, there were doubts about his commitment.

Holyfield–Bowe was nothing less than war, a fierce rolling battle which ebbed and flowed back and forth. Bowe, big, powerful and skilful, formed a battle square which bristled with firepower. Holyfield, eschewing mobility and greater quickness of hand, met him head on with all guns blazing. It made for a superb fight but was perhaps the wrong tactic for the champion. His punches were lightweight by comparison with Bowe's.

For three rounds they fired away at each other on even terms. In the 4th Bowe's juggernaut square began to move forward crashing right after right against Holyfield's head. He dug down deep and survived but took enough punishment for one judge to call it 10–8 for the challenger.

Holyfield came back, not feeling for his openings, not trying to manoeuvre, but launching what soldiers call a 'crumbling' attack. He sought to grind Bowe down by attrition and paid the price. Retaliatory blows bit deep into Evander's reserves. Seven was bad. Holyfield impaled himself on a right uppercut, almost fell, and took more blasts from follow up rights. He again suffered 10–8 on the same judge's card.

The champion's courage shone through in the next two, particularly the 9th, as he willed himself back into the action. Bowe's left eye was beginning to close. By the end it would be little more than a slit.

The 10th lives in the memory of all who saw it. The Bowe fighting square came on relentlessly. Rippling volleys churned into Holyfield giving him an awful hammering. Then, in the last minute, it changed, the champion countering dramatically and effectively, driving Bowe back and causing him to describe Holyfield as a 'crazy man' afterwards.

Holyfield tried to continue his rally in the 11th, but it was Bowe's turn to counter hard and Holyfield dropped for a short count. Bowe was too tired to go for a finish and surrendered the final round. Equally exhausted, the champion — as he still was officially — could only flail away ineffectually.

The scorecards were all for Bowe, two at 117–110 (9–3–0) and the third 115–110 (7–5–0). They were fair, but didn't reflect how hard it had been.

Almost Bowe's first action as champion was to dump the W.B.C.'s belt in a garbage can rather than defend it against official challenger Lennox Lewis.* It set the tone for what was one of the briefest, and certainly the most undignified, reign in history.

Bowe successfully defended the title twice, against Mike Dokes and Jessie Ferguson. There is nothing to be said about either 'fight', which would not

* It had been done before, to a W.B.A. belt, ironically by a British world champion, welterweight Lloyd Honeyghan.

express disgust, so I will take a leaf out of footballer Len Shackleton's book (literally) and leave the next part of this page blank in protest.

Bowe's regime ended where it began, at Las Vegas against Evander Holyfield, only this time only the W.B.A. and I.B.F. titles were involved. Bowe had fragmented the championship again.

November 6th, 1993, — Bowe had held the title exactly 51 weeks — saw another epic struggle, although not the cannonading of the first one. Holyfield boxed a much shrewder fight this time, refusing to be drawn into a punch-up and making more intelligent use of his greater hand and leg speed. Bowe, whose weight during the past months had allegedly zoomed up to obese proportions, entered the ring at a career heaviest 246 lbs and appeared fleshy.

This was a fight of two halves — literally. One minute into the 7th an idiotic parasailer landed on the ring ropes and the contest was halted for 22 minutes.

Holyfield dominated the first half winning all but the 2nd on my card. A yard faster, he consistently beat Bowe's guard with whiplash combinations, moving adroitly out of danger before the champion could counter. He set out his stall in the first minute with a quite superb combination. Bowe jabbed impressively at times but Holyfield's lateral movement prevented him following through with the big shots which had won him the title. It was tense, absorbing and full of quality.

At the end of the 5th Bowe was rocked by well timed combinations which also opened a cut beside his left eye. Blood would continue to flow throughout. In the final minute of the 6th more exquisite combinations left Bowe hurt and befuddled. We began to feel that Holyfield might stop him.

Sparked by his corner, Bowe came out grimly determined for the 7th and for the first time took control. Then the parasailer — perhaps he was enacting a James Bond fantasy — touched down and all was chaos. When the fight eventually resumed it was Holyfield who was more quickly into his rhythm. A round which Bowe had been winning ended up even on my card.

The remainder of the contest was a grim, determined, exciting battle with, I thought, the edge to Bowe. Working beautifully off his jab, he more and more got his punches off. But Holyfield was not outdone. He played the old pro's trick of saving his best for the last minute of each round and then moved in and out with lucid clusters of punches. Even so, I gave four of the last five rounds to Bowe — by a shade — with the other level.

How had the judges seen it? One said draw, 114–114 (6–6), the other two 115–114 (6–5–1) and 115–113 (7–5) for Holyfield which made him the third man in heavyweight history to regain titles he had lost. My card originally read 115–114 to Holyfield; later I changed it to 115–115 (5–5–2). It could not have been closer, but Evander deserved it for the greater variety of his work.

Whether the interruption had an influence is a moot question. Bowe was winning the 7th and then Holyfield resumed better. Evander had suffered a back strain in training and the delay gave his corner the opportunity to massage it. A few minutes before the restart he was up and walking around the ring clearly to keep the muscles supple. In the event, of the two judges who scored for Holyfield, the first (115–114) called the 7th even and the second (115–113) for Holyfield. Had either judge seen it for Bowe then the result would have been a draw.

But such anaemic discussion should not reflect on a fight which is, at this date, the last classic heavyweight title confrontation, a pulsating contest between two men whose contrasting styles will always make for a great clash.*

No classics, but the next three years were to provide plenty of drama and a story tale come true.

The W.B.C., properly in my view, stripped Bowe of their crown for refusing to defend it against No. 1 contender Lennox Lewis. Lewis had achieved his status with a career best performance against 'Razor' Ruddock. Some of the most exhilarating right hand punching ever seen in a British ring chopped Ruddock down inside two rounds.

But that was not a justification for what the W.B.C. next did. Reverting to the Norton prototype, they simply handed Lewis the title, without his fighting for it.

Lennox Claudius Lewis was born of Jamaican parents in the London borough of Newham on September 2nd, 1965. He emigrated to Canada with his mother at the age of six, returned home to live with an aunt until twelve, and then rejoined his mother in Ontario. Manhood found him standing 6′ 4¾″

* In 1995 Bowe stopped Holyfield in the 8th round of another thriller.

and weighing 245 lbs. He boxed as an amateur for Canada and won the Olympic super heavyweight title in Seoul in 1988, controversially stopping Riddick Bowe in the final.

Lewis's British birth gave him dual nationality status. Turning pro he based his career in Britain and by the end of 1992 was unbeaten in 22 fights (19 kayos) which had brought him the British, Commonwealth and European titles.

This brief summary, however, masks the quality of Lewis's opposition. Aside from Ruddock and Gary Mason — from whom he took the British title — it left much to be desired. On the record — with 'Thanks for the Memory' crooning gently in the background — were 'Jaws' Ocasio, eleven years after Holmes, six after leaving his W.B.A. cruiserweight laurel lying around in South Africa; Mike Weaver, just about ready for a bath chair, and Tyrell Biggs, four years down the ham 'n' egg road from Tyson. The only other 'name' was Glenn McCrory, a failed British heavyweight who had scaled down to cruiser, won the I.B.F. title, and subsequently lost it to an American journeyman via a third round kayo. Lewis took one less, which actually was one longer than I had predicted.

Lewis seemed to have learnt precious little from this guided tour of has-beens and never wassers. He appeared to me to have remained amateurish in style, an inconsistent jab and powerful right, with an alarming tendency to drop his left hand. His championship displays did not alter this perception.

Tony Tucker, another trip down memory lane (but not for the last time), provided Lewis's first defence, in Las Vegas on May 8th, 1993. Lewis won a unanimous verdict in a nondescript bout. Tucker was floored twice but survived. Lewis seemed to lack the experience to set him up for the kill.

Frank Bruno was next, at Cardiff Arms Park on October 1st, the first time that two British fighters had contested a version of the heavyweight title.

Witherspoon-Bruno had drawn 40,000 to Wembley, but with the fight live on TV and heavy rain the previous day, only 24,000 were attracted live to Wales' rugby Mecca.

There was, and is, little love lost between the two men, Bruno claiming that Lewis is effectively a Canadian, Lewis berating Bruno for never having boxed for the British title. Both accusations are spurious; family connections took Lewis to Canada, whilst Bruno had no reason and, pre-Gary Mason, no credible British opposition after winning the European crown.

The fight cruelly exposed Lewis's limitations at world level. For the better part of six rounds Bruno gave the younger man a boxing lesson, constantly beating him to the jab and ramming his head back on his shoulders. Lewis looked a seriously flawed fighter, lacking knowledge and adaptability. I gave Bruno five of the first six rounds. Somehow the two American judges managed to score it level. British judge Adrian Morgan's card reflected the general consensus at 59–55.

Bruno, who had been rocked by a right late in the 6th, threw caution to the winds at the start of the next and unleashed a barrage of punches. Lewis, bleeding from the left eye, retreated before him. Roared on by the crowd, who sensed a climax, Bruno wound up a big right. The crowd's instinct was correct; its choice wasn't. Bruno's slowness let him down again. Lewis beat him to the punch with a sizzling left hook and as Bruno reeled into the ropes followed up with a torrent of punches. Right uppercuts almost threatened to tear Frank's head off and he was in desperate straits when referee Mickey Vann intervened.

Lewis had turned what seemed a losing cause around with one dramatic punch, but the rest of the act had been wholly unconvincing.

Atlantic City saw him next, defending against Phil Jackson on May 6th, 1994. Jackson was rated No. 5 by the W.B.C. but his record of winning 30 out of 31 was effectively a paper chase; Jackson's long list of 'opponents' could be collectively summed up as the seven dwarfs. His only class adversary, Ruddock, had stopped him in four.

Lewis gunned him down with a right in just 20 seconds but did not capitalise. He plodded through the next three rounds, decked Jackson again twice in the 5th — the second time a punch which landed after the bell — and finally finished him off in round eight with a cluster bomb to the head. A sparse 5,500 crowd was not overly impressed. Lewis had seemed not to possess the variety of moves needed to quickly dispose of a second rate challenger.

Oliver McCall, his official challenger, came to Wembley on September 24th. He should not have caused Lewis much trouble. A powerfully built 29 year old from Chicago, McCall had been beaten five times in twenty-nine fights.

Lewis may have been over-confident. He speared McCall with his left jab in the 1st, and went on the attack in the 2nd.

The end came with dramatic suddenness.

Lewis moved forward with his chin in the air, dropped his left — both endemic amateur faults — missed with a right, and Christmas came early for Oliver McCall. His right hook to the jaw was a spectacular punch, a bolt from the blue which ended Lewis's championship rule. Lennox arose at '6' but referee Lupe Garcia stopped it. Afterwards, Lewis and manager Frank Maloney complained bitterly that it had been stopped too soon. Well they would wouldn't they.

It may have been poetic justice. If that traumatic 7th round did give Holyfield back his titles, then a round equally as controversial was to remove them from him on his first defence, against Michael Moorer at Las Vegas on April 22nd, 1994.

Almost ninety years earlier two light-heavyweights had boxed for the heavyweight crown. Now a former cruiserweight would put his belts on the line to an ex-light-heavyweight who had won his first (amateur) title at *light-middle-weight.*

Michael Moorer originates from Tyson's part of town, Brooklyn, where he was born on November 12th, 1967. A southpaw — distinctly rare in the upper brigades — he turned pro as light heavy and put together a long run of kayo victories which brought him the W.B.O. light heavyweight crown. He relinquished that title — he would later do the same to the W.B.O.'s heavyweight 'championship' — straddle jumped the cruisers altogether, and landed in the heavyweight pit, where neither the quality of his opposition or his punching power were anywhere near as impressive.

By spring 1994, Moorer was unbeaten in 34 fights with 30 kayos. As a heavyweight however, everything about him seemed to flatter to deceive. Although now 6′ 2½″ and 214 lbs, many doubted that he was really a genuine heavy. His 88% knock-out percentile consisted mainly of light-heavies, and his best win at the premier weight was a three round stoppage of Levi Billups. Billups had taken Lewis the distance but was regarded strictly as a journeyman.

Holyfield therefore appeared to have little to worry about. But at 26 Moorer was five years younger, had not been in the sort of wars which Evander had waged with Bowe, and was an adroit boxer with a perplexing southpaw style. Michael also had a man named Teddy Atlas in his corner.

Holyfield–Moorer was tense and interesting, Moorer giving a masterclass exhibition of the jab, scoring points, breaking up Holyfield's attacks and keeping him off balance. He worked authoritative combinations off it and prevented the champion from establishing any kind of rhythm. Beside Moorer's, Holyfield's own usually reliable jab paled into insignificance. He looked a shop-worn, well-worn fighter. He had sacked his cornermen, Emanuel Steward and his famed Kronk team, in a row over money and was working with new men who seemingly underrated both Moorer and the difficulties posed by a southpaw.

By contrast, Moorer's corner was run by Teddy Atlas who had been associated with Tyson early on in his career. Atlas provided constant motivation: 'Do you want me to fight... do you want me to change places with ya?... If you don't take him the next guy will and then you'll cry. You're gonna cry tomorrow... He's finished; back him up and fight a full round.'

Atlas kept Moorer's concentration going except for one moment near the end of the 2nd when a sudden sharp left hook dropped Moorer to one knee. There had been suggestions that Moorer's jaw was made of less than granite but he appeared perfectly alert as he took the mandatory eight count. Up to that point in the round Moorer had been winning it well, pushing Holyfield back and zeroing in on him with hurting punches. That flash knockdown however was to become the focal point of controversy.

Moorer built up a good lead over the first six rounds. Holyfield made his effort in the next three but it was sporadic, not the rhythmic combinations we had come to associate with him. Then Moorer took over again in the last quarter, that right jab pin-cushioning its target over and over again.

The scorecards made Holyfield an ex-champion, judges Jerry Roth 115–114 (6–5–1), and Chuck Giampa 116–112 (8–4) offsetting Dalby Shirley's 114–114 (6–6).

Now came the controversy. Giampa and Shirley had given the 2nd to Holyfield 10–9 whilst Roth had levelled it at 10–10.

There is an illusion that a knockdown automatically scores a round 10–8 to the perpetrator. TV commentator Ian Darke, for example, scored round two 10–8 Holyfield even though he had Moorer winning the rest of the round big.

In fact, a knockdown is worth one extra point. If boxer 'A' is winning the round and also floors boxer 'B', he wins it 10–8 and not 10–9. Roth, with impeccable logic, went the other way, adding the extra point to Holyfield's tally in a round he otherwise had him losing. Giampa and Shirley certainly did not have Holyfield winning the round, but if they had it very close then, also applying logic, they were entitled to score the knockdown as his margin of victory in it.

Evander's camp complained that if Roth had gone along with Giampa and Shirley then his card would have read 114–114, thus making the result a draw. But then Roth would have been unfair to Moorer. The scoring was just and fair and Holyfield really had no cause for complaint. Jerry Roth incidentally was the judge in Holyfield–Bowe who gave Evander the fight 115–113, scoring the 7th to him.

My own personal card agreed with both Roth's and Giampa's. I scored round two 10–10 and the fight overall to Moorer by four points, 117–113 (7–3–2).

Holyfield's defeat put the kibosh on a money-spinning unification bout with Lewis that autumn. It also brought George Foreman back into the reckoning!

Since losing to Evander, George had ignored appeals to retire and grubbed on. He stopped a club fighter, outpointed Alex Stewart — getting his face busted up in the process — and halted South African Pierre Coatzer who was generally ranked in the bottom half of the top ten. These wins brought him a match with Tommy 'Duke' Morrison for the vacant, synthetic, W.B.O. crown. Morrison, a swashbuckling but limited fighter was a nephew of John Wayne and had starred with Sylvester Stallone in 'Rocky V'.* He appeared to be guiding George to the exit door again by outpointing him over twelve rounds. Foreman stubbornly refused to go through it. He was right.

Moorer took George as his first defence on November 11th at Las Vegas. It figured to be easy; lucrative too, as there was still a lot of sentiment out there for Foreman.

For nine rounds Moorer's right jab systematically demolished Foreman's castle in the air, brick by brick. In the 10th, George parachuted straight down onto Fantasy Island.

* Sadly, Morrison was forced to retire in 1996 after being diagnosed HIV positive.

He had begun to hit Moorer to the body in the 9th, bringing his guard down slightly. It was meant to deceive and did. In the 10th Moorer was caught napping by a jab, followed by a right to the head which hurt him. Foreman followed up with the same mixture, the right this time a little lower and taking Moorer cleanly on the chin. Moorer went down heavily and the count began.

'One-two-three' — the big man with the shiny skull and spreading waistline could only watch and wait. 'Four-five-six' — he began to hope. 'Seven-eight-nine' — the dream beginning to build. 'Ten' — the magic number: Cinderella had gone to the ball, after all.

George Foreman, age 45, became the oldest man ever to win a title in ring history*, and the patron saint of every middle-aged overweight man dreaming of sporting glory.

His was a triumph of hope over adversity, persistence over reality. Somebody once wrote that the true hero is the man who picks himself up and carries on. George Foreman personified that belief.

April 1995. Golden Oldies month tinged with apprehension. Foreman had been stripped of the W.B.A. title for refusing to defend it against a recognised contender. He would defend the I.B.F. crown only, against Germany's Axel Schulz at Las Vegas on the 22nd.** Meanwhile on another Las Vegas bill on the 8th, Bruce Seldon and veteran Tony Tucker would contest the vacant W.B.A. title. Even longer in the tooth than Tucker, Larry Holmes was bidding for a fingertip hold on Foreman's glory by challenging Oliver McCall on the same bill. The heavyweight championship was now fragmented three ways again for the first time since Tyson had unified it. Call it 'Alphabeticus Calamitus'.

The apprehension? That was in the minds of the pretenders. 'Iron' Mike was just weeks away from release. Don King was already back. McCall, Seldon and Tucker were promoted by him.

Seldon, born in Atlantic City on January 30th, 1967, weighing 230 lbs and standing 6′ 3″, had a 31–3 record which included 27 inside the distance victories. It is best described as deceptive. He was regarded as a boxer rather than a puncher and the trade thought him 'chinny', having been kayoed inside a round by Bowe and stopped by McCall. His victories had been primarily over 'opponents'. Tucker, although 36, sported a remarkable 55–2 record and started favourite. Unfortunately — how often that word abounds in boxing — most of Tucker's credit column also consisted of a magical mystery tour of the record books. His two best performances were the losses — going the distance with Tyson and Lewis.

* Possibly also the oldest man to hold one, depending on Archie Moore's real age.
** Schulz was 20 years younger than Foreman creating a new official record for the greatest age disparity in heavyweight title history. Unofficially, Patterson–Moore may still be the greatest.

Seldon made his eight year advantage tell, outspeeding Tucker and beating him to the punch. His left jab beat a constant tattoo on Tucker's features, marking them up and closing his left eye. Tucker's corner retired him, protesting, at the end of the 7th. At that point the ex-I.B.F. champion was only one point behind on two of the scorecards but his handlers were wise. Seldon, quietly dominant, was set fair for victory.

Since the Holyfield loss, Holmes had huffed and puffed his way through seven 'opponents'. He was 45 and other men had always taken the glory, Louis the most defences, Ali three times a champion, Marciano the longest unbeaten run, and now Foreman, the oldest. As titleholder Holmes had lived in Ali's shadow and perhaps now set his heart on winning more championship bouts than the maestro. Two would do it.

He came close. Just how close is evidenced by the judges' scores, 114–113 (6–6), 115–114 (6–5–1) and 115–112 (7–5), the first and third judges giving the 9th to McCall 10–8. Going into the last third of the fight the ex-champion appeared to be marginally ahead by dint of shrewd tactics and crafty boxing, raking McCall with jabs out of defence and taming his inelegant rushes with sharp right hand counters. Holmes was playing to his remaining strengths and exposing McCall's weaknesses. As a matter of personal opinion, McCall is technically the most limited heavyweight champion I have seen. Strength, a good right and not much else. He used his strength, and his youth, to win the last third as Holmes tired, battering him throughout the 9th and pressurising him thereafter.

Holmes did not retire afterwards, as expected. He fought — and won — another four times before finally hanging up his gloves in June, 1996. Those last few years in the ring mellowed him. The grumpy, glowering man who seemed at times to think the world was denying his greatness added a smile and sage philosophy to his repertoire.

The world will not deny Larry Holmes his greatness. In the end he did not rewrite the record books, but then he never needed to. Based on his ability this consummate master boxer was one of the finest champions in history. If there was an elimination tournament of the greatest heavyweight kings then Holmes would be in it alongside Johnson, Dempsey, Tunney, Louis, Marciano, Ali and Tyson.

Many hoped that Foreman would retire after the Moorer victory, the perfect end to the fairy tale. Instead he decided to carry on. Axel Schulz tarnished the legend. A hitherto obscure German, he had answered the call 23 times and held a victory over 'Bonecrusher' Smith. But Smith had regressed a long way and Schulz had subsequently received a boxing lesson from Britain's Henry Akinwande* in a European title fight. The W.B.A. refused to sanction the match. Foreman had had trouble with them before the Moorer fight when they had

* Currently the W.B.O. champion.

originally refused to accept him, Foreman, as a challenger. George took them to court and won. This time he surrendered the belt. The I.B.F. proved considerably more pliant, approving the defence even though Schulz was not one of their ranked contenders; 'rank' might seem the operative word to describe both their behaviour and the challenger's credentials.

The fight was horrid. Foreman plodded after Schulz seeking to land his big punches and failing. Afterwards he confessed that he had looked like 'a junkyard dog'. Schulz kept on the move and appeared to have landed the majority of the punches. The judges disagreed. Two scored it 115–113 (7–5) for Foreman, the third a draw at 114 apiece (6–6). The lustre of the Moorer fight was considerably dimmed.

In the aftermath of Pensioners Month at Las Vegas, Foreman also relinquished his I.B.F. crown,* and Oliver McCall signed to meet the W.B.C.'s No. 6 contender Frank Bruno, in what had to be Bruno's final crack at the title.

Meanwhile, Tyson was out and running.

At first he did not look impressive. They brought on Peter McNeely — son of Patterson challenger Tom — to test him. McNeely's 36 victories were merely notches on a water pistol. It looked like a one round job and it was, McNeely's manager jumping into the ring to save him after 89 seconds.** McNeely's purse of $400,000 was his biggest by $390,000! Tyson received $22 million!

Another 'son of' was Tyson's second comeback victim, in December 1995. Buster Mathis junior's fleeting brush with fame was that he had boxed in a 'no contest' with Bowe, the ex-champion hitting him when he was down. For two rounds Buster stayed out of trouble with Tyson looking awful, his timing completely awry. Then, two minutes into the 3rd, everything seemed to suddenly click and a trio of right hooks put Mathis down for the count.

These two fights were of course simply warm-ups for Tyson to shake off the prison rust and get the cobwebs out of his timing. On the surface the performances seemed unlikely to instil fear in the two men Tyson would need to beat to regain the W.B.A. and W.B.C. titles. Those men were now Seldon and... Frank Bruno.

September 2nd 1995:

It was a night to stroll down to your local and view it over a pint with friends, a warm evening in late summer with autumn knocking on the door.

* Still not retired (officially), he is today recognised by the minuscule W.B.U.
** Technically a disqualification.

Many were surprised that Bruno had qualified for yet another title shot. He was now almost 34 and his only victory of note since being stopped by Lewis was over the very faded Carl Williams. But paradoxically Oliver McCall seemed his best opportunity. McCall had not greatly impressed before beating Lewis and had looked awful against Holmes. In contrast to Bruno's first three attempts I felt he had a chance of beating McCall.

This was certainly British boxing's biggest night since Ali–Cooper in 1966. But, in the smoke-filled beer-flowing pubs and clubs up and down the country, and for the 30,000 spectators at Wembley Stadium, it would be more a great occasion than a great fight.

The opening three rounds saw Bruno taking full advantage of McCall's lack of technique. The American simply walked onto Bruno's best weapon, his jab which he interspersed with short hooks and uppercuts at close range. With McCall, boxing seemed to have regressed almost a century, to what Jim Jacobs termed as 'impaling your face on the other man's glove.' An overarm right in round one, which had McCall stuttering back across the ring, was the best single shot of the fight.

McCall had not endeared himself to the British public before the fight, calling Bruno, whose sparring partner he had been for Tyson, an 'Uncle Tom'. Bruno, as he made clear in his post-fight interview, had taken this derogatory remark to heart. There had always been a suspicion that Bruno was perhaps a little too much of a 'nice guy' for the fight game. On this night he felt not only desire but dislike too and it willed him on. For McCall, his campaign of denigration turned out to be a 'no brainer'.

But he came on in the 4th and 5th, getting inside and taking Bruno out of his rhythm. McCall's jab had all the fluency of a wooden-armed man trying to swat flies but his strength is his strength and he just keeps bludgeoning forward.

Bruno took control again in the 6th, in-fighting well with hooks and uppercuts, outworking the champion. Even allowing for McCall's limitations, Frank was displaying a variety which we had not seen before, actually turning southpaw for much of the 8th, banking on McCall not having the manoeuvrability to take advantage with his right.

Round succeeded round in similar fashion. This was no great fluctuating drama: there were no highlights. But as the points kept on going into Bruno's column excitement and anticipation grew apace. You could feel it, sense it. It was in the air; tangible.

McCall attacked with a desperate intensity in the last two rounds, particularly the 12th when Bruno, exhausted, was out on his feet and hanging on to survive. McCall, however, couldn't create the gaps and Bruno didn't leave any, and that was that. The decision was unanimous and two thirds wide 117–111, 117–111 (9–3), and 115–113 (7–5). My own score read 116–112 (8–4). Bruno — and Britain — had done it. Lumps appeared in throats, Frank cried and the spectators sang 'Land of Hope and Glory' with even more gusto than the Henry Wood promenaders. It was a memorable moment.

The final part of this book fittingly belongs to Mike Tyson.

We left his depositing Buster Mathis jnr. for the count and looking towards Frank Bruno. Bruno's next opponent should have been Lennox Lewis, the official challenger for the W.B.C. title. Bruno stood to make an estimated 10 million against Tyson, over double the amount he could get from fighting Lewis. And of course he had previously lost to Lewis.

The W.B.C. had allowed McCall to make a voluntary defence against Bruno. Now they allowed Bruno to make a voluntary defence against Tyson. There was of course a much bigger sanctioning fee to be made from the latter. True, Bruno–Tyson had much greater appeal but what is the point of a regulatory body which doesn't enforce its own rules? Lewis unsuccessfully took legal action, and it is difficult to avoid the conclusion that he was all round treated very shabbily.

So were the thousands of British fans who shelled out hard earned money to travel to Las Vegas in support of Bruno on March 16th, 1996. Much mayhem was promised. Some thought, on the evidence of Tyson's warm-ups against McNeely and Mathis, that Frank was not without a chance. Bruno himself avowed that he was now punching harder than Tyson. But as he made his way to the ring on that late winter's evening, repeatedly crossing himself, he appeared to be a man walking with death rather than destiny.

Seven years earlier he had provided one brief, electrifying moment of hope. This time there was aught but despair.

Tyson looked devastating. Bruno's strategy — if such it can be called — appeared to be to tie Tyson up and use a two stone weight advantage to wear him down. Or perhaps it was just desperation because for two rounds Bruno hung on for grim death,.

His courage was emasculated by rights in the 1st and he went back to his corner with an ugly gash over his left eye. Tyson, now left hooking like a runaway steam engine on a curving track from Hell, ran amok in the 2nd. Bruno could only cling on to the engine and was deducted a point.

The end came in the 3rd. A left hook began Dante's inferno of punches, 12 hooks and uppercuts, which left Frank sitting on the middle strand of the ropes where he was rescued by Mills Lane.

The 'fear' was back, the 'bully boy' supreme again. Tyson became the sixth man in history to claim a heavyweight title for the second time after Patterson, Ali, Witherspoon, Holyfield and Foreman.

Don King was also back. He controlled as a promoter both Tyson and Seldon. Since Foreman, the I.B.F. heavyweight title had become no more credible than those of the Mickey Mouse bodies.* Effectively, King was undisputed master of the ship again.

Eye problems forced Frank Bruno to retire in the summer. It would be both cruel and unjust to remember him for his last fight. He did much — contributed much — for British boxing. He deserves instead to be recalled for that emotionally charged Wembley night when he made Britain proud of him.

In the summer of 1996 Bruce Seldon was the forgotten man of boxing. He had defended his W.B.A. garland just once since winning it, on August 19th, 1995 against Joe Hipp in Las Vegas.

The fight merited only the historical footnote that Hipp was the first full-blooded Red Indian to box for a version of the heavyweight title. The contest itself was no more than a digit in history. Seldon, boxing behind his jab and stifling yawns with his right, made tunnels of both Hipp's eyes and created an underground river running beneath from his left cheek. Hipp quit midway through the 10th.

Seldon's second defence came on September 7th, 1996, against Tyson at Las Vegas.

As a defending champion (Tyson's W.B.C. title was not at stake) Seldon set records that no other boxer will want to emulate. He was a 20–1 underdog in the betting. Tyson, who also received the lion's share of the purse from the Bruno encounter, this time garnered six to eight times as much as the champion, $30–40 million as opposed to Seldon's $5 million. These differences were to be illustrated in the most graphic terms on September 7th.

Seldon's response to his underdog status was hardly encouraging: 'Nobody,' he said, 'gave King Kong a chance either.' Not against the aeroplanes Bruce, and they were right. But in the jungle Kong had no peers and Tyson, cavorting for publicity stills with a tiger cub, was Kong. Seldon more resembled Fay Wray!

The Spanish call the bull ring the moment of truth. That moment began for Bruce Seldon as he plodded down the aisle to the ring. He smiled; as if saying to the bull, 'look at my lovely suit of lights — please don't gore me.'

Inside the ring he looked around helplessly: 'Why haven't the picadors put their lances in him?' Tyson pawed the ground.

The fight actually ended at the five second mark. That was when Tyson's left horn gored Seldon to the core, a hook which drained every ounce of courage out of him.

Afterwards the audience would chant 'fix — fix'. It wasn't; it was simply the end of a man who had faced his moment of truth and been found wanting.

Just a minute had elapsed when Tyson moved in for the kill. It is only

* See the Appendix.

detectable by playing back the film frame by frame, but Tyson landed a lightning jab. A following right combed Seldon's hair — nothing more. Later it was said that Tyson's elbow had caught him but the film does not evidence it.

Seldon went down on his face. Referee Richard Steele originally waved 'no knockdown' but then he changed his mind and started to count. Seldon arose at '4'.

There are no cowards in a 20 foot square ring but Tyson is a man who inspires fear in even the bravest. He stalked Seldon to the ropes, gunned him with a left hook and floored him again. Seldon got up at '5', and as Richard Steele reached the second of the mandatory count which would send him back into battle, began to shake and shimmy at the legs. Steele waved his arms aloft and the pathos of E. L. Thayer's poem came to mind:

'The band is playing
somewhere, and somewhere
hearts are light,
and somewhere men are
laughing, and somewhere
children shout;
but there is no joy
in Vegas — mighty
Seldon has struck out.'

Mike Tyson had unified the real title for the second time.

Finis Coranat Opus

Postscript

Las Vegas November 9th 1996.

The school bully was trounced again!

Evander Holyfield went into the ring a massive underdog and emerged once more with the W.B.A. crown, the third time he has worn it.

Tyson attempted to repeat the shock tactics of the Seldon fight, tearing across the ring at the opening bell and trying to unhinge Holyfield with a big right. But Holyfield avoided its full force and struck back immediately. It was obvious then that Tyson had a fight on his hands.

They fought four tough, gritty rounds without, I thought, any overall advantage to either man. But ominous signs were there for Tyson. The punches were uncoordinated, the upper body movement static and the timing fractionally off.

Even so, it got better before it got worse. In the 5th Tyson appeared at least to be putting things together, the punches beginning to come through more convincingly as though some encircling cobweb had been torn away from him. Then, in the last 30 seconds of the round, the fight was won and lost. Suddenly Holyfield backed him up and fired in combinations and the champion looked all at sea. Shock was written on Tyson's face. Just when he had looked to be getting on top the man had broken right back at him, hurt him; broken his spirit too.

Holyfield continued it in the 6th, rifling home his shots, building his rhythm, getting his punches off first. One cut Tyson's left eye and he was befuddled and bemused. His answer was a desperation charge and he ran straight into a whip cord of a left hook which left him on his behind, legs splaying upwards as if they wanted to walk on the ceiling. Holyfield did not try to end it then though; there was still much to be done.

Round succeeded round. Holyfield began to use his jab like a trombone, ramming it into Tyson's face to keep him off balance and help push him back. These were the tactics of the Buster Douglas fight being repeated, Tyson bullied around the ring, driven onto his back foot and tied up in close. All rhythm was gone. Holyfield's was clicking away nicely.

At the end of the 9th I noted that on my card Tyson was four points behind. He needed either knock-downs or a knock-out. But it wasn't going to happen. Blood still seeped from his eye, his confidence was long gone and he looked a miserable, beaten fighter.

The 10th was really the last. The bit by bit demolition of Mike Tyson the fighter was now complete and awaiting the coup de grace. Holyfield commenced it with a volley of punches which sent Tyson hurtling back into the ropes. He was being punished on them when the bell went, arguably a split second before the referee intended stopping it. In his corner Tyson sat like a man who sees without seeing, a groggy, defeated figure. He came out for the 11th but that was all. Holyfield drove him to the ropes and was teeing off when the referee jumped between them. Mike Tyson was an ex-champion for the second time; Evander Holyfield had won the W.B.A. belt for the third.

Holyfield fought his greatest fight. Does it make him one of the great champions? On his overall record, undisputed cruiserweight and heavyweight champion followed by two superb performances to regain versions of the heavyweight title it does. On his skill and bravery too. But I feel judgement must yet wait. He has never looked impressive in defending the premier crown, Bowe has twice beaten him, Moorer also. As for Tyson, whether he can come back from this defeat will represent the supreme test of his character and will.

Appendix: The W.B.O and I.B.F.

Although regarded in some quarters as the fourth major sponsoring body, the W.B.O. has yet to achieve credibility, particularly in the heavyweight division where its only three meritorious champions, Ray Mercer, Michael Moorer and Riddick Bowe treated the bauble with disdain, giving it up when it suited them. A chronological listing of W.B.O. champions is as follows:

Francesco Damiani	(Italy)
Ray Mercer	(U.S.A.)
Michael Moorer	(U.S.A.)
Tommy Morrison	(U.S.A.)
Michael Bentt	(Jamaica)
Herbie Hide	(Britain)
Riddick Bowe	(U.S.A.)
Henry Akinwande	(Britain)

The I.B.F. heavyweight title fell into decay after Foreman relinquished it. Francois Botha, a South African of French descent, won the vacant crown outpointing Axel Schulz. Botha was stripped of the title after failing a drug test and Moorer won the vacant-again crown beating Schulz. At the moment the title has no real credulity and since 1995 can be regarded as being on a par with the W.B.O.'s.

It remains to be seen whether Michael Moorer can re-establish its credentials.

Select Bibliography

Books

Astor Gerald, *Gloves Off: The Joe Louis Story*, Pelham, 1974

Batchelor Denzil, *The Boxing Companion*, Eyre & Spottiswoode 1964 and *Jack Johnson & His Times*, The Sportsman's Book Club, 1956.

Butler Frank, *A History of Boxing*, Arthur Barker, 1972 and (with James Butler) *The Fight Game*, The World's Work, 1954

Cantwell Robert, *The Real McCoy*, Auerbach, 1971

Carpentier Georges, *Carpentier*, Hutchinson, 1955

Cooper Henry, *Henry Cooper*, Cassell, 1972

Corbett James J., *The Roar of the Crowd*, Grosset & Dunlap, 1925

Cottrell John, *Man of Destiny*, Frederick Muller, 1967

Durrant John, *The Heavyweight Champions*, Hastings House, 1960

Farr Finis, *Black Champion*, Macmillan, 1964

Farr Tommy, *Thus Farr*, W.H. Allen, 1989

Fleischer Nat, *Fifty Years at Ringside*, Corgi, 1960; *Black Dynamite*, Ring Books, Volume One 1938 and Volume Five 1947; *Jack Dempsey*, Arlington House, 1972; *Max Baer*, Ring Books, 1970; *The Ring Record Book*

Foreman George, *By George*, Stanley Paul, 1995

Golding Louis, *Bareknuckle Breed*, Hutchinson, 1952

Gorn Elliot J., *The Manly Arts*, Robson, 1986

Hauser Thomas, *The Black Lights* and *Muhammad Ali*, Robson 1986 and 1991

Hellier Peter, *In This Corner* and *Tyson*, Robson, 1975 and 1989

Illingworth Montieth, *Mike Tyson*, Grafton, 1992

Isenberg Michael T., *John L. Sullivan and His Times*, Robson,1988

Johansson Ingemar, *Seconds Out of the Ring*, Stanley Paul, 1960

Johnson Dick, *Barefist Fighters of the 18th and 19th Centuries*, The Book Guild, 1987

Johnson Jack, *Jack Johnson in the Ring and Out*, Citadel Press, 1969

Leigh-Lye Terry, *In the Corner* and *A Century of Great Boxing Drama*, Mayflower, 1963 and 1970

Lewis Lennox, *Lennox Lewis*, Faber & Faber, 1993

Lloyd Alan, *The Great Prizefight*, Cassell, 1977

Loubet Nat, Andre Sam and Fleischer Nat, *The Pictorial History of Boxing*, Hamlyn 1981

Mace Jem, *The Life Story of Jem Mace*, Peter McInnes, 1989

Mead Chris, *Champion Joe Louis*, Robson, 1986

Moore Archie, *The Archie Moore Story*, Nicholas Kaye Ltd, 1960
Morrison Ian, *Guinness World Championship Boxing Book*, Guinness, 1990
Mullally Frederic, *Primo*, Robson, 1991
Mullan Harry, *Fighting Words*, Colebridge, 1993
Odd Gilbert, *Great Moments in Heavyweight Boxing* and *The Fighting Blacksmith*, Pelham, 1973 and 1976
Patterson Floyd, *Victory Over Myself*, Pelham, 1962
Pepe Phil, *Come Out Smokin'*, Coward, McCann and Geo Chegan, 1972
Roberts Randy, *Papa Jack* and *Jack Dempsey*, Robson, 1986 and 1987
Sanford Harry and Steeber Max, *The Square Jungle*, Panther, 1960
Schoor Gene, *The Jack Dempsey Story*, Nicholas Kaye Ltd, 1960
Shaw Mark, *Down for the Count*, Sagamore Publishing, 1993
Shipley Stan, *Bombardier Billy Wills*, Bewick Press, 1993
Skehan Everett M., *Rocky Marciano*, Robson, 1977
Steen Rob, *Sonny Boy*, Methuen, 1993
Sullivan John L. *I Can Lick Any Sonofabitch in the House*, Proteus, 1979
Suster Gerald, *Champions of the Ring*, Robson, 1992
Torres Jose, *Sting Like a Bee*, Abelard Schuman 1972 and *Fire and Fear*, Warner Books, 1989
Treharne Evan R., *British Heavyweight Champions*, F. C. Avis, 1959
Whiting George, *Great Fights of the Sixties*, Leslie Frewin, 1967
Wilson Peter, *Ringside Seats*, Rich and Cowan, 1949; *More Ringside Seats* and *Boxing's Greatest Prize*, Stanley Paul 1960 and 1980; *King Henry*, Daily Mirror Books, 1971
Wright Alan, *Tom Sayers*, The Book Guild, 1994

Newspapers and Periodicals

Boxing Illustrated
Boxing International
Boxing News
Herald Tribune
News Week
The Ring
Sports Illustrated
Time